ASP.NET 4 24-HOUR TRAINER

ASP.NET 4 24-Hour Trainer

ASP.NET 4 24-Hour Trainer

Toi B. Wright

WILEY

Wiley Publishing, Inc.

ASP.NET 4 24-Hour Trainer

Published by
Wiley Publishing, Inc.
10475 Crosspoint Boulevard
Indianapolis, IN 46256
www.wiley.com

Copyright © 2010 by Wiley Publishing, Inc., Indianapolis, Indiana

Published simultaneously in Canada

ISBN: 978-0-470-59691-3

Manufactured in the United States of America

10 9 8 7 6 5 4 3 2 1

For my boys — Jim, Frederick and Franklin.

ABOUT THE AUTHOR

TOI B. WRIGHT owns her own consulting business, One Stop Designs, which does web development for small- to medium-sized businesses all over the United States. She has a BS in Computer Science and Engineering from the Massachusetts Institute of Technology and an MBA from Carnegie Mellon University. She has worked as a professional software developer for over 25 years and has been a Microsoft MVP in ASP.NET since 2005.

Toi has been a leader and organizer of technical user groups in the Dallas, Texas area for over a decade. She is the Founder and President of the Dallas ASP.NET User Group, `http://www.dallasasp.net`. She is also the Founder and President of Geeks in Pink, `http://www.geeksinpink.org`, which is a support organization for women in technology. In 2008, she organized the first WE ARE MICROSOFT - Charity Challenge Weekend, `http://www.wearemicrosoft.com`, which is a three-day event in which software developers donate their time to work on projects (such as a new website) for non-profit organizations. Since 2008, she has organized two more events and Microsoft has sponsored numerous similar events under the name GiveCamp, `http://www.givecamp.org`.

Toi lives in Dallas, Texas with her loving husband and two beautiful sons.

CREDITS

EXECUTIVE EDITOR
Robert Elliott

PROJECT EDITOR
Christopher J. Rivera

TECHNICAL EDITOR
Carsten Thomsen

PRODUCTION EDITOR
Rebecca Anderson

COPY EDITOR
Kim Cofer

EDITORIAL DIRECTOR
Robyn B. Siesky

EDITORIAL MANAGER
Mary Beth Wakefield

ASSOCIATE DIRECTOR OF MARKETING
David Mayhew

PRODUCTION MANAGER
Tim Tate

**VICE PRESIDENT AND
EXECUTIVE GROUP PUBLISHER**
Richard Swadley

VICE PRESIDENT AND EXECUTIVE PUBLISHER
Barry Pruett

ASSOCIATE PUBLISHER
Jim Minatel

PROJECT COORDINATOR, COVER
Lynsey Stanford

COMPOSITOR
James D. Kramer, Happenstance Type-O-Rama

PROOFREADER
Josh Chase, Word One New York

INDEXER
Johnna VanHoose Dinse

COVER DESIGNER
Michael E. Trent

COVER PHOTO
© Felix Alim/istockphoto

ACKNOWLEDGMENTS

I WOULD LIKE TO THANK EVERYONE that helped to make this book a reality. First, I would like to thank Bob Elliott at Wiley who brought the concept for this book to my attention. As far as I know, this is the first book to offer the reader a direct comparison between ASP.NET Web Forms and ASP.NET MVC. Next, I would like to thank my technical editors. Rachel Appel at Microsoft helped me to organize the various sections of the book and Carsten Thomsen made sure all of my code examples were accurate and followed best practices. Also, I would like to thank my Project Editor, Christopher Rivera, for keeping me on schedule. Finally, I would like to thank my husband, Jim Wright, for providing me valuable feedback on each of the tutorials and for putting the kids to bed by himself when I was forced to work late to meet a deadline.

CONTENTS

PREFACE

The Internet is here to stay. Every day, more and more web sites are added to the World Wide Web. Everyday web sites become more sophisticated. Indeed, in our Web 2.0 world, many web sites look and feel just like Windows applications. This book, ASP.NET 4 24-Hour Trainer, will teach you the skills you need to become a web developer.

There are currently two different frameworks used to develop web sites with ASP.NET 4. The first framework is referred to as the ASP.NET Web Forms framework. The ASP.NET Web Forms framework has been in use since the first version of ASP.NET was released in 2002. As such, it is well tested and quite robust. The other framework is the ASP.NET MVC framework. The ASP.NET MVC framework is much newer; it was released in 2009. Many programmers prefer the ASP.NET MVC framework because it gives them more control than traditional ASP.NET Web Forms.

This book covers ASP.NET 4 web development using both the ASP.NET Web Forms framework and the ASP.NET MVC 2 framework. As such, it is a great resource to compare and contrast the two technologies.

WHO THIS BOOK IS FOR

This book is for anyone who wants to be shown how to develop web applications using ASP.NET 4 with Microsoft Visual Studio 2010. Since this book covers both the ASP.NET Web Forms framework and the ASP.NET MVC framework, it is also useful to the developer who is considering moving from Web Forms to MVC.

This is a beginning ASP.NET book. Nevertheless, it is assumed that you have some development experience using Microsoft Visual Studio. Also, since all of the sample code is written in C#, it is assumed that you have some experience with C#. However, due to the unique structure of the book, novices will also be able to understand and learn from the lessons.

HOW THIS BOOK IS STRUCTURED

This is not a reference book. The intent of this book is to teach you how to do the tasks that are required for web development. This book is uniquely structured to cover ASP.NET 4 web development using both the ASP.NET Web Forms framework and the ASP.NET MVC 2 framework.

By the time you finish this book you will know how to create a fully functional web site using the ASP.NET Web Forms framework, and you will know how to create a fully functional web site using the ASP.NET MVC 2 framework. While some tasks are done the same way using either technology, most tasks are accomplished in different ways. There are three types of lessons.

1. Lessons that are relevant to all ASP.NET developers.

2. Lessons that are only relevant to developers using the ASP.NET Web Forms framework.

3. Lessons that are only relevant to developers using the ASP.NET MVC 2 framework.

Every lesson concludes with a tutorial designed to demonstrate the information that was covered in that lesson. An important component of this book is the DVD full of videos that accompanies the book. All of the tutorials are demonstrated in the videos.

WHAT THIS BOOK COVERS

This book covers the two frameworks that Microsoft provides developers for developing ASP.NET 4 web sites using Microsoft Visual Studio 2010; the ASP.NET Web Forms framework and the ASP. NET MVC framework. It contains 48 lessons that are grouped into 10 sections. Each lesson is associated with one subject. Each lesson begins with an explanation of the subject and is followed by a tutorial that walks you through that subject.

➤ **Section I: Introduction to Web Development** — This section introduces static HTML pages. You will create and style your first web page. You will also explore the stateless nature of the web and configure a web application.

➤ **Section II: Getting Started** — This section guides you through creating your first web sites using Microsoft Visual Web Developer 2010 Express. You will create two identical web sites; one web site will use the ASP.NET Web Forms framework and the other web site will use the ASP.NET MVC 2 framework. You will also follow the life cycle that each type of web site uses to process requests.

➤ **Section III: Developing Forms and Views** — It's time to add forms and views to your web site. This section will teach you how to construct the user interface for your web site.

➤ **Section IV: Maintaining a Consistent Page Layout** — Many pages of a web site share elements such as the placement of their logo and their site navigation. This section demonstrates how to use styles to layout a page. You will also learn how to reuse commonly used code on multiple pages.

➤ **Section V: Controlling the Flow** — It's time to add some code to your web sites. This section will teach you to use code to respond to your user's inputs.

➤ **Section VI: Validating User Input** — We have all heard the expression, "Garbage In, Garbage out." In this section you will learn to validate data on both the client and the server.

➤ **Section VII: Reading and Displaying Data** — You use the ADO.Net Entity Framework to access your data in this section. You will learn to display and edit both simple data and tabular data.

➤ **Section VIII: Managing Data** — Most web sites need to manipulate data. This section will show you how to use Dynamic Data in Web Forms and templates in MVC to both edit your existing data and to insert new data.

➤ **Section IX: Client-Side Programming** — The more that your web application can leverage the processing power of the client, the fewer round trips your web content has to make. This is accomplished using client-side programming. This section covers JavaScript and asynchronous JavaScript and XML (AJAX).

➤ **Section X: Securing Your Application** — Due to the nature of the Internet, security is always very important when you are developing a web site. This section teaches you how to secure your web sites.

➤ **Appendix A: Ajax Control Toolkit** — This section will demonstrate some of the more popular controls in this free library of client-side controls.

➤ **Appendix B: What's on the DVD?** — This section goes into more detail about using the DVD that comes with this book.

INSTRUCTIONAL VIDEOS ON DVD

All of the lessons in this book are brought to life through hours of instructional video that are included on the DVD. Every lesson concludes with a tutorial. Both the content of the lesson and the accompanying tutorial are covered in the video. You may want to watch the video before you read each lesson or vice versa. The choice is up to you.

CONVENTIONS

I use a number of conventions throughout the book.

> *Boxes like this one contain important information pertaining to the surrounding text.*

> *Notes and asides are offset and italicized like this.*

> *References like this one refer you to the relevant video on the DVD.*

➤   As for styles in the text:

New terms and important words are *highlighted* when I first use them.

URLs and code are shown in the text like so: `www.wrox.com`.

Code is presented using a fixed-width font.

```
This is a code sample.
```

SUPPORTING WEB SITES AND CODE

As you work through each lesson I recommend that you create the web sites and type in all of the code. However, depending on how you learn, you may prefer to download the code. The code is available at `www.wrox.com`. You can use the search box on the web site to locate this title. After you have located this book, click the **Download Code** link to access the files that can be downloaded. You can download the files via HTTP or FTP. All of the files are stored as ZIP files.

 The ISBN for this book is 978-0-470-59691-3. You may find it easier to search by the ISBN than by the title of the book.

You can also download the code from the main WROX download page, `http://www.wrox.com/dynamic/books/download.aspx`. Click the link to the ASP.NET 4 24-Hour Trainer to access the files that can be downloaded.

ERRATA

I have made every effort to ensure that this book is error-free. Nevertheless, mistakes do occur. If you find an error in the book, like faulty code or a misspelled word, please let me know. The errata is available on `www.wrox.com`. You can use the search box on the web site to locate this title. After you have located this book, click the **Errata** link to access the errata page.

If you don't see "your" error, please complete the Errata Form. After you submit the Errata Form, your information will be checked and, if appropriate, an update will be made to the errata page.

You can also reach the errata page via the `www.wrox.com/misc-pages/booklist.shtml` page. Simply locate this title and click the **Errata** link.

P2P.WROX.COM

For continuing discussions about this book and other technical topics, you are invited to join the P2P Programmer Forums. The forums are hosted by Wrox books and are available at p2p.wrox.com. The forums are a community of over 40,000 computer programmers including Wrox authors, editors, other industry leaders and readers like you.

As a guest, you can read any of the posts on the forum. You can even subscribe to a particular discussion. However, if you want to post a question or respond to other programmer's questions, you must register. Registration is fast and, best of all, it is free.

To join the P2P Programmer Forums please follow these steps:

1. Go to p2p.wrox.com and click the **Register Now** link.

2. Read and agree to abide by the p2p.wrox.com Forums rules.

3. Complete the form and click the **Complete Registration** button.

4. You will receive an email in your inbox. You MUST follow the link in that email before you can post to the forums. Until you do that, you will be told that you do not have permission to post.

For more information about the P2P Programmer Forums please refer to the FAQ page located at p2p.wrox.com/faq.php. The FAQ page includes information on general forum usage as well as information on how to read and post messages.

ASP.NET 4 24-Hour Trainer

Welcome

ASP.NET 4 is a powerful framework for building dynamic web sites. This book walks you through the subjects that you need to learn in order to develop web applications using the ASP.NET 4 framework with Microsoft Visual Studio 2010.

I have always been fascinated with computer programming. When I was 12, I took my first programming class at our local junior college. I went on to get a degree in Computer Science from the Massachusetts Institute of Technology (MIT). In the '90s I became enamored with Rapid Application Development. This led me to programming in both Borland Delphi and Microsoft Visual Basic. At the time, I developed retail software for computers running Windows. A large percent of time on each project was spent writing the installer and testing the software on each version of the operating system, with and without each of the patches associated with that particular version. I thought, "There has to be a better way!"

In the late '90s I was given the opportunity to write an application for the Internet. I found that developing the pages took half the time of a traditional Windows application. Also, the time to deploy was next to nothing. A few weeks after I deployed that first web application, the users requested some reports be added to their system. In the past, I would have had to write an installation routine and send everyone the new setup file. On the Internet, I just updated the web site and everyone had access to the new files immediately. I was hooked. I actually was so excited about developing for the Internet that I started the Dallas ASP.NET User Group, www.dallasasp.net, because I decided that all I wanted to do was ASP.NET.

I hope that this book will imbue you with the same enthusiasm that I have found for developing web applications. Before I dive into the lessons, this introductory chapter sets the stage. Some of the questions that this chapter will attempt to answer are:

- ➤ What is unique about web development?
- ➤ What is ASP.NET?
- ➤ What are ASP.NET Web Forms?
- ➤ What is the ASP.NET MVC framework?

➤ Which one should I use, the ASP.NET Web Forms framework or the ASP.NET MVC framework?

➤ What do I need to get started?

WEB DEVELOPMENT 101

The Internet is the largest computer network in the world. It was originally developed as a military research project, but has grown into a tool that millions use every day. They use it to send emails, buy books, read blogs, and share all types of information.

When you "surf" the Internet, you use a browser. The browser requests pages from a web server. The web server responds by sending the pages back to the browser, as shown in Figure 1. The pages that the web server sends back to the browser contain markup that the browser then renders on the page using HyperText Markup Language (HTML). Lessons 1 and 2 both cover HTML.

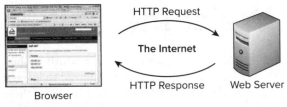

FIGURE 1

Internet Explorer is one of the most popular browsers, but many people use other browsers such as Firefox, Safari, and Chrome. More and more people are using browsers on their mobile devices to access the Internet. When a browser accesses your web site, ASP.NET automatically determines the capabilities of that browser. This is the list of browsers that ASP.NET 4 inherently recognizes:

➤ Blackberry

➤ Chrome

➤ Firefox

➤ Gateway

➤ Generic

➤ Internet Explorer

➤ Internet Explorer Mobile

➤ iPhone

➤ Opera

➤ Safari

Hypertext Transfer Protocol (HTTP) is what browsers and web servers use to communicate. The most important thing to know about HTTP is that it is a stateless protocol. This means that from the web server's perspective, no two requests are related; it thinks that every request is from a new user. It does not maintain state.

There are many scenarios where maintaining state is important. For example, if you are writing an application for a hotel to take reservations you will need your web application to recognize the user over multiple page requests. ASP.NET provides a number of ways to maintain state. Lesson 4 covers state management in ASP.NET 4.

ASP.NET FRAMEWORK

The ASP.NET framework is the web application framework developed by Microsoft. It sits on top of Microsoft's .NET Framework, which is Microsoft's framework for building all types of software applications. The .NET Framework contains a huge number of classes that provide the core functionality to the applications that are developed using it.

Because the ASP.NET framework is built on top of the Microsoft .NET Framework, any experience you have using the Microsoft .NET Framework can be leveraged when you are developing for the ASP.NET framework. For example, when using the ASP.NET framework you can code your application using any of the .NET languages, including C# and Microsoft Visual Basic. I will be using C# for all of the examples in this book.

The ASP.NET framework contains a set of classes that Microsoft developed specifically for building web applications. Some of the functionality that is included in the ASP.NET framework includes:

- The ASP.NET compiler
- Security infrastructure to provide authentication and authorization
- State management
- Application configuration
- Health monitoring and performance features
- Debugging support
- An XML Web services framework
- Extensible hosting environment and application life cycle management
- An extensible designer environment
- Caching
- The Microsoft Ajax Library
- Dynamic Data
- URL Routing

The ASP.NET framework runs on a web server that has the Microsoft .NET Framework installed on it. ASP.NET dynamically renders markup to the requesting browser. When you are "surfing" the

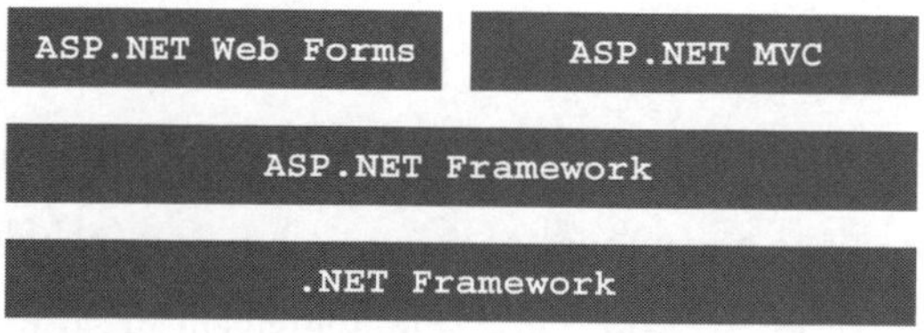

ASP.NET Web Forms	ASP.NET MVC
ASP.NET Framework	
.NET Framework	

FIGURE 2

Internet, one way you can tell that you are visiting a site that uses ASP.NET is that the page you are visiting ends with the .aspx file extension.

You can use either the ASP.NET Web Forms framework or the ASP.NET MVC framework to develop applications using ASP.NET. Both of these frameworks are built on top of the ASP.NET framework, as shown in Figure 2.

ASP.NET Web Forms Framework

When ASP.NET was first developed, most Microsoft developers only had experience developing Windows applications. To make the transition from Windows developer to Web developer as painless as possible, Microsoft developed the ASP.NET Web Forms framework (Web Forms). To ease the transition, Web Forms use the same event-driven model that is used by Windows Forms.

As I mentioned, the Internet uses HTTP to communicate and HTTP is a completely stateless protocol. If a user requests a page, updates a value on that page, and submits the page, the web server does not recognize that the two pages are related. It is up to the developer to relate the two events. Web Forms strive to make this state management transparent to the developer. They do this by introducing server-side controls and a page life-cycle that each element on the page must complete.

The ASP.NET Web Forms framework simplified a number of everyday tasks and, more importantly, enabled developers to work at a higher level of abstraction. This allowed them to focus more on the core functions of the web application rather than on common tasks around Web page design.

Nevertheless, as developers became more knowledgeable about HTTP they began to resent the high level of abstraction that Web Forms provides. They wanted to manage state themselves and have absolute control over the HTML that their pages render. Therefore, in 2009 Microsoft released the first version of the ASP.NET MVC framework. The second version of the ASP.NET MVC framework was released in April, 2010. This book covers MVC 2.

ASP.NET MVC Framework

The ASP.NET MVC framework (MVC) is a framework for building web applications that use a *model-view-controller* pattern. This pattern is very common in software development. The objective of this pattern is to separate the application's logic from the application's user interface.

Unlike Web Forms, MVC does not strive to hide the stateless nature of the Web. Instead, its objective is to return control back to the developer.

Web Forms vs. MVC

Advantages and disadvantages are associated with both frameworks.

The advantages of using Web Forms include:

➤ Automatic state management

➤ Extensive library of controls provided by both Microsoft and third-party vendors

➤ Robust and time-tested technology

➤ Rapid Application Development

➤ Event-driven model

➤ HTML is automatically generated by the server controls

➤ Less coding than MVC

The advantages of using MVC include:

➤ Provides a clear separation between your logic and your user interface

➤ Complete control over the HTML that is rendered

➤ Easier to test, which enables test-driven development

➤ Easier to maintain

You must decide for yourself which framework is right for you. This book is organized in a way to make that comparison easy. Each lesson that uses the ASP.NET Web Forms framework is followed by a similar lesson that uses the ASP.NET MVC 2 framework. I recommend that you do all of the lessons in the book and decide which framework you prefer after you have completed all of the lessons.

> *The ASP.NET Web Forms framework and the ASP.NET MVC framework can be used together in the same web application.*

GETTING STARTED

To get the most out of this book, you should plan to complete all of the lessons. To do so, you need to install a version of Microsoft Visual Studio 2010 and a version of Microsoft SQL Server 2008.

> *All of the videos and screenshots in this book use Microsoft Visual Web Developer 2010 Express and SQL Server 2008 Express Edition. They are both free.*

You can install both Microsoft Visual Web Developer 2010 Express and SQL Server 2008 Express Edition by using the Microsoft Web Platform Installer 2.0. available at www.microsoft.com/express/Web/.

> *SQL Server 2008 Express Edition uses the same database engine as the full versions of Microsoft SQL Server. The main limitation is that the size of the database is limited to 4GB.*

Microsoft Visual Web Developer 2010 Express Setup

The setup for Microsoft Visual Web Developer 2010 Express requires Microsoft Web Platform Installer 2.0 to be installed. To install Microsoft Web Platform Installer 2.0 download it from `www.microsoft.com/express/Web/`. Figure 3 shows the installation screen for Microsoft Visual Web Developer 2010 Express.

These are the steps you should follow to install Microsoft Visual Web Developer 2010 Express on your computer:

1. Click the Install button on the Microsoft Web Platform Installer 2.0 to start the installation process.

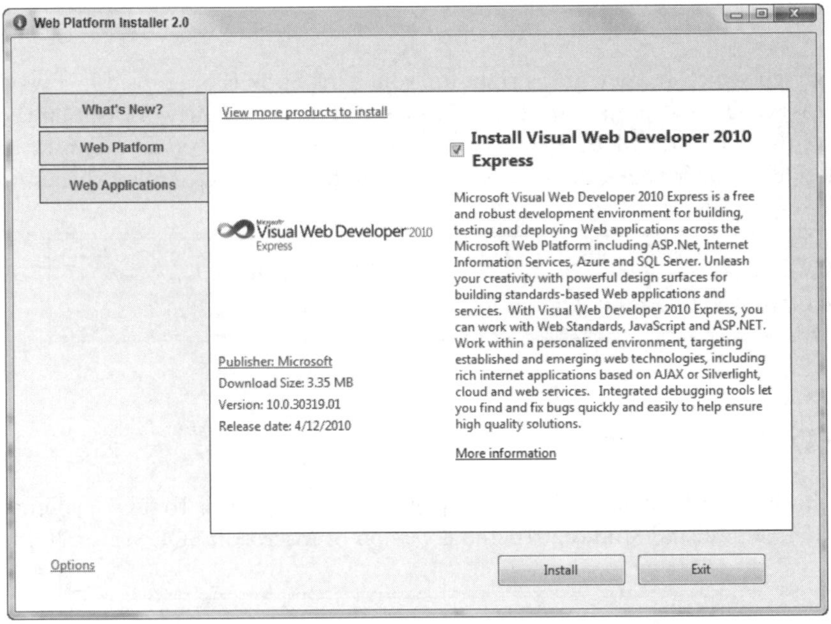

FIGURE 3

2. Click the I Accept button to accept the license terms (see Figure 4).

3. Wait for the download and installation to complete (see Figure 5). It took my computer almost 20 minutes to download and install all of the files.

4. Open Microsoft Visual Web Developer 2010 Express.

5. Select Tools ➪ Settings from the menu to enable all of the menus and toolbars that are available with Microsoft Visual Web Developer 2010 Express.

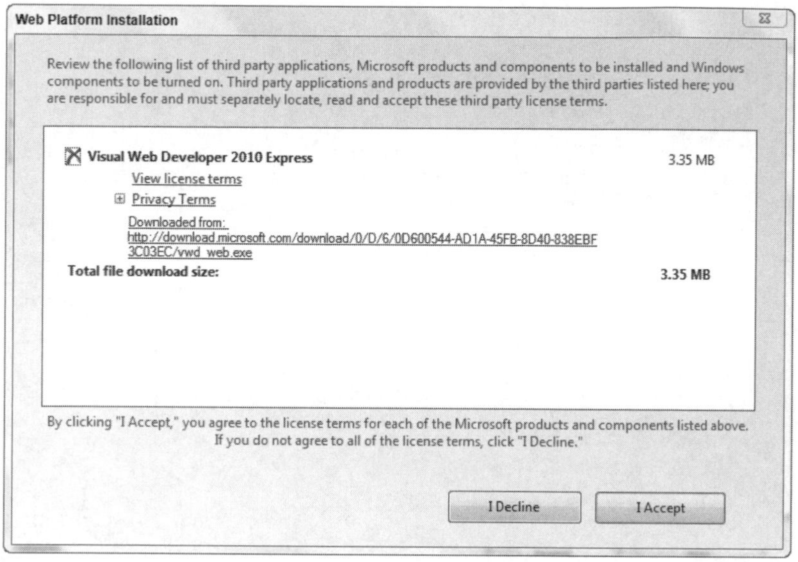

FIGURE 4

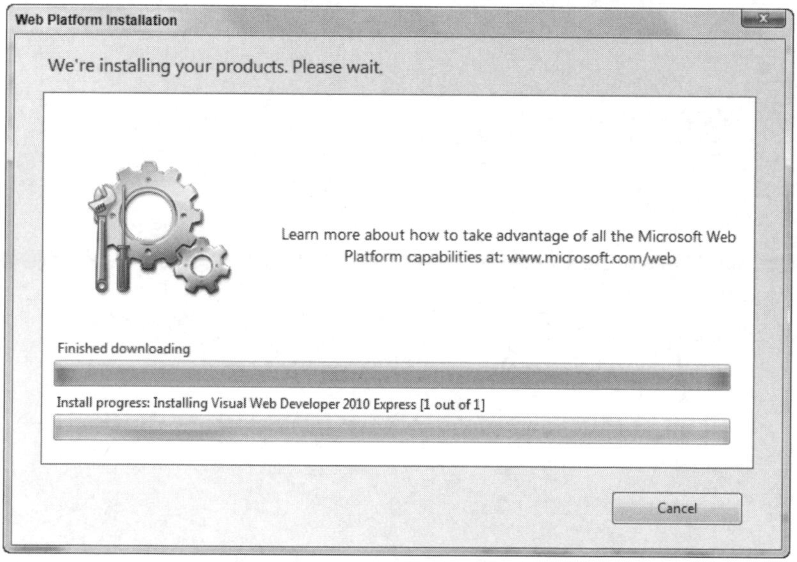

FIGURE 5

SECTION I
Introduction to Web Development

- ▶ **LESSON 1:** Anatomy of an HTML Page

- ▶ **LESSON 2:** Using Common HTML Tags

- ▶ **LESSON 3:** Adding Style to an HTML Page

- ▶ **LESSON 4:** State Management in ASP.NET 4

- ▶ **LESSON 5:** Configuring Your Web Application

1

Anatomy of an HTML Page

HyperText Markup Language (HTML) is the language of the Internet. The web server uses it to communicate the structure of the page to the browser, and it is the language that all browsers use to render pages. Therefore, it is very important that you are familiar with HTML.

HTML defines only the structure of a page. It does not define how a page looks when it is viewed. Cascading style sheets (CSS) are used to define the styles on a page. I talk more about CSS in Lesson 3.

Figure 1-1 shows the default markup that is generated when a new HTML page is created using Microsoft Visual Web Developer 2010 Express.

```
DOCTYPE Declaration

        <!DOCTYPE html PUBLIC "-//W3C//DTD XHTML 1.0 Transitional//EN"
        "http://www.w3.org/TR/xhtml1/DTD/xhtml1-transitional.dtd">

        <html xmlns="http://www.w3.org/1999/html">
        <head>
            <title>Untitled page</title>    Head Element
HTML    </head>
Element <body>
                    Body Element
        </body>
        </html>
```

FIGURE 1-1

As you can see, the default page begins with a DOCTYPE declaration and is followed by the HTML element.

DOCTYPE DECLARATION

The DOCTYPE declaration tells the browser the exact version of HTML the browser should use to render the page. If you do not include the DOCTYPE declaration, the browser must guess which version of HTML to use. All modern browsers have multiple modes that correspond to the different versions of HTML, and the mode that the browser uses is determined by the DOCTYPE declaration. Therefore, for the browser to render your pages correctly, the DOCTYPE declaration must appear at the top of every single one of your web pages.

This is the default DOCTYPE declaration that Microsoft Visual Web Developer 2010 Express uses:

```
<!DOCTYPE html PUBLIC "-//W3C//DTD XHTML 1.0 Transitional//EN"
    "http://www.w3.org/TR/xhtml1/DTD/xhtml1-transitional.dtd">
```

The default document declaration identifies the document as XHTML 1.0 Transitional. XHTML is a standard that defines HTML as a well-formed XML (eXtensible Markup Language) document. Some of the requirements of XHTML are that all elements must be lowercase, have an end tag or be self-closing and nest properly. I explain more about well-formed XML later in this lesson.

Microsoft Visual Web Developer 2010 Express supports the validation of a number of document type declarations within the Integrated Development Environment (IDE). In the HTML Source Editing toolbar, you can select a different schema from the Target Schema for Validation drop-down list. The options include Internet Explorer 6.0, HTML 4.01, XHTML 1.0 Transitional, XHTML 1.0 Frameset, and XHTML 1.1. The different document types are defined by the World Wide Web Consortium (www.w3.org).

When you are in the Source view, the editor continually checks that your document is valid. If it finds any markup that is not valid, it underlines it with a wavy green line and adds the error to the Error List.

> *The Error List window displays errors, warnings and messages. If you double-click an error in the Error List, you will go directly to the line of code that is causing the error. To open the Error List click Ctrl+\, Ctrl+E or select it from the View menu.*

The editor determines what is valid based on the target schema for validation. For XTML 1.0 Transitional it means that the following will be marked as errors and will appear on the Error List:

- ➤ Client tags are not lowercase
- ➤ Tags are not well-formed
- ➤ Attribute values are not quoted
- ➤ Element or attribute is deprecated

The following table lists the validation that is performed for each of the target schemas that are provided by Visual Studio 2010.

TARGET SCHEMA	VALIDATION
Internet Explorer 6.0	Quirks mode. Displays pages as if they were viewed by older versions of the browser.

TARGET SCHEMA	VALIDATION
HTML 4.01	The elements are not case sensitive, empty elements do not need closing tags, and attributes do not need to be in quotes.
XHTML 1.0 Transitional	The markup is well-formed XML. Allows all HTML elements and attributes. However, framesets are not allowed.
XHTML 1.0 Frameset	Same as XHTML 1.0 Transitional, except that framesets are allowed.
XHTML 1.1	The markup is well-formed XML. Allows all HTML elements and attributes, but does not include presentational or deprecated elements (like font). Framesets are not allowed.

You can also modify the target schema from the Tools ⇨ Options ⇨ Validation dialog box. Using this dialog box you can fine-tune validation by selecting the types of errors against which you want the editor to validate.

> *The DOCTYPE declaration is case sensitive. If it is not typed correctly, it will be ignored by the browser.*

HTML ELEMENT

The HTML element is the root element of the document, and as such, it contains all of the other elements. As you can see in the following example, the HTML element begins with `<html>` and ends with `</html>`:

```
<html xmlns="http://www.w3.org/1999/xhtml">
<head>
    <title>Untitled Page</title>
</head>
<body>

</body>
</html>
```

The HTML element contains both a head element and a body element. The `xmlns` attribute identifies the XML namespace that the page uses. By default, the `xmlns` attribute refers to the XHTML namespace per the World Wide Web Consortium.

Head Element

The head element contains the processing information and metadata for the document. The text within this element is not rendered by the browser. The default HTML example only includes a title element because the title element is required. If you do not include a title for your page, you will receive a warning in the Error List.

This table lists the elements that can be included in the head element:

ELEMENT	FUNCTION
link	Specifies a link to another document. This element is commonly used to link external style sheets. You learn about external style sheets in Lesson 3.
meta	Specifies metadata about the document such as keywords, its expiration date, copyright and author. The metadata is used by the browser and by search engines.
script	Contains client script, such as JavaScript. Section 9 of this book covers JavaScript.
style	Contains style information. You learn about inline styles in Lesson 3.
title	Specifies the text that appears in the title bar. It is also used to refer to the page when the page is bookmarked or referenced by a search engine. It is required.

Body Element

The body element contains the markup that is displayed by the browser. Two types of elements can be in the body element: inline or block. Inline elements are treated as part of the flow of the document, whereas block elements force a line break. An example of an inline element is the select element. An example of a block element is the div element. The following table lists the elements that are used in this lesson. You learn more elements in the next lesson.

ELEMENT	FUNCTION
input	Input. This element is used to input information. Depending on its type attribute is can be a button, a textbox, a checkbox and more.
div	Division. This element defines a logical division in your page. It is used to provide a container for other elements.
h1	Header 1. This is the highest level heading.
h2	Header 2. This is the second-level heading.
select	Selection. Used with `<option>` to render a drop-down list.
hr	Horizontal rule. This is a horizontal line.

Syntax

An element in HTML represents a structure. It consists of a start tag, content, and an end tag. Some elements, such as the HTML element, contain other elements:

➤ `<div>` — This is a sample start tag.

➤ `<div color="red">` — This is a sample start tag with an attribute. In this case the attribute of color has been set to red. Each element has a different set of attributes associated with it.

➤ `</div>` — This is a sample end tag.

➤ `<div>Welcome</div>` — This is a div element. It includes a start tag, some content, and an end tag.

➤ `<hr />` — This is an empty element. It uses a self-closing tag.

> *Sometimes HTML elements are referred to as tags. However, the term "tag" actually refers to the markup at the start and end of an element.*

Earlier in the lesson I mentioned that HTML elements must have a closing tag and be properly nested. The following markup is incorrect because the closing tags are missing:

```
<p>This is a paragraph.
<p>This is another paragraph.
```

This is correct:

```
<p>This is a paragraph.</p>
<p>This is another paragraph.</p>
```

In older browsers, the closing tags were assumed. However, in newer browsers, markup that is missing its closing tags will not render the way you expect and may result in an unintelligible page. Empty elements must also have a closing tag. In the past, empty elements such as <hr> were not required to have a closing tag. It was just assumed by the browser. Now, all HTML elements, including empty elements, must have a closing tag.

Nesting describes the relationship between tags in HTML markup. For Tag A to be properly nested inside of Tag B, Tag A must be both opened and closed before Tag B is closed. This is an example of incorrect nesting:

```
<h1><div>These tags are improperly nested.</h1></div>
```

This is correct:

```
<div><h1>These tags are correctly nested.</h1></div>
```

TRY IT

In this lesson you create your first HTML page, complete with JavaScript and a little styling.

Lesson Requirements

To complete this lesson you need to install Microsoft Visual Web Developer 2010 Express.

Hints

➤ Enter **HTML** in the Search Installed Templates search box to find the HTML Page template.

➤ Add elements to the HTML page by dragging them from the Toolbox.

Step-by-Step

1. Open Microsoft Visual Web Developer 2010 Express.

2. Click New Web Site to open the New Web Site dialog box.

3. Select **Visual C#.**

4. Select **Empty Web Site** from the list of installed templates.

 Do not double-click the Empty Web Site template, because if you do, you will not be given the opportunity to select the name and location for the new web site.

5. Verify that File System is selected and type **c:\ASPNETTrainer\Lesson1** for the Web Location (see Figure 1-2).

FIGURE 1-2

6. Click OK.

7. Click Web site ➪ Add New Item and select the HTML Page template from the Add New Item dialog box.

8. Type **HelloWorld.htm** for the Name of the HTML page (see Figure 1-3).

9. Click Add.

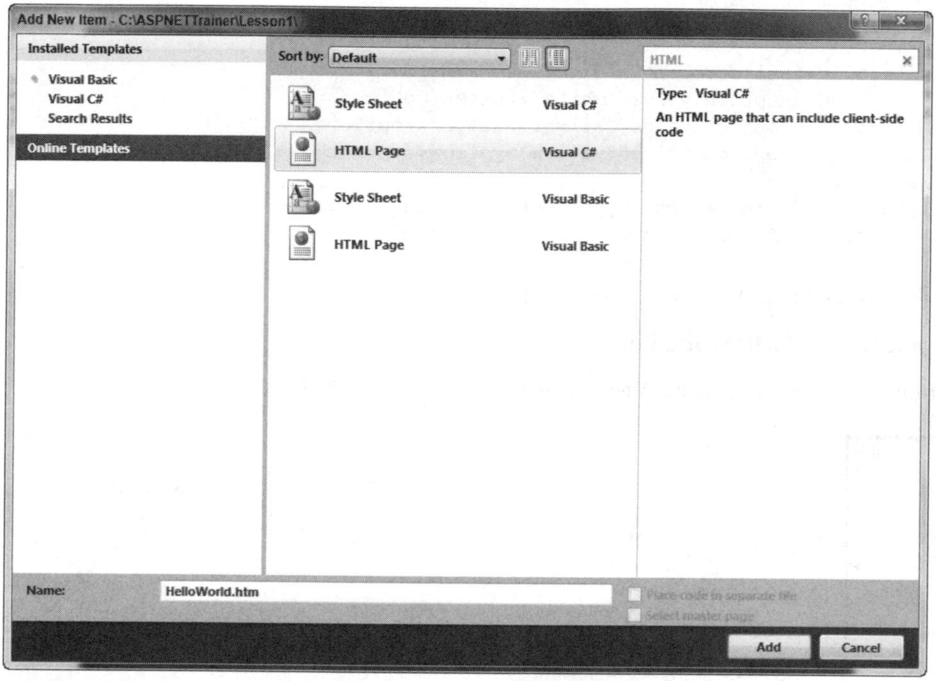

FIGURE 1-3

10. Type **Hello World** in the title element.

11. Click View ⇨ Toolbox to display the Toolbox.

> *If the Toolbox is not on the View menu, click Tools ⇨ Settings ⇨ Expert Settings to add it to the View menu.*

12. Drag a div element from the Toolbox (see Figure 1-4) and add the following attribute to your new div element:

```
id="BodyContent"
```

13. Type the following markup within the div element:

```
<h1>Hello World</h1>
<h2>Welcome</h2>
This is my first web page.
```

14. Drag a Horizontal Rule element from the Toolbox.

15. Type **Please select a color:**.

16. Drag a Select element from the Toolbox and add the following markup:

```
<select id="SelectColor">
        <option value="white">white</option>
        <option value="silver">silver</option>
        <option value="yellow">yellow</option>
</select>
<input id="ButtonSelect" type="button" value="Select"
   onclick="ShowSelection()" />
```

17. Click Edit ⇨ Format Document to format the document.

18. Click File ⇨ Save HelloWorld.htm.

19. Right-click the page and select View in Browser (see Figure 1-5).

FIGURE 1-4   **FIGURE 1-5**

20. Close the browser.

21. Add the following code to the head element:

```
<style type="text/css">
        h1 {color: Blue; }
</style>
<script type="text/javascript">
        function ShowSelection() {
            alert('You have selected ' + SelectColor.value);
            BodyContent.style.backgroundColor = SelectColor.value;
        }
</script>
```

22. Verify that your code matches the following:

```
<!DOCTYPE html PUBLIC "-//W3C//DTD XHTML 1.0 Transitional//EN"
    "http://www.w3.org/TR/xhtml1/DTD/xhtml1-transitional.dtd">
<html xmlns="http://www.w3.org/1999/xhtml">
<head>
    <title>Hello World</title>
    <style type="text/css">
        h1
        {
            color: Blue;
        }
    </style>
    <script type="text/javascript">
        function ShowSelection() {
            alert('You have selected ' + SelectColor.value);
            BodyContent.style.backgroundColor = SelectColor.value;
        }
    </script>
</head>
<body>
    <div id="BodyContent">
        <h1>
            Hello World</h1>
        <h2>
            Welcome</h2>
        This is my first web page.
        <hr />
        <select id="SelectColor">
            <option value="white">white</option>
            <option value="silver">silver</option>
            <option value="yellow">yellow</option>
        </select>
        <input id="ButtonSelect" type="button" value="Select"
            onclick="ShowSelection()" />
    </div>
</body>
</html>
```

23. Click File ⇨ Save HelloWorld.htm.

24. Right-click the page and select View in Browser.

25. Select a color from the drop-down list of colors.

26. Close the browser.

Please select Lesson 1 on the DVD to view the video that accompanies this lesson.

2

Using Common HTML Tags

In this lesson I introduce some common HTML tags. However, this is not a book on HTML. For more information about HTML please see the Wrox book *Beginning HTML, XHTML, CSS, and JavaScript* (Duckett, 2009, Wrox).

> *The best way to learn HMTL is to study how other people use it. For example, in Internet Explorer 8, you can view the source of a web page by selecting View Source from the Page menu.*

HEADINGS

Headings are used to divide sections of text in a hierarchical manner. HTML defines six levels of headings, ranging from `<h1>` for the most important to `<h6>` for the least important:

```
<h1>Heading 1</h1>
<h2>Heading 2</h2>
<h3>Heading 3</h3>
<h4>Heading 4</h4>
<h5>Heading 5</h5>
<h6>Heading 6</h6>
```

Figure 2-1 shows each of the six levels of headings. An important thing to notice about headings is that they always appear on their own line. They are considered block-level elements.

Once you have your added your headings, it's time to add some text. Text is divided into paragraphs, and the HTML tag for paragraph is `<p>`:

```
<p>This is my first paragraph. It is a very short paragraph by design.</p>
```

The paragraph element automatically creates some space before and after itself, therefore it is also a block-level element. Many people are tempted to use the line break element (<br />) to create paragraphs. They do this by placing two line breaks in a row. However, you should avoid this temptation. If you separate your paragraphs using line breaks, you will not be able to apply styles to them. You learn more about applying styles in the next lesson.

At this point you may be asking yourself, why should I bother with using any elements at all? Why not just use the Enter key to create line breaks? The reason that you must use the appropriate element is that *any* extra white space in your HTML is automatically stripped out by the browser and therefore is completely ignored. For example, if you painstakingly format the text shown in Figure 2-2 by using the Enter key, you will end up with the gibberish that is shown in Figure 2-3 when the page is rendered in the browser.

FIGURE 2-1

```
Client Objects & Events                        (No Events)
 1  <!DOCTYPE html PUBLIC "-//W3C//DTD XHTML 1.0 Transitional//EN"
 2    "http://www.w3.org/TR/xhtml1/DTD/xhtml1-transitional.dtd">
 3  <html xmlns="http://www.w3.org/1999/xhtml">
 4  <head>
 5      <title>Whitespace</title>
 6  </head>
 7  <body>
 8  This is my first paragraph.
 9
10  This is my second paragraph. It is a little longer.
11
12  This is a short list of items:
13    1. First Item
14    2. Second Item
15    3. Third Item
16  </body>
17  </html>
18
100 %
```

FIGURE 2-2

FIGURE 2-3

> If you need to retain the white space use the <pre> tag. The <pre> tag is for pre-formatted text. It is usually displayed using a fixed-width font and it preserves both spaces and line breaks. It's great for displaying sample code.

DIVIDING TEXT

I briefly introduced the <div> tag in the first lesson. This tag defines a block of content and is used to create logical divisions on your page. This is an example of how you would use the <div> tag to lay out a web page:

```
<div id="header"></div>
<div id="body">
```

```
        <div id="navigation"></div>
        <div id="content"></div>
    </div>
    <div id="footer">
    </div>
```

You will be using the `<div>` tag later in this lesson's tutorial to lay out your web page.

> ✖ *If you view the preceding code in a browser, you will get a blank page. You must add content to each of the `<div>` tags, and I show you how to do this in Lesson 3.*

If you want to add a dividing line between sections of your page, you can use a horizontal rule. The horizontal rule uses a self-closing tag, `<hr />`, and renders a horizontal line. The horizontal rule is a block-level element.

LISTS

The two most common types of lists are unordered lists and ordered lists. Unordered lists are bulleted lists, whereas ordered lists can be either numerical or alphabetical lists.

The `<ul>` tag is used to designate an unordered list, and each item within the list must be enclosed in a list item (`<li>`) tag. The bullets are automatically added by the browser, and you use the `Style` attribute to designate the shape of the bullet that is used.

This markup renders the unordered list shown in Figure 2-4:

```
<h1>Unordered List</h1>
<ul>
    <li>Item One</li>
    <li>Item Two</li>
    <li>Item Three</li>
</ul>
```

The `<ol>` tag is used to designate an ordered list, and just like the unordered list, each item within the list must be enclosed in a list item (`<li>`) tag. The numbers or letters are automatically added by the browser. You can designate the starting number for the list and the type of number to use via a cascading style sheet. The default type of number is Arabic numerals, but your list can use uppercase letters, lowercase letters, uppercase Roman Numerals, or lowercase Roman Numerals instead of Arabic numerals. Cascading style sheets are covered in Lesson 3.

This markup renders the ordered list shown in Figure 2-5:

```
<h1>Ordered List</h1>
<ol>
    <li>Item One</li>
    <li>Item Two</li>
    <li>Item Three</li>
</ol>
```

FIGURE 2-4

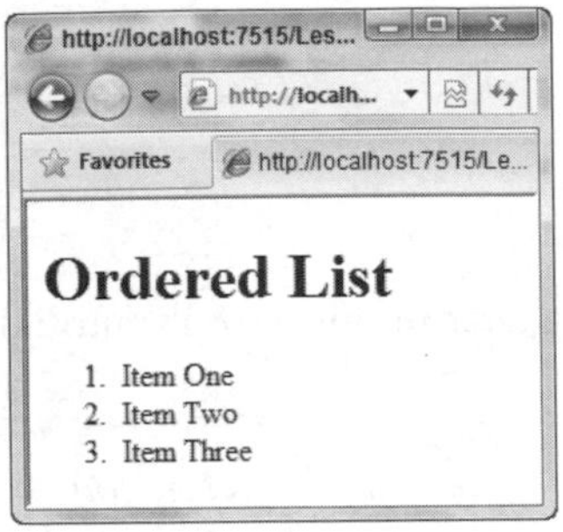

FIGURE 2-5

LINKS

A link is a connection from one web page to another. Although links are simple to use, or perhaps because they are simple to use, they have been a driving force behind the success of the Internet.

A link uses an `<a>` tag, which stands for anchor. The `href` attribute is used to designate the link's destination. Href stands for **H**ypertext **Ref**erence. The following example redirects the user to the home page for Wrox:

```
<a href="http://www.wrox.com">WROX</a>
```

This example uses an absolute link, which requires a complete web address. However, you can also use links to redirect a user to pages within your own web site. These types of links are referred to as relative links. They take advantage of the fact that the page already knows its location relative to the page to which it is linking. If I wanted to create a link to the home page of my web site, I might use the following code:

```
<a href="Home.aspx">Home</a>
```

However, this example assumes that the home page is in the same folder as the current web page. If my current web page is in a subfolder of the folder that contains the home page, this example will not work. In that case, I will need to direct the browser to go up one folder in order to find the home page. The following code will correctly link to the home page from a page that is in a subfolder:

```
<a href="../Home.aspx">Home</a>
```

The `../` directs the browser to move up one folder, and I can add more `../`'s for deeper levels of subfolders. What if I want to add a link to the home page from all of my pages? In that case I would use a root-relative link. To create a root-relative link all I have to do is add a forward slash (/) to the beginning of the path. This is an example of a root-relative link:

```
<a href="/Home.aspx">Home</a>
```

In the preceding example, the link is directing the browser to return to the root folder of the web site to find the `Home.aspx` page.

IMAGES

Images are an important component of most web pages. The <img> tag is used to add an image to a web page. The source of the image and the alternate text for the image are both required attributes. The most widely used image formats on the Internet are GIF, JPEG, and PNG.

This is an example of an image element:

```
<img src="Telephone.gif" alt="Telephone" title="This is a telephone."/>
```

The src attribute is used to designate the source of the image. It is a hypertext reference, like the href attribute used with links. The source of the image can be an absolute link or a relative link. The alt attribute is used to designate the alternative text, which is displayed instead of the image if the image cannot be displayed. For example, the image cannot be displayed if the image file has been deleted.

> The alt *attribute should be used as the alternative text that is displayed if the image is not available, not as a tooltip. Use the* title *attribute to add a tooltip.*

TABLES

Tables are meant to display tabular data. They allow you to arrange your data into rows and columns, and they are incredibly flexible. Each cell of a table can contain just about any type of data from text, images, and links to entire tables.

Tables are very easy to add to your web pages. The <table> tag is used to define a table. Within a table the table row (<tr>) tag is used to distinguish each row. Within each row the table header (<th>) tag is used to enter the header for each column and the table data (<td>) tag is used to enter the data into each cell. 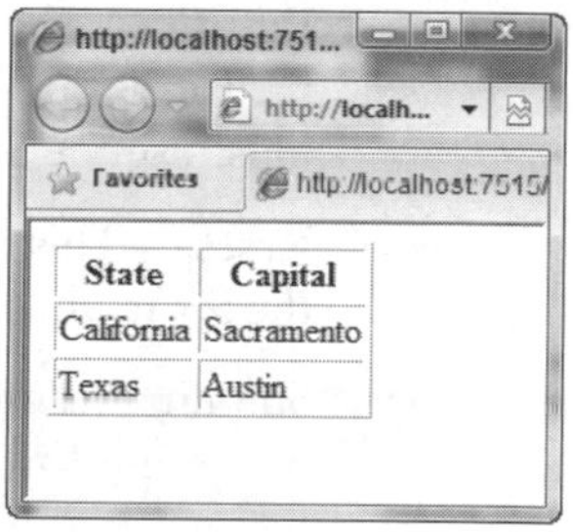

FIGURE 2-6

Figure 2-6 shows the table that is rendered as a result of this HTML:

```
<table border="1">
    <tr>
        <th>State</th>
        <th>Capital</th>
    </tr>
    <tr>
        <td>California</td>
        <td>Sacramento</td>
    </tr>
    <tr>
        <td>Texas</td>
        <td>Austin</td>
    </tr>
</table>.
```

> *Though it may be tempting to use tables to lay out your web pages, you should resist the temptation. You should use <div> elements and cascading style sheets to lay out your pages. Tables should be used only for tabular data.*

FORMS

Forms are used to send data to the server. They can contain all types of input elements. The <form> tag is used to create a form and the action attribute is required for each form. The action attribute is used to designate where to send the data when the form is submitted. By default, the form is submitted to itself.

Input elements are used to input data into the form. Figure 2-7 shows the contents of the HTML tab of the Toolbox. As you can see there are quite a few ways to input data into a form.

This is the markup for a button:

```
<input id="Button1" type="button" value="button" />
```

The type attribute is used to designate the type of input element that is rendered. This is a short description of each of the input types:

FIGURE 2-7

➤ **Button** — This type renders a clickable button that does not submit the form to the server. In order to submit the form to the server, you must use the Submit type.

➤ **Reset** — This type renders a reset button that clears all of the text in the form when it is clicked.

➤ **Submit** — This type renders a submit button. A submit button submits the information on the form to the server.

➤ **Text** — This type renders a one-line input field.

➤ **File** — This type is used to upload files to the server.

➤ **Password** — This type renders a one-line input field where all of the characters are displayed as asterisks or circles.

➤ **Checkbox** — This type renders a checkbox.

➤ **Radio** — This type renders a radio button.

➤ **Hidden** — This type renders a field that is not visible to the user. Hidden fields are often used to store default data.

Figure 2-8 shows how each type of input element is rendered.

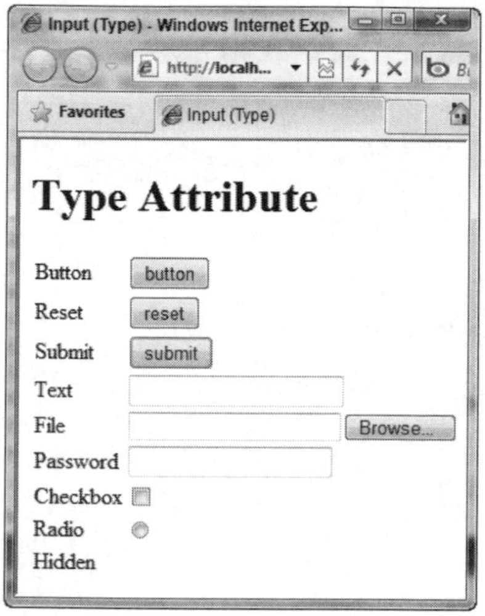

FIGURE 2-8

TRY IT

In this lesson you create an HTML page that uses most of the HTML tags that you have learned.

Lesson Requirements

To complete this lesson you need to download the `SuperEasyRecipesLogo.gif` image.

Hints

➤ Use HTML Snippets to add HTML elements to the page.

➤ Use Ctrl+K, Ctrl+D to format your document.

Step-by-Step

1. Open Microsoft Visual Web Developer 2010 Express.

2. Click New Web Site.

3. Select **Visual C#**.

4. Select **Empty Web Site** from the list of installed templates.

5. Verify that File System is selected and type **c:\ASPNETTrainer\Lesson2** for the Web Location.

6. Click OK.

7. Click Web site ⇨ Add New Item and select the HTML Page template from the Add New Item dialog box.

8. Type **CheeseSandwich.htm** for the Name of the HTML page.

9. Click Add.

10. Enter **Cheese Sandwich** in the title element.

11. Enter the following code into the body element:

```
<div class="header"></div>
<div class="sidebar"></div>
<div class="content"></div>
```

12. Click Web site ➪ Add Existing Item to open the Add Existing Item dialog box.

13. Navigate to the `SuperEasyRecipesLogo.gif` file, select it, and click Add (see Figure 2-9).

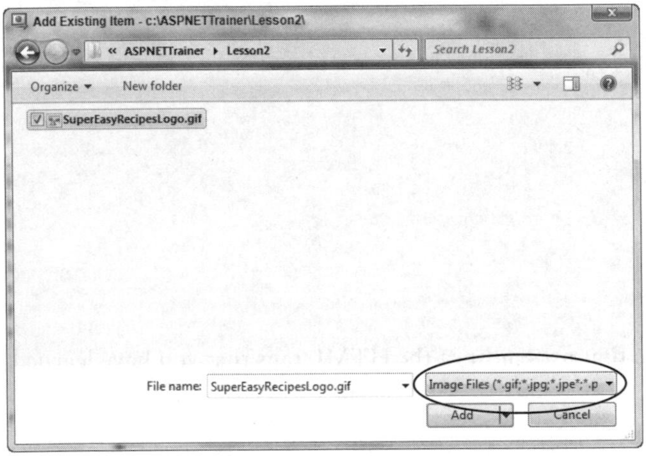

FIGURE 2-9

> Select Image Files from the drop-down list located in the lower right-hand corner of the Add Existing Item dialog box to view only the images.

14. Enter the following code into the div element where `class="header"`:

```
<img src="SuperEasyRecipesLogo.gif" />
```

15. View the Error List (see Figure 2-10).

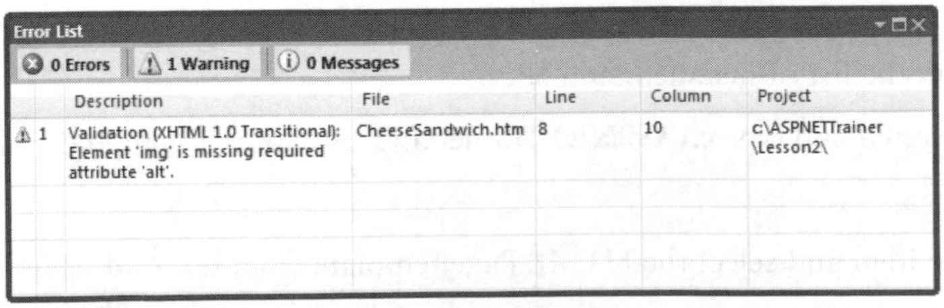

FIGURE 2-10

> *If the Error List window is not open, click View ⇨ Error List to open it. If the Error List is not on the View menu, click Tools ⇨ Settings ⇨ Expert Settings to add it to the View menu.*

16. Add the following `alt` attribute to the img element to remove the error:

```
alt="Super Easy Recipes"
```

17. Enter the following code into the div element where `class="sidebar"`:

```
<h2>Tools</h2>
<ol>
    <li>Saucepan</li>
    <li>Spatula</li>
</ol>
```

18. Enter the following code into the div element where `class="content"`:

```
<h1>Grilled Cheese Sandwich</h1>
<table>
    <tr>
        <td>Prep Time:</td>
         <td>Cook Time:</td>
           <td>Ready In:</td>
    </tr>
    <tr>
        <td>5 Min</td>
        <td>15 Min</td>
        <td>20 Min</td>
    </tr>
</table>
<h2>Ingredients</h2>
<ul>
    <li>2 slices of bread</li>
    <li>2 slices of American cheese</li>
    <li>Butter</li>
</ul>
<h2>Directions</h2>
<p>
    Preheat skillet over medium heat.
</p>
<p>
    Generously butter one side of a slice of bread and add 2 slices of
    cheese. Generously butter both sides of the other piece of bread and add
    it to the top. Place bread butter-side-down onto the skillet bottom and
    butter the top piece of bread.
</p>
<p>
Grill until lightly browned on both sides. Serve immediately.
</p>
```

19. Verify that your code matches the following:

```
<!DOCTYPE html PUBLIC "-//W3C//DTD XHTML 1.0 Transitional//EN"
    "http://www.w3.org/TR/xhtml1/DTD/xhtml1-transitional.dtd">
<html xmlns="http://www.w3.org/1999/xhtml">
<head>
    <title>Cheese Sandwich</title>
</head>
<body>
    <div class="header">
        <img src="SuperEasyRecipesLogo.gif" alt="Super Easy Recipes" />
    </div>
    <div class="sidebar">
        <h2>
            Tools</h2>
        <ol>
            <li>Saucepan</li>
            <li>Spatula</li>
        </ol>
    </div>
    <div class="content">
        <h1>
            Grilled Cheese Sandwich</h1>
        <table>
            <tr>
                <td>
                    Prep Time:
                </td>
                <td>
                    Cook Time:
                </td>
                <td>
                    Ready In:
                </td>
            </tr>
            <tr>
                <td>
                    5 Min
                </td>
                <td>
                    15 Min
                </td>
                <td>
                    20 Min
                </td>
            </tr>
        </table>
        <h2>
            Ingredients</h2>
        <ul>
            <li>2 slices of bread</li>
            <li>2 slices of American cheese</li>
            <li>Butter</li>
        </ul>
        <h2>
```

```
                        Directions</h2>
            <p>
                Preheat skillet over medium heat.
            </p>
            <p>
                Generously butter one side of a slice of bread and add 2 slices
                of cheese. Generously butter both sides of the other piece of
                bread and add it to the top. Place bread butter-side-down onto
                the skillet bottom and butter the top piece of bread.
            </p>
            <p>
                Grill until lightly browned on both sides. Serve immediately.
            </p>
        </div>
    </body>
    </html>
```

20. Save the file.

21. Right-click the page and select View in Browser (see Figure 2-11).

FIGURE 2-11

 Please select Lesson 2 on the DVD to view the video that accompanies this lesson.

3

Adding Style to an HTML Page

In this lesson you learn how to use cascading style sheets (CSS) to add style to an HTML page. As I said in Lesson 1, HTML defines the structure of a page, while cascading style sheets define the styles on a page. They can be used to define colors, fonts, and background images and they can be used for page layout. There are over 90 properties that you can use to style your HTML.

CSS RULES

A cascading style sheet is made-up of a collection of CSS rules. This is the CSS rule to modify the colors used by the `<h1>` tag:

```
h1 {color:White; background-color:Silver}
```

This CSS rule sets the text color of all of your `<h1>` tags to white and their background color to silver, as shown in Figure 3-1.

A CSS rule consists of a selector and one or more declarations. Each declaration is made up of a property and a value, as shown in Figure 3-2.

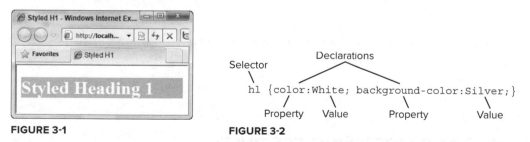

FIGURE 3-1

FIGURE 3-2

As you can see in Figure 3-2 each declaration is separated by a semicolon. Another way to write this CSS rule is to type each declaration on its own line:

```
h1
{
    color: White;
```

```
        background-color: Silver;
    }
```

In the preceding example, all of the <h1> tags on the entire page will be displayed using the new H1 style. If you do not want your style to be applied to every instance of a particular HTML element, you can specify your own selectors. You can specify both class selectors and ID selectors.

Class Selectors

Class selectors allow you to select certain elements on the basis of the value that is assigned to their class attribute. Multiple elements on the same page can share the same class attribute. The following CSS rule defines a warning class selector that will change the text to red and make it bold:

```
.warning
{
    color:Red;
    font-weight:bold;
}
```

This is an example of an element that uses the warning class:

```
<p class="warning">This is a warning.</p>
```

ID Selectors

The ID selector matches an element that has a specific attribute value. Because each ID must be unique, an ID selector will never match more than one element in a document. ID selectors are typically used for page layout. The following CSS rule defines a sidebar ID selector that will float the element to the right side of the page and set its background color to silver:

```
#sidebar
{
    float:right;
    width:200px;
    background-color: Silver;
}
```

This is an example of an element that uses the sidebar ID selector:

```
<div id="sidebar">
    This is the sidebar.
</div>
```

CREATING AND MODIFYING CSS RULES

Creating CSS rules is easy with Microsoft Visual Web Developer 2010. You can use the Add Style Rule dialog box to add a new CSS rule. The Add Style Rule dialog box, shown in Figure 3-3, can be used to add any of the three types of rules.

You do not need to use the Add Style Rule dialog box to add new rules. You can type them directly into your code. As you become more proficient with CSS rules you probably will not use the Add Style Rule dialog box at all.

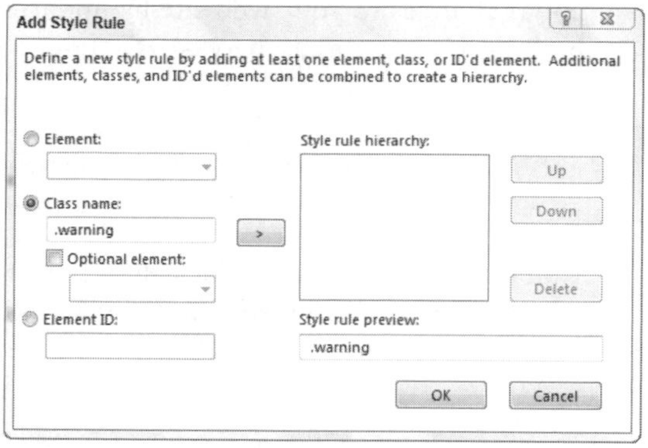

Once you have created your CSS rule, you can use the Modify Style dialog box to edit it. This dialog box, as shown in Figure 3-4, includes most of the commonly used properties. An added feature of the Modify Style dialog box is that it provides a preview pane that shows how the sample text will be displayed.

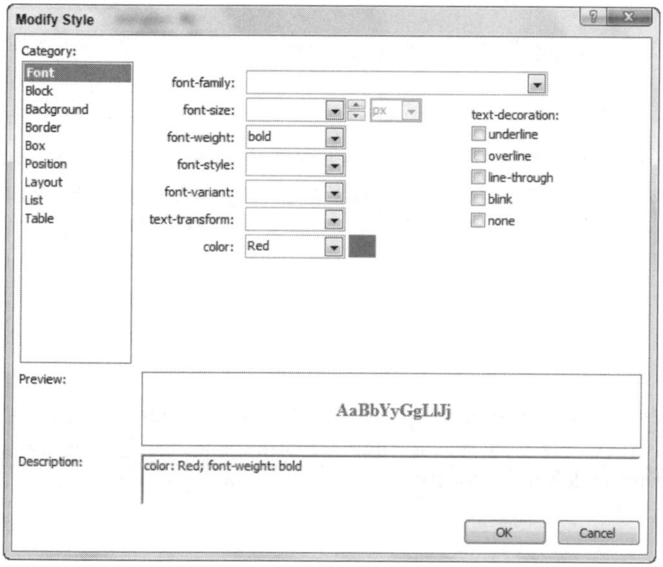

FIGURE 3-3

FIGURE 3-4

APPLYING CSS RULES

Now that you know how to define your CSS rules, you need to apply them to your pages. Your CSS rules can be associated with a particular page in three ways. You can use an external style sheet, an internal style sheet, or inline styles. External style sheets are the preferred method. However, I briefly cover all three methods.

An external style sheet has the .css file extension. As the name implies it is a separate file that only contains CSS rules. The advantage of using an external style sheet is that you can make global changes to your web site by updating only one file. It is linked to your documents by using the following syntax, where `StyleSheet.css` refers to the name of your particular style sheet:

```
<head>
    ...
    <link href="StyleSheet.css" rel="stylesheet" type="text/css" />
<head>
```

An internal style sheet includes all of the CSS rules in the head element of the HTML page. All of the CSS rules are included in a `<style>` tag. The following code sets all of the H1 elements to blue:

```
<head>
    ...
    <style type="text/css">
        h1
        {
            color: Blue;
        }
    </style>
</head>
```

The last way to apply CSS rules is to use inline styles. Inline styles apply the style to the individual tag. They should be avoided because they mix structure with style; however, they can be a very handy tool to use when you are initially designing a page. The following code centers the text within the `<p>` element:

```
<p style="text-align: center">
    This text is centered.
</p>
```

Now you are probably wondering whether you can use external style sheets, internal styles, and inline styles on the same page. The answer is yes. The reason they are called cascading style sheets is that the styles can cascade. The style that is defined closest to the object is the style that is applied. This is the how they are prioritized:

1. Inline Style

2. Internal Style Sheet

3. External Style Sheet

4. Browser Default

A style defined inline overrides a style that is defined in an internal style sheet or an external style sheet.

> *The order of the links in the head element also impacts the style that will be used. Any links in the head element will be overwritten by styles in a preceding link. Also, if an internal style sheet is before an external style sheet, the CSS rules in the external style sheet take precedence over the rules in the internal style sheet.*

MANAGING CSS RULES

The cascading nature of cascading style sheets can get quite confusing. If you have more than one location where you define your CSS rules, you may experience unexpected results due to the order of the rules. Microsoft Visual Web Developer 2010 provides three really helpful windows that help you manage your styles:

➤ CSS Properties window

➤ Manage Styles window

➤ Apply Styles window

The CSS Properties window lists all of the styles that are used by the currently selected element. It includes the order of precedence of those styles and all of their properties and values (see Figure 3-5). If you need to open the CSS Properties window, select View ➪ CSS Properties.

The Manage Styles window is used to apply, modify, rename, and delete styles (see Figure 3-6). You can also use the Manage Styles window to change the location or order of styles. You can move styles from an internal style sheet into an external style sheet and vice versa. If you need to open the Manage Styles window, select View ➪ Manage Styles.

The Apply Styles window is used to apply styles to a particular page. The Apply Styles window lists all of the styles used on the currently selected page. This window is easy to use because it displays each style according to the rules of that style (see Figure 3-7). To apply a style, all you need to do is select the element and then click the style that you want to apply. If you need to open the Apply Styles window, select View ➪ Apply Styles.

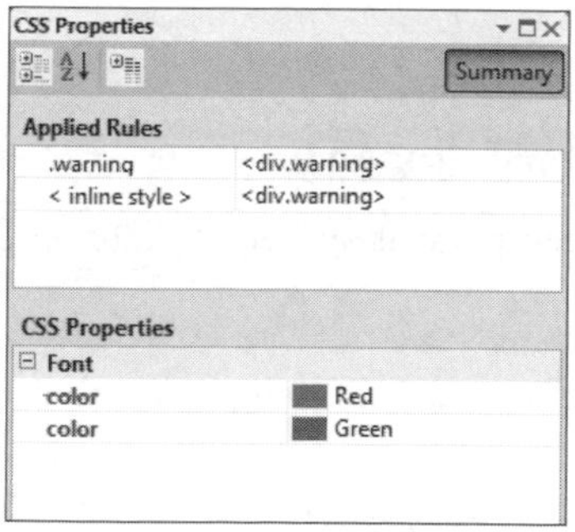

FIGURE 3-5

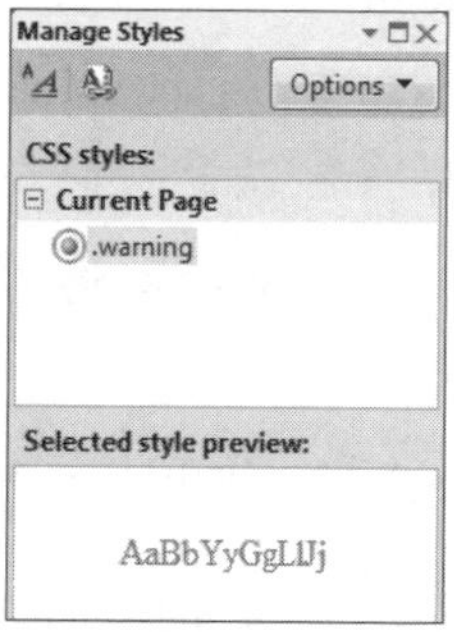

FIGURE 3-6

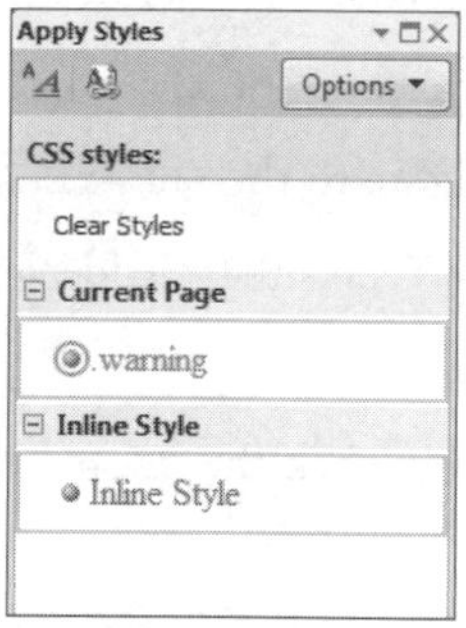

FIGURE 3-7

My favorite web site that demonstrates the power of CSS rules is CSS Zen Garden, www.csszengarden.com. This web site allows people to submit custom CSS files that are all applied to the same HTML document.

TRY IT

In this lesson you apply styles to the HTML document that you created in Lesson 2.

Lesson Requirements

➤ The `CheeseSandwich.htm` file that you created in the previous lesson.

➤ The `SuperEasyRecipesLogo.gif` file.

Hints

➤ Use the Manage Styles window to manage your styles.

Step-By-Step

1. Open Microsoft Visual Web Developer 2010 Express.

2. Click New Web Site.

3. Select **Visual C#**.

4. Select **Empty Web Site** from the list of installed templates.

5. Verify that File System is selected and type **c:\ASPNETTrainer\Lesson3** for the Web Location.

6. Click OK.

7. Click Web site ➪ Add Existing Item.

8. Navigate to the `CheeseSandwich.htm` file, select it, and click Add.

9. Navigate to the `SuperEasyRecipesLogo.gif` file, select it, and click Add.

10. Click Web site ➪ Add New Item and select the Style Sheet template as shown in Figure 3-8.

11. Click Add.

12. Double-click the `CheeseSandwich.htm` file to open it and enter the following link into its head element:

```
<link href="StyleSheet.css" rel="stylesheet" type="text/css" />
```

13. Verify that the head element matches the following code:

```
<head>
    <title>Cheese Sandwich</title>
    <link href="StyleSheet.css" rel="stylesheet" type="text/css" />
</head>
```

14. Save the file.

15. Add the following CSS rules to the `StyleSheet.css` file:

```
body
{
    margin: 0 auto;
    width: 800px;
}
h1
{
    color: #663399;
}
td
{
    background-color: #FFFF66;
    padding: 5px;
}
p
{
    width: 500px;
}
```

FIGURE 3-8

16. Save the file.

17. View the `CheeseSandwich.htm` file in the browser (see Figure 3-9).

FIGURE 3-9

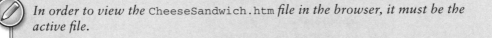
In order to view the CheeseSandwich.htm *file in the browser, it must be the active file.*

18. Add the following CSS rules to StyleSheet.css and save the file:

```
.content
{
    float: left;
}
.sidebar
{
    float: right;
    background-color: #9966CC;
    padding: 10px;
    color: White;
    width: 250px;
}
.header
{
    background-color: #FFCC66;
}
```

19. View the `CheeseSandwich.htm` file in the browser (see Figure 3-10).

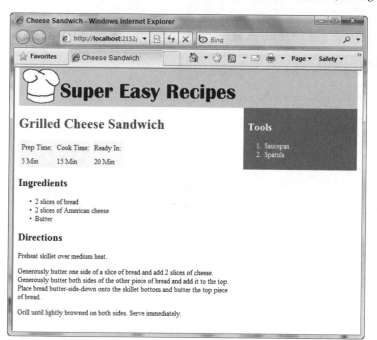

FIGURE 3-10

20. Reverse the position of the sidebar on the `CheeseSandwich.htm` file by changing the sidebar CSS rule to the following:

```
.sidebar
{
    float: left;
    background-color: #9966CC;
    padding: 10px;
    color: White;
    width: 250px;
}
```

21. Save the file.

22. View the `CheeseSandwich.htm` file in the browser (see Figure 3-11).

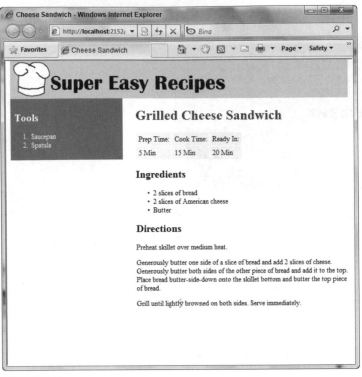

FIGURE 3-11

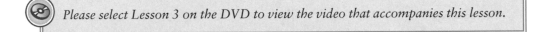

Please select Lesson 3 on the DVD to view the video that accompanies this lesson.

4

State Management in ASP.NET 4

As I mentioned in the Welcome, the Internet uses the **Hypertext Transfer Protocol (HTTP)** to enable browsers and web servers to communicate with each other. The problem with HTTP is that it is an inherently stateless protocol. This means that every page request is unrelated to every other page request. If you are building a web application that does more than display static data, you need to be able to associate data with a particular user over multiple page requests. Therefore, your web application requires state management.

In this lesson I show you how the ASP.NET framework is able to overcome the stateless nature of HTTP and simulate state. I also show you a few methods that the ASP.NET framework provides for storing data about a particular user.

SESSION ID

ASP.NET simulates state by assigning each user a randomly generated Session ID and sending that Session ID to the user's browser via a cookie. A cookie is a very small text file stored on a user's computer by a web browser. The browser sends the cookie back to the web site with any subsequent requests. In this manner, your web site is able to recognize returning users.

By default, ASP.NET stores the Session ID for each session in a cookie on the browser. The Session ID is generated by a random number generator that returns a sequence of randomly generated numbers that are mapped to valid URL characters and returned as a 120-bit string. This is the code to view the Session ID for the current user:

```
string mySessionID = Session.SessionID;
```

I ran this code during a recent session, and this is the Session ID that the system generated:

```
nsta5xi5pciit4zrsiwsscpq
```

> *If users disable cookies, ASP.NET will not be able to store their Session IDs in a cookie. However, if cookies are disabled, the ASP.NET framework can be configured to store the Session ID in the URL.*

COOKIES

Each browser stores its cookies in a different location. That means that Internet Explorer does not have access to the cookies stored by Firefox and vice versa. Also, each cookie is associated with only one domain. That means that Travelocity.com cannot read the cookies from Orbitz.com and vice versa.

On Windows 7, Internet Explorer stores cookies in the following folder:

```
C:\Users\Toi\AppData\Roaming\Microsoft\Windows\Cookies
```

If you navigate to your cookies folder you will find a collection of text files. On my computer the most recent cookie has the filename `toi@support.microsoft[1].txt`. This is the content of that cookie:

```
.ASPXANONYMOUS
bP8X7mbJygEkAAAANGJiOWM1ZmYtMDJjZC00NmFhLTg2Y2YtNGU2NWQzMzA5OTNm3Al2cXuMSGj8iI1-Zb0
OFc25KwU1
support.microsoft.com/
9216
3992672384
30067046
395540208
30053077
*
```

 Cookies are stored in clear text. Therefore, you do not want to store any sensitive data in a cookie.

In the past, cookies have been unfairly maligned. Because cookies are stored on the user's machine, they raise security concerns; however, they are safe. Cookies store only text. As such, they are not executable. Also, cookies can store only a very small amount of text — 4096 bytes on most browsers. On top of that, most browsers limit the number of cookies that a particular web site can store on your machine to 20.

Although cookies are safe to use, all modern browsers allow users to disable them. If your application relies on cookies you must be prepared to handle requests from browsers that do not have cookies enabled.

Each cookie is made up of a name/value pair. You add a cookie by adding it to the Response. Cookies collection. The following code creates a cookie named Theme:

```
Response.Cookies["Theme"].Value = "Retro";
```

To read your cookies, use the Request.Cookies collection. This is the code to read the preceding cookie:

```
if (Request.Cookies["Theme"] != null)
{
    string theme =  Request.Cookies["Theme"].Value;
}
```

It is very important that you make sure your cookie exists before you try to read it. If the cookie does not exist, you will get the `Object reference not set to an instance of an object` exception. Also, it is important to remember that the name of a cookie is case-sensitive. Therefore a cookie named Theme is different from a cookie named theme.

There are two types of cookies: session and persistent. Session cookies are deleted when the user closes the browser. By default, cookies created by ASP.NET are session cookies. If you want to create a persistent cookie you must specify an expiration date. The following code sets the expiration date for the cookie to be one month in the future:

```
Response.Cookies["Theme"].Expires = DateTime.Now.AddMonths(1);
```

Overall, cookies are simple to use. However, because cookies can be disabled and are stored in clear text, they should not be used to store sensitive data. Also, it is important to remember that cookies are transmitted with each request, which means they can negatively impact the amount of time that your page takes to load.

SESSION OBJECT

Session state is another tool you can use to store information about the current user. Whereas cookies are stored on the client, session state is stored on the server. Also, unlike cookies, session state is not limited to small amounts of text.

The Session object is used to store session state. Each Session object is made up of a name/value pair. This is the code to save the value of the user's shopping cart to a Session object:

```
Session["ShoppingCart"] = ShoppingCart;
```

To read this Session object use the following code:

```
Cart shoppingCart = New Cart();
if (Session["ShoppingCart"] != null)
{
    shoppingCart = (Cart)Session["ShoppingCart"];
}
```

It is very important that you make sure that your Session object exists before you try to retrieve it. If the Session object does not exist, you will get the Object reference not set to an instance of an object exception. Also, like with cookies, the name of a Session object is case-sensitive. Therefore, a Session object named ShoppingCart is different from a Session object named shoppingcart. Finally, because the Session object stores data of type object, you must cast the value that is returned by the Session object. In the preceding example, I cast the returned object to Cart.

By default, the Session object is configured to expire after 20 minutes of inactivity. This means that if the user has not requested a page for more than 20 minutes, the session will time out. You can modify the Session timeout through code and in the web configuration file. The following code sets the Session timeout to 30 minutes:

```
Session.Timeout = 30;
```

> *The maximum length of time to which you can set the Session timeout value is one year (525,600 minutes).*

Also by default, the Session state is configured to be stored in the memory of the web server that served the document. This is referred to as InProc or in-process mode. The advantage of storing the Session object in-process is that it is very fast. However, because it is stored in the same process as the ASP.NET process, if your application restarts, you will lose the session data for *all* of your users. You can modify the Session state mode in the web configuration file.

> *Your application will be forced to restart for many reasons. For example, modifying the web configuration file, updating a DLL in the bin folder, or updating the* `Global.aspx` *file will all cause your application to restart.*

If you store your Session state in-process, your application is not scalable. The reason for this is that the Session object is stored on one particular server. Therefore storing Session state in-process will not work with a web farm. In addition to storing the Session state in-process, you can store Session state in a state server, an SQL server, or a custom location. There is a performance tradeoff if you do not store the data in-process, because storing Session state in memory does not require any database calls and therefore is faster.

The Session object is very easy to use. It can store all types of objects; however, it is not persistent. Once the user's session ends, it is destroyed.

PROFILE OBJECT

The Profile object is another object that the ASP.NET framework provides to store user data. The advantages of the Profile object over the Session object are that it stores the user's data over multiple sessions and it is strongly typed. To create a Profile object you must define its properties. The easiest way to define its properties is by updating the web configuration file.

This is the code to define a profile that contains the user's full name and category:

```xml
<?xml version="1.0"?>
<configuration>
  <system.web>
    <compilation debug="true" targetFramework="4.0"/>
    <profile>
      <properties>
        <add name="FullName"/>
        <add name="Category" type="Int32" defaultValue ="0"/>
      </properties>
    </profile>
  </system.web>
</configuration>
```

In this case `FullName` is a string, and `Category` is an integer with a default value of 0. If the `type` attribute is not provided, the property is assumed to be a string.

Once you have defined the properties, the Profile object can be accessed from anywhere in your application. This is the code to update the Profile properties that are defined in the preceding example:

```
Profile.FullName = "Toi B Wright";
Profile.Category = 2;
```

This is the code to read the Profile properties:

```
string fullName = Profile.FullName;
int category = Profile.Category;
```

If you want to define a large number of properties, you may want to organize them into groups. The following code creates a group for the user's preferences:

```
<?xml version="1.0"?>
<configuration>
  <system.web>
    <compilation debug="true" targetFramework="4.0"/>
    <profile>
      <properties>
        <group name="Preferences">
          <add name="Theme"/>
          <add name="Currency"/>
        </group>
      </properties>
    </profile>
  </system.web>
</configuration>
```

This is the code to set the `Theme` within the `Preferences` group using the Profile object:

```
Profile.Preferences.Theme = "Retro";
```

This is the code to read the `Theme` within the `Preferences` group using the Profile object:

```
String theme = Profile.Preferences.Theme;
```

> *I have been using Web Site projects (WSP) in these demonstrations. In future lessons I will be using Web Application projects (WAP). If you are using a Web Application project, you must define the ProfileCommon class before you can use the Profile object.*

You are probably wondering where the web site is storing the profile data. The profile data is stored in a Microsoft SQL Server Express database named ASPNETDB.mdf. By default this database is located in the App_Data folder. However, you can configure your application to use a different database to store the profile data by modifying the web configuration file.

TRY IT

In this lesson you examine the Session ID and manage user data using both the Session object and the Profile object.

Lesson Requirements

None.

Hints

➤   Use code completion for faster, more accurate data entry.

➤   Use Ctrl+Shift+W to view the current page in the browser.

Step-By-Step

1.   Open Microsoft Visual Web Developer 2010 Express.

2.   Select New Web Site from the File menu.

3.   Select **Visual C#**.

4.   Select **Empty Web Site** from the list of installed templates and verify that File System is selected for the Web location.

5.   Type **c:\ASPNETTrainer\Lesson4** for the Web Location.

6.   Click the OK button.

7.   Click Web site ➪ Add New Item and select the Web Form template from the Add New Item dialog box.

8.   Type **SessionID.aspx** for the Name, verify that the `Place code in separate file` checkbox is checked, and click the `Add` button (see Figure 4-1).

9.   Update the title element to the following:

```
<title>Session ID</title>
```

10.   Enter the following text into the `div` element:

```
<h1>Session ID</h1>
Your Session ID:
<asp:Literal ID="LiteralSessionID" runat="server" />
```

11.   Right-click the page and select View Code to open the code page.

12.   Type the following code into the `Page_Load` event:

```
this.LiteralSessionID.Text = Session.SessionID;
```

13.   Save both files and view the `Session.aspx` page in the browser (see Figure 4-2).

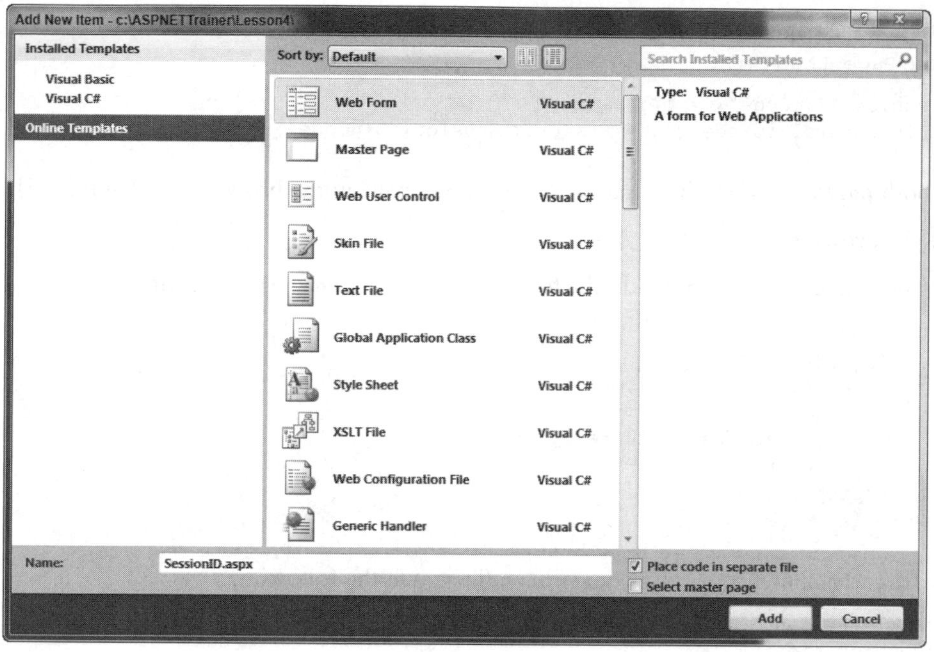

FIGURE 4-1

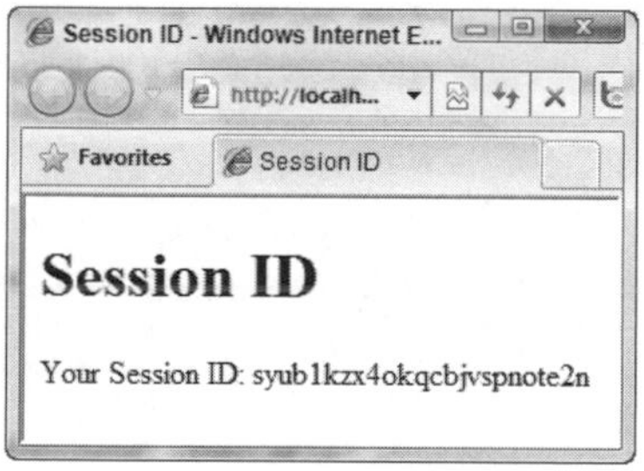

FIGURE 4-2

14. Close the browser.

15. Select Add New Item from the Web site menu and select the Web Form template.

16. Type **SessionObject.aspx** for the Name property, verify that the `Place code in separate file` checkbox is checked, and click `Add`.

17. Update the title element to the following:

```
<title>Session Object</title>
```

18. Enter the following code into the `div` element:

```
<h1>Session Object</h1>
Your Zip Code:
<asp:Literal ID="LiteralZipCode" runat="server" />
```

19. Right-click the page, select View Code to open the code page and type the following code into the `Page_Load` event:

```
Session["ZipCode"] = "75034";
this.LiteralZipCode.Text = (string)Session["ZipCode"];
```

20. Save both pages and view the `SessionObject.aspx` page in the browser (see Figure 4-3).

21. Close the browser.

22. Open the `web.config` file and add the following to the `system.web` element:

```
<profile>
    <properties>
        <group name="Preferences">
            <add name="Theme"/>
            <add name="Currency"/>
        </group>
    </properties>
</profile>
```

23. Verify that the contents of your `web.config` file match the following:

```
<?xml version="1.0"?>
<configuration>
    <system.web>
        <compilation debug="false" targetFramework="4.0" />
        <profile>
            <properties>
                <group name="Preferences">
                    <add name="Theme"/>
                    <add name="Currency"/>
                </group>
            </properties>
        </profile>
    </system.web>
</configuration>
```

24. Select Add New Item from the Web site menu and select the Web Form template.

25. Type **ProfileObject.aspx** for the Name, verify that the `Place code in separate file` checkbox is checked, and click Add.

26. Update the `title` element to the following:

```
<title>Profile Object</title>
```

27. Enter the following code into the `div` element:

```
<h1>Profile Object</h1>
Your Selected Theme:
<asp:Literal ID="LiteralTheme" runat="server" />
```

28. Type the following code into the `Page_Load` event:

```
Profile.Preferences.Theme = "Retro";
this.LiteralTheme.Text = Profile.Preferences.Theme;
```

29. Save the files and view the `ProfileObject.aspx` page in the browser (see Figure 4-4).

30. Close the browser.

31. On the Solution Explorer window click the refresh button to view the App_Data folder that was automatically created (see Figure 4-5).

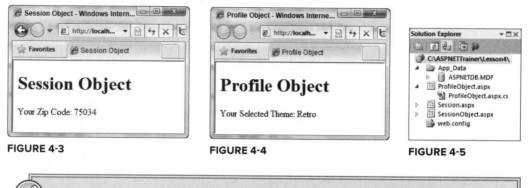

FIGURE 4-3

FIGURE 4-4

FIGURE 4-5

> *Microsoft Visual Web Developer 2010 Express automatically creates the ASPNETDB.MDF database file to store the profile information.*

32. Double-click the `ASPNETDB.MDF` file in the Solution Explorer to view the Database Explorer and view the aspnet_Profile table (see Figure 4-6).

Database Explorer

- Data Connections
  - ASPNETDB.MDF
    - Database Diagrams
    - Tables
      - aspnet_Applications
      - aspnet_Membership
      - aspnet_Paths
      - aspnet_PersonalizationAllUsers
      - aspnet_PersonalizationPerUser
      - aspnet_Profile
        - UserId
        - PropertyNames
        - PropertyValuesString
        - PropertyValuesBinary
        - LastUpdatedDate
      - aspnet_Roles
      - aspnet_SchemaVersions
      - aspnet_Users
      - aspnet_UsersInRoles
      - aspnet_WebEvent_Events
    - Views
    - Stored Procedures
    - Functions
    - Synonyms
    - Types
    - Assemblies

FIGURE 4-6

> *Please select Lesson 4 on the DVD to view the video that accompanies this lesson.*

5

Configuring Your Web Application

Configuration files are used to define Profile properties, store connection strings, configure debugging, define default error pages, and store a host of other settings that control how ASP.NET applications behave. Their primary purpose is to store the settings that you do not want to store in your compiled code.

In this lesson you learn how to configure your web application. I cover the hierarchical nature of web configuration files, how to use the ASP.NET Web site Administration Tool, and how to read a web configuration file programmatically.

WEB CONFIGURATION FILES

At the application level your web configuration is stored in the root folder in a file called web.config. This is an empty web.config file:

```
<?xml version="1.0"?>
<configuration>
</configuration>
```

As you can see, the web.config file is an XML text file with a root element of <configuration>.

ASP.NET uses a system of configuration files that is hierarchical. At the top of the hierarchy is the machine.config file. The machine.config file is located in the following folder:

```
C:\Windows\Microsoft.NET\Framework\v4.0.21006\Config
```

The machine.config file contains hundreds of settings. The settings in the machine.config file are inherited by all of the applications on the machine that use the .NET Framework. This includes both web applications and other types of applications.

In the same folder as the `machine.config` file is a `web.config` file. The `web.config` file contains settings related to web applications. The settings in the `web.config` file override the settings in the `machine.config` file.

As you have seen in the previous lessons, each application has its own `web.config` file in its root folder. The `web.config` file in the applications' root folder overrides the settings in the higher-level configuration files. You can also place a `web.config` file in a subfolder. In that case, the settings apply to that folder and all of the folders below it. Figure 5-1 shows the hierarchal relationship of the configuration files.

When an ASP.NET application starts, all of the configuration settings are merged and cached into memory. If you make a change to any of the configuration files, the application is restarted so that the new configuration settings can be updated in memory.

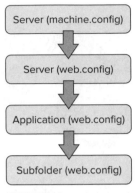

FIGURE 5-1

ASP.NET WEB SITE ADMINISTRATION TOOL

As you have seen, you can modify your web configuration files directly from the Integrated Development Environment (IDE) that is provided by Microsoft Visual Web Developer 2010 Express. ASP.NET also provides a tool specifically designed to update your `web.config` files. The ASP.NET Web Site Administration Tool (WSAT) is a standalone web application for modifying your web configuration files. To open the WSAT select ASP.NET Configuration from the Web site menu. The WSAT is shown in Figure 5-2.

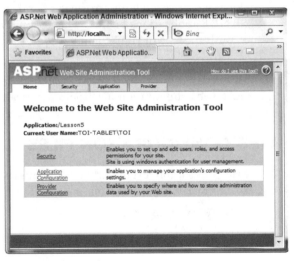

FIGURE 5-2

The WSAT has four tabs:

➤ **Home** — This tab contains links to the other three tabs.

➤ **Security** — This tab is used to manage the users, roles, and access rules used by your application.

➤ **Application** — This tab is used to manage the application settings, SMTP setting, application status, configure debugging and tracing, and define a default error page.

➤ **Provider** — This tab is used to configure how web site management data is stored and retrieved.

The WSAT is a full application that the ASP.NET installation routine installs in the following folder:

```
C:\Windows\Microsoft.NET\Framework\v4.0.30319\ASP.NETWebAdminFiles
```

This folder includes the full source code for the tool. Also, because it is a separate tool, you can run it directly from this folder. You do not need to run it from the IDE. This can be handy if you need to update configuration files on a machine without using the IDE. This is the URL to run the WSAT for Lesson 5 on my machine:

```
http://localhost:2805/asp.netwebadminfiles/default.aspx?applicationPhysicalPath=
    c:\ASPNETTrainer\Lesson5\&applicationUrl=/Lesson5
```

From the Application tab you can manage your application's configuration settings, as shown in Figure 5-3.

When you click the `Configure debugging and tracing` link the page shown in Figure 5-4 is displayed.

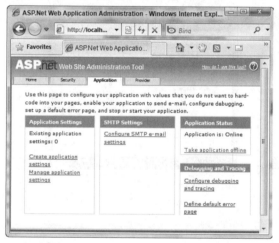

FIGURE 5-3

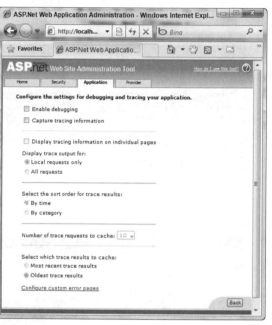

FIGURE 5-4

To enable debugging using this page, all you need to do is click the Enable debugging checkbox. Clicking this checkbox *immediately* submits the page and updates your `web.config` file. This is the updated `web.config` file:

```xml
<?xml version="1.0"?>
<configuration>
    <system.web>
        <compilation debug="true" targetFramework="4.0" />
    </system.web>
</configuration>
```

> *If you make changes to your* `web.config` *file directly in the IDE while the WSAT is open, the WSAT will not read the updated* `web.config` *settings. You must re-open the WSAT to see the updated* `web.config` *settings.*

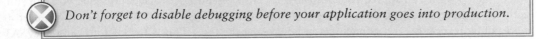

Don't forget to disable debugging before your application goes into production.

Application settings can be managed from the Application tab of the WSAT. Select the `Create application settings` link to add a new application setting. Application settings are name/value pairs. Figure 5-5 demonstrates how to add an Application setting. In this case a ServerType setting is being added with the value Staging.

Click Save to update the `web.config` file. After you click Save, you will receive the confirmation shown in Figure 5-6.

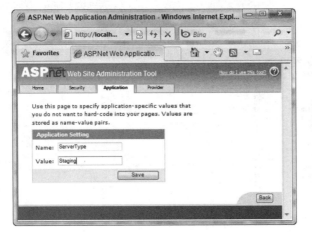

FIGURE 5-5

FIGURE 5-6

This is the updated `web.config` file:

```xml
<?xml version="1.0"?>
<configuration>
    <appSettings>
      <add key="ServerType" value="Staging" />
    </appSettings>
    <system.web>
        <compilation debug="true" targetFramework="4.0" />
    </system.web>
</configuration>
```

When using the WSAT, some changes occur immediately, whereas others require you to click a Save button. Also, some changes provide a confirmation dialog, whereas others do not.

PROGRAMMATICALLY READING A WEB.CONFIG FILE

You can access the ServerType programmatically. First, add the following `using` statement to the top of the code page:

```
using System.Configuration;
```

Now that you have added the `using` statement, you can use the following code to access the ServerType:

```
string serverType = ConfigurationManager.AppSettings["ServerType"];
```

Connection strings are often stored in the `web.config` file. The reason for this is that during development your application typically uses a different SQL Server from when your application is in production. Storing the connection strings in the `web.config` file makes it very easy to update the connection strings when the application is deployed. Connection strings are stored so frequently in the `web.config` file that there is a section that is specifically designed for storing connection strings. The following code shows a `web.config` file with a sample connection string:

```
<?xml version="1.0"?>
<configuration>
    ...
    <connectionStrings>
        <add name="OSD"
            connectionString="server=(local);database=onestop;
            Trusted_Connection=yes;" providerName="System.Data.SqlClient" />
    </connectionStrings>
    ...
<configuration>
```

This is the code to access the connection string named OSD:

```
String connStr = ConfigurationManager.ConnectionStrings["OSD"].ConnectionString;
```

Because your web configuration files contain sensitive information, such as connection strings, they must be protected. ASP.NET automatically protects configuration files from being accessed over the Internet. If anyone tries to browse to a file with a `.config` extension, they get the "Forbidden" error message shown in Figure 5-7.

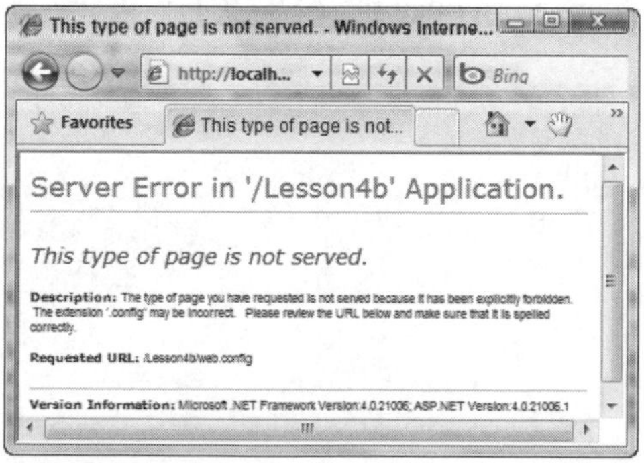

FIGURE 5-7

> *Do not rename your backup* web.config *file to* web.config.backup. *If you do, the file is no longer protected.*

TRY IT

In this lesson you use the ASP.NET Web Site Administration Tool to update the application's root web.config file and programmatically read that web.config file.

Lesson Requirements

> The ASP.NET Web Site Administration Tool must be installed.

Hints

> You can access the ASP.NET Web Site Administration Tool from the toolbar of the Solution Explorer window.

Step-By-Step

1. Open Microsoft Visual Web Developer 2010 Express.

2. Select **New Web site** from the File menu.

3. Select **Visual C#** on the left side of the dialog box.

4. Select **Empty Web Site** from the list of installed templates and verify that File System is selected for the Web location.

5. Type **c:\ASPNETTrainer\Lesson5** for the Web Location property.

6. Click the OK button.

7. Double-click the web.config file to open it and notice that debug="false".

8. Select ASP.NET Configuration from the Web site menu to open the ASP.NET Web site Administration Tool (WSAT).

9. Select the Application tab.

10. Click the Configure debugging and tracing link.

11. Click the Enable debugging checkbox.

12. Return to Microsoft Visual Web Developer 2010 Express without closing the WSAT.

13. Click the Yes button on the dialog box in Figure 5-8.

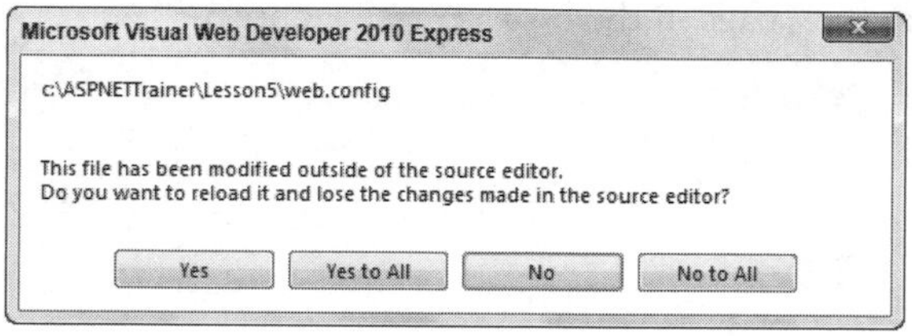

FIGURE 5-8

14. Notice that `debug="true"` in the web.config file.

15. Return to the WSAT and click the Back button to return to the Application tab.

16. Click the `Create application settings` link.

17. Enter **ServerType** for the Name and **Staging** for the Value of the new application setting.

18. Click the Save button.

19. Close the WSAT.

20. Return to Microsoft Visual Web Developer 2010, click the Yes button and view the updated `web.config` file.

21. Select Add New Item from the Web site menu and select the Web Form template from the Add New Item dialog box.

22. Type **ReadConfig.aspx** for the Name, verify that the `Place code in separate file` checkbox is checked, and click the Add button.

23. Update the title element to the following:

```
<title>Read Configuration File</title>
```

24. Enter the following text into the `div` element:

```
<h1>Read Configuration File</h1>
Server Type:
<asp:Literal ID="LiteralServerType" runat="server" />
```

25. Right-click the page and select View Code to open the code page.

26. Add the following `using` statement:

```
using System.Configuration;
```

27. Type the following code into the `Page_Load` event:

```
this.LiteralServerType.Text = ConfigurationManager.AppSettings["ServerType"];
```

28. Save the files and view the `ReadConfig.aspx` page in the browser (see Figure 5-9).

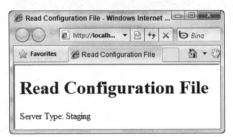

FIGURE 5-9

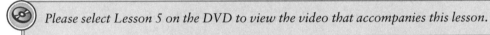

Please select Lesson 5 on the DVD to view the video that accompanies this lesson.

SECTION II
Getting Started

- ▶ **LESSON 6:** Web Site Projects vs. Web Application Projects

- ▶ **LESSON 7A:** Your First ASP.NET Web Forms Web Application

- ▶ **LESSON 7B:** Your First ASP.NET MVC Web Application

- ▶ **LESSON 8A:** The Page Lifecycle in Web Forms

- ▶ **LESSON 8B:** The Request Lifecycle in MVC

6

Web Site Projects vs. Web Application Projects

Microsoft Visual Web Developer 2010 Express is a powerful tool for developing all types of web applications. In this lesson you learn about the different types of projects that you can build using Microsoft Visual Web Developer 2010 Express.

Microsoft Visual Web Developer 2010 Express provides two types of projects to build web applications: Web Site projects and Web Application projects. It is important to understand the difference between these two types of projects. In all of the preceding lessons I have used Web Site projects, however, in most of the remaining lessons I use Web Application projects. The reason for this is that Web Site projects are perfect for doing small applications and simple demonstrations, but they are not as robust as Web Application projects.

From the File menu you have the option to either create a New Project or a New Web Site, as shown in Figure 6-1.

File	Edit	View	Debug	Tools	Window	Help	
	New Project...						Ctrl+Shift+N
	New Web Site...						Shift+Alt+N
	New File...						Ctrl+N
	Open Project...						Ctrl+Shift+O
	Open Web Site...						Shift+Alt+O
	Open File...						Ctrl+O
	Close						
	Close Project						
	Save Selected Items						Ctrl+S
	Save Selected Items As...						
	Save All						Ctrl+Shift+S
	Export Template...						
	Page Setup...						
	Print...						Ctrl+P
	Recent Files						▶
	Recent Projects and Solutions						▶
	Exit						Alt+F4

FIGURE 6-1

> *On the File menu, New Project refers to a new Web Application project and New Web Site refers to a new Web Site project.*

WEB SITE PROJECTS

Web Site projects (WSP) use a folder-based approach to web development. Every file that is in the folder or subfolders of the project is part of the application. Applications built with Web Site projects are compiled dynamically when a user first requests a page. This means that you do not need to compile your files before you deploy them. For these reasons, Web Site projects are very easy to deploy; all you have to do to deploy this type of project is to copy the files to the web server. There is even a handy Copy Web Site button on the Solution Explorer window to make deployment super easy.

Figure 6-2 shows the dialog box that is used to create a new Web Site project.

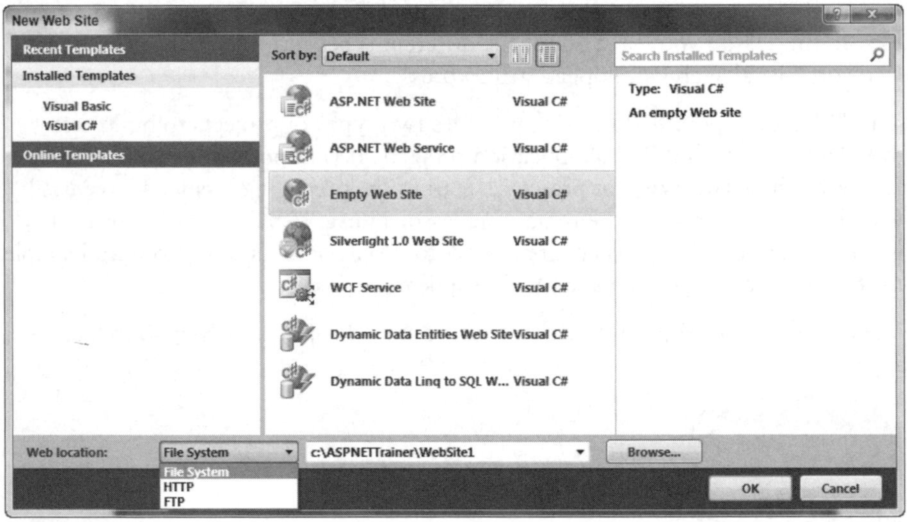

FIGURE 6-2

At the bottom of the New Web Site dialog box is the Web Location field. In all of the previous lessons I have selected File System. That is not always necessary. Via the Web Location field, you have the option to create new Web Site projects on your local copy of IIS, a remote computer's IIS, or on an FTP server. All of these options are available because the pages are not compiled ahead of time. The downside to this flexibility is that the first person to hit your site has to wait for the entire site to compile.

With Web Site projects, individual files do not need to be written in the same language. This is another reason they are really good for doing demonstrations. Nevertheless, trying to maintain a project that has pages written in both C# and Visual Basic is not realistic.

Another interesting benefit of using Web Site projects is that you can instruct the compiler to create a separate assembly (DLL) for each page in your web site. This means that you do not need to compile the entire project successfully in order to test an individual page.

The last thing I would like to show you is the Property Pages dialog box provided by Web Site projects, shown in Figure 6-3.

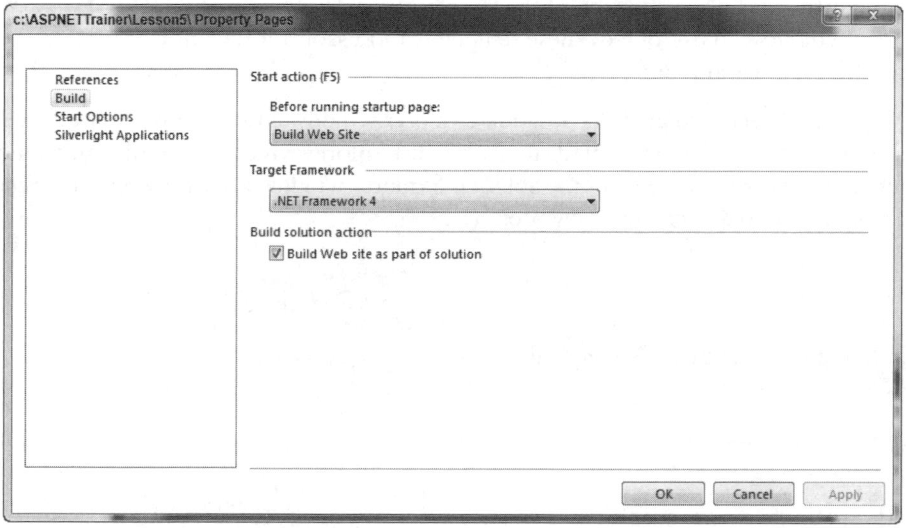

FIGURE 6-3

You access the Property Pages dialog box by clicking the name of the project and selecting Property Pages from the View menu. You can also access this dialog box by right-clicking the project's name and selecting Properties. As you can see, because a project is simply defined as all of the files in the folder, you cannot set many properties at the project level.

The Property Pages dialog box has only four tabs:

➤ **References** — This tab is used to add and remove references.

➤ **Build** — This tab, shown in Figure 6-3, is used to set the start action and the target framework.

➤ **Start Options** — This tab is used to select where to start the application, which server to use, and which debuggers to use.

➤ **Silverlight Applications** — This tab is used add and remove Silverlight applications.

WEB APPLICATION PROJECTS

Web Application projects (WAP) use a project-based approach to web development. Only files that are referred to by the project file are part of the project. This makes it very simple to exclude files from a project. Applications built with Web Application projects are compiled into a single assembly which, by default, is placed into the bin folder. You can specify the name and version of the assembly. You can also specify pre-build and post-build steps to occur during compilation.

Figure 6-4 shows the dialog box that is used to create a new Web Application project.

The first thing that you notice is that many more templates are available for Web Application projects than for Web Site projects. Also, there is no location option, as on the New Web Site dialog box. The most interesting difference is the addition of the templates for developing ASP.NET MVC 2 Web Applications. I show you how to use one of these templates in Lesson 7B. For now, I will use the ASP.NET Empty Web Application template.

After an empty Web Site project is created the Solution Explorer window contains only a `web.config` file. When a Web Application project is created, the Solution Explorer window contains much more information. Figure 6-5 shows the contents of the Solution Explorer window after the ASP.NET Empty Web Application template is used to create a new project.

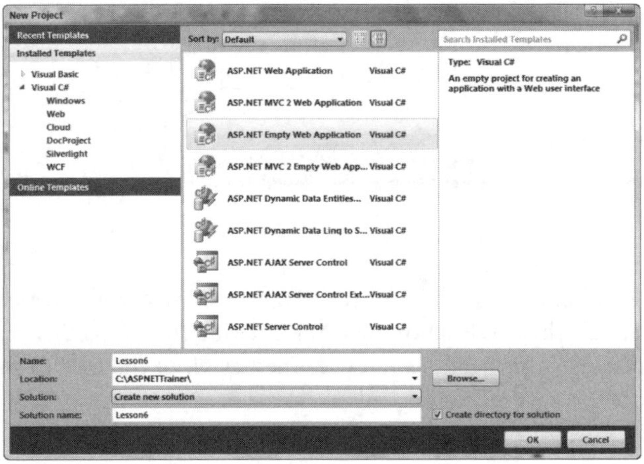

FIGURE 6-4

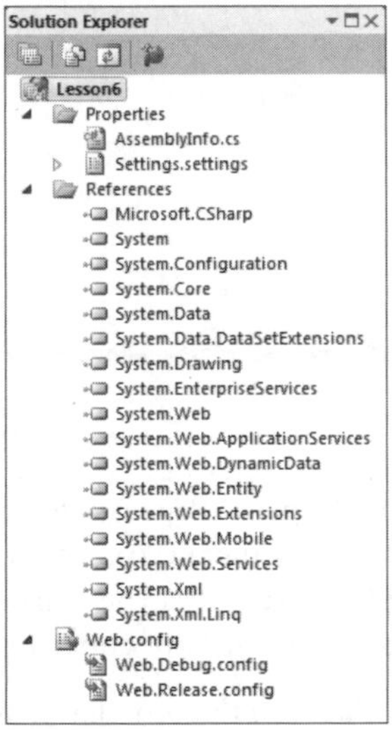

FIGURE 6-5

For comparison purposes I would like to show you the Project Properties window for Web Application projects. You can access this window by either clicking the name of the project and selecting Property Pages from the View menu, or by right-clicking the project's name and selecting Properties. The Project Properties window for Web Application projects is shown in Figure 6-6.

The Project Properties window has 11 pages:

➤ **Application** — This page is used to configure your assembly, select the target framework, and specify how application resource files will be managed.

➤ **Build** — This page, shown in Figure 6-6, is used to configure the build process, manage how errors and warnings are handled, select your output path, and designate your XML documentation file.

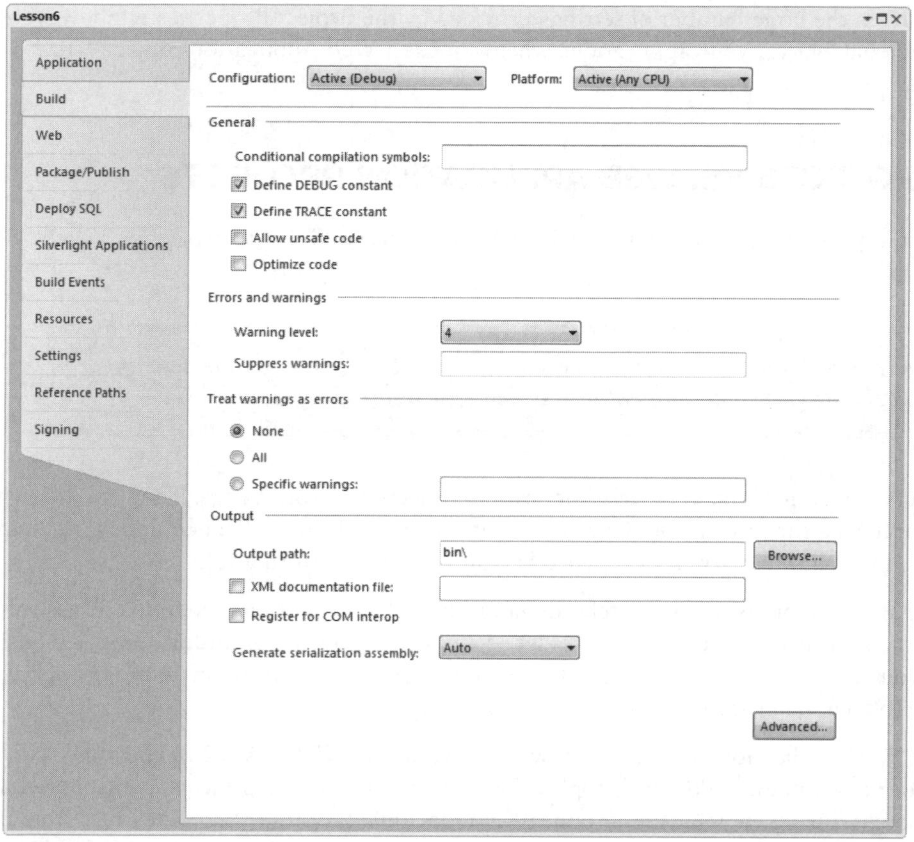

FIGURE 6-6

➤ **Web** — This page is used to select where to start the application, which server to use, and which debuggers to use.

➤ **Package/Publish** — This page is used to configure the options for packaging and publishing your web application.

➤ **Deploy SQL** — This page is used to enter information about the databases that you will be deploying.

➤ **Silverlight Applications** — This page is used to add and remove Silverlight applications.

➤ **Build Events** — This page is used to designate both pre-build and post-build events.

➤ **Resources** — This page is used to add and remove resources.

➤ **Settings** — This page is used to manage application settings.

➤ **Reference Paths** — This page is used to add and remove reference paths.

➤ **Signing** — This page is used to sign your assembly.

As you can see from the large number of settings provided by the Project Properties window, you have much more control over your applications when you use a Web Application project versus a Web Site project.

WEB SITE PROJECTS VS. WEB APPLICATION PROJECTS

Before you start any web project, you must decide whether to use a Web Site project or a Web Application project.

> *You can convert a project from one type to another, but it is very time consuming. You should put some thought into which type of project you will use.*

Web Site projects are from Mars, and Web Application projects are from Venus. They are different tools for accomplishing the same thing. Once a web site has been deployed and compiled, not many scenarios exist in which the user will experience any difference in performance.

You should use Web Site projects if you prefer dynamic compilation, need to generate one assembly for each page, or want instantly to open any folder as a project. They are great for doing demonstrations because you can mix both C# and Visual Basic in one project and your entire project does not need to be able to compile in order to view an individual page.

You should use Web Application projects if you want to build ASP.NET MVC 2 applications, control the names of your assemblies, build a web application comprising multiple projects, control pre-build and post-build steps during compilation, produce XML documentation, or "exclude" files from the project. This is really just the short list of reasons that I prefer Web Application projects for developing production web sites.

TRY IT

In this lesson you create an empty ASP.NET Web Application and use the Project Properties window to update the assembly information.

Lesson Requirements

None.

Hints

➤ Don't forget to select the project by clicking the project's name in the Solution Explorer window.

➤ You can use Shift+F4 to open the Project Properties window.

Step-By-Step

1. Open Microsoft Visual Web Developer 2010 Express.

2. Click New Project from the File menu.

3. Select **Visual C#** on the left side of the dialog box.

4. Select **ASP.NET Empty Web Application** from the list of templates.

5. Enter **Lesson6** in the Name field and enter **c:\ASPNETTrainer** in the Location field as shown in Figure 6-4.

6. Click the OK button.

7. Right-click the name of the project in the Solution Explorer and click Properties to open the Project Properties window.

8. Select the Application page (see Figure 6-7).

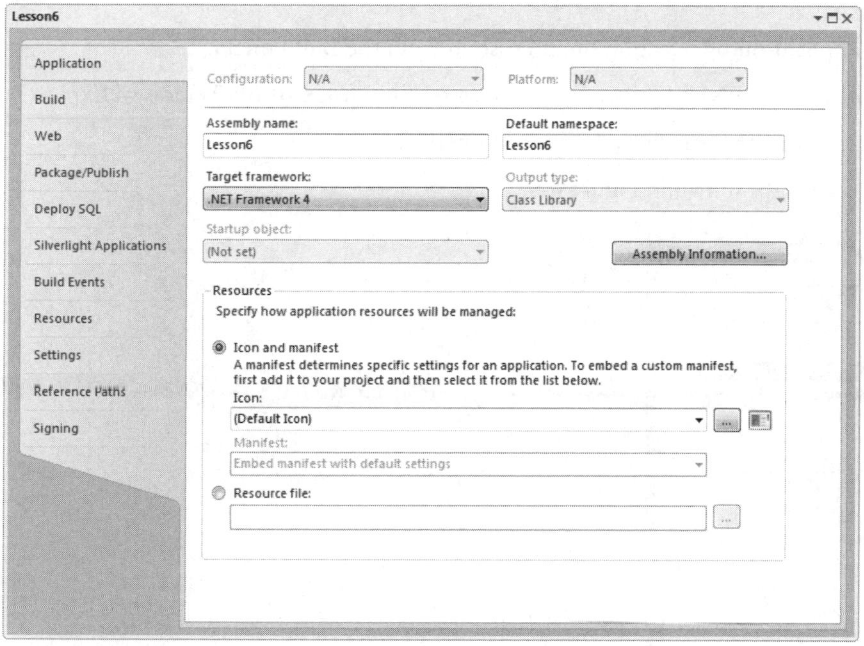

FIGURE 6-7

9. Click the Assembly Information button to open the Assembly Information dialog box shown in Figure 6-8.

10. Replace "Microsoft" with your name in both the Company field and the Copyright field.

11. Update both the Assembly version and the File version to 2.0.1.1.

12. Click the OK button.

FIGURE 6-8

13. Build your application by selecting Build Lesson6 from the Build menu.

14. Navigate to the C:\ASPNETTrainer\Lesson6\Lesson6\bin folder using Windows Explorer.

15. Right-click the Lesson6.dll file and select Properties.

16. Click the Details tab, shown in Figure 6-9.

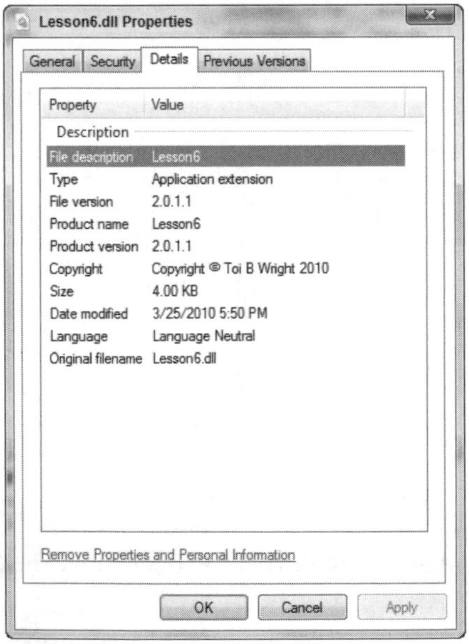

FIGURE 6-9

Please select Lesson 6 on the DVD to view the video that accompanies this lesson.

7A

Your First ASP.NET Web Forms Web Application

In this lesson you learn how to develop your first web application using the ASP.NET Web Forms framework. I also review the files that are automatically generated by the ASP.NET Web Application template and explain the structure of a Web Form.

THE SAMPLE ASP.NET WEB FORMS APPLICATION

To create the sample ASP.NET Web Forms application, follow these steps:

1. Select New Project from the File menu.

2. Select the ASP.NET Web Application template.

3. Click the OK button (see Figure 7A-1).

FIGURE 7A-1

When you use the ASP.NET Web Application template, Microsoft Visual Web Developer 2010 Express automatically creates a complete sample web application. Select Start Debugging from the Debug menu or press the F5 key to start the sample application. Figure 7A-2 shows the Home page of the sample application.

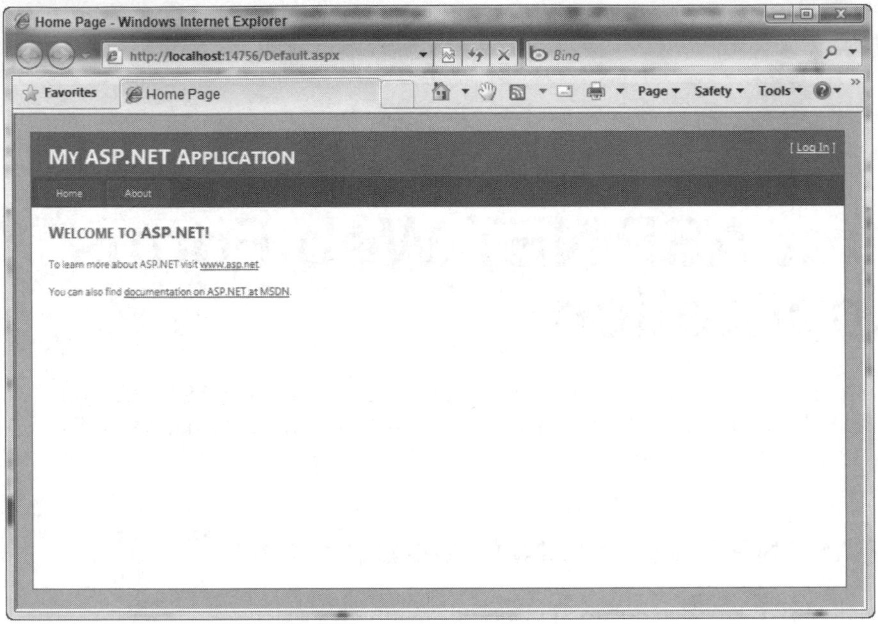

FIGURE 7A-2

You can use the tabs at the top of the page to navigate between the Home page and the About Us page. Notice how the layout of the Home page and the About Us page are identical. This is accomplished using master pages, which are covered in Lesson 11.

You click the Log In link in the upper right-hand corner to access the Log In page. If you click the Log In button on the Log In page before you have entered any text in the fields, you will get the error messages shown in Figure 7A-3. In this example the sample web site is performing data validation. I cover validating user input in Lessons 21 and 22.

After you create a new account and log into that account the form is updated to show your name and the Log In link is replaced by a Log Out link as shown in Figure 7A-4.

You can use the Change Password page to change your password as shown in Figure 7A-5.

> *To view the Change Password page you must first log into the application and then navigate to the* Account/ChangePassword.aspx *page.*

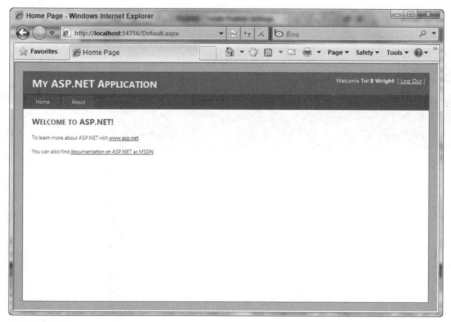

FIGURE 7A-3

FIGURE 7A-4

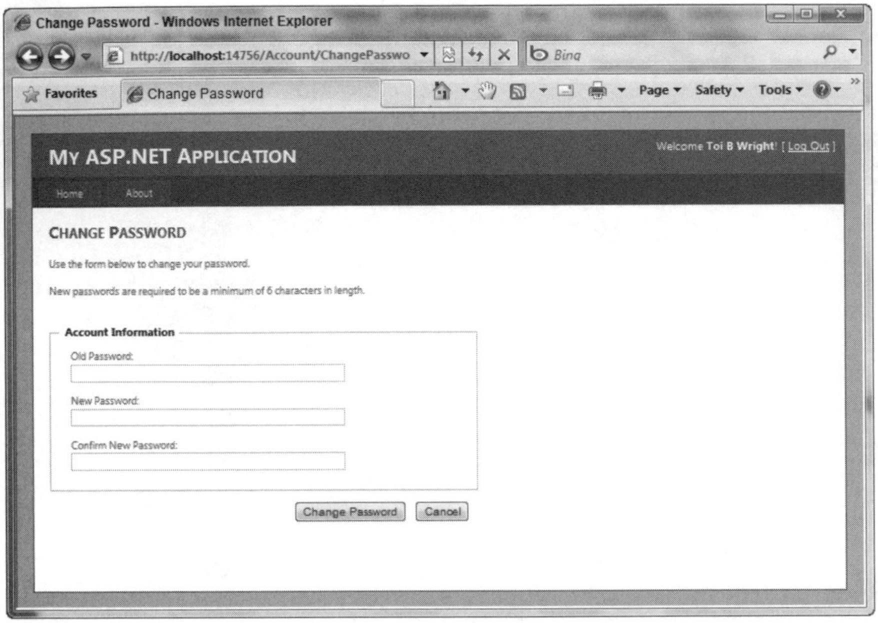

FIGURE 7A-5

After you have successfully changed your password, the Change Password Success page is displayed (Figure 7A-6).

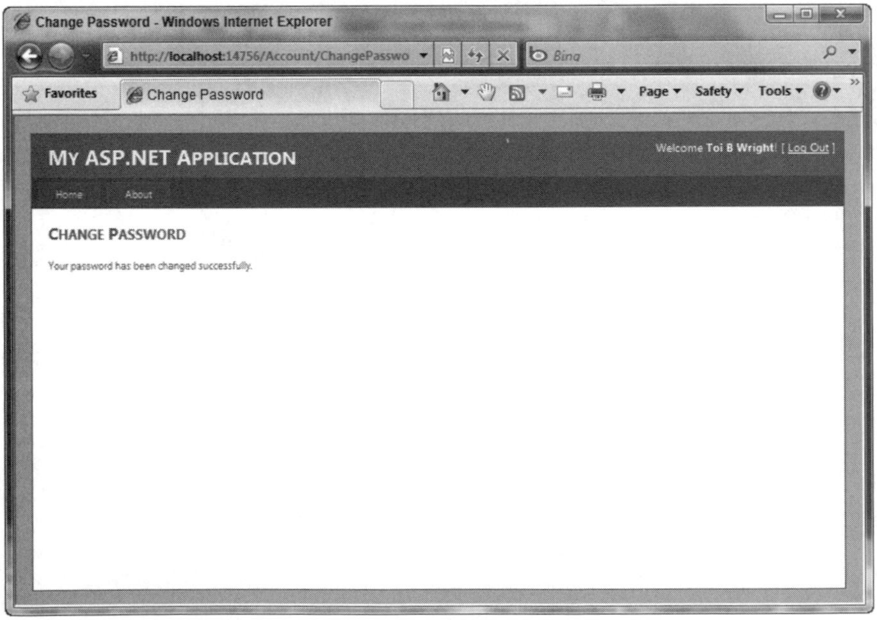

FIGURE 7A-6

STRUCTURE OF A WEB FORMS APPLICATION

Now, look at the list of files that were created in order to produce the sample application by viewing the Solution Explorer window. The Solution Explorer window is shown in Figure 7A-7.

The Solution Explorer window shows that the root of the application contains assorted folders and files. The following lists information about those folders and files:

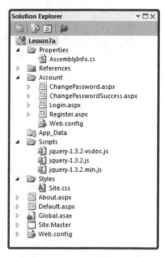

FIGURE 7A-7

➤ **Properties folder** — This folder contains the `AssemblyInfo.cs` file. This is the file that contains the assembly information that you configured in Lesson 6.

➤ **References folder** — This folder lists all of the assemblies (DLLs) that this application references.

➤ **Account folder** — This folder includes the following web pages:

  ➤ `ChangePassword.aspx`

  ➤ `ChangePasswordSuccess.aspx`

  ➤ `Login.aspx`

  ➤ `Register.aspx`

Each of these files ends with the ASPX file extension, which identifies them as web pages. Web pages are discussed in more detail later in this lesson. This folder also contains a `web.config` file. The `web.config` file is being used to deny anonymous users access to some of the pages in this folder. I cover authentication and authorization in Lesson 26.

➤ **App_Data folder** — This is the folder that is designated by ASP.NET to contain the data files for the application. You cannot rename this folder. In this example, this folder contains the SQL Server 2008 Express database, named ASPNETDB.MDF, which was automatically created to store user credentials. This is the same database that was created in Lesson 4 to store the Profile properties.

➤ **Scripts folder** — This folder contains the JQuery JavaScript files. As you can see, JavaScript files end with the JS file extension. JavaScript is covered in Lesson 23.

➤ **Styles folder** — This folder contains the cascading style sheet used by this project. Style sheets are covered in Lesson 3.

➤ **About.aspx file** — This is the About Us page.

➤ **Default.aspx file** — This is the Home page.

➤ **Global.asax file** — This is the ASP.NET application file. It is an optional file for responding to application-level and session-level events.

➤ **Site.Master file** — This is the master page that is used to lay out the site.

➤ **Web.config file** — This is the root `web.config` file.

If you compare the Solution Explorer window's content to the content in the folder (Figure 7A-8), you will notice some discrepancies.

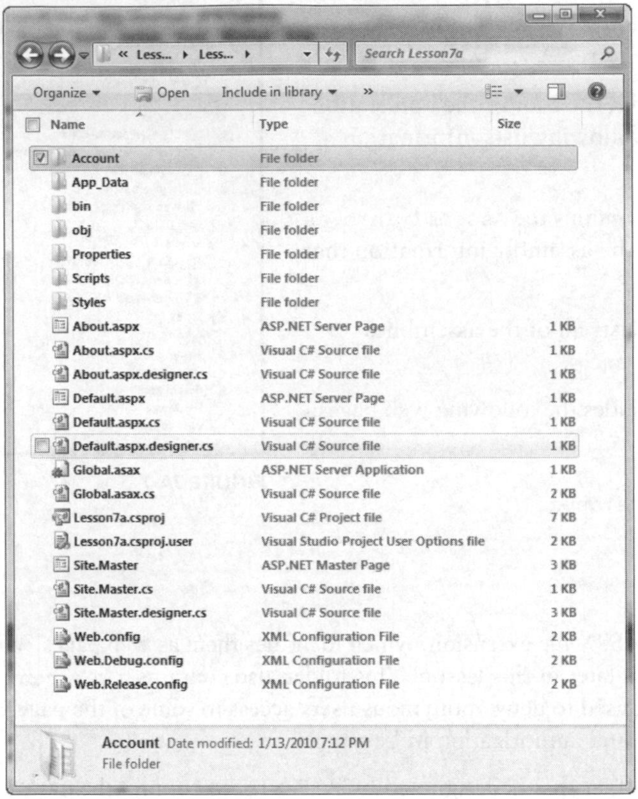

FIGURE 7A-8

The bin and obj folders and a couple of files are missing from the Solution Explorer window. The following lists information about the files that were not displayed:

➤ **bin folder** — The bin folder contains both the `Lesson7a.dll` and the `Lesson7a.pdb` files. The DLL file is the assembly that the compiler created when it compiled the C# code. The PDB file is the project database file. It contains the information needed by the debugger to debug the application. This file is only created when you compile the application in Debug mode.

➤ **obj folder** — The obj folder is used to store temporary files.

➤ **Lesson7a.csproj file** — This is the project file, which contains information about all of the items in the project. The `.csproj` file is an XML file. If you change the file extension from `.csproj` to `.xml` you can view the contents of this file.

➤ **Lesson7a.csproj.user file** — This is the project user option file and it is unique to each user. This is also an XML file. If you change the `.user` file extension to `.xml`, you can view the contents of this file.

> You can view the bin folder and the other hidden folders in the Solution Explorer window by clicking the Show All Files button on the toolbar.

COMPONENTS OF A WEB FORM

Look closer at the About Us page. It is generated by the `About.aspx` file, which represents a web page. Each web page has two files associated with it. In the case of the `About.aspx` file, it has the following two files:

➤ `About.aspx.cs`

➤ `About.aspx.designer.cs`

The `About.aspx.cs` file contains C# code that is used by this page. `About.aspx.designer.cs` is a system-generated file that also contains C# code that is used by this page. The reason for the two separate code files is that the `About.aspx.cs` file is updated by the developer, whereas the `About.aspx.designer.cs` file is updated by the system. In earlier versions of the ASP.NET framework, all of the code was in one file, but this caused many problems because it was too easy for the developer to accidentally overwrite the code generated by the system and vice versa.

> The C# code can be included in the ASPX file, but it is a better practice to use the code-behind model that is used in all of the lessons.

This is the content of the `About.aspx` file:

```
<%@ Page Title="About Us" Language="C#" MasterPageFile="~/Site.master"
AutoEventWireup="true" CodeBehind="About.aspx.cs" Inherits="Lesson7a.About" %>

<asp:Content ID="HeaderContent" runat="server" ContentPlaceHolderID="HeadContent">
</asp:Content>
<asp:Content ID="BodyContent" runat="server" ContentPlaceHolderID="MainContent">
    <h2>
        About
    </h2>
    <p>
        Put content here.
    </p>
</asp:Content>
```

The `About.aspx` file begins with an `@Page` directive. The `@Page` directive can only be used in ASPX pages and each ASPX page can include only one `@Page` directive. The purpose of the `@Page` directive is to define the attributes that are specific to each page.

Dozens of attributes can be used with the @Page directive. In this example, the following @Page attributes were used:

➤ **Title** — This is the title of the page. It has the same effect as using the title element within HTML. If your page includes both a title attribute and a title element, the text within the title attribute is the text that is displayed.

➤ **Language** — This is the programming language used with the page.

➤ **MasterPageFile** — This is the location of the master page.

➤ **AutoEventWireup** — This indicates whether page events are automatically enabled. The default is true.

➤ **CodeBehind** — This is the location of the file that contains the C# code that is not automatically created by the designer.

➤ **Inherits** — This is the base class that the page inherits. It must be derived from the System.Web.UI.Page class.

Because this page does not do anything, the About.aspx.cs file is basically empty. This is the content of the About.aspx.cs file:

```
using System;
using System.Collections.Generic;
using System.Linq;
using System.Web;
using System.Web.UI;
using System.Web.UI.WebControls;

namespace Lesson7a
{
    public partial class About : System.Web.UI.Page
    {
        protected void Page_Load(object sender, EventArgs e)
        {

        }
    }
}
```

The About.asp.cs file starts with the list of using statements followed by the namespace. After the namespace is the definition for the About partial class that inherits from the System.Web.UI.Page class. It is important to note that the About class is defined as a partial class.

The About.aspx.designer.cs file contains the field declarations for the controls on the page. This is the content of the About.aspx.designer.cs file:

```
//------------------------------------------------------------------------------
// <auto-generated>
//     This code was generated by a tool.
//
//     Changes to this file may cause incorrect behavior and will be lost if
```

```
//      the code is regenerated.
// </auto-generated>
//------------------------------------------------------------------------------

namespace Lesson7a {


    public partial class About {
    }
}
```

At the top of this file is a warning that says that changes to this file may cause incorrect behavior and will be lost if the code is regenerated. That means that you should never edit the designer.cs file. This file also contains the definition for the About partial class. Because both the About.aspx.cs page and the About.aspx.designer.cs page contain the same partial class, the compiler merges them into a single class at compile time.

Because this page does not have any server controls on it, the partial About class is empty. If you drag a Calendar control to the About page, the About.aspx.designer.cs file will automatically be updated to the following:

```
//------------------------------------------------------------------------------
// <auto-generated>
//      This code was generated by a tool.
//
//      Changes to this file may cause incorrect behavior and will be lost if
//      the code is regenerated.
// </auto-generated>
//------------------------------------------------------------------------------

namespace Lesson7a {


    public partial class About {

        /// <summary>
        /// Calendar1 control.
        /// </summary>
        /// <remarks>
        /// Auto-generated field.
        /// To modify move field declaration from designer file to code-behind file
        /// </remarks>
        protected global::System.Web.UI.WebControls.Calendar Calendar1;
    }
}
```

In the updated version of the About.designer.cs file the field declaration for the Calendar1 control has been added. Because it has been added as part of the partial class, you can now refer to the Calendar1 control from the About.cs file.

TRY IT

In this lesson you create your first ASP.NET Web Forms web application.

Lesson Requirements

None.

Hints

> ➤ Click the F5 button to start the application in Debug mode.

Step-By-Step

1. Open Microsoft Visual Web Developer 2010 Express.

2. Select New Project from the File menu.

3. Select **Visual C#** on the left side of the dialog box.

4. Select the **ASP.NET Web Application** template.

5. Enter **Lesson7a** in the Name field and **c:\ASPNETTrainer** in the Location field.

6. Click the OK button.

7. Select Start Debugging from the Debug menu.

8. Explore the sample application.

Please select Lesson 7A on the DVD to view the video that accompanies this lesson.

7B

Your First ASP.NET MVC Web Application

In this lesson you learn how to develop your first web application using the ASP.NET MVC framework. I also introduce the folder structure that is required when using the MVC framework and explain the components of a page.

THE SAMPLE ASP.NET MVC APPLICATION

To create the sample ASP.NET MVC application, follow these steps:

1. Select New Project from the File menu.

2. Select the ASP.NET MVC 2 Web Application template.

3. Click the OK button (see Figure 7B-1).

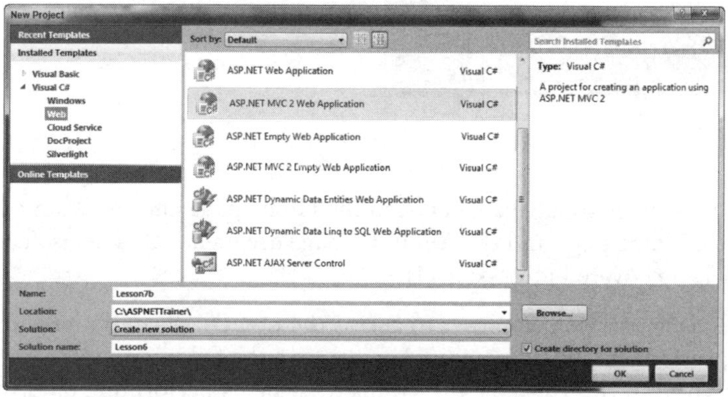

FIGURE 7B-1

When you use the ASP.NET MVC 2 Web Application template, Microsoft Visual Web Developer 2010 Express automatically creates a complete sample web application. Select Start Debugging from the Debug menu or press the F5 key to start the sample application.

The default for MVC is to run in debug mode. Nevertheless, the first time you run the sample web application you may receive the Debugging Not Enabled dialog box shown in Figure 7B-2. If you do, click the OK button to enable debugging.

FIGURE 7B-2

Figure 7B-3 shows the Home page of the sample application.

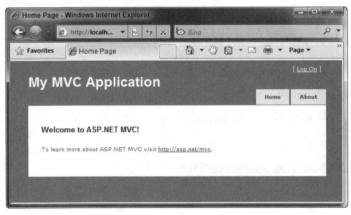

FIGURE 7B-3

You can use the tabs at the top of the page to navigate between the Home page and the About Us page. Notice how the layout of the Home page and the About Us page are identical. This is accomplished using master pages, which are covered in Lesson 11.

You click the Log On link in the upper right-hand corner to access the Log On page. If you click the Log On button on the Log On page before you have entered any text in the fields, you will get the error messages shown in Figure 7B-4. In this example the sample web site is performing data validation. I cover validating user input in Lessons 21 and 22.

After you create a new account and log onto that account the form is updated to show your name and the Log On link is replaced by a Log Off link as shown in Figure 7B-5.

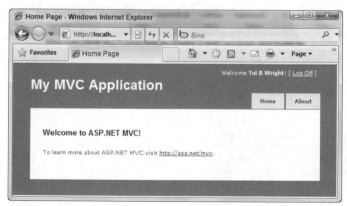

FIGURE 7B-4

FIGURE 7B-5

You can use the Change Password page to change your password as shown in Figure 7B-6.

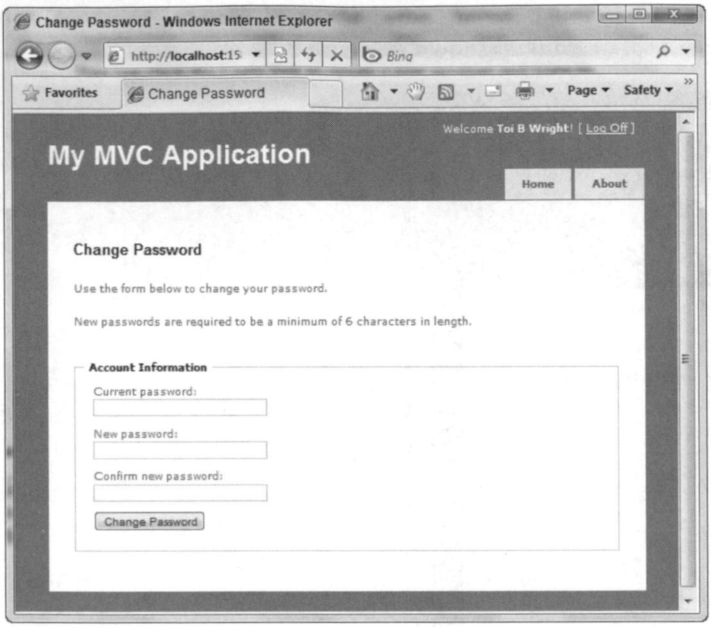

FIGURE 7B-6

To view the Change Password page you must first log onto the application and then navigate to the Account/ChangePassword *page.*

After you have successfully changed your password, the Change Password Success page is displayed (Figure 7B-7).

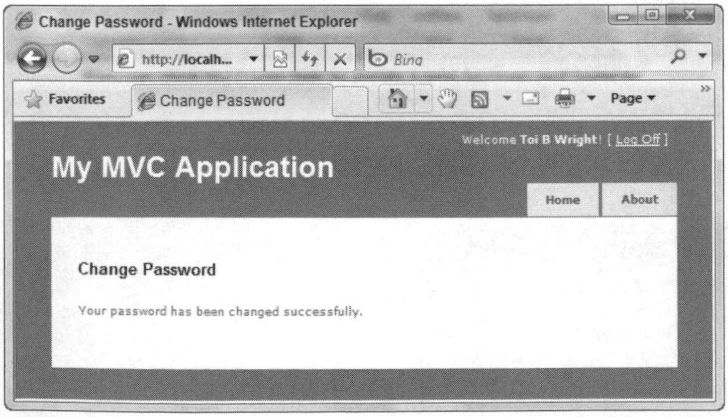

FIGURE 7B-7

STRUCTURE OF AN MVC APPLICATION

Now, look at the list of files that were created in order to produce the sample application by viewing the Solution Explorer window. The Solution Explorer window is shown in Figure 7B-8.

The Solution Explorer window shows that the root of the application contains assorted folders and files. Information about those folders and files follows:

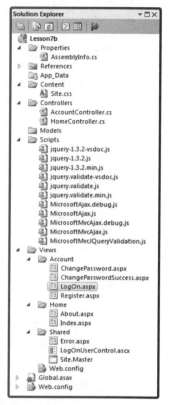

FIGURE 7B-8

> ➤ **Properties folder** — This folder contains the `AssemblyInfo.cs` file. This is the file that contains the same assembly information that you configured in Lesson 6.

> ➤ **References folder** — This folder lists all of the assemblies (DLLs) that this application references.

> ➤ **App_Data folder** — This is the folder that is designated by ASP.NET to contain the data files for the application. You cannot rename this folder. In the example, this folder contains the SQL Server 2008 Express database, named ASPNETDB. MDF, which was automatically created to store user credentials. This is the same database that was created in Lesson 4 to store the Profile properties.

> ➤ **Content folder** — The Content folder is used to store static content such as cascading style sheets and images. In this example, the Content folder contains the cascading style sheet used by this project. I cover style sheets in Lesson 3.

> ➤ **Controllers folder** — This folder contains the controller classes. These are code files, and I explain them later in the lesson.

> ➤ **Models folder** — This folder contains the model classes. These are code files, and I explain them later in the lesson.

> ➤ **Scripts folder** — This folder contains the JavaScript files. As you can see, JavaScript files end with the JS file extension. I cover JavaScript in Lesson 23.

> ➤ **Views folder** — This folder contains the views. I explain them later in the lesson.

> ➤ **Global.asax file** — This is the ASP.NET application file. It is an optional file for responding to application-level and session-level events.

> ➤ **Web.config file** — This is the root `web.config` file.

If you compare the Solution Explorer window's content to the actual content in the folder (Figure 7B-9), you will notice some discrepancies.

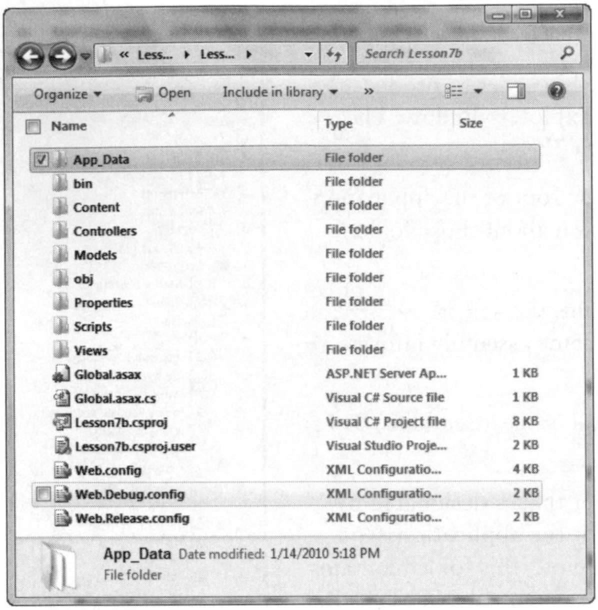

FIGURE 7B-9

The bin and obj folders and a couple of files are missing from the Solution Explorer window. This is information about the files that were not displayed:

➤ **bin folder** — The bin folder contains both the `Lesson7b.dll` and the `Lesson7b.pdb` files. The DLL file is the assembly that the compiler created when it compiled the C# code. The PDB file is the project database file. It contains the information needed by the debugger to debug the application. This file is only created when you compile the application in Debug mode.

➤ **obj folder** — The obj folder is used to store temporary files.

➤ **Lesson7b.csproj file** — This is the project file, which contains information about all of the items in the project. The `.csproj` file is an XML file. If you change the file extension from `.csproj` to `.xml` you can view the contents of this file.

➤ **Lesson7b.csproj.user file** — This is the project user option file and it is unique to each user. It is also an XML file. If you change the `.user` file extension to `.xml`, you can view the contents of this file.

> *You can view the bin folder and the other hidden folders in the Solution Explorer window by clicking the Show All Files button on the toolbar.*

The Models, Views, and Controllers folders are all required when you are developing MVC applications.

COMPONENTS OF AN MVC PAGE

MVC stands for Model-View-Controller. The following is an explanation of each of the components of an MVC page:

➤ **View** — The view is the simplest component of an MVC page to understand. It is simply the user interface. In the sample application, an ASPX page is used to render the view.

➤ **Controller** — The controller is a set of classes that controls the flow of the application.

➤ **Model** — The model is a set of classes that describe and manage the data.

Look closer at the About Us page. In the sample application the About Us page uses the `About.aspx` file in the Home subfolder of the Views folder and the `HomeControllers.cs` file in the Controllers folder. It does not use a model because there is no data associated with this page.

This is the markup from the `About.aspx` file:

```
<%@ Page Language="C#" MasterPageFile="~/Views/Shared/Site.Master"
    Inherits="System.Web.Mvc.ViewPage" %>

<asp:Content ID="aboutTitle" ContentPlaceHolderID="TitleContent"
    runat="server">
    About Us
</asp:Content>
<asp:Content ID="aboutContent" ContentPlaceHolderID="MainContent"
    runat="server">
    <h2>
        About</h2>
    <p>
        Put content here.
    </p>
</asp:Content>
```

The `About.aspx` file begins with an `@Page` directive. The `@Page` directive can only be used in ASPX pages and each ASPX page can include only one `@Page` directive. The purpose of the `@Page` directive is to define the attributes that are specific to each page.

Dozens of attributes can be used with the `@Page` directive. In this example, the following `@Page` attributes were used:

➤ **Language** — This is the programming language of the page.

➤ **MasterPageFile** — This is the location of the master page.

➤ **Inherits** — This is the base class that the page inherits. It must be derived from the `System.Web.Mvc` class.

This is the code from the `HomeControllers.cs` file:

```
using System;
using System.Collections.Generic;
using System.Linq;
using System.Web;
```

```
using System.Web.Mvc;

namespace Lesson7b.Controllers
{
    [HandleError]
    public class HomeController : Controller
    {
        public ActionResult Index()
        {
            ViewData["Message"] = "Welcome to ASP.NET MVC!";

            return View();
        }

        public ActionResult About()
        {
            return View();
        }
    }
}
```

The HomeController class includes two methods: the Index method and the About method. The Index method is invoked when the user requests the Home page by clicking the Home tab. The About method is invoked when the user requests the About Us page by clicking the About tab. In this example, the About method simply returns the view.

TRY IT

In this lesson you create your first ASP.NET MVC web application.

Lesson Requirements

None.

Hints

➤   Click the F5 button to start the application in Debug mode.

Step-By-Step

1.   Open Microsoft Visual Web Developer 2010 Express.

2.   Select New Project from the File menu.

3.   Select **Visual C#** on the left side of the dialog box.

4.   Select the **ASP.NET MVC 2 Web Application** template.

5.   Enter **Lesson7b** in the Name field and **c:\ASPNETTrainer** in the Location field.

6.   Click the OK button.

7. Select Start Debugging from the Debug menu.

8. Explore the sample application.

 Please select Lesson 7B on the DVD to view the video that accompanies this lesson.

8A

The Page Life Cycle in Web Forms

Every time a browser requests a page from a web application using the ASP.NET Web Forms framework, the page must complete the full page life cycle. In this lesson I list all of the steps in the page life cycle, show you how to run a trace of your page to see what is happening during each stage of the page's life cycle, and show you how to determine if a page is a postback.

All of the lessons so far have only used the Page_Load() event to add code to the page. Many more events are available during the page's life cycle. This is the sequence of events, in the order that they are raised, whenever a page is requested:

➤ PreInit

➤ Init

➤ InitComplete

➤ PreLoad

➤ Load

➤ LoadComplete

➤ PreRender

➤ PreRenderComplete

➤ SaveStateComplete

➤ Render

➤ Unload

> *Render is included on the list of events even though it is not an event; it is a method. The Page object calls the Render method on each control to write out the control's markup to the page.*

PAGE-LEVEL TRACING

A simple way to view the page life cycle for your page is to enable tracing. You enable page-level tracing by adding a `trace="true"` attribute to the `@Page` directive at the top of the page. This is an example of an `@Page` directive that has been modified to enable tracing:

```
<%@ Page Title="Home Page" Language="C#" MasterPageFile="~/Site.master"
    AutoEventWireup="true" CodeBehind="Default.aspx.cs"
    Inherits="Lesson8a._Default" Trace="true" %>
```

Figure 8A-1 shows the Request Details and Trace Information that is added to the bottom of the page when the trace attribute is set to true.

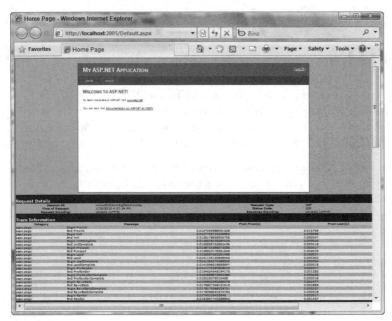

FIGURE 8A-1

The Request Details section displays the current Session ID among the other session details. The Trace Information section lists all of the states that the page goes through. For each state, both the elapsed time in seconds that have passed as well as the amount of time between the current state and the previous state are shown.

You use `Trace.Warn()` and `Trace.Write()` to add your own custom trace messages. The difference between `Trace.Warn()` and `Trace.Write()` is that the `Trace.Warn()` method writes the custom trace message in red. This is the code to add a custom trace message to the `Page_Load()` event:

```
protected void Page_Load(object sender, EventArgs e)
{
    Trace.Warn("My Page_Load Event");
}
```

The resulting Trace Information section is shown in Figure 8A-2.

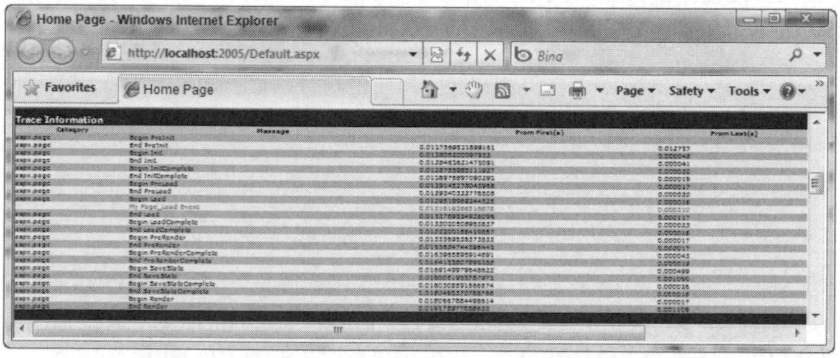

FIGURE 8A-2

APPLICATION-LEVEL TRACING

Tracing is a very powerful tool for understanding the stages that a Web Forms page goes through. When you enable tracing, however, everyone who views the page can see the tracing information. To prevent this, you can enable application-level tracing by updating the web configuration file to include a trace element with the attribute of `enabled`, set to true, as shown in the following code:

```
<configuration>
    <system.web>
        <trace enabled="true"/>
    </system.web>
</configuration>
```

To view the application-level tracing information you need to navigate to the `trace.axd` page in the root of your application. The `trace.axd` page is shown in Figure 8A-3.

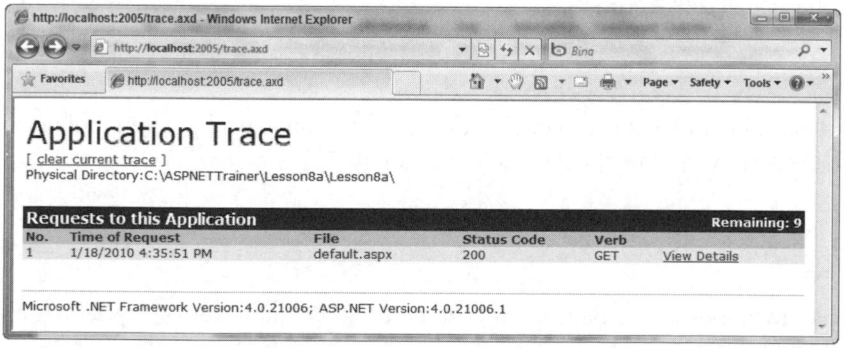

FIGURE 8A-3

By clicking the View Details page on the Application Trace page you can view the Tracing Information for the page, as shown in Figure 8A-1.

By default, the Application Trace page lists only the first 10 page requests that were made since application tracing was enabled. However, if you set the `mostRecent` attribute to true, the 10 most recent page requests are listed. The following code shows how to set the `mostRecent` attribute:

```
<configuration>
    <system.web>
        <trace enabled="true" mostRecent="true"/>
    </system.web>
</configuration>
```

> *You can disable tracing by setting* `<deployment retail=true>` *in the root* web `.config` *file for the machine. It is a good idea to add this setting to the root* web.config *file of your production servers to disable tracing for all of the web applications on the server. This setting not only disables tracing and debugging, it also enables remote custom errors.*

ISPOSTBACK PROPERTY

As I mentioned earlier, all of the events in the page's life cycle are raised every single time a page is requested. To determine whether a page has already been requested, use the `IsPostBack` property. The following example only initializes a list box if it is the first request for the page by using the `Page.IsPostBack` property:

```
protected void Page_Load(object sender, EventArgs e)
{
    if (!Page.IsPostBack)
    {
        ListBoxColors.Items.Add("Blue");
        ListBoxColors.Items.Add("Red");
        ListBoxColors.Items.Add("Yellow");
    }
}
```

If the preceding `Page_Load` did not test to see whether the page was a postback, three more items would be added to the list box every time the page was submitted.

TRY IT

In this lesson you enable tracing on a web page in order to better understand the life cycle that a page goes through and you use the `IsPostback` property of a page to determine if the page has already been requested.

Lesson Requirements

None.

Hints

➤ Use the `Page.IsPostback` property to determine whether this is the first time the page has been requested.

Step-By-Step

1. Open Microsoft Visual Web Developer 2010 Express.

2. Select New Project from the File menu.

3. Select **Visual C#** on the left side of the dialog box.

4. Select the **ASP.NET Web Application** template.

5. Enter **Lesson8a** in the Name field and **c:\ASPNETTrainer** in the Location field.

6. Click the OK button.

7. Add a `Trace` attribute to the `@Page` directive of the `Default.aspx` page:

```
<%@ Page Title="Home Page" Language="C#" MasterPageFile="~/Site.master"
    AutoEventWireup="true" CodeBehind="Default.aspx.cs"
    Inherits="Lesson8a._Default" Trace="true" %>
```

8. Click the F5 button to start debugging and scroll to the bottom of the rendered page to see the Trace Information.

9. Close the browser.

10. Add the following code to the `_Default` class located in the Default.aspx.cs file:

```
protected void Page_PreInit(object sender, EventArgs e)
{
    Trace.Warn("My Page_PreInit Event");
}
```

11. Add the following code to the `Page_Load` event:

```
Trace.Warn("My Page_Load Event");
```

12. Verify that your code matches the following:

```
using System;
using System.Collections.Generic;
using System.Linq;
using System.Web;
using System.Web.UI;
using System.Web.UI.WebControls;

namespace Lesson8a
{
    public partial class _Default : System.Web.UI.Page
    {
        protected void Page_PreInit(object sender, EventArgs e)
        {
            Trace.Warn("My Page_PreInit Event");
```

```
                    }

                    protected void Page_Load(object sender, EventArgs e)
                    {
                        Trace.Warn("My Page_Load Event");
                    }
                }
            }
```

13. Click the F5 button to start debugging and scroll to the bottom of the page to see the Trace Information.

14. Close the browser.

15. Replace the `Put content here.` text on the `About.aspx` page with the following:

```
<asp:ListBox ID="ListBoxColors" runat="server" />
<asp:Button ID="ButtonSelectColor" runat="server" Text="Select Color" />
```

16. Update the `Page_Load` event on the `About.aspx.cs` page to the following:

```
protected void Page_Load(object sender, EventArgs e)
{
    ListBoxColors.Items.Add("Blue");
    ListBoxColors.Items.Add("Red");
    ListBoxColors.Items.Add("Yellow");
    ListBoxColors.Rows = ListBoxColors.Items.Count;
}
```

17. Click the F5 button to start debugging and click the Select Color button three times (see Figure 8A-4). Every time the page is requested, three more items are added to the list box.

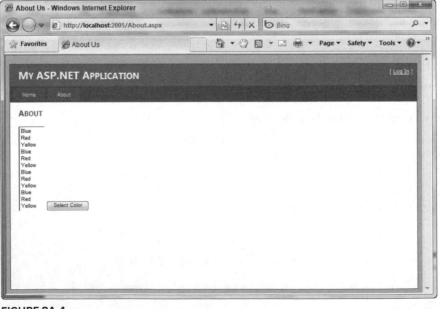

FIGURE 8A-4

18. Close the browser.

19. Use `Page.IsPostBack` to ensure that the list box items are added to the page only once by updating the Page_Load() event to the following:

```
protected void Page_Load(object sender, EventArgs e)
{
    if (!Page.IsPostBack)
    {
        ListBoxColors.Items.Add("Blue");
        ListBoxColors.Items.Add("Red");
        ListBoxColors.Items.Add("Yellow");
        ListBoxColors.Rows = ListBoxColors.Items.Count;
    }
}
```

20. Click the F5 button to start debugging and click the Select Button three times to verify that the list box now works correctly.

 Please select Lesson 8A on the DVD to view the video that accompanies this lesson.

The Request Life Cycle in MVC

Every time a page is requested using the ASP.NET MVC framework, it must complete a request life cycle. In this lesson I describe the steps in a page's request life cycle.

ROUTING

This is a sample URL that is used to request a page using the ASP.NET MVC framework (see Figure 8B-1):

```
http://localhost:1585/Home/About
```

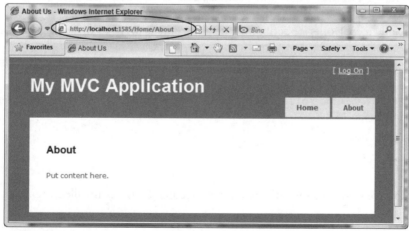

FIGURE 8B-1

Notice that the URL does not refer to a specific page. Instead, the ASP.NET MVC framework uses a routing table to determine how the request should be handled. When you create an MVC application, routing is automatically enabled in the Global.asax.cs file.

This is the routing information included in the `Global.asax.cs` file that is used by the sample MVC application that you created in the previous lesson:

```
routes.MapRoute(
    "Default",                                            // Route name
    "{controller}/{action}/{id}",                         // URL with parameters
    new { controller = "Home", action = "Index", id = "" }  // Defaults
);
```

The route is used to determine which controller and action should be used to process the request. When the "Default" route is applied to the following request the route dictates that the HomeController should be used with the `About` action. See Figure 8B-2.

FIGURE 8B-2

> ✏️ The word Controller is automatically added to the name of the controller. Therefore, it does not need to be included in the URL.

If the URL does not include a controller or action, the default route is used. In this case, this is the default route:

```
new { controller = "Home", action = "Index", id = "" }
```

This route indicates that the `HomeController` should be used with the `Index` action method. I cover routing in more detail in Lesson 15.

THE CONTROLLER

Once the appropriate controller is identified, the request is executed by the controller (see Figure 8B-3).

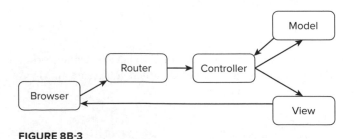

FIGURE 8B-3

The controller validates the user input and delegates execution to the model, if there is one associated with the controller. The controller then determines which view to return to the user. The view, in turn, displays the information returned from the model by sending a response back to the browser.

As you can see from Figure 8B-3, the controller is the brains of the operation. It acts as a bridge between the model and the view. This is a sample controller:

```
using System;
using System.Collections.Generic;
using System.Linq;
using System.Web;
using System.Web.Mvc;

namespace Lesson7b.Controllers
{
    [HandleError]
    public class HomeController : Controller
    {
        public ActionResult Index()
        {
            ViewData["Message"] = "Welcome to ASP.NET MVC!";

            return View();
        }

        public ActionResult About(int id)
        {
            ViewData["Message"] = String.Format("{0} Squared = {1}", id,
                Models.Math.Square(id));
            return View();
        }
    }
}
```

The sample controller contains two action methods: Index and About. An action method is a method that responds to user requests and returns a view. Each view can have one or more action methods associated with it. The Index action method returns data to the Index View while the About action method returns data to the About View.

The sample controller is decorated by the HandleError attribute. This attribute is used to direct the user to an appropriate error page when the application encounters an error. You will enable a custom error page as part of the tutorial at the end of this lesson.

THE MODEL

The model is made up of classes that define the data objects and the business logic for the web application. The classes used to define the model are stored in the Models folder. This is a very simple model:

```
namespace Lesson8b.Models
{
    public class Math
    {
```

```
        public static int Square(int value)
        {
            return value * value;
        }
    }
}
```

THE VIEW

The view is the user interface. This book relies on the same ASPX pages that ASP.NET Web Forms uses to create the views. In the case of ASP.NET MVC, however, the views have no code beyond the logic that is required to display the information returned to the view by the controller. This is some sample code for a view:

```
<%@ Page Language="C#" MasterPageFile="~/Views/Shared/Site.Master"
    Inherits="System.Web.Mvc.ViewPage" %>

<asp:Content ID="aboutTitle" ContentPlaceHolderID="TitleContent" runat="server">
    About Us
</asp:Content>

<asp:Content ID="aboutContent" ContentPlaceHolderID="MainContent" runat="server">
    <h2>About</h2>
    <p>
        <%= Html.Encode(ViewData["Message"]) %>
    </p>
</asp:Content>
```

> *You should never trust input that is provided by a user. Therefore, you should always HTML-encode any user input before you display it. The ASP.NET MVC framework provides the* Html.Encode *method to HTML-encode the text. This method uses* HttpUtility.HtmlEncode *to remove any HTML that a malicious user may be attempting to inject into your web application. Instead of returning a string,* Html.Encode *returns an* MvcHtmlString.

Another way to HTML-encode a string is to use the following code block:

```
<%: %>
```

Using this code block, this markup:

```
<%= Html.Encode(ViewData["Message"]) %>
```

can be replaced by the following:

```
<%: ViewData["Message"] %>
```

> *When a string is HTML-encoded the less than symbol, (<), and the greater than symbol, (>), are replaced with* `&lt;` *and* `&gt;` *respectively. For example, <html> becomes* `&lt;html&gt;`*.*

How the views are organized is very important. Each view must be located in a folder with the same name as its controller. For example, the view that is associated with the `About` action method of the `HomeController` needs to be in the Home subfolder of the Views folder. The appropriate folder structure is shown in Figure 8B-4.

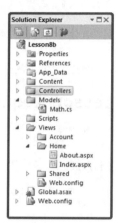

HTTP VERBS

Another factor to take into consideration in the life cycle of a request is the HTTP verb associated with the request. The most commonly used HTTP verbs are HTTP GET and HTTP POST. An HTTP GET occurs when a page is first requested. An HTTP POST occurs when a page, with an HTML form, is submitted.

FIGURE 8B-4

The action method in the controller can be decorated with the `AcceptVerbs` attribute to designate one or more HTTP verbs that are associated with the request. This is an example of an action method that responds to an HTTP POST:

```
[AcceptVerbs(HttpVerbs.Post)]
public ActionResult About(string TextName)
{
    ViewData["Message"] = String.Format("Welcome {0}!", TextName);
    return View();
}
```

Instead of using the `AcceptVerbs` attribute to designate which HTTP verbs are associated with the request, you can also use the following attributes:

➤   `HttpDeleteAttribute`

➤   `HttpGetAttribute`

➤   `HttpPostAttribute`

➤   `HttpPutAttribute`

➤   `NotActionAttribute`

This is an example of an action method that responds to an HTTP Post:

```
[HttpPost]
public ActionResult About(string TextName)
```

```
    {
        ViewData["Message"] = String.Format("Welcome {0}!", TextName);
        return View();
    }
```

TRY IT

In this lesson you explore the request life cycle for an ASP.NET MVC 2 web application. You create a very simple model that will be accessed by the controller to update a view and you experience first-hand how updating the request URL affects the routing of the request.

Lesson Requirements

None.

Hints

➤ Use the `<%: %>` code block to HTML-encode any data entered by the user.

Step-By-Step

1. Open Microsoft Visual Web Developer 2010 Express.

2. Select New Project from the File menu.

3. Select **Visual C#** on the left side of the dialog box.

4. Select the **ASP.NET MVC 2 Web Application** template.

5. Enter **Lesson8b** in the Name field and **c:\ASPNETTrainer** in the Location field.

6. Click the OK button.

7. Add a new model named Math by right-clicking the Models folder in the Solution Explorer window, selecting Class from the Add menu, entering Math.cs into the Name field and clicking the OK button (see Figure 8B-5).

FIGURE 8B-5

8. Add the following code to the Math class:

```
public static int Square(int value)
{
    return value * value;
}
```

9. Verify that the Math.cs file matches the following:

```
using System;
using System.Collections.Generic;
using System.Linq;
using System.Web;

namespace Lesson8b.Models
{
    public class Math
    {
        public static int Square(int value)
        {
            return value * value;
        }
    }
}
```

10. Open the HomeController.cs file in the Controllers folder by double-clicking it and update the About action method of the HomeController to use the new model by changing the About action method to the following:

```
public ActionResult About(int id)
{
    ViewData["Message"] = String.Format("{0} Squared = {1}", id,
        Models.Math.Square(id));
    return View();
}
```

11. Open the About.aspx file in the Home subfolder of the Views folder by double-clicking it and update the About.aspx file to display the message returned by the About action method by replacing the "Put content here." string with the following:

```
<%:ViewData["Message"] %>
```

12. Click the F5 button to start debugging.

13. Navigate to the updated About Us page by adding the following string in the address. See Figure 8B-6.

```
Home/About/7
```

14. Now replace the number 7 with the word "text" (see Figure 8B-7) and review the exception that is thrown because the code expects an integer.

15. Close the browser to stop debugging.

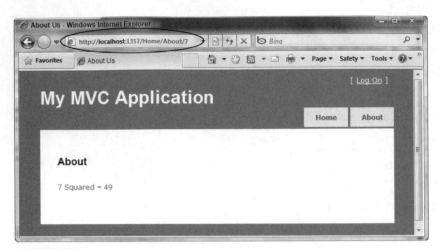

FIGURE 8B-6

FIGURE 8B-7

16. To enable custom errors open the `web.config` file and add the following line to the system. web element:

```
<customErrors mode="On" />
```

17. Click the F5 button.

18. Navigate to the updated About Us page by adding the following string in the address (see Figure 8B-6):

```
Home/About/7
```

19. Now try the following string:

```
Home/About/Text
```

20. Figure 8B-8 shows the custom error page that is rendered. In this example, the custom error page, Error.aspx, is located in the Shared subfolder of the Views folder.

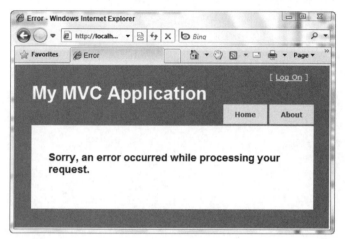

FIGURE 8B-8

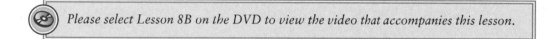

Please select Lesson 8B on the DVD to view the video that accompanies this lesson.

SECTION III
Developing Forms and Views

9A

Server Controls in Web Forms

In the ASP.NET Web Forms framework, a *server control* is a special type of control that is processed on the server and participates in the same life cycle as the Web Form. Its job is both to render HTML and JavaScript to the browser. Microsoft Visual Web Developer 2010 Express comes with dozens of server controls for performing common tasks such as displaying data, collecting data, submitting data, and validating data. Some of the server controls map 1-1 with HTML elements, but most of them are much more complex. Also, many, many libraries of server controls can be obtained from third parties.

In this lesson I introduce the different categories of server controls, show you the markup that is generated by some of the server controls, show you how to use some of the server controls, and show you how programmatically to update a property of a server control. I cover both simple and complex server controls.

SERVER CONTROL CATEGORIES

The server controls are conveniently located in the Toolbox and are divided into categories via separate tabs in the Toolbox, as shown in Figure 9A-1.

You can open the Toolbox by selecting Toolbox from the View menu or using the Ctrl+Alt+X key combination.

The following is information about each of the categories of server controls that are provided in the Toolbox:

> ➤ **Standard** — These are the standard controls. Some of the standard controls that you will use quite often are Label, Button, TextBox, and DropDownList. I show you how to use a number of these server controls later in this lesson.

> ➤ **Data** — These are the controls used to access and view data. You use many of these controls in the later lessons.

FIGURE 9A-1

➤ **Validation** — These controls are used to validate the data that the user enters via your Web Form. I cover the validation server controls in Lessons 16 and 17.

➤ **Navigation** — These controls are used to provide site navigation. You start using site navigation in Lesson 11.

➤ **Login** — These are the controls used to create and manage users and their passwords. I cover these server controls in Lesson 27.

➤ **WebParts** — These controls are used to create and manage WebParts. I do not cover WebParts in this book.

➤ **AJAX Extensions** — These are the controls used to enable and use Ajax with your Web Form. I cover Ajax in Lessons 24 and 25.

➤ **Dynamic Data** — These are the controls used by Dynamic Data. I cover Dynamic Data in Lessons 21 and 22.

➤ **HTML** — These are the standard HTML elements. They are not server controls because they do not include the `runat="server"` attribute. You can easily convert an HTML element into a server control by adding the `runat="server"` attribute. I cover the standard HTML elements in Lesson 2.

➤ **General** — This category is empty. It is provided for any controls that you want to add to the Toolbox. You do not need to use this category because you can create more categories any time you want by right-clicking the Toolbox and selecting Add Tab.

See Figure 9B-2 for the complete list of server controls that are provided on the Standard tab of the Toolbox.

FIGURE 9A-2

SIMPLE SERVER CONTROLS

One of the simplest and most commonly used server controls is the `Label` server control, which is used to update text programmatically on a web page. This is the syntax of a `Label` server control:

```
<asp:Label ID="Label1" runat="server">My Text</asp:Label>
```

The `Label` server control shown here includes two attributes: `ID` and `runat`. The `ID` attribute is used to assign a unique ID to the server control and is required. The `runat` attribute is used to determine if the control is easily accessible from code executed on the server. The only option for `runat` is `server`; however, even though there are no other options, the `runat` attribute is still required.

> All server controls require both an `ID` attribute and a `runat` attribute. The `runat` attribute must be set to `server`.

This is the HTML that is generated by the `Label` server control:

```
<span id="Label1">My Text</span>
```

> *You can view the HTML that is generated by selecting View Source from the Page menu in Internet Explorer. Most browsers provide a means for you to view the source of the web page that is being rendered.*

As you can see, the `Label` server control renders a span element on the browser. Another way to format the Label server control is to add a `Text` attribute explicitly like in the following code:

```
<asp:Label ID="Label1" runat="server" Text="My Text" />
```

The HTML that is generated is exactly the same as using this syntax:

```
<asp:Label ID="Label1" runat="server">My Text</asp:Label>
```

The second version of the `Label` server control uses both an opening tag and a closing tag. The first version of the `Label` server control uses a self-closing tag. I prefer to use self-closing tags whenever possible because they take less room on the Web Form; however, they both render the same exact HTML.

The most basic server control is the `Literal` server control. This is the syntax for a `Literal` server control:

```
<asp:Literal ID="Literal1" runat="server" Text="My Literal Text" />
```

The `Literal` server control shown here renders the following HTML:

```
My Literal Text
```

The HTML generated is simply the text that is included within the `Text` attribute with nothing added. The Literal server control is the simplest server control — it is used to display static text programmatically.

The declarative syntax for a control includes all of its attributes and their values. This is the declarative syntax for the `Literal` server control:

```
<asp:Literal
    EnableTheming="True|False"
    EnableViewState="True|False"
    ID="string"
    Mode="Transform|PassThrough|Encode"
    OnDataBinding="DataBinding event handler"
    OnDisposed="Disposed event handler"
    OnInit="Init event handler"
    OnLoad="Load event handler"
    OnPreRender="PreRender event handler"
    OnUnload="Unload event handler"
    runat="server"
    SkinID="string"
    Text="string"
    Visible="True|False"
/>
```

I have already discussed the ID, runat, and Text attributes. The Visible attribute can be used to hide the control. A server control with its Visible attribute set to false is not rendered on the browser. All server controls include the Visible attribute. An attribute that most server controls include is the CSSClass attribute. The CSSClass attribute gets or sets the cascading style sheet class that is used by the control. In this example, the Label server control is using the bold class that has been defined on the cascading style sheet that is linked to the web page:

```
<asp:Label ID="Label1" runat="server" CssClass="bold" />
```

The following attributes are used to designate the event handlers for the respective events: OnDataBinding, OnDisposed, OnInit, OnLoad, OnPreRender, and OnUnload. It is very important to understand that the life cycle of the page and the lifecycle of the server control are linked together. They both participate in the same page life cycle. I cover more of the attributes in the declarative syntax in coming lessons.

For comparison purposes, this is the declarative syntax for the Label server control:

```
<asp:Label
    AccessKey="string"
    AssociatedControlID="string"
    BackColor="color name|#dddddd"
    BorderColor="color name|#dddddd"
    BorderStyle="NotSet|None|Dotted|Dashed|Solid|Double|Groove|Ridge|
        Inset|Outset"
    BorderWidth="size"
    CssClass="string"
    Enabled="True|False"
    EnableTheming="True|False"
    EnableViewState="True|False"
    Font-Bold="True|False"
    Font-Italic="True|False"
    Font-Names="string"
    Font-Overline="True|False"
    Font-Size="string|Smaller|Larger|XX-Small|X-Small|Small|Medium|
        Large|X-Large|XX-Large"
    Font-Strikeout="True|False"
    Font-Underline="True|False"
    ForeColor="color name|#dddddd"
    Height="size"
    ID="string"
    OnDataBinding="DataBinding event handler"
    OnDisposed="Disposed event handler"
    OnInit="Init event handler"
    OnLoad="Load event handler"
    OnPreRender="PreRender event handler"
    OnUnload="Unload event handler"
    runat="server"
    SkinID="string"
    Style="string"
    TabIndex="integer"
    Text="string"
```

```
        ToolTip="string"
        Visible="True|False"
        Width="size"
/>
```

> Although most of the server controls include attributes that can be used to style the control, you should not use them. You should use cascading style sheets instead. I covered cascading style sheets in Lesson 3.

A commonly used server control is the TextBox server control. This is the syntax for a TextBox:

```
<asp:TextBox ID="TextBox1" runat="server"></asp:TextBox>
```

This is the HTML that is generated by this TextBox server control:

```
<input name="TextBox1" type="text" id="TextBox1" />
```

Another commonly used server control is the Button server control. This is the syntax for a Button:

```
<asp:Button ID="Button1" runat="server" Text="Submit" />
```

This is the HTML that is generated by this Button server control:

```
<input type="submit" name="Button1" value="Submit" id="Button1" />
```

Typically when a user clicks a button something happens. The easiest way to add an event to a button is to double-click the button in Design view (see Figure 9A-3).

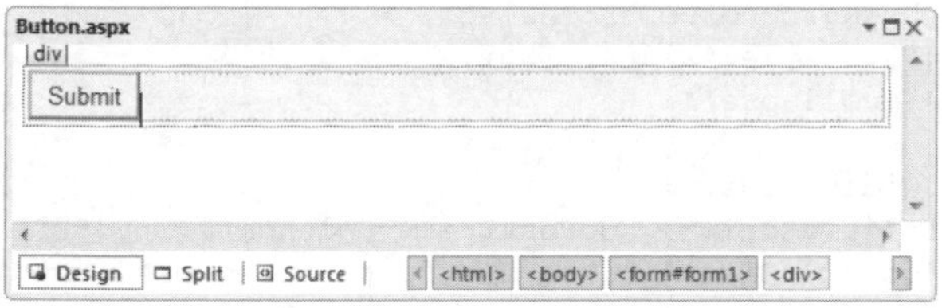

FIGURE 9A-3

After you double-click the button, the following empty method is automatically generated:

```
protected void Button1_Click(object sender, EventArgs e)
{

}
```

Also, the Button server control is automatically updated to include a reference to the new method:

```
<asp:Button ID="Button1" runat="server" Text="Submit" onclick="Button1_Click" />
```

COMPLEX SERVER CONTROLS

So far, you have been looking at server controls that map 1-1 with HTML elements, but many server controls create more than one HTML element. A prime example is the Calendar server control. This is the syntax for the Calendar shown in Figure 9A-4:

```
<asp:Calendar ID="Calendar1" runat="server" />
```

FIGURE 9A-4

This is the HTML that the Calendar server control renders:

```
<table id="Calendar1" cellspacing="0" cellpadding="2" title="Calendar"
    style="border-width: 1px;
        border-style: solid; border-collapse: collapse;">
        <tr>
            <td colspan="7" style="background-color: Silver;">
                <table cellspacing="0" style="width: 100%;
                    border-collapse: collapse;">
                    <tr>
                        <td style="width: 15%;">
                            <a href="javascript:__doPostBack('Calendar1','V3622')"
                            style="color: Black" title="Go to the previous month">
                                &lt;</a>
                        </td>
                        <td align="center" style="width: 70%;">
                            January 2010
                        </td>
                        <td align="right" style="width: 15%;">
                            <a href="javascript:__doPostBack('Calendar1','V3684')"
                            style="color: Black" title="Go to the next month">
                                &gt;</a>
                        </td>
                    </tr>
                </table>
            </td>
        </tr>
        <tr>
            <th align="center" abbr="Sunday" scope="col">
                Sun
```

```
        </th>
        <th align="center" abbr="Monday" scope="col">
            Mon
        </th>
        <th align="center" abbr="Tuesday" scope="col">
            Tue
        </th>
        <th align="center" abbr="Wednesday" scope="col">
            Wed
        </th>
        <th align="center" abbr="Thursday" scope="col">
            Thu
        </th>
        <th align="center" abbr="Friday" scope="col">
            Fri
        </th>
        <th align="center" abbr="Saturday" scope="col">
            Sat
        </th>
    </tr>
    <tr>
        <td align="center" style="width: 14%;">
            <a href="javascript:__doPostBack('Calendar1','3648')"
                style="color: Black" title="December 27">
                27</a>
        </td>
        <td align="center" style="width: 14%;">
            <a href="javascript:__doPostBack('Calendar1','3649')"
                style="color: Black" title="December 28">
                28</a>
        </td>
        <td align="center" style="width: 14%;">
            <a href="javascript:__doPostBack('Calendar1','3650')"
                style="color: Black" title="December 29">
                29</a>
        </td>
        <td align="center" style="width: 14%;">
            <a href="javascript:__doPostBack('Calendar1','3651')"
                style="color: Black" title="December 30">
                30</a>
        </td>
        <td align="center" style="width: 14%;">
            <a href="javascript:__doPostBack('Calendar1','3652')"
                style="color: Black" title="December 31">
                31</a>
        </td>
        <td align="center" style="width: 14%;">
            <a href="javascript:__doPostBack('Calendar1','3653')"
                style="color: Black" title="January 01">
                1</a>
        </td>
        <td align="center" style="width: 14%;">
            <a href="javascript:__doPostBack('Calendar1','3654')"
                style="color: Black" title="January 02">
                2</a>
```

```
            </td>
        </tr>
        <tr>
            <td align="center" style="width: 14%;">
                <a href="javascript:__doPostBack('Calendar1','3655')"
                    style="color: Black" title="January 03">
                    3</a>
            </td>
            <td align="center" style="width: 14%;">
                <a href="javascript:__doPostBack('Calendar1','3656')"
                    style="color: Black" title="January 04">
                    4</a>
            </td>
            <td align="center" style="width: 14%;">
                <a href="javascript:__doPostBack('Calendar1','3657')"
                    style="color: Black" title="January 05">
                    5</a>
            </td>
            <td align="center" style="width: 14%;">
                <a href="javascript:__doPostBack('Calendar1','3658')"
                    style="color: Black" title="January 06">
                    6</a>
            </td>
            <td align="center" style="width: 14%;">
                <a href="javascript:__doPostBack('Calendar1','3659')"
                    style="color: Black" title="January 07">
                    7</a>
            </td>
            <td align="center" style="width: 14%;">
                <a href="javascript:__doPostBack('Calendar1','3660')"
                    style="color: Black" title="January 08">
                    8</a>
            </td>
            <td align="center" style="width: 14%;">
                <a href="javascript:__doPostBack('Calendar1','3661')"
                    style="color: Black" title="January 09">
                    9</a>
            </td>
        </tr>
        <tr>
            <td align="center" style="width: 14%;">
                <a href="javascript:__doPostBack('Calendar1','3662')"
                    style="color: Black" title="January 10">
                    10</a>
            </td>
            <td align="center" style="width: 14%;">
                <a href="javascript:__doPostBack('Calendar1','3663')"
                    style="color: Black" title="January 11">
                    11</a>
            </td>
            <td align="center" style="width: 14%;">
                <a href="javascript:__doPostBack('Calendar1','3664')"
                    style="color: Black" title="January 12">
                    12</a>
            </td>
```

```
        <td align="center" style="width: 14%;">
            <a href="javascript:__doPostBack('Calendar1','3665')"
                style="color: Black" title="January 13">
                13</a>
        </td>
        <td align="center" style="width: 14%;">
            <a href="javascript:__doPostBack('Calendar1','3666')"
                style="color: Black" title="January 14">
                14</a>
        </td>
        <td align="center" style="width: 14%;">
            <a href="javascript:__doPostBack('Calendar1','3667')"
                style="color: Black" title="January 15">
                15</a>
        </td>
        <td align="center" style="width: 14%;">
            <a href="javascript:__doPostBack('Calendar1','3668')"
                style="color: Black" title="January 16">
                16</a>
        </td>
    </tr>
    <tr>
        <td align="center" style="width: 14%;">
            <a href="javascript:__doPostBack('Calendar1','3669')"
                style="color: Black" title="January 17">
                17</a>
        </td>
        <td align="center" style="width: 14%;">
            <a href="javascript:__doPostBack('Calendar1','3670')"
                style="color: Black" title="January 18">
                18</a>
        </td>
        <td align="center" style="width: 14%;">
            <a href="javascript:__doPostBack('Calendar1','3671')"
                style="color: Black" title="January 19">
                19</a>
        </td>
        <td align="center" style="width: 14%;">
            <a href="javascript:__doPostBack('Calendar1','3672')"
                style="color: Black" title="January 20">
                20</a>
        </td>
        <td align="center" style="width: 14%;">
            <a href="javascript:__doPostBack('Calendar1','3673')"
                style="color: Black" title="January 21">
                21</a>
        </td>
        <td align="center" style="width: 14%;">
            <a href="javascript:__doPostBack('Calendar1','3674')"
                style="color: Black" title="January 22">
                22</a>
        </td>
        <td align="center" style="width: 14%;">
            <a href="javascript:__doPostBack('Calendar1','3675')"
                style="color: Black" title="January 23">
```

```
                23</a>
        </td>
    </tr>
    <tr>
        <td align="center" style="width: 14%;">
            <a href="javascript:__doPostBack('Calendar1','3676')"
                style="color: Black" title="January 24">
                24</a>
        </td>
        <td align="center" style="width: 14%;">
            <a href="javascript:__doPostBack('Calendar1','3677')"
                style="color: Black" title="January 25">
                25</a>
        </td>
        <td align="center" style="width: 14%;">
            <a href="javascript:__doPostBack('Calendar1','3678')"
                style="color: Black" title="January 26">
                26</a>
        </td>
        <td align="center" style="width: 14%;">
            <a href="javascript:__doPostBack('Calendar1','3679')"
                style="color: Black" title="January 27">
                27</a>
        </td>
        <td align="center" style="width: 14%;">
            <a href="javascript:__doPostBack('Calendar1','3680')"
                style="color: Black" title="January 28">
                28</a>
        </td>
        <td align="center" style="width: 14%;">
            <a href="javascript:__doPostBack('Calendar1','3681')"
                style="color: Black" title="January 29">
                29</a>
        </td>
        <td align="center" style="width: 14%;">
            <a href="javascript:__doPostBack('Calendar1','3682')"
                style="color: Black" title="January 30">
                30</a>
        </td>
    </tr>
    <tr>
        <td align="center" style="width: 14%;">
            <a href="javascript:__doPostBack('Calendar1','3683')"
                style="color: Black" title="January 31">
                31</a>
        </td>
        <td align="center" style="width: 14%;">
            <a href="javascript:__doPostBack('Calendar1','3684')"
                style="color: Black" title="February 01">
                1</a>
        </td>
        <td align="center" style="width: 14%;">
            <a href="javascript:__doPostBack('Calendar1','3685')"
                style="color: Black" title="February 02">
                2</a>
```

```
        </td>
        <td align="center" style="width: 14%;">
            <a href="javascript:__doPostBack('Calendar1','3686')"
                style="color: Black" title="February 03">
                3</a>
        </td>
        <td align="center" style="width: 14%;">
            <a href="javascript:__doPostBack('Calendar1','3687')"
                style="color: Black" title="February 04">
                4</a>
        </td>
        <td align="center" style="width: 14%;">
            <a href="javascript:__doPostBack('Calendar1','3688')"
                style="color: Black" title="February 05">
                5</a>
        </td>
        <td align="center" style="width: 14%;">
            <a href="javascript:__doPostBack('Calendar1','3689')"
                style="color: Black" title="February 06">
                6</a>
        </td>
    </tr>
</table>
```

TRY IT

In this lesson you create a simple web page that includes a number of server controls. You write code to handle the `OnClick` event of the Button server control and programmatically update a property of a server control.

Lesson Requirements

None.

Hints

➤ Double-click a `Button` server control in Design view to automatically add a `Click` event handler.

➤ Use the Properties window to update the attributes of a server control.

Step-By-Step

1. Open Microsoft Visual Web Developer 2010 Express.

2. Select New Project from the File menu.

3. Select **Visual C#** on the left side of the dialog box.

4. Select the **ASP.NET Web Application** template.

5. Enter **Lesson9a** in the Name field and **c:\ASPNETTrainer** in the Location field.

6. Click the OK button.

7. Open the `About.aspx` page.

8. Replace the "Put content here." string on the `About.aspx` page with the following three server controls:

```
<asp:TextBox ID="TextBoxName" runat="server" />
<asp:Button ID="ButtonSubmit" runat="server" Text="Submit Name" />
<asp:Label ID="LabelHello" runat="server" />
```

9. Click the F5 button (see Figure 9A-5).

10. Click the Submit Name button. Notice that although the page does a postback to the server, nothing changes on the page when you click the button.

11. Stop debugging by closing the browser.

12. View `About.aspx` in Design view and double-click the Submit Name button to create the `ButtonSubmit_Click` event.

13. Add the following code to the `ButtonSubmit_Click` event:

FIGURE 9A-5

```
this.LabelHello.Text = String.Format("Hello {0}!", this.TextBoxName.Text);
```

14. Verify that the code for the About.aspx.cs file matches the following:

```csharp
using System;
using System.Collections.Generic;
using System.Linq;
using System.Web;
using System.Web.UI;
using System.Web.UI.WebControls;

namespace Lesson9a
{
    public partial class About : System.Web.UI.Page
    {
        protected void Page_Load(object sender, EventArgs e)
        {

        }

        protected void ButtonSubmit_Click(object sender, EventArgs e)
        {
            this.LabelHello.Text = String.Format("Hello {0}!", this.
TextBoxName.Text);
        }
    }
}
```

15. Click the F5 button.

16. Enter your name and click the Submit Name button (see Figure 9A-6).

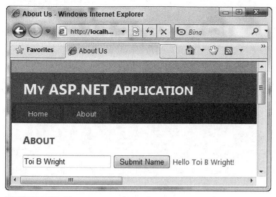

FIGURE 9A-6

17. Stop debugging by closing the browser.

18. Set the CSSClass property for the LabelHello server control to **bold**.

19. Verify that the markup for the About.aspx page matches the following:

```
<%@ Page Title="About Us" Language="C#" MasterPageFile="~/Site.master"
    AutoEventWireup="true" CodeBehind="About.aspx.cs"
    Inherits="Lesson9a.About" %>

<asp:Content ID="HeaderContent" runat="server"
    ContentPlaceHolderID="HeadContent">
</asp:Content>
<asp:Content ID="BodyContent" runat="server"
    ContentPlaceHolderID="MainContent">
    <h2>
        About
    </h2>
    <p>
        <asp:TextBox ID="TextBoxName" runat="server" />
        <asp:Button ID="ButtonSubmit" runat="server" Text="Submit Name"
            OnClick="ButtonSubmit_Click" />
        <asp:Label ID="LabelHello" runat="server" CssClass="bold" />
    </p>
</asp:Content>
```

20. Click the F5 button.

21. Enter your name and click the Submit Name button. Your name now appears in a bold font.

Please select Lesson 9A on the DVD to view the video that accompanies this lesson.

9B

HTML Helpers in MVC

HTML helpers are an easy way to render the appropriate HTML markup in a view and the ASP.NET MVC framework provides a wide selection of them. An HTML helper method returns an HTML-encoded string of the type `MvcHtmlString`. The string can be used to render something as simple as a `CheckBox` or as complicated as a complete table of data. In this lesson I show you how to use both the standard HTML helpers and the strongly-typed HTML helpers to render HTML in a web page.

> *An `MvcHtmlString` is a string that has already been HTML-encoded and therefore should not be encoded again.*

STANDARD HTML HELPERS

This is the HTML used to render a `TextBox`:

```
<input id="Text1" type="text" value="My TextBox" />
```

This is the code, used by a view, to render the same `TextBox` using an HTML helper:

```
<%: Html.TextBox("Text1", Model.Value) %>
```

In this example, the view is using the `Html.TextBox` helper method. The first parameter provides the name and id for the `TextBox` and the second parameter provides the value.

> *The script delimiters `<%` and `%>` are used to mark the beginning and end of a script. The equal sign within the script delimiters, `<%=` and `%>`, is a shortcut for `Response.Write`. If you forget the equal sign, the text will not be displayed because the `Reponse.Write` method is not called. The colon within the script delimiters, `<%:` and `%>`, is also a shortcut for `Response.Write`. But, in this case the string is automatically HTML-encoded.*

HTML helpers are really simple to use. They are all `HtmlHelper` methods that return an HTML-encoded string of type `MvcHtmlString` and they are included in IntelliSense (see Figure 9B-1).

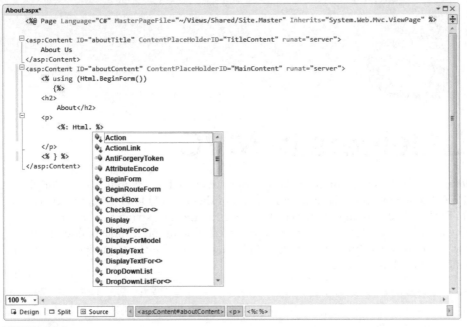

FIGURE 9B-1

This is a partial list of the standard HTML helpers, organized by class, that are included with the ASP.NET MVC framework:

➤ **Form Extensions** — These methods are used to render the HTML form element:

  ➤ `Html.BeginForm()`

  ➤ `Html.BeginRouteForm()`

  ➤ `Html.EndForm()`

➤ **Input Extensions** — These methods are used to render the HTML input elements:

  ➤ `Html.CheckBox()`

  ➤ `Html.Hidden()`

  ➤ `Html.Password()`

  ➤ `Html.RadioButton()`

  ➤ `Html.TextBox()`

➤ **Label Extensions** — This method is used to render the HTML label element:

  ➤ `Html.Label()`

➤ **Link Extensions** — These methods support HTML links:

   ➤ `Html.ActionLink()`

   ➤ `Html.RouteLink()`

➤ **Select Extensions** — These methods support making selections in a list:

   ➤ `Html.DropDownList()`

   ➤ `Html.ListBox()`

➤ **TextArea Extensions** — This method renders an HTML textarea:

   ➤ `Html.TextArea()`

➤ **Validation Extensions** — These methods support validating input from a form. I cover validation in Lessons 21 and 22.

   ➤ `Html.Validate()`

   ➤ `Html.ValidationMessage()`

   ➤ `Html.ValidationSummary()`

Most of the standard HTML helpers have a one-to-one relationship with their HTML counterpart. The `Html.TextBox` method I showed you at the beginning of the lesson is a case in point.

Another HTML helper is the `Html.CheckBox` method. This is the code used by a view to render a `CheckBox` using the `Html.Checkbox` method:

```
<%: Html.CheckBox("My Sample Checkbox")%>
```

This is the HTML that is rendered:

```
<input id="My Sample Checkbox" name="My Sample Checkbox" type="checkbox"
    value="true" />
<input name="My Sample Checkbox" type="hidden" value="false" />
```

The `Html.Checkbox` method renders a checkbox input element and a hidden input element. The hidden input element is used to ensure that an unselected checkbox returns false. An advantage of using the `Html.Checkbox` method over using a checkbox input element is that it is much easier to bind to either view data or model data by using the `Html.Checkbox` method.

> *You are not required to use HTML helpers — they are provided to make rendering HTML, from a view, simpler.*

The `Html.ActionLink` method is used to render an HTML link to an action method. This sample code uses the `Html.ActionLink` method:

```
<%: Html.ActionLink("Return Home", "Index", "Home") %>
```

In the preceding example, the first parameter of the `Html.ActionLink` method is the text of the link, the second parameter is the name of the action method and the third parameter is the name of the controller. This is the HTML that is rendered by the preceding `Html.ActionLink` method:

```
<a href="/">Return Home</a>
```

> The `Html.RouteLink` method is used to render an HTML link to a URL instead of an action method. The URL can represent a file, an image, an action link, or some other resource.

The `Html.DropDownList` method is an example of a more complicated method. It is a member of the `SelectExtensions` class that is designed to support making selections in a list. This is the sample code that is used by the view:

```
<%: Html.DropDownList("Colors")%>
```

This is the code that has been added to the action method to return the data that will be displayed in the drop-down list:

```
List<string> colors = new List<string> { "Blue", "Red", "Yellow" };
ViewData["Colors"] =  new  SelectList(colors);
```

Finally, this is the HTML that is rendered:

```
<select id="Colors" name="Colors">
    <option>Blue</option>
    <option>Red</option>
     <option>Yellow</option>
</select>
```

An important pair of HTML helpers are the `Html.BeginForm` and the `Html.EndForm` methods. They are used to render a `form` element. These are examples that use them:

```
<% Html.BeginForm();%>
…
<% Html.EndForm(); %>
```

or

```
<% using (Html.BeginForm()) {%>
…
<% }; %>
```

In these examples, the view renders an `MvcForm` that posts back to the same action method as the action method that had called the view. Of course, there are properties that you can set to modify the action method that is used.

Sample HTML that is rendered looks like this:

```
<form action="/Home/About" method="post"></form>
```

> *The Form Extensions use <% and %> without the equal sign or a colon because they do not return a string; they return an* `MvcForm`.

STRONGLY-TYPED HTML HELPERS

Most of the HTML helpers that I have shown you take a string as their first parameter. However, they are expecting a certain type of data to be returned. If the correct type of data is not returned, the user will receive an error at runtime. Of course, it would be better to get the error at compile-time instead. Strongly-typed HTML helpers provide a way to do compile-time checking of your views. Strongly-typed HTML helpers use lambda expressions when referring to the model that has been passed to the view.

> *A lambda expression is an anonymous function that calculates and returns a single value. Lambda expressions use the lambda operation, =>, which is read as "goes to".*

This is a partial list of the strongly-typed HTML helper methods:

➤ **Input Extensions** — These methods are used to render the HTML input elements:

  ➤ `Html.CheckBoxFor()`

  ➤ `Html.HiddenFor()`

  ➤ `Html.PasswordFor()`

  ➤ `Html.RadioButtonFor()`

  ➤ `Html.TextBoxFor()`

➤ **Label Extensions** — This method is used to render the HTML label element:

  ➤ `Html.LabelFor()`

➤ **Select Extensions** — These methods support making selections in a list:

  ➤ `Html.DropDownListFor()`

  ➤ `Html.ListBoxFor()`

➤ **TextArea Extensions** — This method renders an HTML textarea:

  ➤ `Html.TextAreaFor()`

➤ **Validation Extensions** — These methods support validating input from a form. I cover validation in Lessons 21 and 22.

  ➤ `Html.ValidateFor()`

  ➤ `Html.ValidationMessageFor()`

The best way to learn how to use the strongly-typed HTML helpers is to study an example. This is the simple model that I am using for the example:

```
namespace Lesson9b.Models
{
    public class CustomerModel
    {
        public string FirstName { get; set; }
        public string LastName { get; set; }
    }
}
```

This is a sample view that uses strongly-typed HTML helpers:

```
<%@ Page Title="" Language="C#" MasterPageFile="~/Views/Shared/Site.Master"
    Inherits="System.Web.Mvc.ViewPage<Lesson9b.Models.CustomerModel>" %>

<asp:Content ID="Content1" ContentPlaceHolderID="TitleContent" runat="server">
    Customer
</asp:Content>

<asp:Content ID="Content2" ContentPlaceHolderID="MainContent" runat="server">

    <h2>Customer</h2>

    <% using (Html.BeginForm()) {%>
        <%: Html.ValidationSummary(true) %>

        <fieldset>
            <legend>Fields</legend>

            <div class="editor-label">
                <%: Html.LabelFor(model => model.FirstName) %>
            </div>
            <div class="editor-field">
                <%: Html.TextBoxFor(model => model.FirstName) %>
                <%: Html.ValidationMessageFor(model => model.FirstName) %>
            </div>

            <div class="editor-label">
                <%: Html.LabelFor(model => model.LastName) %>
            </div>
            <div class="editor-field">
                <%: Html.TextBoxFor(model => model.LastName) %>
                <%: Html.ValidationMessageFor(model => model.LastName) %>
            </div>

            <p>
                <input type="submit" value="Create" />
            </p>
        </fieldset>

    <% } %>

    <div>
```

```
        <%: Html.ActionLink("Back to List", "Index") %>
    </div>

</asp:Content>
```

 The preceding code is for the Create *view that you will be writing as part of this lesson's tutorial.*

TRY IT

In this lesson you use a few of the standard HTML helpers to create a simple view and you create a new view that uses the strongly-typed HTML helpers.

Lesson Requirements

None.

Hints

➤   Make sure you use <%: %> script delimiter with the HTML helpers that return a string.

Step-By-Step

1.   Open Microsoft Visual Web Developer 2010 Express.

2.   Select New Project from the File menu.

3.   Select **Visual C#** on the left side of the dialog box.

4.   Select the **ASP.NET MVC 2 Web Application** template.

5.   Enter **Lesson9b** in the Name field and **c:\ASPNETTrainer** in the Location field.

6.   Click the OK button.

7.   Open the About.aspx file in the Home subfolder of the Views folder and use HTML helpers to add a form to the page.

8.   Verify that the code in the About.aspx file matches the following:

```
<%@ Page Language="C#" MasterPageFile="~/Views/Shared/Site.Master"
    Inherits="System.Web.Mvc.ViewPage" %>

<asp:Content ID="aboutTitle" ContentPlaceHolderID="TitleContent" runat="server">
    About Us
</asp:Content>

<asp:Content ID="aboutContent" ContentPlaceHolderID="MainContent" runat="server">
```

```
<% using (Html.BeginForm()) {%>

    <h2>About</h2>
    <p>
        Put content Here.
    </p>

<% } %>
</asp:Content>
```

9. Replace the "Put content here." string with the following code:

```
<%: Html.TextBox("TextBoxName") %>
<input type="submit" value="Enter Name" />
<%: ViewData["Message"] %>
```

10. Open the HomeController.cs file and **add** the following About action method after the existing About action method:

```
[HttpPost]
public ActionResult About(string TextBoxName)
{
    ViewData["Message"] = String.Format("Welcome {0}!", TextBoxName);
    return View();
}
```

11. Click the F5 button.

12. View the About Us page. Enter some data in the text box and click the Enter Name button (see Figure 9B-2).

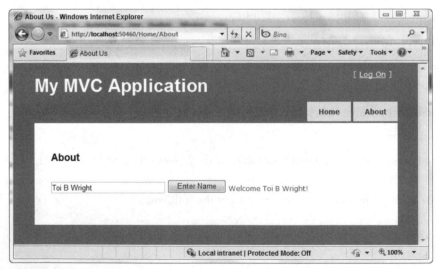

FIGURE 9B-2

13. View the source code of the page.

> In Internet Explorer you can view the source code of the page by right-clicking the page and selecting View Source.

14. Stop debugging by closing the browser.

15. Add a new model by right-clicking the Models folder and selecting Class from the Add menu. Name the new file **CustomerModel.cs** and click the Add button.

16. Update the `CustomerModel` class to the following:

```
using System;
using System.Collections.Generic;
using System.Linq;
using System.Web;

namespace Lesson9b.Models
{
    public class CustomerModel
    {
        public string FirstName { get; set; }
        public string LastName { get; set; }
    }
}
```

17. Select Build Lesson9b from the Build menu to build the project.

18. Add a new view by right-clicking the Home sub-folder of the Views folder and selecting View from the Add menu. This opens the Add View dialog box.

19. Enter **Customer** in the View Name field, click the `Create a strongly-typed view` checkbox, select **Lesson9b.Models.CustomerModel** from the View data class drop-down list, and select **Create** from the View content drop-down list, as shown in Figure 9B-3.

20. Click the Add button.

21. Add the following action method to the HomeController.cs file:

```
public ActionResult Customer()
{
    return View();
}
```

FIGURE 9B-3

22. Verify that the code in the `HomeController.cs` file matches the following:

```
using System;
using System.Collections.Generic;
using System.Linq;
using System.Web;
using System.Web.Mvc;

namespace Lesson9b.Controllers
{
    [HandleError]
    public class HomeController : Controller
    {
        public ActionResult Index()
        {
            ViewData["Message"] = "Welcome to ASP.NET MVC!";

            return View();
        }

        public ActionResult About()
        {
            return View();
        }

        [HttpPost]
        public ActionResult About(string TextBoxName)
        {
            ViewData["Message"] = String.Format("Welcome {0}!", TextBoxName);
            return View();
        }

        public ActionResult Customer()
        {
            return View();
        }
    }
}
```

23. Open the `Site.Master` page located in the Shared subfolder of the Views folder and add a Customer tab by adding an `Html.ActionLink` method to the menu:

```
<ul id="menu">
    <li><%: Html.ActionLink("Home", "Index", "Home")%></li>
    <li><%: Html.ActionLink("About", "About", "Home")%></li>
    <li><%: Html.ActionLink("Customer", "Customer", "Home")%></li>
</ul>
```

24. Click the F5 button.

25. Click the Customer tab (see Figure 9B-4).

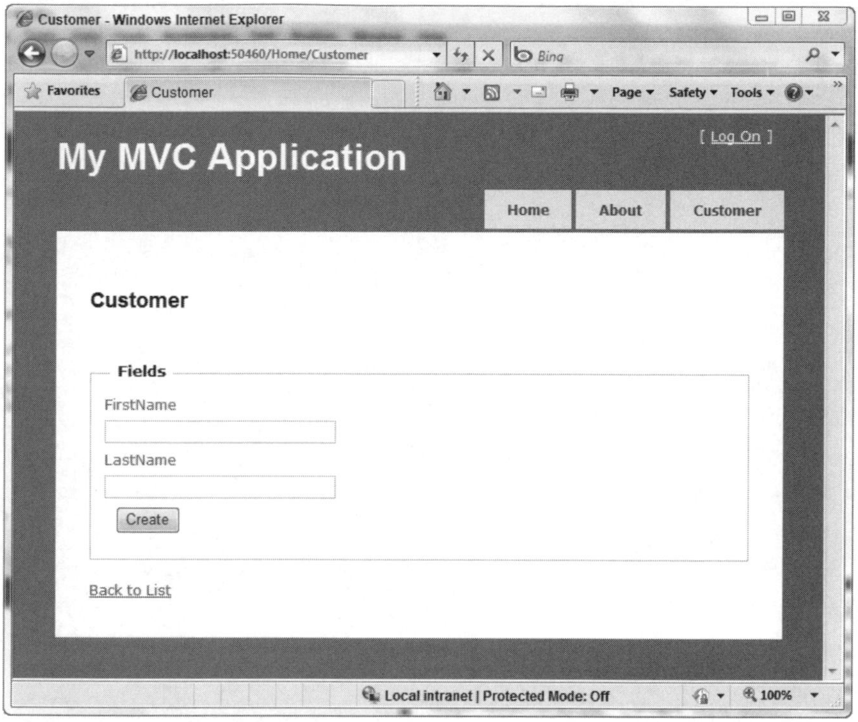

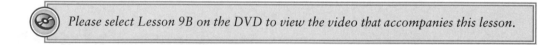

FIGURE 9B-4

Please select Lesson 9B on the DVD to view the video that accompanies this lesson.

10A

View State in Web Forms

View state is used to preserve the state of controls on a Web Form across postbacks. In this lesson I show you how view state is stored on a web page, why it is useful, and how to turn it off.

VIEWING VIEW STATE

This is the code for a simple web page that has only one server control on it:

```
<%@ Page Language="C#" AutoEventWireup="true" CodeBehind="Label.aspx.cs"
    Inherits="Lesson10a.Label" %>

<!DOCTYPE html PUBLIC "-//W3C//DTD XHTML 1.0 Transitional//EN"
    "http://www.w3.org/TR/xhtml1/DTD/xhtml1-transitional.dtd">

<html xmlns="http://www.w3.org/1999/xhtml">
<head runat="server">
    <title></title>
</head>
<body>
    <form id="form1" runat="server">
    <div>
        <asp:Label ID="Label1" runat="server" Text="Label" />
    </div>
    </form>
</body>
</html>
```

When the preceding page is rendered on a browser, this is the HTML source for the page:

```
<!DOCTYPE html PUBLIC "-//W3C//DTD XHTML 1.0 Transitional//EN"
    "http://www.w3.org/TR/xhtml1/DTD/xhtml1-transitional.dtd">

<html xmlns="http://www.w3.org/1999/xhtml">
<head><title>

</title></head>
```

```
<body>
    <form method="post" action="Label.aspx" id="form1">
<div class="aspNetHidden">
<input type="hidden" name="__VIEWSTATE" id="__VIEWSTATE"
    value="/wEPDwUJOTczNTMyNjI5ZGTL47vwelS4H7Q78eBnfVHkSleBV1ii753zaCBSWQAKKw==" />
</div>
    <div>
        <span id="Label1">Label</span>
    </div>
    </form>
</body>
</html>
```

The view state is stored in the hidden field named __VIEWSTATE. View state is a Base64-encoded string. In this example the amount of text stored in the view state is rather small, but this page is only displaying a simple label. It is easy to see that as more and more controls are added to the page, the view state will grow bigger.

> *A Base64 encoded string is a string that is used to store a base 64 representation of binary data.*

The easiest way to see how big the view state is for each control is to add a `Trace="true"` attribute to the `@Page` directive at the top of the Web Form, view the page in a browser, and examine the Control Tree. The Control Tree for my simple page with only one label is shown in Figure 10A-1.

Control Tree

Control UniqueID	Type	Render Size Bytes (including children)	ViewState Size Bytes (excluding children)	ControlState Size Bytes (excluding children)
__Page	ASP.label_aspx	646	0	0
ctl02	System.Web.UI.LiteralControl	172	0	0
ctl00	System.Web.UI.HtmlControls.HtmlHead	32	0	0
ctl01	System.Web.UI.HtmlControls.HtmlTitle	19	0	0
ctl03	System.Web.UI.LiteralControl	14	0	0
form1	System.Web.UI.HtmlControls.HtmlForm	408	0	0
ctl04	System.Web.UI.LiteralControl	21	0	0
Label1	System.Web.UI.WebControls.Label	59	64	0
ctl05	System.Web.UI.LiteralControl	18	0	0
ctl06	System.Web.UI.LiteralControl	20	0	0

FIGURE 10A-1

The view state for the `Label1` server control is 64 bytes. Because the view state is part of the page, the larger it gets the longer it takes for the page to render.

> *The following server controls do not use view state: TextBox, RadioButton, CheckBox, and DropDownList. This is because they map 1-1 with HTML elements that return their state by default as part of the HTTP request.*

The ListBox server control uses view state to maintain its list of items. This is a sample ListBox:

```
<asp:ListBox ID="ListBoxColors" runat="server" />
```

This is code used to populate the list in the ListBox:

```
protected void Page_Load(object sender, EventArgs e)
{
    if (!Page.IsPostBack)
    {
        ListBoxColors.Rows = 3;
        ListBoxColors.Items.Add("Blue");
        ListBoxColors.Items.Add("Red");
        ListBoxColors.Items.Add("Yellow");
    }
}
```

Thanks to view state, when this page is submitted to the server, all of the values in the ListBox are retained. Without view state, the ListBox would need to be repopulated on each postback. If the data were coming from a database, the database call would need to be made every time the page was submitted if view state were not available. This is an advantage of using view state.

DISABLING VIEW STATE

View state is definitely a handy tool for persisting and restoring the values of your server controls between postbacks. However, as you have seen, it is not free. It is stored on the page and must be sent to the browser as part of the response and returned to the web server as part of the request. As a web developer, you should always strive to make your page as small as possible. You may want to disable view state for either some or all of the server controls on a page.

You can disable view state at the page level, at the container level, and at the control level. By default, view state is enabled for every page in your web application. Two properties are used to disable and enable view state:

➤ **EnableViewState** — This property can be set to either True or False. By default, it is set to True.

➤ **ViewStateMode** — This property can be set to Enabled, Disabled, or Inherit. By default, it is set to Inherit.

View state for a control is only enabled if all of the following conditions are met:

➤ The EnableViewState property for the page is set to True.

➤ The EnableViewState property for the control is set to True.

➤ The ViewStateMode property for the control is set to Enabled or inherits from a control that has its ViewStateMode property set to Enabled.

> ⊗ *If you set the EnableViewState property for the page to False, you will not be able to enable view state for any of the controls on the page.*

When developing a Web Form, the goal is to enable view state only for the controls that need to have it enabled and to disable it for all of the other controls. For example, on a page where I want to enable view state for only a few controls I would do the following:

1. Set `ViewStateMode="Disabled"` in the `@Page` directive.

2. Add a PlaceHolder server control and set `ViewStateMode="Enabled"` for the PlaceHolder.

3. Add all the controls that need ViewState enabled to the PlaceHolder. Because the default value of the `ViewStateMode` property is Inherit, you do not need to set the `ViewStateMode` property for the controls that are within the PlaceHolder control.

This is an example of a page that used the preceding three-step process to enable view state for only certain controls:

```
<%@ Page Language="C#" AutoEventWireup="true" CodeBehind="EnableViewState.aspx.cs"
    Inherits="Lesson10a.EnableViewState" ViewStateMode="Disabled"  %>

<!DOCTYPE html PUBLIC "-//W3C//DTD XHTML 1.0 Transitional//EN"
    "http://www.w3.org/TR/xhtml1/DTD/xhtml1-transitional.dtd">
<html xmlns="http://www.w3.org/1999/xhtml">
<head runat="server">
    <title>ViewState</title>
</head>
<body>
    <form id="form1" runat="server">
    <asp:PlaceHolder ID="PlaceHolder1" runat="server" ViewStateMode="Enabled">
        <asp:Label ID="Label1" runat="server" />
        <asp:ListBox ID="ListBox1" runat="server" />
    </asp:PlaceHolder>
    <asp:Button ID="Button1" runat="server" Text="Button" />
    </form>
</body>
</html>
```

> The `PlaceHolder` *server control is simply a container for other controls. It does not produce any output on the page.*

TRY IT

In this lesson you populate a `ListBox`, use view state to restore its value on a postback, and see what happens when view state is disabled.

Lesson Requirements

None.

Hints

➤ Set `Trace="true"` in the `@Page` directive to see how large the view state is for each control on the page.

Step-By-Step

1. Open Microsoft Visual Web Developer 2010 Express.

2. Select New Project from the File menu.

3. Select **Visual C#** on the left side of the dialog box.

4. Select the **ASP.NET Web Application** template.

5. Enter **Lesson10a** in the Name field and **c:\ASPNETTrainer** in the Location field.

6. Click the OK button.

7. Open the About.aspx page and replace the "Put content here." string with the following server controls: a `ListBox`, a `Button`, and a `Label`.

> You can drag each of these server controls from the Toolbox.

8. Update the new controls to match the following:

```
<asp:ListBox ID="ListBoxColors" runat="server"></asp:ListBox>
<asp:Button ID="ButtonSelectColor" runat="server" Text="Select Color" />
<asp:Label ID="LabelColor" runat="server"></asp:Label>
```

9. View the `About.aspx` page in Design view and double-click the Select Color button.

10. Add the following code to the `ButtonSelectColor_Click` event:

```
LabelColor.Text = String.Format("You have selected the color {0}.",
        ListBoxColors.SelectedValue);
```

11. Add the following code to the `Page_Load` event:

```
if (!Page.IsPostBack)
{
    ListBoxColors.Rows = 3;
    ListBoxColors.Items.Add("Blue");
    ListBoxColors.Items.Add("Red");
    ListBoxColors.Items.Add("Yellow");
}
```

12. Verify that the code on the About.aspx.cs page matches the following:

```
using System;
using System.Collections.Generic;
```

```
using System.Linq;
using System.Web;
using System.Web.UI;
using System.Web.UI.WebControls;

namespace Lesson10a
{
    public partial class About : System.Web.UI.Page
    {
        protected void Page_Load(object sender, EventArgs e)
        {
            if (!Page.IsPostBack)
            {
                ListBoxColors.Rows = 3;
                ListBoxColors.Items.Add("Blue");
                ListBoxColors.Items.Add("Red");
                ListBoxColors.Items.Add("Yellow");
            }
        }

        protected void ButtonSelectColor_Click(object sender, EventArgs e)
        {
            LabelColor.Text = String.Format("You have selected the color {0}.",
            ListBoxColors.SelectedValue);
        }
    }
}
```

13. Click the F5 button.

14. View the About Us page, select a color, and click the Select Color button. Although you are not repopulating the ListBox on the postback of the page, it still maintains its original values (see Figure 10A-2).

15. Stop debugging by closing the browser.

16. Add Trace="true" to the @Page directive to view the size of the ViewState that the controls are using.

17. Click the F5 button.

18. View the About Us page.

FIGURE 10A-2

19. Scroll down to the bottom of the page to view the Control Tree.

20. Scroll back up to the top of the page, select a color and click the Select Color button.

21. Scroll down the page to view the Control Tree again and try to identify the changes.

22. Stop debugging by closing the browser.

23. Add EnableViewState="false" to the @Page directive.

24. Click the F5 button.

25. View the About Us page, select a color, and click the Select Color button. Because view state is disabled, the ListBox is now empty (see Figure 10A-3).

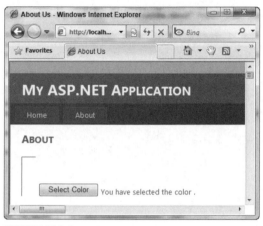

FIGURE 10A-3

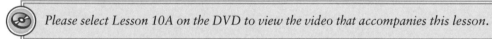

Please select Lesson 10A on the DVD to view the video that accompanies this lesson.

10B

Custom HTML Helpers in MVC

There is a large set of HTML Helpers that come with the ASP.NET MVC framework. Nevertheless, you can write your own custom HTML Helpers. In this lesson I show you how to write both a simple HTML Helper and how to write an HTML Helper using an extension method.

CREATING AN HTML HELPER

The ASP.NET MVC framework does not come with an HTML Helper to generate an ordered list. This is the HTML for a sample ordered list:

```
<ol>
    <li>Item One</li>
    <li>Item Two</li>
    <li>Item Three</li>
</ol>
```

The following class builds a string to output an `MvcHtmlString` that contains the HTML required to render an ordered list:

```
public class OrderedListHelper
{
    public static MvcHtmlString OrderedList(Object items)
    {
        var builder = new StringBuilder();
        builder.Append("<ol>");
        var enumItems = (IEnumerable<Object>)items;
        foreach (Object item in enumItems)
            builder.AppendFormat("<li>{0}</li>",
                HttpUtility.HtmlEncode(item.ToString()));
        builder.Append("</ol>");
        return MvcHtmlString.Create(builder.ToString());
    }
}
```

> *An* `MvcHtmlString` *is an HTML-encoded string that should not be encoded again.*

This is the code the view uses to call this new static method:

```
<%: OrderedListHelper.OrderedList(ViewData.Model) %>
```

CREATING AN HTMLHELPER EXTENSION METHOD

A better way to create a new HTML Helper is to use an extension method. An extension method is a new method for an existing class, and in order to create one you need to do two things:

1. Create a static class with a static method.

2. Set the type of the first parameter to the name of the class that is being extended followed by the word `this`.

By following these two steps, it is very simple to modify the `OrderedList` code to make it into an extension method of the `HtmlHelper` class. This is the updated code:

```
public static class OrderedListHelper
{
    public static MvcHtmlString OrderedList(this HtmlHelper helper, Object items)
    {
        var builder = new StringBuilder();
        builder.Append("<ol>");
        var enumItems = (IEnumerable<Object>)items;
        foreach (Object item in enumItems)
            builder.AppendFormat("<li>{0}</li>",
                HttpUtility.HtmlEncode(item.ToString()));
        builder.Append("</ol>");
        return MvcHtmlString.Create(builder.ToString());
    }
}
```

> *All of the standard HTML Helpers are implemented as extension methods of the* `HtmlHelper` *class.*

Instead of using `StringBuilders`, all of the standard `HtmlHelper` extension methods use the `TagBuilder` class to generate the appropriate HTML. The `TagBuilder` class is a special class specifically designed for building HTML tags.

These are the methods of the `TagBuilder` class:

➤ **AddCssClass** — This method is used to add a `Class` attribute.

➤ **GeneratedId** — This method is used to generate an id for the tag.

➤ **MergeAttribute** — This method is used to add attributes to the tag.

➤ **SetInnerText** — This method is used to set the inner text of the tag. Before this method sets the inner text of the tag, it HTML-encodes the text.

The OrderedList method can easily be rewritten to use the TagBuilder class. This is the updated OrderedList code:

```
public static string OrderedList(this HtmlHelper helper, Object items)
{
    // Create list items
    var itemsBuilder = new StringBuilder();
    foreach (Object item in (IEnumerable<Object>)items)
    {
        var itemTagBuilder = new TagBuilder("li");
        itemTagBuilder.SetInnerText(item.ToString());
        itemsBuilder.Append(itemTagBuilder.ToString());
    };

    // Create ordered list
    var orderedListTagBuilder = new TagBuilder("ol");

    // Add list items to ordered list
    orderedListTagBuilder.InnerHtml = itemsBuilder.ToString();

    return orderedListTagBuilder.ToString();
}
```

The TagBuilder class is a very handy class. It makes adding attributes to a tag much easier. Also, when building a complicated tag, it is easier to use the properties and methods of the TagBuilder than to concatenate a bunch of strings.

TRY IT

In this lesson you create an HTML Helper method by creating an extension method of the HtmlHelper class.

Lesson Requirements

None.

Hints

➤ Use the @Import directive to import a namespace into a view.

➤ Make sure your method returns an MvcHtmlString.

Step-By-Step

1. Open Microsoft Visual Web Developer 2010 Express.

2. Select New Project from the File menu.

3. Select **Visual C#** on the left side of the dialog box.

4. Select the **ASP.NET MVC 2 Web Application** template.

5. Enter **Lesson10b** in the Name field and **c:\ASPNETTrainer** in the Location.

6. Right-click the name of the project in the Solution Explorer window and select New Folder from the Add menu to create a new folder. Name the new folder **Helpers.**

7. Right-click the Helpers folder and select Class from the Add menu. Name the new class **OrderedListHelper.cs** and click the Add button.

8. Add the following `using` statements to the top of the `OrderedListHelper.cs` file:

```
using System.Web.Mvc;
using System.Text;
```

9. Add the following method to the `OrderedListHelper` class:

```
public static MvcHtmlString OrderedList(Object items)
{
    var itemsBuilder = new StringBuilder();
    foreach (Object item in (IEnumerable<Object>)items)
    {
        var itemTagBuilder = new TagBuilder("li");
        itemTagBuilder.SetInnerText(item.ToString());
        itemsBuilder.Append(itemTagBuilder.ToString());
    };

    var orderedListTagBuilder = new TagBuilder("ol");
    orderedListTagBuilder.InnerHtml = itemsBuilder.ToString();

    return MvcHtmlString.Create(orderedListTagBuilder.ToString());

}
```

10. Update the `About` action method of the HomeController to the following:

```
public ActionResult About()
{
    List<string> Colors = new List<string> { "Blue", "Red", "Yellow" };
    return View(Colors);
}
```

11. Update the About view to use the new `OrderedListHelper` by replacing the "Put content here." string with the following code:

```
<%: Lesson10b.Helpers.OrderedListHelper.OrderedList(ViewData.Model) %>
```

12. Click the F5 button.

13. View the About Us page (see Figure 10B-1).

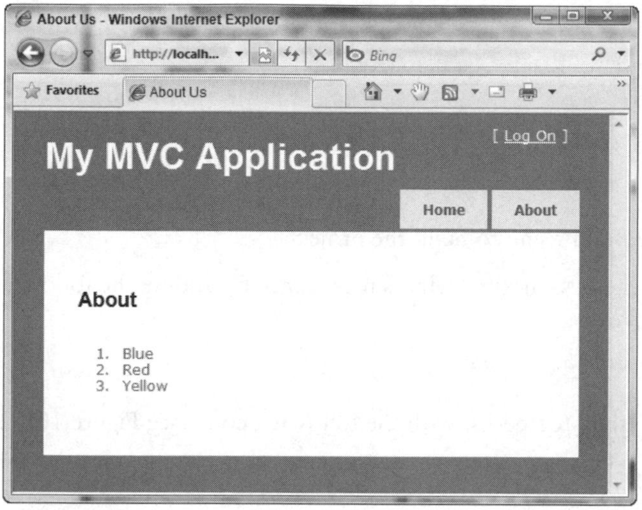

FIGURE 10B-1

14. Stop debugging by closing the browser.

15. To convert the method that you created into an extension method, make the OrderedListHelper class into a static class and update the definition of OrderedList to include HtmlHelper as its first parameter, as shown below:

```
public static MvcHtmlString OrderedList(this HtmlHelper helper, Object items)
```

16. Verify that the code in the OrderListHelper.cs file matches the following:

```
using System;
using System.Collections.Generic;
using System.Linq;
using System.Web;
using System.Web.Mvc;
using System.Text;

namespace Lesson10b.Helpers
{
    public static class OrderedListHelper
    {
        public static MvcHtmlString OrderedList(this HtmlHelper helper, Object items)
        {
            var itemsBuilder = new StringBuilder();
            foreach (Object item in (IEnumerable<Object>)items)
            {
                var itemTagBuilder = new TagBuilder("li");
                itemTagBuilder.SetInnerText(item.ToString());
                itemsBuilder.Append(itemTagBuilder.ToString());
            };

            var orderedListTagBuilder = new TagBuilder("ol");
```

```
                        orderedListTagBuilder.InnerHtml = itemsBuilder.ToString();

                        return MvcHtmlString.Create(orderedListTagBuilder.ToString());
                    }

                }
            }
```

17. Select Build Lesson10b from the Build menu to build the project.

18. In the About.aspx page, import the Lesson10b. Helpers namespace by adding the following statement after the @Page directive:

```
<%@ Import Namespace="Lesson10b.Helpers" %>
```

19. Replace the code used to display the ordered list with the following code (see Figure 10B-2):

```
<%: Html.OrderedList(ViewData.Model) %>
```

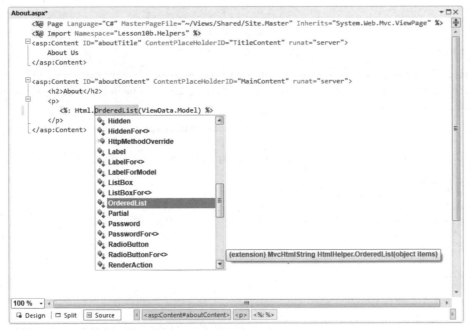

FIGURE 10B-2

20. Verify that the code on the About.aspx page matches the following:

```
<%@ Page Language="C#" MasterPageFile="~/Views/Shared/Site.Master"
    Inherits="System.Web.Mvc.ViewPage" %>
<%@ Import Namespace="Lesson10b.Helpers" %>

<asp:Content ID="aboutTitle" ContentPlaceHolderID="TitleContent" runat="server">
    About Us
</asp:Content>
```

```
<asp:Content ID="aboutContent" ContentPlaceHolderID="MainContent" runat="server">
    <h2>
        About</h2>
    <p>
        <%: Html.OrderedList(ViewData.Model) %>
    </p>
</asp:Content>
```

21.   Click the F5 button and view the About Us page.

Please select Lesson 10B on the DVD to view the video that accompanies this lesson.

SECTION IV
Maintaining a Consistent Page Layout

11

Master Pages

Many pages on a web site share common elements. For example, most pages on a web site share a header, some type of page navigation, and a footer. *Master pages* are used to store the shared elements on your page in one location. They enable you to create a consistent look and feel for your web application. In this lesson I illustrate some of the shared sections of a web page and explain how a generic master page works.

Figure 11-1 shows a typical web page with a header, a menu for navigation, some content, and a footer.

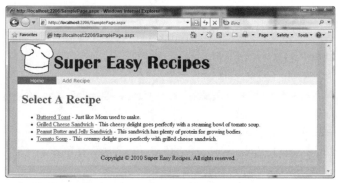

FIGURE 11-1

Figure 11-2 points out the different sections of the page.

The best way to lay out your web pages is to use a cascading style sheet. The first thing that I do when I am creating a new web site is to lay out a sample page using HTML. The page shown in Figure 11-1 used the following HTML:

```
<!DOCTYPE html PUBLIC "-//W3C//DTD XHTML 1.0 Transitional//EN"
    "http://www.w3.org/TR/xhtml1/DTD/xhtml1-transitional.dtd">
<html xmlns="http://www.w3.org/1999/xhtml">
<head>
    <title></title>
```

```
        <link href="StyleSheet.css" rel="stylesheet" type="text/css" />
    </head>
    <body>
        <form id="form1" runat="server">
        <div id="header">
        </div>
        <div id="navigation">
            Top-Level Menu
        </div>
        <div id="content">
            Content goes here.
        </div>
        <div id="footer">
            Copyright &copy; 2010 Super Easy Recipes. All rights reserved.
        </div>
        </form>
    </body>
</html>
```

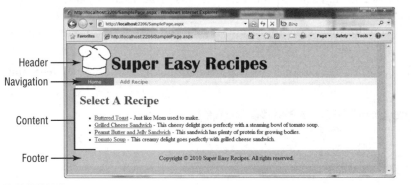

FIGURE 11-2

I have replaced the navigation menu and the content with short strings to make the HTML easier to read.

Figure 11-3 shows the page that is generated by the preceding HTML before any styles are applied.

After the page is laid out, I use a cascading style sheet to style the HTML elements on the page. This page uses a cascading style sheet named StyleSheet.css. These are the contents of the cascading style sheet used by the page shown in Figure 11-1:

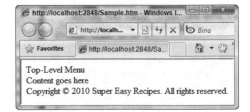

FIGURE 11-3

```
body
{
    margin: 0 auto;
```

```
    width: 800px;
    padding: 0;
    background: #CCCCCC;
}
#header
{
    background-color: #FFCC66;
    height: 90px;
    width: 800px;
    background-image: url('images/SuperEasyRecipesLogo.gif');
    background-repeat: no-repeat;
}
#navigation
{
    background-color: #F7F6F3;
}
#content
{
    padding:5x;
    background: White;
}
#footer
{
    padding: 10px;
    margin:0px;
    width: 780px;
    text-align: center;
    background-color: #FFCC66;
}
```

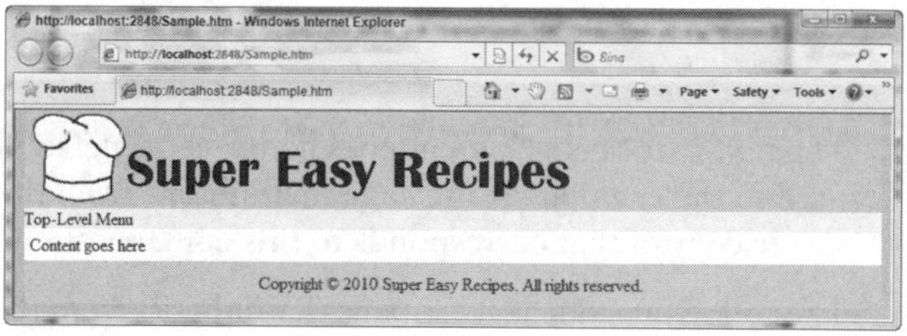

Figure 11-4 shows the page that is rendered when the HTML markup is combined with the cascading style sheet.

FIGURE 11-4

To have all of your pages share the same header, navigation, and footer, you could copy those elements to each of your individual pages. However, any time that you wanted to change any of those elements, you would need to update every page in your web application. Master pages solve this problem by providing a class that can be inherited by all of your pages.

A master page is a special type of page. Following are the three major differences between a regular page and a master page:

1. A master page ends with the .MASTER file extension.

2. On a master page the @Page directive at the top of the page is replaced by an @Master directive.

3. One or more ContentPlaceHolder server controls are included on the master page.

The `ContentPlaceHolder` server control is used by the pages that inherit from the master page to display their unique content. The following code shows a master page that was created by using the original HTML example as a template:

```
<%@ Master Language="C#" AutoEventWireup="true" CodeBehind="Site1.master.cs"
    Inherits="Lesson11.Site1" %>

<!DOCTYPE html PUBLIC "-//W3C//DTD XHTML 1.0 Transitional//EN"
    "http://www.w3.org/TR/xhtml1/DTD/xhtml1-transitional.dtd">
<html xmlns="http://www.w3.org/1999/xhtml">
<head runat="server">
    <title></title>
    <link href="Stylesheet.css" rel="stylesheet" type="text/css" />
</head>
<body>
    <form id="form1" runat="server">
    <div id="header">
    </div>
    <div id="navigation">
        Top-Level Menu
    </div>
    <div id="content">
        <asp:ContentPlaceHolder ID="ContentPlaceHolder1" runat="server">
            Content goes here.
        </asp:ContentPlaceHolder>
    </div>
    <div id="footer">
        Copyright &copy; 2010 Super Easy Recipes. All rights reserved.
    </div>
    </form>
</body>
</html>
```

The text that says "Content goes here." is the default content of the `ContentPlaceHolder` that is used in the example. If the page that inherits from this master page includes content in the `Content` server control that corresponds to this `ContentPlaceHolder`, the default content will be replaced.

The following code is for a page that inherits from the proceeding master page:

```
<%@ Page Title="" Language="C#" MasterPageFile="~/Site1.Master" AutoEventWireup="true"
    CodeBehind="Content.aspx.cs" Inherits="Lesson11.Content" %>

<asp:Content ID="Content1" ContentPlaceHolderID="ContentPlaceHolder1" runat="server">
    New content.
</asp:Content>
```

Web pages developed using both the ASP.NET Web Forms framework and the ASP.NET MVC framework can take advantage of master pages. I examine how each of the frameworks uses master pages, in more detail, in Lessons 11A and 11B.

11A

Master Pages in Web Forms

In this lesson I show you how to use master pages in an ASP.NET Web Form application.

MASTER PAGES

To create a new master page, select the Add New Item option from the Project menu to open the Add New Item dialog box. Select the Master Page template from the dialog box and click the Add button (see Figure 11A-1).

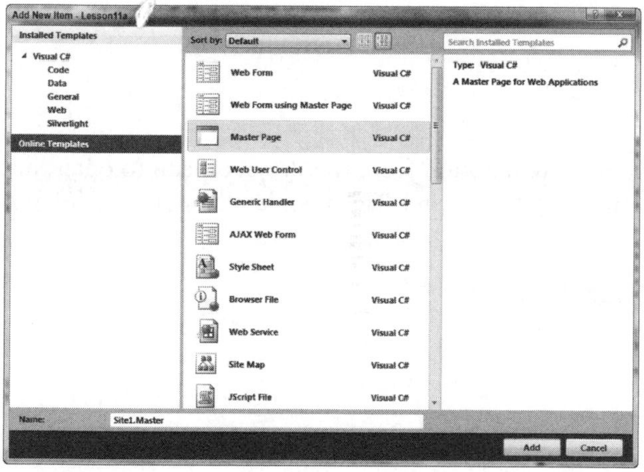

FIGURE 11A-1

This is markup that is generated in the default master page:

```
<%@ Master Language="C#" AutoEventWireup="true" CodeBehind="Site1.master.cs"
    Inherits="Lesson11.Site1" %>

<!DOCTYPE html PUBLIC "-//W3C//DTD XHTML 1.0 Transitional//EN"
    "http://www.w3.org/TR/xhtml1/DTD/xhtml1-transitional.dtd">
<html xmlns="http://www.w3.org/1999/xhtml">
```

```
<head runat="server">
    <title></title>
    <asp:ContentPlaceHolder ID="head" runat="server">
    </asp:ContentPlaceHolder>
</head>
<body>
    <form id="form1" runat="server">
    <div>
        <asp:ContentPlaceHolder ID="ContentPlaceHolder1" runat="server">
        </asp:ContentPlaceHolder>
    </div>
    </form>
</body>
</html>
```

The default master page looks like a regular page except that it includes an @Master directive at the top of the page instead of an @Page directive, it includes a ContentPlaceHolder server control in its head element and it includes a ContentPlaceHolder server control in its body element. The ContentPlaceHolder server controls are used by the pages that are based on the master page.

> *A master page can have as many* ContentPlaceHolder *server controls as your design requires. You are not limited to the two* ContentPlaceHolder *server controls that are provided by default.*

CONTENT PAGES

To create a content page, select the Add New Item option from the Project menu to open the Add New Item dialog box. Select the Web Form using the Master Page template from the dialog box and click the Add button (see Figure 11A-2).

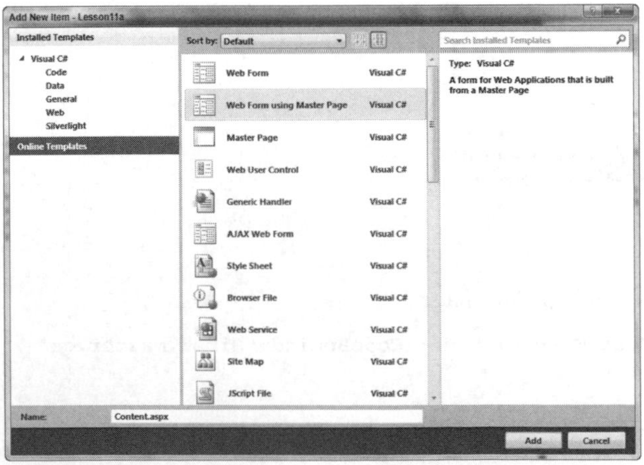

FIGURE 11A-2

After you have clicked the Add button you will be asked to identify the master page that you would like to use with this page, because your application can have more than one master page (see Figure 11A-3).

FIGURE 11A-3

Use the Select a Master Page dialog box to navigate to the master page that you want to use and click the OK button. This is the content of the content page that is generated:

```
<%@ Page Title="" Language="C#" MasterPageFile="~/Site1.Master"
    AutoEventWireup="true" CodeBehind="Content.aspx.cs"
    Inherits="Lesson11a.Content" %>

<asp:Content ID="Content1" ContentPlaceHolderID="head" runat="server">
</asp:Content>
<asp:Content ID="Content2" ContentPlaceHolderID="ContentPlaceHolder1"
    runat="server">
</asp:Content>
```

The @Page directive of a content page includes the MasterPageFile attribute, which is used to identify which master page to use. In my example, there are two Content server controls that correspond to the two ContentPlaceHolder server controls on the master page. However, the content page does not need to include references to all of the ContentPlaceHolder server controls that are on the master page. If the content page does not include a reference to a particular ContentPlaceHolder server control, the markup in that ContentPlaceHolder server control on the master page will be inherited by the content page.

NESTED MASTER PAGES

A really cool feature of master pages is that they can be nested. Many web sites use a root master page that only includes the web site's header and footer. *Nested master pages* are then used to further customize the layout of the web pages used by that web site.

To create a nested master page, select the Add New Item option from the Project menu to open the Add New Item dialog box. Select the Nested Master Page template and click the Add button (see Figure 11A-4).

FIGURE 11A-4

Just like when you added a content page, you will be asked to identify the master page that you would like to use with this page, because your application can have more than one master page (see Figure 11A-5).

FIGURE 11A-5

This is the content of the page that is generated:

```
<%@ Master Language="C#" MasterPageFile="~/Site1.Master" AutoEventWireup="true"
    CodeBehind="NestedMasterPage1.master.cs"
    Inherits="Lesson11a.NestedMasterPage1" %>

<asp:Content ID="Content1" ContentPlaceHolderID="head" runat="server">
</asp:Content>
<asp:Content ID="Content2" ContentPlaceHolderID="ContentPlaceHolder1"
    runat="server">
</asp:Content>
```

A nested master page uses an `@Master` directive just like a regular master page and includes a `MasterPageFile` attribute just like a content page.

Page navigation is often included via a nested master page. The Navigation tab of the Toolbox includes both a `Menu` server control and a `TreeView` server control that can be used to provide navigation for your web site.

THE MASTER PROPERTY

The `Master` property of a page returns the `MasterPage` object associated with that page. If the page does not reference a master page, a null reference is returned.

This is a very simple master page that only includes a `Menu` server control:

```
<%@ Master Language="C#" AutoEventWireup="true" CodeBehind="Simple.master.cs"
    Inherits="Lesson11a.Simple" %>

<!DOCTYPE html PUBLIC "-//W3C//DTD XHTML 1.0 Transitional//EN"
    "http://www.w3.org/TR/xhtml1/DTD/xhtml1-transitional.dtd">
<html xmlns="http://www.w3.org/1999/xhtml">
<head runat="server">
    <title></title>
</head>
<body>
    <form id="form1" runat="server">
    <div>
        <asp:Menu ID="Menu1" runat="server">
            <Items>
                <asp:MenuItem Text="Home" Value="Home"></asp:MenuItem>
                <asp:MenuItem Text="Add Recipe" Value="Add Recipe"></asp:MenuItem>
            </Items>
        </asp:Menu>
        <asp:ContentPlaceHolder ID="ContentPlaceHolder1" runat="server">
        </asp:ContentPlaceHolder>
    </div>
    </form>
</body>
</html>
```

There are two different approaches that you can take, that use the `Master` property of the content page, to access a control on the master page from the content page:

1. Add a public property to the master page.

2. Use the `FindControl` method from the content page.

To add a public property to the master page that can be used to access the `Menu` server control, add the following code to the master page:

```
public string MenuSelectedItem
{
    get { return Menu1.SelectedValue; }
}
```

This new public property, `MenuSelectedItem`, can be accessed from the content page by using the following code:

```
((Simple)Master).MenuSelectedItem
```

> ✎ *If you do not want to cast the `MasterPage` object each time you refer to it, you can add an `@MasterType` directive to the top of the content page to create a strongly-typed reference to the master page.*

If you prefer not to add a public property, you can also access a control on the master page by using the `FindControl` method. This is the `FindControl` method that returns the same value as the preceding `MenuSelectedItem` public property:

```
((Menu)Master.FindControl("Menu1")).SelectedValue
```

> ✖ *Master pages treat relative URLs from server controls and HTML controls differently. Relative URLs from server controls are interpreted relative to the master page, whereas relative URLs from HTML controls are interpreted relative to their content page.*

TRY IT

In this lesson you create a master page with navigation and a content page that uses that master page.

Lesson Requirements

➤ The `Styles.css` file.

➤ The `SuperEasyRecipesLogo.gif` file.

Hints

➤ Format the Menu server control by selecting the Professional theme on the AutoFormat dialog box.

Step-by-Step

1. Open Microsoft Visual Web Developer 2010 Express.

2. Select New Project from the File menu.

3. Select **Visual C#** on the left side of the dialog box.

4. Select the **ASP.NET Empty Web Application** template.

5. Enter **Lesson11a** in the Name field and **c:\ASPNETTrainer** in the Location field.

> I use the ASP.NET Empty Web Application template in this lesson.

6. Click the OK button.

7. Right-click the name of the project in the Solution Explorer window, and select New Folder from the Add menu to add a new folder called **Helpers**.

8. Right-click the Helpers folder and select Existing Item from the Add menu to add the `Styles.css` file.

9. Right-click the name of the project in the Solution Explorer window, and select New Folder from the Add menu to add a new folder called **images**.

10. Right-click the images folder and select Existing Item from the Add menu to add the `SuperEasyRecipesLogo.gif` file.

11. Right-click the Helpers folder and select the New Item option from the Add menu.

12. Select the Master Page template and click the Add button to create the **Site1.Master** page.

13. Add a reference to the `Styles.css` file in the `head` element of the `Site1.Master` page:

    ```
    <link href="Styles.css" rel="stylesheet" type="text/css" />
    ```

14. Add the following markup before the `ContentPlaceHolder1` server control:

    ```
    <div id="header">
    </div>
    <div id="navigation">
    </div>
    <div id="content">
    ```

15. Add the following markup after the `ContentPlaceHolder1` server control:

    ```
    </div>
    <div id="footer">
        Copyright &copy; 2010 Super Easy Recipes. All rights reserved.
    </div>
    ```

16. Drag a `Menu` server control from the Toolbox into the navigation `div` element (see Figure 11A-6).

17. Add an `Orientation` attribute to the `Menu` control and set its value to **Horizontal** as shown in the following code:

    ```
    <asp:Menu ID="Menu1" runat="server" Orientation="Horizontal">

    </asp:Menu>
    ```

18. Add the following two items to the `Menu` server control:

    ```
    <Items>
        <asp:MenuItem Text="Home" Value="Home"></asp:MenuItem>
        <asp:MenuItem Text="Add Recipe" Value="Add Recipe"></asp:MenuItem>
    </Items>
    ```

19. Format the menu by viewing the page in Design view and using the Menu Tasks smart tag, shown in Figure 11A-7, to open the AutoFormat dialog box and apply the **Professional** scheme to the menu.

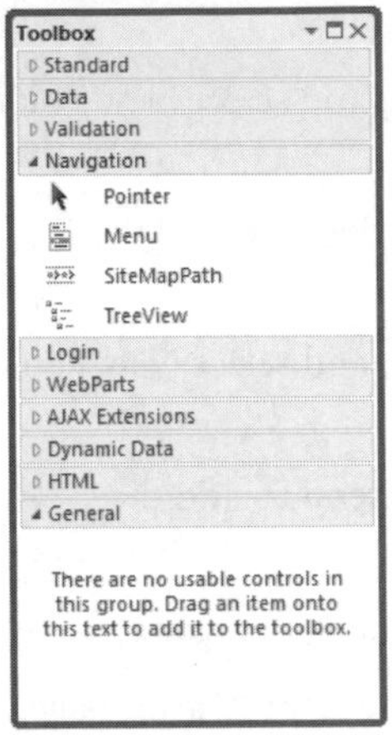

FIGURE 11A-6

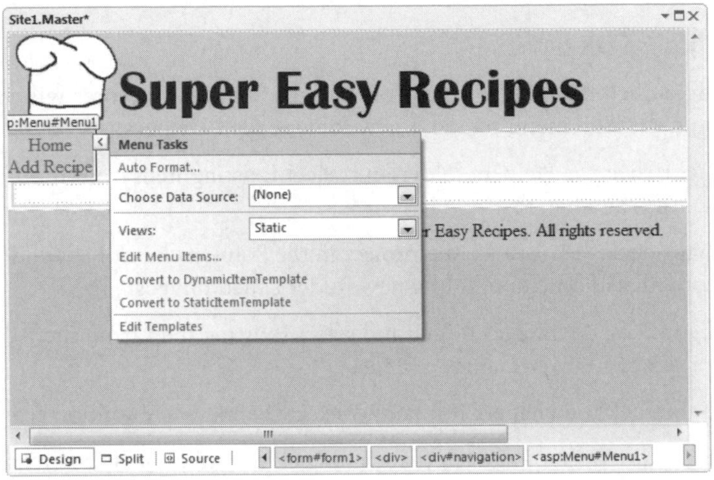

FIGURE 11A-7

20. Return to Source view, add a `Width` attribute to the `StaticMenuItemStyle` element of the menu and set its value to **100px**.

21. Verify that the code in your `Site1.Master` page matches the following:

```
<%@ Master Language="C#" AutoEventWireup="true" CodeBehind="Site1.master.cs"
    Inherits="Lesson11a.Helpers.Site1" %>

<!DOCTYPE html PUBLIC "-//W3C//DTD XHTML 1.0 Transitional//EN"
    "http://www.w3.org/TR/xhtml1/DTD/xhtml1-transitional.dtd">
<html xmlns="http://www.w3.org/1999/xhtml">
<head runat="server">
    <title></title>
    <link href="Styles.css" rel="stylesheet" type="text/css" />
    <asp:ContentPlaceHolder ID="head" runat="server">
    </asp:ContentPlaceHolder>
</head>
<body>
    <form id="form1" runat="server">
    <div>
        <div id="header">
        </div>
        <div id="navigation">
            <asp:Menu ID="Menu1" runat="server" Orientation="Horizontal"
                BackColor="#F7F6F3" DynamicHorizontalOffset="2"
                    Font-Names="Verdana"
                Font-Size="0.8em" ForeColor="#7C6F57"
                StaticSubMenuIndent="10px">
                <DynamicHoverStyle BackColor="#7C6F57" ForeColor="White" />
                <DynamicMenuItemStyle HorizontalPadding="5px"
```

```
                    VerticalPadding="2px" />
                <DynamicMenuStyle BackColor="#F7F6F3" />
                <DynamicSelectedStyle BackColor="#5D7B9D" />
                <Items>
                    <asp:MenuItem Text="Home" Value="Home"></asp:MenuItem>
                    <asp:MenuItem Text="Add Recipe" Value="Add Recipe">
                        </asp:MenuItem>
                </Items>
                <StaticHoverStyle BackColor="#7C6F57" ForeColor="White" />
                <StaticMenuItemStyle HorizontalPadding="5px"
                    VerticalPadding="2px"
                    Width="100px" />
                <StaticSelectedStyle BackColor="#5D7B9D" />
            </asp:Menu>
        </div>
        <div id="content">
            <asp:ContentPlaceHolder ID="ContentPlaceHolder1" runat="server">
            </asp:ContentPlaceHolder>
        </div>
        <div id="footer">
            Copyright &copy; 2010 Super Easy Recipes. All rights reserved.
        </div>
    </div>
    </form>
</body>
</html>
```

22. Right-click the name of the project in the Solution Explorer window and select New Item from the Add menu to open the Add New Item dialog box. Select the Web Form using Master Page template and click the Add button to create a **WebForm1.aspx** page.

23. Set the `Title` attribute of the `@Page` directive to **Super Easy Recipes**.

24. Add some text to the second `ContentPlaceHolder` control on the `WebForm1.aspx` page:

```
<asp:Content ID="Content2" ContentPlaceHolderID="ContentPlaceHolder1"
    runat="server">
    Your content here …
</asp:Content>
```

25. Verify that the code for the `WebForm1.aspx` page matches the following:

```
<%@ Page Title="Super Easy Recipes" Language="C#"
    MasterPageFile="~/Helpers/Site1.Master"
    AutoEventWireup="true" CodeBehind="WebForm1.aspx.cs"
    Inherits="Lesson11a.WebForm1" %>

<asp:Content ID="Content1" ContentPlaceHolderID="head" runat="server">
</asp:Content>
<asp:Content ID="Content2" ContentPlaceHolderID="ContentPlaceHolder1"
    runat="server">
    Your content here …
</asp:Content>
```

26. Click the F5 button (see Figure 11A-8).

FIGURE 11A-8

Please select Lesson 11A on the DVD to view the video that accompanies this lesson.

11B

Master Pages in MVC

In this lesson I show you how to use master pages in an ASP.NET MVC application.

MASTER PAGES

To create a new master page, select the Add New Item option from the Project menu to open the Add New Item dialog box. Select the MVC 2 View Master Page template from the dialog box and click the Add button (see Figure 11B-1).

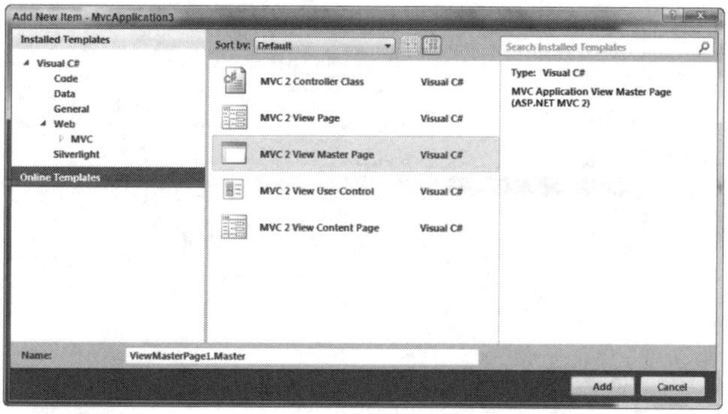

FIGURE 11B-1

This is the markup that is generated in the default master page:

```
<%@ Master Language="C#" Inherits="System.Web.Mvc.ViewMasterPage" %>

<!DOCTYPE html PUBLIC "-//W3C//DTD XHTML 1.0 Transitional//EN"
    "http://www.w3.org/TR/xhtml1/DTD/xhtml1-transitional.dtd">
<html xmlns="http://www.w3.org/1999/xhtml">
<head runat="server">
    <title>
        <asp:ContentPlaceHolder ID="TitleContent" runat="server" />
```

```
        </title>
    </head>
    <body>
        <div>
            <asp:ContentPlaceHolder ID="MainContent" runat="server">
            </asp:ContentPlaceHolder>
        </div>
    </body>
</html>
```

The default master page looks like a regular page except that it includes an @Master directive at the top of the page instead of an @Page directive, it includes a ContentPlaceHolder control in its head element and it includes a ContentPlaceHolder control in its body element. The ContentPlaceHolder controls are used by the pages that inherit from the master page.

> *A master page can have as many* ContentPlaceHolder *controls as your design requires. You are not limited to the two* ContentPlaceHolder *controls that are provided by default.*

CONTENT PAGES

To create a content page, select the Add New Item option from the Project menu to open the Add New Item dialog box. Select the MVC 2 View Content Page template and click the Add Button (see Figure 11B-2).

After you have clicked the Add button you will be asked to identify the master page that you would like to use with this particular content page, because your application may have more than one master page (see Figure 11B-3).

FIGURE 11B-2

Use the Select a Master Page dialog box to navigate to the master page that you want to use and click the OK button.

> *By convention you should store all of your Master Pages in a subfolder under the Views folder named Shared.*

FIGURE 11B-3

This is the content of the page that is generated:

```
<%@ Page Title="" Language="C#"
    MasterPageFile="~/Views/Shared/ViewMasterPage1.Master"
    Inherits="System.Web.Mvc.ViewPage" %>

<asp:Content ID="Content1" ContentPlaceHolderID="TitleContent" runat="server">
</asp:Content>
<asp:Content ID="Content2" ContentPlaceHolderID="MainContent" runat="server">
</asp:Content>
```

The @Page directive of a content page includes the MasterPageFile attribute, which is used to identify which master page to use. In my example, there are two Content controls that correspond to the two ContentPlaceHolder controls on the master page. However, the content page does not need to include references to all of the ContentPlaceHolder controls that are on the master page. If a content page does not include a reference to a particular ContentPlaceHolder control, the markup in that ContentPlaceHolder will be inherited by the content page.

NESTED MASTER PAGES

A really cool feature of master pages is that they can be nested. Many web sites use a root master page that only includes the web site's header and footer. *Nested master pages* are then used to further customize the layout of the web pages used by that web site.

To add a nested master page to your project you need to convert a regular master page into a nested master page. To convert a regular master page, first add a MasterPageFile attribute to the @Master directive of the master page where the MasterPageFile points to an existing master page. Finally, add at least one `ContentPlaceHolder` control to the new nested master page. This is the code for a sample nested master page:

```
<%@ Master Language="C#" Inherits="System.Web.Mvc.ViewMasterPage"
   MasterPageFile="~/Views/Shared/Outer.Master" %>

<asp:Content ID="Content1" ContentPlaceHolderID="TitleContent" runat="server">
</asp:Content>
<asp:Content ID="Content2" ContentPlaceHolderID="MainContent" runat="server">
   <asp:ContentPlaceHolder ID="MainContent" runat="server">
   </asp:ContentPlaceHolder>
</asp:Content>
```

UPDATING MASTER PAGE CONTENT

At times a content page will need to output data to a master page. This is very easy to do using the ASP.NET MVC framework and can be accomplished in two easy steps. In the following example I use `ViewData["Content"]` to transfer the data:

1. Add the following code to the content page's action method to send data to the master page:

```
ViewData["Content"] = "This message is from the content page";
```

2. Add the following code to the master page to consume the data:

```
<%: ViewData["Content"] %>
```

Sometimes all of the action methods associated with a particular controller need to send data to the master page. In that case, you should not update each action method because that would result in too much redundant code. Instead, you should create an abstract controller from which your controller will inherit. This is an example of an abstract controller:

```
using System.Web.Mvc;

namespace Lesson11b.Controllers
{
    public abstract class ApplicationController : Controller
    {
        public ApplicationController()
        {
            ViewData["Content"] = "This message is from the content page";
        }

    }
}
```

This is a controller that inherits from that abstract controller:

```
using System.Web.Mvc;

namespace _11b.Controllers
{
```

```
[HandleError]
public class HomeController : ApplicationController
{
    public ActionResult Index()
    {
        return View();
    }

    public ActionResult About()
    {
        return View();
    }
}
```

Finally, you need to add the following code to the master page:

```
<%: ViewData["Content"] %>
```

Now, all of the action methods for the controller will return the same data to the master page.

TRY IT

In this lesson you create a master page with navigation and you create a content page that uses that master page.

Lesson Requirements

➤ The Styles.css file.

➤ The SuperEasyRecipesLogo.gif file.

Hints

None.

Step-by-Step

1. Open Microsoft Visual Web Developer 2010 Express.

2. Select New Project from the File menu.

3. Select **Visual C#** on the left side of the dialog box.

4. Select the **ASP.NET MVC 2 Empty Web Application** template.

> *I am using the ASP.NET MVC 2 Empty Web Application template in this lesson.*

5. Enter **Lesson11b** in the Name field and **c:\ASPNETTrainer** in the Location field.

6. Right-click the Content folder and select Existing Item from the Add menu to add the `Styles.css` file.

7. Right-click the Content folder and select New Folder from the Add menu to add a new folder called **images**.

8. Right-click the images folder and select Existing Item from the Add menu to add the `SuperEasyRecipesLogo.gif` file.

9. Right-click the Shared subfolder, under the Views folder, and select the New Item option from the Add menu.

10. Select the **MVC 2 View Master Page** template and click the Add button to create the **ViewMasterPage1.Master** page.

11. Add a reference to the `Styles.css` file in the `head` element of the `ViewMasterPage1 .Master` page:

```
<link href="../../Content/Styles.css" rel="stylesheet" type="text/css" />
```

12. Add the following markup before the `ContentPlaceHolder` control with `id="MainContent"`:

```
<div id="header">
</div>
<div id="navigation">
    <ul id="menu">
        <li>
            <%= Html.ActionLink("Home", "Index", "Home")%>
        </li>
        <li>
            <%= Html.ActionLink("Add Recipe", "AddRecipe", "Home")%>
        </li>
    </ul>
</div>
<div id="content">
```

13. Add the following markup after the `ContentPlaceHolder` with `id="MainContent"`:

```
</div>
<div id="footer">
        Copyright &copy; 2010 Super Easy Recipes. All rights reserved.
</div>
```

14. Verify that the code in the `ViewMasterPage1.Master` page matches the following:

```
<%@ Master Language="C#" Inherits="System.Web.Mvc.ViewMasterPage" %>

<!DOCTYPE html PUBLIC "-//W3C//DTD XHTML 1.0 Transitional//EN"
    "http://www.w3.org/TR/xhtml1/DTD/xhtml1-transitional.dtd">
<html xmlns="http://www.w3.org/1999/xhtml">
<head runat="server">
    <title>
        <asp:ContentPlaceHolder ID="TitleContent" runat="server" />
    </title>
```

```
            <link href="../../Content/Styles.css" rel="stylesheet" type="text/css" />
    </head>
    <body>
        <div>
            <div id="header">
            </div>
            <div id="navigation">
                <ul id="menu">
                    <li>
                        <%= Html.ActionLink("Home", "Index", "Home")%>
                    </li>
                    <li>
                        <%= Html.ActionLink("Add Recipe", "AddRecipe", "Home")%>
                    </li>
                </ul>
            </div>
            <div id="content">
                <asp:ContentPlaceHolder ID="MainContent" runat="server">
                </asp:ContentPlaceHolder>
            </div>
            <div id="footer">
                Copyright &copy; 2010 Super Easy Recipes. All rights reserved.
            </div>
        </div>
    </body>
</html>
```

15. Right-click the Controllers folder, select Controller from the Add menu, enter **HomeController** as the name of the new controller and click the Add button (see Figure 11B-4).

FIGURE 11B-4

16. Add the following action method to the Home controller.

```
public ActionResult AddRecipe()
{
    return View();
}
```

17. Add a **Home** subfolder under the Views folder.

18. Right-click the Home folder and select New Item from the Add menu, select the **MVC 2 View Content Page** template, enter **Index.aspx** for the name of the new page, and click the Add button.

19. Select **ViewMasterPage1.Master** from the Select Master Page dialog box and click OK.

20. Add a title to the Index.aspx page by adding some text to the ContentPlaceHolder control with ID="Content1":

```
<asp:Content ID="Content1" ContentPlaceHolderID="TitleContent"
runat="server">
    Home
</asp:Content>
```

21. Add some content to the `Index.aspx` page by adding some text to the `ContentPlaceHolder` control with `ID="Content2"`:

```
<asp:Content ID="Content2" ContentPlaceHolderID="MainContent" runat="server">
    <h2>Home</h2>
</asp:Content>
```

22. Right-click the Home folder and select View from the Add menu to open the Add View dialog box.

23. Enter **AddRecipe** for the view name, check the `Select master page` checkbox, select **ViewMasterPage1.Master** as the master page, and click the Add button (see Figure 11B-5).

24. Click the F5 button (see Figure 11B-6).

25. Click the Add Recipe menu item to navigate to the Add Recipe page.

FIGURE 11B-5

FIGURE 11B-6

Please select Lesson 11B on the DVD to view the video that accompanies this lesson.

12A

Skins and Themes in Web Forms

Themes are used to give your web site a consistent appearance. They do not impact the content; rather they focus on the rendered format of the controls on your web site. A theme consists of skins, cascading style sheets, images, and resource files. In this lesson I show you how to create a theme for your web site.

THEMES

Each theme must be placed in a subfolder of the App_Themes folder (see Figure 12A-1).

If your application does not include an App_Themes folder you can create one easily by right-clicking the name of the project and selecting Add ⇨ Add ASP.NET Folder ⇨ Theme from the menu (see Figure 12A-2).

In my example I have set up two themes: the Yellow Theme and the Blue Theme. Both themes consist of a folder of images, a `Button.skin` file, and a cascading style sheet. You are already very familiar with cascading style sheets, but, you are probably wondering, what is a skin?

FIGURE 12A-1

SKINS

As you know, cascading style sheets are used to format HTML elements. Skins, similarly, are used to format server controls. To create a new skin file, right-click the folder that contains the theme to which you want to add the skin, select the Skin File template, name your skin, and click the Add button (see Figure 12A-3).

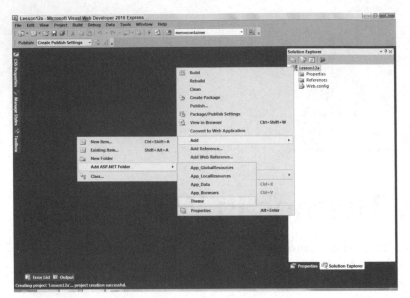

FIGURE 12A-2

FIGURE 12A-3

The name that you select for your skin should be based on the name of the server control to which the skin will be applied. In my example, I have named the new skin **Button.skin**, because it will be applied to buttons. This is the default content of a skin file:

```
<% —
Default skin template. The following skins are provided as examples only.

1. Named control skin. The SkinId should be uniquely defined because
   duplicate SkinId's per control type are not allowed in the same theme.

<asp:GridView runat="server" SkinId="gridviewSkin" BackColor="White" >
   <AlternatingRowStyle BackColor="Blue" />
</asp:GridView>
```

2. Default skin. The SkinId is not defined. Only one default
   control skin per control type is allowed in the same theme.

```
<asp:Image runat="server" ImageUrl="~/images/image1.jpg" />
— %>
```

This is the content of the `Button.skin` file that creates the blue button shown in Figure 12A-4:

```
<asp:Button runat="server" BackColor="Blue" BorderColor="#003399"
    BorderStyle="Dotted" BorderWidth="2px" ForeColor="White" />
```

The easiest way to format a skin file is to drag the control that you want to format to a Web Form and use the Property window to format it. When you have it looking just right, copy the entire control to the skin file. Finally, remove the ID and any other non-appearance-related properties. That's it.

FIGURE 12A-4

> The skin for a button should not include the `Text` property, unless you want all of your buttons to use the same text.

APPLYING THEMES

To use the theme, you can either apply it to the entire web site or just to a single page. To apply the BlueTheme to the entire web site, update the `system.web` section of the `web.config` file:

```
<system.web>
    <compilation debug="true" targetFramework="4.0" />
    <pages theme="BlueTheme" />
</system.web>
```

Once the `web.config` file has been updated to apply a certain theme, every page in the web site will use that theme (see Figure 12A-5).

When a theme is applied to an entire web site, all of the cascading style sheets and skins in the folder for that theme are, by default, applied to *every* Web Form in the web application. You have two ways to override the default theme:

FIGURE 12A-5

1. Set `EnableTheming="false"` at either the page level or the control level.

2. Apply a different theme at the page level.

To apply a theme at the page level set the `Theme` attribute of the `@Page` directive. Because themes are applied in a hierarchical manner, if there is already a theme applied via the `web.config`, the theme

that is applied at the page level will override it. This is the code to override the BlueTheme for the
`Default.aspx` page:

```
<%@ Page Language="C#" AutoEventWireup="true" CodeBehind="Default.aspx.cs"
    Inherits="Lesson12a.Default" Theme="OrangeTheme" %>
```

A theme can also be applied to a page programmatically. To do so, the theme must be applied during
the `Page_PreInit` event:

```
Protected Sub Page_PreInit()
    Page.Theme = OrangeTheme;
End Sub
```

TRY IT

In this lesson you create a theme and apply it to your entire web application.

Lesson Requirements

None.

Hints

➤ Format the server control using the Properties window and then copy the markup to create a
new skin.

Step-by-Step

1. Open Microsoft Visual Web Developer 2010 Express.

2. Select New Project from the File menu.

3. Select **Visual C#** on the left side of the dialog box.

4. Select the **ASP.NET Empty Web Application** template.

> *I use the ASP.NET Empty Web Application template in this lesson.*

5. Enter **Lesson12a** in the Name field and **c:\ASPNETTrainer** in the Location field.

6. Click the OK button.

7. Right-click the name of the project in the Solution Explorer window, select Add ➪ Add
ASP.NET Folder ➪ Theme from the popup menu and name the new theme **BlueTheme**.

8.   Right-click the name of the project and select New Item from the Add menu to open the Add New Item dialog box. Select the Style Sheet template, enter **BlueTheme.css** for the name, and click the Add button.

9.   Drag the `BlueTheme.css` file into the BlueTheme folder and add the following code to the `BlueTheme.css` file:

```
h1
{
    color:Blue;
}
```

10.   Right-click the BlueTheme folder and select New Item from the Add menu to open the Add New Item dialog box. Select the Skin File template, enter **Button.skin** for the name, and click the Add button.

11.   Replace the default code in the `Button.skin` file with the following code:

```
<asp:Button runat="server" BackColor="Blue" BorderColor="#003399"
    BorderStyle="Dotted" BorderWidth="2px" ForeColor="White" />
```

12.   Update the `system.web` section of the `web.config` file to include the following:

```
<pages theme="BlueTheme" />
```

13.   Right-click the name of the project in the Solution Explorer window and select New Item from the Add menu to open the Add New Item dialog box. Select the Web Form template and click the Add button to add a **WebForm1.aspx** page.

14.   Add **Blue Theme** to the `title` element.

15.   Add the following markup to the `div` element:

```
<h1>Blue Theme</h1>
<asp:Button ID="Button1" runat="server" Text="Button" />
```

16.   Verify that the markup on the `WebForm1.aspx` page matches the following:

```
<%@ Page Language="C#" AutoEventWireup="true" CodeBehind="WebForm1.aspx.cs"
    Inherits="Lesson12a.WebForm1" %>

<!DOCTYPE html PUBLIC "-//W3C//DTD XHTML 1.0 Transitional//EN"
    "http://www.w3.org/TR/xhtml1/DTD/xhtml1-transitional.dtd">
<html xmlns="http://www.w3.org/1999/xhtml">
<head runat="server">
    <title>Blue Theme</title>
</head>
<body>
    <form id="form1" runat="server">
    <div>
        <h1>Blue Theme</h1>
        <asp:Button ID="Button1" runat="server" Text="Button" />
    </div>
    </form>
</body>
</html>
```

17.   View the Web Form in Design view (see Figure 12A-6).

> *The theme is not applied in Design mode; you must view the page in the browser to see how the page looks with the theme applied.*

18.   Click the F5 button.

19.   Marvel at the blue text and blue button (see Figure 12A-7).

FIGURE 12A-6   **FIGURE 12A-7**

> *Please select Lesson 12A on the DVD to view the video that accompanies this lesson.*

12B

Design Templates in MVC

To make your MVC web application look more professional, I recommend that you apply a design template. A gallery of design templates is located at www.asp.net/MVC/Gallery. In this lesson I teach you how to apply a design template to your MVC web application.

Microsoft provides a functional tabbed interface in the default MVC application that is created by the ASP.NET MVC 2 Web Application template (see Figure 12B-1). However, using design templates can really make your MVC web application pop.

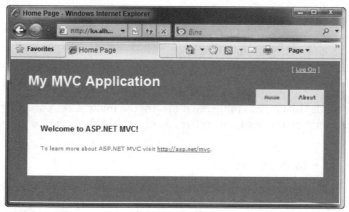

FIGURE 12B-1

The first thing that you must do, and arguably the most difficult part of this project, is to select the design template that you want to use. An ever growing number of design templates are available. For this lesson, I have selected the Rounded Red design template shown in Figure 12B-2.

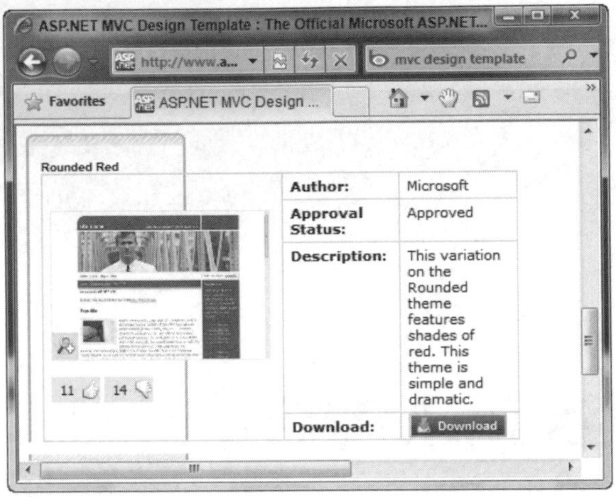

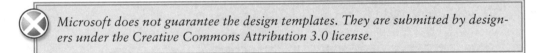

FIGURE 12B-2

Each template includes the following information about that template: Author, Approval Status, and Description. Although the gallery is hosted by Microsoft, most of the templates have not been authored by Microsoft. Instead, there is a vibrant community of graphic artists who submit design templates to the design template gallery.

> Microsoft does not guarantee the design templates. They are submitted by designers under the Creative Commons Attribution 3.0 license.

The design template is a compressed file. Inside the compressed file are the images, the cascading style sheet, and the master page required by the design template. Applying the design template is a three-step process:

1. Extract all files from the `DesignPattern.zip` file.

2. Add all of the files under the DesignTemplateCS\Content folder into the Content folder of your application.

3. Add all of the files under the DesignTemplateCS\Views\Shared folder into the Views\Shared folder of your application.

The design template has now been applied to your application (see Figure 12B-3).

> Each design template includes dummy data in the `Site.Master` file that you will need to delete.

FIGURE 12B-3

TRY IT

In this lesson you apply the Rounded Red design template.

Lesson Requirements

➤ The RoundedRed.zip file.

Hints

➤ Use the Ctrl key to select more than one file from the Add Existing Item dialog box.

Step-by-Step

1. Open Microsoft Visual Web Developer 2010 Express.

2. Select New Project from the File menu.

3. Select **Visual C#** on the left side of the dialog box.

4. Select the **ASP.NET MVC 2 Web Application** template.

5. Enter **Lesson12b** in the Name field and **c:\ASPNETTrainer** in the Location field and click the OK button.

6. Extract all of the files in the RoundedRed.zip file.

7. Right-click the Content folder, select Existing Item from the Add menu, and navigate to the RoundedRed\DesignTemplateCS\Content folder shown in Figure 12B-4.

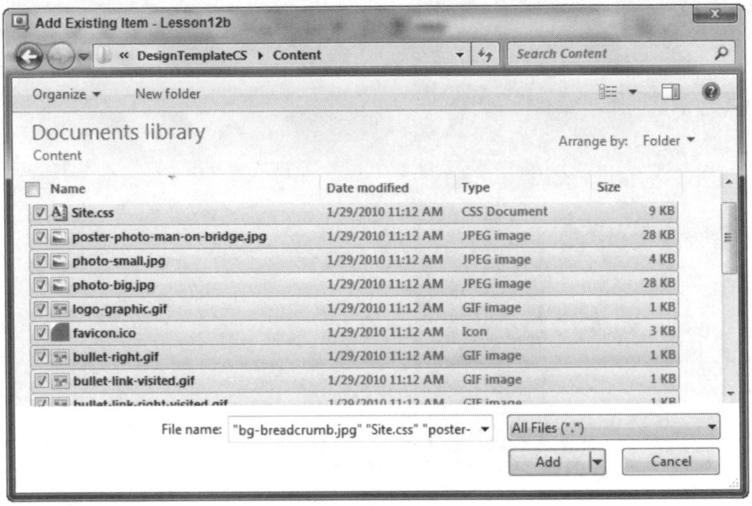

FIGURE 12B-4

8. Use the Ctrl key to highlight all of the files in the Add Existing Item dialog box and click the Add button.

9. Click the Yes button when asked if you want to replace the Site.css file that already exists (see Figure 12B-5).

10. Right-click the Shared subfolder that is under the Views folder, select Existing Item from the Add menu and navigate to the RoundedRed\DesignTemplateCS\Views\Shared folder, select the **Site.Master** file, and click the Add button.

11. Click the Yes button when asked if you want to replace the Site.Master file that already exists (see Figure 12B-6).

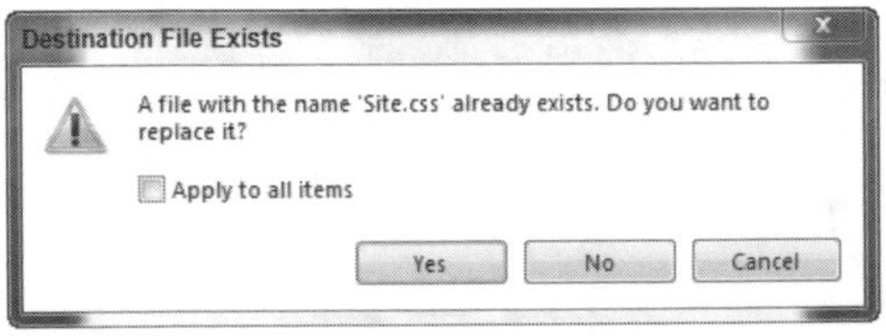

FIGURE 12B-5

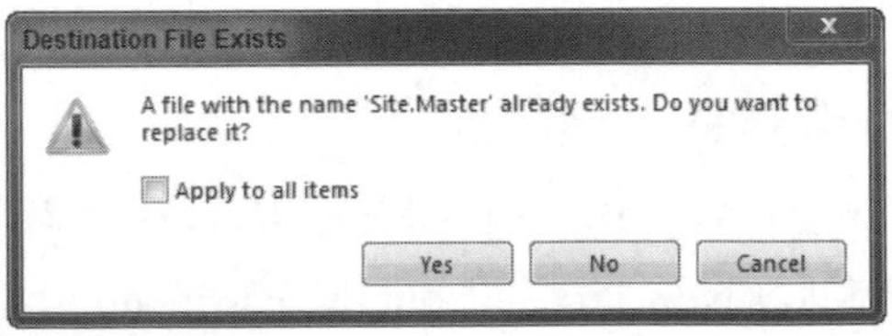

FIGURE 12B-6

12. Click the F5 button.

Please select Lesson 12B on the DVD to view the video that accompanies this lesson.

13A

User Controls in Web Forms

ASP.NET user controls are custom, reusable controls that are both easy to create and use. User controls are a collection of controls, such as text boxes and buttons, and can include custom properties and methods that are exposed to the container of the user control. In this lesson I show you how to create and use a user control. I also show you how to expose properties on a user control.

Whenever you find that you are using the same markup in two or more places, it is time to consider copying that markup to a user control. The page shown in Figure 13A-1 collects both a mailing address and a billing address. The fields for both types of addresses, however, are identical. The address information on this form can be converted into a user control.

FIGURE 13A-1

CREATING A USER CONTROL

To create a user control, select the Web User Control template from the Add New Item dialog box (see Figure 13A-2).

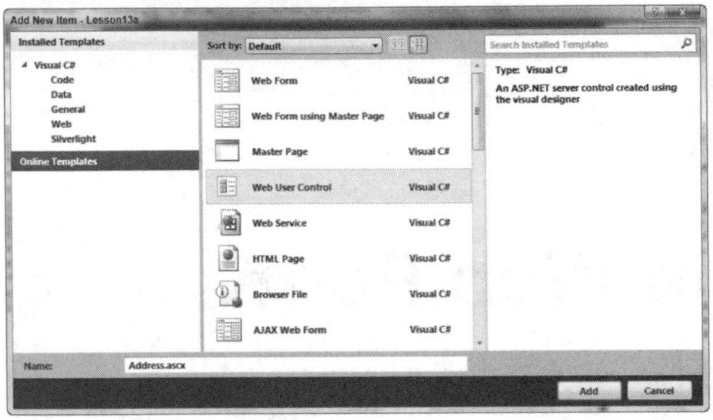

FIGURE 13A-2

> Because a page that uses a user control and the user control itself cannot be in the same folder, it is a best practice to create a folder especially for your user controls.

A user control has the ASCX file extension. This is the default markup that is created for a user control:

```
<%@ Control Language="C#" AutoEventWireup="true" CodeBehind="Address.ascx.cs"
    Inherits="Lesson13a.UserControls.Address" %>
```

As you can see, a user control uses the @Control directive at the top of its page, instead of the @Page directive. The @Control directive has most of the same properties as the @Page directive.

This is the sample user control that is created by copying the block of markup for the Billing Address from the Web Form to the user control:

```
<%@ Control Language="C#" AutoEventWireup="true" CodeBehind="Address.ascx.cs"
    Inherits="Lesson13a.UserControls.Address" %>
<div>
    <label for="TextBoxAddress1">Address 1</label>
    <asp:TextBox ID="TextBoxAddress1" runat="server" Columns="50" MaxLength="50" />
</div>
<div>
    <label for="TextBoxAddress2">Address 2</label>
    <asp:TextBox ID="TextBoxAddress2" runat="server" Columns="50" MaxLength="50" />
</div>
```

```
<div>
    <label for="TextBoxCity">City</label>
    <asp:TextBox ID="TextBoxCity" runat="server" Columns="25" MaxLength="25" />
</div>
<div>
    <label for="TextBoxState">State</label>
    <asp:TextBox ID="TextBoxState" runat="server" Columns="2" MaxLength="2" />
</div>
<div>
    <label for="TextBoxZipCode">Zip Code</label>
    <asp:TextBox ID="TextBoxZipCode" runat="server" Columns="10" MaxLength="10" />
</div>
```

> *Because a user control cannot be viewed directly in a page, the easiest way to design a user control is to create a Web Form with the markup that you want for the user control and then copy that markup to the user control.*

REGISTERING A USER CONTROL

For a page to use a user control the user control must first be registered in the page. You do this by adding an @Register directive to the page. This is a sample @Register directive:

```
<%@ Register Src="~/UserControls/Address.ascx" TagName="Address"
    TagPrefix="uc1" %>
```

The @Register directive contains three attributes that are relevant to a user control:

➤ **Src** — This is the virtual path to the ASCX file that defines the user control.

➤ **TagName** — This is the name that will be used in the current form to refer to the user control. You can use whatever text you want for the TagName, but it is convention to use the name of the user control.

➤ **TagPrefix** — This is the alias that will be used in the current form to refer to the user control. The default is uc1, but I usually change this to my initials. You can change it to whatever you want.

> *ASP.NET uses the "mobile" TagPrefix to identify the Web controls in the* System.Web.UI.MobileControls *namespace. Therefore, you should avoid using that prefix.*

This is the updated page that uses the new user control:

```
<%@ Page Language="C#" AutoEventWireup="true"
    CodeBehind="AddressWithUserControl.aspx.cs"
```

```
        Inherits="Lesson13a.AddressWithUserControl" %>

<%@ Register Src="UserControls/Address.ascx" TagName="Address" TagPrefix="uc1" %>

<!DOCTYPE html PUBLIC "-//W3C//DTD XHTML 1.0 Transitional//EN"
    "http://www.w3.org/TR/xhtml1/DTD/xhtml1-transitional.dtd">
<html xmlns="http://www.w3.org/1999/xhtml">
<head runat="server">
    <title>Addresses</title>
</head>
<body>
    <form id="form1" runat="server">
    Mailing Address
    <uc1:Address ID="AddressMailing" runat="server" />
    <br />
    Billing Address
    <uc1:Address ID="AddressBilling" runat="server" />
    <br />
    <asp:Button ID="ButtonSubmit" runat="server" Text="Submit" />
    </form>
</body>
</html>
```

Instead of registering the user control in each page, you can register the user control in the `system.web` section of the `web.config` file. This is how to register a user control in the `web.config` file:

```
<system.web>
    …
    <pages>
        <controls>
            <add src="UserControls/Address.ascx" tagName="Address"
                tagPrefix="uc1"/>
        </controls>
    </pages>
</system.web>
```

ACCESSING CONTROLS IN A USER CONTROL

You can use the `FindControl` method to access a control that is on the user control. For example, the following code refers to the `Text` attribute of the `TextBox` control used to input Address 1:

```
((TextBox)this.AddressMailing.FindControl("TextBoxAddress1")).Text
```

This method will work, but it is a better practice to expose the `Text` attribute of the `TextBox` control by using a property. If you click the current user control, you see that there are not many properties exposed (see Figure 13A-3).

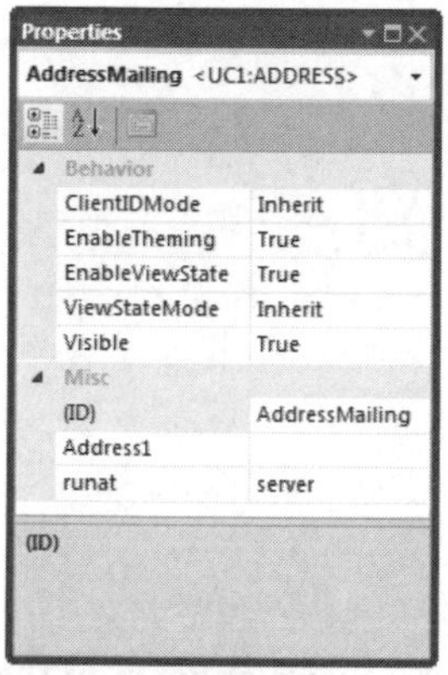

FIGURE 13A-3

The following code will add properties for the Text value of each of the TextBoxes contained in the user control:

```csharp
using System;

namespace Lesson13a.UserControls
{
    public partial class Address : System.Web.UI.UserControl
    {
        [System.ComponentModel.Category("Data")]
        public string Address1
        {
            get {return TextBoxAddress1.Text;}
            set { TextBoxAddress1.Text = value; }
        }

        [System.ComponentModel.Category("Data")]
        public string Address2
        {
            get { return TextBoxAddress2.Text; }
            set { TextBoxAddress2.Text = value; }
        }

        [System.ComponentModel.Category("Data")]
        public string City
        {
            get { return TextBoxCity.Text; }
            set { TextBoxCity.Text = value; }
        }

        [System.ComponentModel.Category("Data")]
        public string State
```

```
        {
            get { return TextBoxState.Text; }
            set { TextBoxState.Text = value; }
        }

        [System.ComponentModel.Category("Data")]
        public string ZipCode
        {
            get { return TextBoxZipCode.Text; }
            set { TextBoxZipCode.Text = value; }
        }
    }
}
```

Now, the `Text` value for each of the `TextBox` controls contained in the user control appears in the Property window (see Figure 13A-4).

FIGURE 13A-4

> I decorated each of the properties in the user control with `[System.Component Model.Category("Data")]` so that they would be separated into a Data category in the Property window.

The following code refers to the `Text` attribute of the `TextBox` control used to input Address 1:

```
this.AddressMailing.Address1 = "123 Main"
```

TRY IT

In this lesson you create and use a user control.

Lesson Requirements

➤ The `InputAddress.apx` file.

➤ The `InputAddress.aspx.cs` file.

➤ The `InputAddress.aspx.designer.cs` file.

➤ The `DefaultStyles.css` file.

Hints

➤ Drag the user control to the Design view directly from the Solution Explorer window to register the user control on the page automatically.

Step-by-Step

1. Open Microsoft Visual Web Developer 2010 Express.

2. Select New Project from the File menu.

3. Select **Visual C#** on the left side of the dialog box.

4. Select the **ASP.NET Empty Web Application** template.

5. Enter **Lesson13a** in the Name field and **c:\ASPNETTrainer** in the Location field.

6. Click the OK button.

7. Right-click the name of the project in the Solution Explorer window and select Add ⇨ Add ASP.NET Folder ⇨ Theme from the popup menu and name the new theme **Default**.

8. Right-click the Default theme and select Existing Item from the New menu to add the **DefaultStyles.css** file.

9. Right-click the name of the project in the Solution Explorer window and select Existing Item from the New menu to add the **InputAddress.aspx** file.

10. Right-click the `InputAddress.aspx` file and select Set As Start Page from the menu.

11. Click the F5 button to view the `InputAddress.aspx` page in the browser.

12. Close the browser.

13. Right-click the name of the project in the Solution Explorer window and select New Folder from the Add menu to add a folder named **UserControls**.

14. Right-click the UserControls folder, select New Items from the Add menu, select the Web User Control template, enter **Address.ascx** for the Name, and click the Add button.

15. Open the `InputAddress.aspx` file and copy all of the markup for the mailing address to the `Address.ascx` file.

16. Replace the "Mailing Address" text with a Literal server control named **LiteralTitle**.

17. Verify that the markup in the `Address.ascx` file matches the following:

```
<%@ Control Language="C#" AutoEventWireup="true" CodeBehind="Address.ascx.cs"
    Inherits="Lesson13a.UserControls.Address" %>
<h2>
    <asp:Literal ID="LiteralTitle" runat="server" />
</h2>
<div>
    <label for="TextBoxAddress1">Address 1</label>
    <asp:TextBox ID="TextBoxAddress1" runat="server" Columns="50" MaxLength="50" />
</div>
<div>
    <label for="TextBoxAddress2">Address 2</label>
    <asp:TextBox ID="TextBoxAddress2" runat="server" Columns="50"
        MaxLength="50" />
</div>
<div>
    <label for="TextBoxCity">City</label>
    <asp:TextBox ID="TextBoxCity" runat="server" Columns="25" MaxLength="25" />
</div>
<div>
    <label for="TextBoxState">State</label>
    <asp:TextBox ID="TextBoxState" runat="server" Columns="2" MaxLength="2" />
</div>
<div>
    <label for="TextBoxZipCode">Zip Code</label>
    <asp:TextBox ID="TextBoxZipCode" runat="server" Columns="10"
        MaxLength="10" />
</div>
```

18. Add the following code to the `Address.ascx.cs` file:

```
public string Title
{
    get { return LiteralTitle.Text; }
    set { LiteralTitle.Text = value; }
}
```

19. Verify that the code in the `Address.ascx.cs` file matches the following:

```
using System;
using System.Collections.Generic;
using System.Linq;
using System.Web;
using System.Web.UI;
using System.Web.UI.WebControls;

namespace Lesson13a.UserControls
{
    public partial class Address : System.Web.UI.UserControl
    {
        public string Title
```

```
            {
                get { return LiteralTitle.Text; }
                set { LiteralTitle.Text = value; }
            }
            protected void Page_Load(object sender, EventArgs e)
            {

            }
        }
    }
```

20. Select Build Lesson13a from the Build menu to build the application.

21. Register the `Address.ascx` user control on the `InputAddress.aspx` page:

```
<%@ Register Src="~/UserControls/Address.ascx" TagName="Address"
    TagPrefix="uc1" %>
```

22. Replace both the Mailing Address and the Billing Address with an `Address` user control.

23. Set the `Title` property for the mailing address to **Mailing Address** and the `Title` property for the billing address to **Billing Address**.

24. Verify that the markup in the `InputAddress.aspx` file matches the following:

```
<%@ Page Language="C#" AutoEventWireup="true" CodeBehind="InputAddress.aspx.cs"
    Inherits="Lesson13a.InputAddress" %>

<%@ Register Src="~/UserControls/Address.ascx" TagName="Address" TagPrefix="uc1" %>

<!DOCTYPE html PUBLIC "-//W3C//DTD XHTML 1.0 Transitional//EN"
    "http://www.w3.org/TR/xhtml1/DTD/xhtml1-transitional.dtd">
<html xmlns="http://www.w3.org/1999/xhtml">
<head runat="server">
    <title>Input Address Form</title>
    <link href="App_Themes/Default/DefaultStyles.css" rel="stylesheet"
        type="text/css" />
</head>
<body>
    <form id="form1" runat="server">
    <h1>Input Address Form</h1>
    Please enter your mailing address and your billing address.
    <uc1:Address ID="Address1" runat="server" Title="Mailing Address" />
    <uc1:Address ID="Address2" runat="server" Title="Billing Address" />
    <hr />
    <asp:Button ID="ButtonSubmit" runat="server" Text="Submit" />
    </form>
</body>
</html>
```

25. Click the F5 button (see Figure 13A-5).

FIGURE 13A-5

Please select Lesson 13A on the DVD to view the video that accompanies this lesson.

13B

Partial Views in MVC

Partial views are reusable views that are both easy to create and use. Whenever you need to use the same markup in two different places, it is time to consider using a partial view. In this lesson I will show you how to create and use a partial view.

CREATING A PARTIAL VIEW

The first step when creating a partial view is to create the model for the view. I use the following model in this lesson:

```
namespace Lesson13b.Models
{
    public class Address
    {
        public string Address1 { get; set; }
        public string Address2 { get; set; }
        public string City { get; set; }
        public string State { get; set; }
        public string ZipCode { get; set; }
    }
}
```

Partial views are usually stored in the Shared subfolder of the Views folder. To create a new partial view right-click the Shared folder and select View from the Add menu to open the Add View dialog box (see Figure 13B-1). Make sure to click the `Create a partial view (.ascx)` checkbox before you click the Add button.

The Add View dialog box creates a file with an ASCX file extension. These are the contents of the `Address.ascx` file that has been created by the Add View dialog box:

```
<%@ Control Language="C#"
    Inherits="System.Web.Mvc.ViewUserControl<Lesson13b.Models.Address>" %>

<% using (Html.BeginForm()) {%>
    <%: Html.ValidationSummary(true) %>

    <fieldset>
```

```
        <legend>Fields</legend>

        <div class="editor-label">
            <%: Html.LabelFor(model => model.Address1) %>
        </div>
        <div class="editor-field">
            <%: Html.TextBoxFor(model => model.Address1) %>
            <%: Html.ValidationMessageFor(model => model.Address1) %>
        </div>

        <div class="editor-label">
            <%: Html.LabelFor(model => model.Address2) %>
        </div>
        <div class="editor-field">
            <%: Html.TextBoxFor(model => model.Address2) %>
            <%: Html.ValidationMessageFor(model => model.Address2) %>
        </div>

        <div class="editor-label">
            <%: Html.LabelFor(model => model.City) %>
        </div>
        <div class="editor-field">
            <%: Html.TextBoxFor(model => model.City) %>
            <%: Html.ValidationMessageFor(model => model.City) %>
        </div>

        <div class="editor-label">
            <%: Html.LabelFor(model => model.State) %>
        </div>
        <div class="editor-field">
            <%: Html.TextBoxFor(model => model.State) %>
            <%: Html.ValidationMessageFor(model => model.State) %>
        </div>

        <div class="editor-label">
            <%: Html.LabelFor(model => model.ZipCode) %>
        </div>
        <div class="editor-field">
            <%: Html.TextBoxFor(model => model.ZipCode) %>
            <%: Html.ValidationMessageFor(model => model.ZipCode) %>
        </div>

        <p>
            <input type="submit" value="Save" />
        </p>
    </fieldset>

<% } %>

<div>
    <%: Html.ActionLink("Back to List", "Index") %>
</div>
```

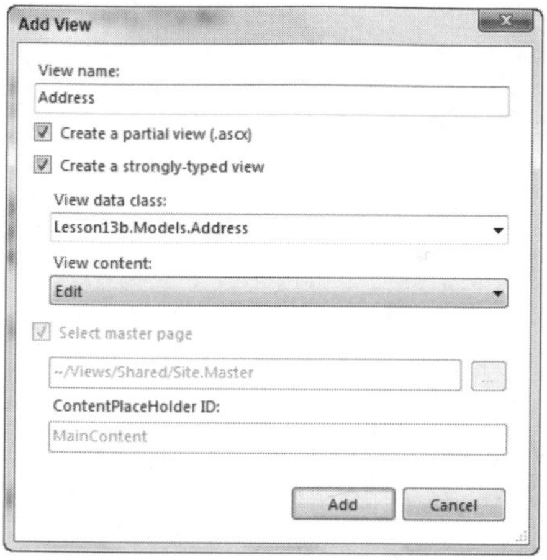

FIGURE 13B-1

As you can see, a partial view uses the `@Control` directive instead of the `@Page` directive. The `@Control` directive has most of the same properties as the `@Page` directive.

RENDERING A PARTIAL VIEW

To add a partial view to an existing view you use the `Html.RenderPartial` method. The following code renders the `Address` partial view:

```
<% Html.RenderPartial("Address"); %>
```

Figure 13B-2 shows the page that is generated when I add the `Address` partial view to the `About` view that is provided by the sample MVC application.

In this example I only passed `Html.RenderPartial` the name of the partial view. I can also use `Html.RenderPartial` to pass both the name of the partial view and the model or the `ViewData Dictionary` that it uses. This is the code to render the Address partial view using the data in the model:

```
<% Html.RenderPartial("Address", Model); %>
```

Now, if I update the `About` action method to the following:

```
public ActionResult About()
{
    var address = new Models.Address();

    address.Address1 = "123 Main Street";
    address.City = "Frisco";
    address.State = "TX";
    address.ZipCode = "75034";

    return View(address);
}
```

FIGURE 13B-2

the About Us page displays the data from the model as shown in Figure 13B-3.

FIGURE 13B-3

> When a partial view is instantiated it has access to the same data as the parent view. However, if the partial view updates the data, the parent view does not have access to those updates.

TRY IT

In this lesson you create and use a partial view.

Lesson Requirements

None.

Hints

None.

Step-by-Step

1. Open Microsoft Visual Web Developer 2010 Express.

2. Select New Project from the File menu.

3. Select **Visual C#** on the left side of the dialog box.

4. Select the **ASP.NET MVC 2 Web Application** template.

5. Enter **Lesson13b** in the Name field and **c:\ASPNETTrainer** in the Location field.

6. Right-click the Models folder on the Solution Explorer window and select Class from the Add menu to open the Add New Item dialog box.

7. Enter **Address.cs** for the Name and click the Add button.

8. Enter the following code in the `Address.cs` file:

   ```
   public string Address1 { get; set; }
   public string Address2 { get; set; }
   public string City { get; set; }
   public string State { get; set; }
   public string ZipCode { get; set; }
   ```

9. Verify that the code in the `Address.cs` file matches the following:

   ```
   using System;
   using System.Collections.Generic;
   using System.Linq;
   using System.Web;

   namespace Lesson13b.Models
   ```

```
    {
        public class Address
        {
            public string Address1 { get; set; }
            public string Address2 { get; set; }
            public string City { get; set; }
            public string State { get; set; }
            public string ZipCode { get; set; }
        }
    }
```

10. Select Build Lesson13b from the Build menu.

11. Right-click the Shared subfolder under the Views folder and select View from the Add menu to open the Add View dialog box.

12. Enter **Address** for the View Name, click the `Create a partial view (.ascx)` checkbox, click the `Create a strongly-typed view` checkbox, select **Lesson13b.Models.Address** as the View data class, select **Edit** as the View content and click the Add button (see Figure 13B-4).

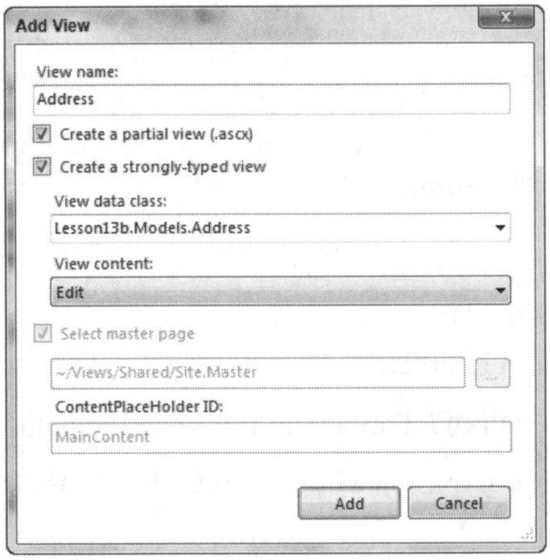

FIGURE 13B-4

13. Replace the "Put content here." text in the `About` view with the following code:

```
<% Html.RenderPartial("Address", Model); %>
```

14. Click the F5 button.

15. Navigate to the About Us page.

 Please select Lesson 13B on the DVD to view the video that accompanies this lesson.

SECTION V
Controlling the Flow

14A

Event Model in Web Forms

An event is something that occurs in response to an action. The ASP.NET Web Form framework provides a rich event model for the developer. In previous lessons you have seen that by simply double-clicking a button the IDE adds an event handler for the button's click event. In this lesson I show you how to handle other types of events, use one event handler for multiple objects, and force a postback to occur when a certain event is triggered.

Lesson 8A covered the page's life cycle. This is the sequence of events that are raised whenever a page is requested:

➤ PreInit

➤ Init

➤ InitComplete

➤ PreLoad

➤ Load

➤ LoadComplete

➤ PreRender

➤ PreRenderComplete

➤ SaveStateComplete

➤ Unload

By default, page events are automatically bound to methods with the name Page_*event*. This is true because by default AutoEventWireup="true" is included in the @Page directive for every page. If AutoEventWireup is set to false, you have to wire-up the events yourself. This is the code to add an event handler called LoadMyPage to handle the Load event of the page:

```
protected override void OnInit(EventArgs e)
{
    base.OnInit(e);
    this.Load += new EventHandler(LoadMyPage);
}
```

Like pages, server controls also have a life cycle. Server control events are processed after the pages `Page_Init` and `Page_Load` events. This is the sequence of events that is followed for every server control whenever a page is requested:

➤ Init

➤ Load

➤ PreRender

➤ DataBinding

➤ Unload

➤ Disposed

However, most server controls include additional events in their life cycle. For example, the `Button` server control also includes the following events:

➤ Click

➤ Command

When you double-click a `Button` server control in Design view, the event handler for the default event is automatically generated:

```
protected void Button1_Click(object sender, EventArgs e)
{

}
```

All page and control events follow a standard pattern for their event-handler methods. The following two arguments are passed by every event:

➤ **sender** — This is the object that raised the event.

➤ e — This is an object of type `EventArgs`, or a derived type, that contains state information pertinent to the event.

In the case of the `Button` server control, e is of type `EventArgs` and is empty because the event handler does not require any state information. However, in the case of an ImageButton, e is of type `ImageClickEventArgs` and includes the coordinates of where the button was clicked.

> *Page events can accept the standard two arguments; however, because no values are passed in these arguments, they are not required.*

You already know that you can create an event handler for a control by double-clicking that control. Unfortunately, this method only allows you to create the default method for that control. The easiest way to create event handlers for the other events is to select the control and click the Events button on the toolbar of the Property window. Figure 14A-1 shows the Property window after the Event button on the toolbar has been clicked for a button.

Using the Property window you can create any of the listed events by double-clicking the event's name. Or, you can associate an event with an event that you have already written by clicking the drop-down list next to the event's name and selecting the event from the choices on the list.

When an event is added to a server control, an attribute is added to the markup for that server control. This is the updated markup for the `Button1` server control:

FIGURE 14A-1

```
<asp:Button ID="Button1" runat="server" Text="Button" OnClick="Button1_Click" />
```

In this case the `OnClick` event calls the `Button1_Click` event handler. Unlike with page events, there is not a strict naming convention associated with server controls. Nevertheless, it is a best practice to name your event handlers using the following convention: *ControlName_<event name>*, where *ControlName* is the name of the control, and *<event name>* is the name of the event.

> *When you are writing event handlers, it is very important to remember that while event handlers use the following naming convention:* ControlName_<event name>, *the attribute on the server control that actually calls the event uses this naming convention:* On<event name>.

One event can be associated with more than one control. For example, all of the buttons in the following code use the same event handler for their `OnClick` event:

```
<asp:Button ID="Button1" runat="server" Text="Button 1" OnClick="Button_Click" />
<asp:Button ID="Button2" runat="server" Text="Button 2" OnClick="Button_Click" />
<asp:Button ID="Button3" runat="server" Text="Button 3" OnClick="Button_Click" />
```

In the case of a button, if you want to call the same event handler for multiple buttons, you should use the `OnCommand` event instead of the `OnClick` event. The `OnCommand` event requires that the button include a `Command` attribute.

```
<asp:Button ID="Button1" runat="server" Text="Button" CommandName="Sort"
    OnCommand="Button_Command" />
<asp:Button ID="Button2" runat="server" Text="Button" CommandName="Edit"
    OnCommand="Button_Command" />
```

This is the blank event handler that is created automatically for the `OnCommand` event:

```
protected void Button_Command(object sender, CommandEventArgs e)
{

}
```

The second argument of the `OnCommand` event handler is `CommandEventArgs` instead of `EventArgs`. The `CommandEventArgs` type includes the `CommandName` and the `CommandArguments` for the `Button`. It is better to use the `OnCommand` event than the `OnClick` event of the `Button` if you want to use the same event handler for multiple buttons because it includes a built-in way for you to identify the appropriate command, or the `Button` control that was clicked. Otherwise, you must rely on either the name or the text of the button to identify the command that is associated with the button.

By default, the `OnClick` event of a `Button` causes the page to be posted back immediately to the server for processing. This is not true for all server controls. Figure 14A-2 shows the events associated with a textbox.

In the case of the textbox, the default event is the `TextChanged` event. Unless you change the value of the `AutoPostback` property of the textbox to true, a postback will not automatically occur. Instead, the event will not be raised until the next postback occurs.

FIGURE 14A-2

You can determine whether a request is a postback by checking the `Page.IsPostback` *property.*

An `AutoPostBack` property is included for all controls that support a change event. This is a textbox with the `AutoPostBack` property set to true:

```
<asp:TextBox ID="TextBox1" runat="server" AutoPostBack="true" />
```

The `AutoPostBack` *property will not work properly if the user's browser disallows scripting.*

You do not want to perform more postbacks than is absolutely required, because every postback requires a roundtrip to the server for processing. Therefore, they can affect the performance of the page and the server. To limit the number of postbacks, server controls do not support events that occur often, such as the `OnMouseOver` event. These events must be handled on the client.

Some server controls, such as the Repeater and GridView controls, can contain items with button controls that can themselves raise events. Figure 14A-3 shows the events associated with a Repeater.

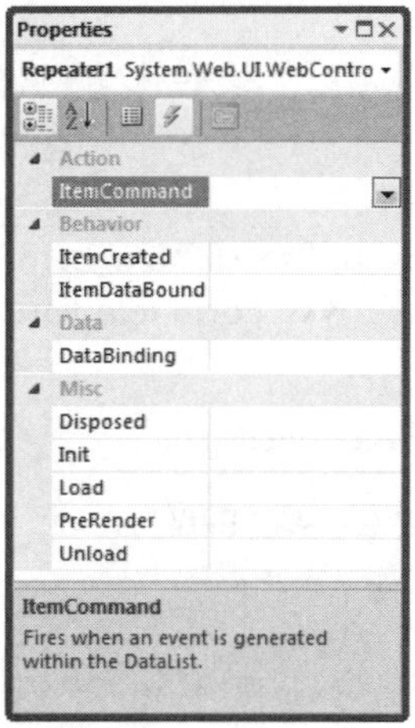

FIGURE 14A-3

The `OnItemCommand` event is raised whenever any button on the Repeater is clicked. This is the empty event handler for the Repeater `OnItemCommand` event:

```
protected void Repeater1_ItemCommand(object source, RepeaterCommandEventArgs e)
{

}
```

The second argument is a `RepeaterCommandEventArgs`. The `RepeaterCommandEventArgs` type includes the `CommandName`, `CommandSource`, and `CommandArguments` for the button that was clicked.

TRY IT

In this lesson you create a page with multiple buttons that all call the same event handler.

Lesson Requirements

None.

Hints

➤ Use the Properties window to select the event handler to use for a particular event.

Step-by-Step

1. Open Microsoft Visual Web Developer 2010 Express.

2. Select New Project from the File menu.

3. Select **Visual C#** on the left side of the dialog box.

4. Select the **ASP.NET Web Application** template.

5. Enter **Lesson14a** in the Name field and **c:\ASPNETTrainer** in the Location field.

6. Click the OK button.

7. Right-click the name of the project in the Solution Explorer window and select New Item from the Add menu to open the Add New Item dialog box. Select the **Web Form** template, enter **ButtonCommand.aspx** for the Name, and click the Add button.

8. Add **OnCommand Event** to the `title` element on the `ButtonCommand.aspx` page.

9. Add the following markup to the `div` element on the `ButtonCommand.aspx` page:

```
<h1><asp:Literal id="LiteralButtonClicked" runat="server" /></h1>
```

10. Add a Button server control with the following attributes to the `ButtonCommand.aspx` page:

```
ID="ButtonSortAsc"
Text="Sort Ascending"
CommandName="Sort"
CommandArgument ="Ascending"
```

11. Add the following event handler for the `OnCommand` event of a button to the `ButtonCommand.aspx.cs` file:

```
protected void Sort_Command(object sender, CommandEventArgs e)
{
    this.LiteralButtonClicked.Text = String.Format("You clicked the {0}
        button.", e.CommandName);
}
```

12. Associate the `OnCommand` event of the button with the `Sort_Command` event handler by using the Property window.

13. Click the F5 button.

14. Click the Sort Ascending button.

15. Stop debugging by closing the browser.

16. Add another button to the `ButtonCommand.aspx` page with the following attributes:

```
ID="ButtonSortDesc"
Text="Sort Descending"
CommandName="Sort"
CommandArgument ="Descending"
```

17. Associate the `OnCommand` event of the new button with the existing `Sort_Command` method.

18. Verify that the markup on the `ButtonCommand.aspx` page matches the following:

```
<%@ Page Language="C#" AutoEventWireup="true" CodeBehind="ButtonCommand.aspx.cs"
    Inherits="Lesson14a.ButtonCommand" %>

<!DOCTYPE html PUBLIC "-//W3C//DTD XHTML 1.0 Transitional//EN"
    "http://www.w3.org/TR/xhtml1/DTD/xhtml1-transitional.dtd">
```

```
<html xmlns="http://www.w3.org/1999/xhtml">
<head runat="server">
    <title>OnCommand Event</title>
</head>
<body>
    <form id="form1" runat="server">
    <div>
        <h1>
            <asp:Literal ID="LiteralButtonClicked" runat="server" />
        </h1>
        <asp:Button ID="ButtonSortAsc" runat="server" Text="Sort Ascending"
            CommandName="Sort" CommandArgument="Ascending"
            oncommand="Sort_Command" />
        <asp:Button ID="ButtonSortDesc" runat="server" Text="Sort Descending"
            CommandName="Sort" CommandArgument="Descending"
            oncommand="Sort_Command" />
    </div>
    </form>
</body>
</html>
```

19. Update the Sort_Command method in the ButtonCommand.aspx.cs file to the following:

```
protected void Sort_Command(object sender, CommandEventArgs e)
{
    this.LiteralButtonClicked.Text = String.Format("You clicked the {0} button,
        with the following argument: {1}.", e.CommandName, e.CommandArgument);
}
```

20. Click the F5 button.

21. Click the Sort Ascending button (see Figure 14A-4).

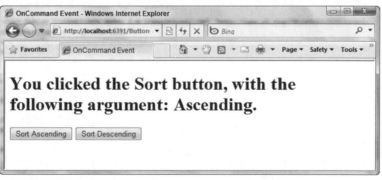

FIGURE 14A-4

 Please select Lesson 14A on the DVD to view the video that accompanies this lesson.

14B

Controllers in MVC

In the ASP.NET MVC framework, a controller is a class that takes a browser request and returns a response. The controller can issue any set of commands to the model and it can render any view back to the browser. In short — it is the boss. In this lesson I explain each of the different types of results that a controller can return, introduce the action filter attributes that can be applied to a controller, and I show you how to create a controller.

This is the code for a sample controller called `HomeController`:

```
using System.Web.Mvc;

namespace Lesson14b.Controllers
{
    [HandleError]
    public class HomeController : Controller
    {
        public ActionResult Index()
        {
            ViewData["Message"] = "Welcome to ASP.NET MVC!";

            return View();
        }

        public ActionResult About()
        {
            return View();
        }
    }
}
```

 All controllers must end with the "Controller" suffix. If you omit the "Controller" suffix you will not be able to invoke the controller.

ACTION METHODS

Each controller contains one or more action methods, which is a special type of method that can pass data to a view. The `HomeController` includes two action methods: `Index` and `About`. In the preceding sample code, both of these action methods return an `ActionResult`. Action methods all return an instance of a class that is derived from the `ActionResult` class. Different action result types are provided to handle the different tasks that the action method might want to perform. These are the built-in action result types:

➤ **ContentResult** — This represents raw text.

➤ **EmptyResult** — This represents a result that does nothing.

➤ **FileResult** — This represents a file.

➤ **JavaScriptResult** — This represents a JavaScript script.

➤ **JsonResult** — This represents a serialized JavaScript Object Notation object.

➤ **PartialViewResult** — This renders a partial view.

➤ **RedirectResult** — This represents a redirect to a new URL.

➤ **RedirectToRouteResult** — This represents a redirect that uses the route table.

➤ **ViewResult** — This renders a view.

> *An action method can return any type of object; however, the object will be wrapped in the appropriate* `ActionResult` *type before it is rendered to the response stream.*

The most commonly used action result type is the `ViewResult`. This class contains properties that identify the name of the view, the name of the master view, the view data and the temporary data.

PASSING DATA TO THE VIEW

These are the intrinsic ways that a controller can pass data to the view:

➤ **ViewData Property**

➤ **TempData Property**

➤ **Strongly-Typed Views**

The controller uses its `ViewData` property to pass an instance of the `ViewDataDictionary` class to the view. This is an action method that uses the `ViewData` property to pass data to the view:

```
public ActionResult Index()
{
    ViewData["Message"] = "Welcome to ASP.NET MVC!";

    return View();
}
```

The controller can also use its `TempData` property to pass data to the view. This property works just like the `ViewData` property except that it passes an instance of the `TempDataDictionary` class and the data persists until it is either read or the session times out. The `TempDataDictionary` class is great for displaying confirmation messages and providing useful information to error pages.

Another way to pass data to the view is to pass a strongly-typed object in the `View` method. This is the code to pass a collection of Categories to the view:

```
public ActionResult Index()
{
    var categories = from c in _entity.Categories
                     orderby c.Name
                     select c;

    return View(categories);
}
```

ACTION FILTERS

An action method of a controller class must be public. In fact, the ASP.NET MVC framework treats all public methods in a controller as action methods. This can be a problem if your controller contains a public method that you do not want to be treated as an action method. To designate that you do not want a public class of a controller to be treated as an action method, you must decorate it with the `NonActionAttribute` attribute. This is an example of a class that is decorated with the `NonActionAttribute` attribute:

```
[NonAction]
public void IgnoreMe()
{

}
```

The `NonActionAttribute` attribute is only one of the built-in action filters that can control how an action method is defined. Two more are the `ActionNameAttribute` attribute and the `AcceptVerbs Attribute` attribute. The `ActionNameAttribute` attribute is used to change the name of an action method. The following code changes the name of the action method from `MyView` to `View`:

```
[ActionName("View")]
public ActionResult MyView()
{
    return View();
}
```

The `AcceptVerbsAttribute` attribute sets the HTTP verbs to which the action method can respond. Generally, an HTTP GET occurs when a page is first requested, and an HTTP POST occurs when the page is submitted. The HTTP verbs are GET, POST, PUT, and DELETE. This is an action result that only responds to a POST:

```
[AcceptVerbs(HttpVerbs.Post)]
public ActionResult Day()
```

```
    {
        return View();
    }
```

Instead of using the `AcceptVerbsAttribute` attribute to identify to which HTTP verbs the action method responds, you can use one or more of the following, slightly shorter attributes:

➤ **HttpDeleteAttribute**

➤ **HttpGetAttribute**

➤ **HttpPostAttribute**

➤ **HttpPutAttribute**

> *When an HTTP request is received, the ASP.NET MVC framework first looks for an action method that explicitly supports the incoming HTTP verb. If one is not found, it uses the action method that does not explicitly specify an HTTP verb.*

Action filters can be applied to either an individual action method or the entire controller. If an action filter decorates a controller, it is applied to all of the action methods in the controller. There are four types of action filters and each type of action filter includes a collection of attributes. You can use the existing attributes or write your own. These are the four types of action filters:

Authorization — These filters are for authentication and authorization. For example, the `AuthorizeAttribute` attribute can be used to restrict access to a particular action method.

Action — These filters wrap the action method's execution. The `AcceptVerbsAttribute` attribute is an example of an action filter.

Result — These filters perform additional processing of the result. For example, the `OutputCacheAttribute` attribute can be used to cache the results of the action method.

Exception — These filters are executed when there is an unhandled exception. For example, the `HandleErrorAttribute` attribute is used to redirect the user to an error page in the event of an unhandled exception.

CONTROLLER METHODS

Action methods do not directly return an `ActionResult`. Instead, they call a method of the `Controller` class. This is a list of the methods of the `Controller` class that return an `ActionResult`:

➤ **View** — Returns a `ViewResult`.

➤ **PartialView** — Returns a `PartialViewResult`.

➤ **Redirect** — Returns a `RedirectResult`.

➤ **RedirectToAction** — Returns a `RedirectToRouteResult`.

- ➤ **RedirectToRoute** — Returns a `RedirectToRouteResult`.

- ➤ **Json** — Returns a `JsonResult`.

- ➤ **JavaScript** — Returns a `JavaScriptResult`.

- ➤ **Content** — Returns a `ContentResult`.

- ➤ **File** — Returns a `FileResult`.

- ➤ **EmptyResult** — Returns `null`.

In the sample controller, both action methods call the `View` method of the controller to return a `ViewResult` to the browser. The following action method calls the `RedirectToAction` method that returns a `RedirectToRouteResult` to the browser and redirects the user to the `Index` action method of the `HomeController`:

```
public ActionResult ReturnHome()
{
    return RedirectToAction("Index", "Home");

}
```

RETRIEVING DATA FROM THE REQUEST

An action method can take one or more parameters. In the following example, the action method expects a parameter called `date` of type `DateTime`:

```
[HttpPost]
public ActionResult Day(DateTime date)
{
    ViewData["day"] = String.Format("{0} is a {1}", date.ToString("MMMM dd, yyyy"),
        date.DayOfWeek);
    return View();
}
```

The value for the parameter is automatically mapped from the data collection for the request. The data collection for the request includes routing values, request data, query string values, and cookie values. If the parameter cannot be found and it is not a nullable-type, an exception of type `System .ArgumentException` is thrown.

CREATING A CONTROLLER

To create a new controller, right-click the Controllers folder and select Controller from the Add menu to open the Add Controller dialog box show in Figure 14B-1.

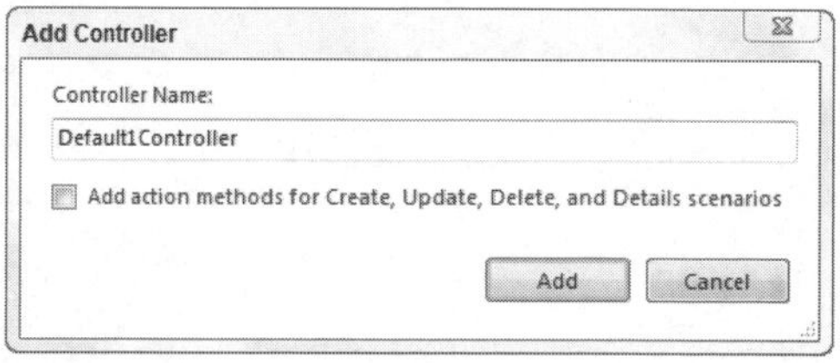

FIGURE 14B-1

The name of the controller must end with the "Controller" suffix, so be careful not to delete the "Controller" suffix accidentally when using the Add Controller dialog box.

When using the Add Controller dialog box you have the option to add action methods automatically for create, update, delete and details scenarios. If you click the `Add action methods for Create, Update, Delete and Details scenarios` checkbox this is the controller that will be created:

```
using System;
using System.Collections.Generic;
using System.Linq;
using System.Web;
using System.Web.Mvc;

namespace Lesson14b.Controllers
{
    public class Default1Controller : Controller
    {
        //
        // GET: /Default1/

        public ActionResult Index()
        {
            return View();
        }

        //
        // GET: /Default1/Details/5

        public ActionResult Details(int id)
        {
            return View();
        }

        //
        // GET: /Default1/Create

        public ActionResult Create()
        {
            return View();
        }

        //
        // POST: /Default1/Create

        [HttpPost]
        public ActionResult Create(FormCollection collection)
        {
            try
            {
```

```
        // TODO: Add insert logic here

        return RedirectToAction("Index");
    }
    catch
    {
        return View();
    }
}

//
// GET: /Default1/Edit/5

public ActionResult Edit(int id)
{
    return View();
}

//
// POST: /Default1/Edit/5

[HttpPost]
public ActionResult Edit(int id, FormCollection collection)
{
    try
    {
        // TODO: Add update logic here

        return RedirectToAction("Index");
    }
    catch
    {
        return View(),
    }
}

//
// GET: /Default1/Delete/5

public ActionResult Delete(int id)
{
    return View();
}

//
// POST: /Default1/Delete/5

[HttpPost]
public ActionResult Delete(int id, FormCollection collection)
{
    try
    {
        // TODO: Add delete logic here

        return RedirectToAction("Index");
```

```
                }
                catch
                {
                    return View();
                }
            }
        }
    }
```

TRY IT

In this lesson you update an existing action method to see the impact of changing the `ActionResult` that is returned by the action method and use the `HandleErrorAttribute` attribute to redirect the user to an error page in the event of an unhandled error.

Lesson Requirements

None.

Hints

None.

Step-by-Step

1. Open Microsoft Visual Web Developer 2010 Express.

2. Select New Project from the File menu.

3. Select **Visual C#** on the left side of the dialog box.

4. Select the **ASP.NET MVC 2 Web Application** template.

5. Enter **Lesson14b** in the Name field and **c:\ASPNETTrainer** in the Location field.

6. Open the HomeController.cs file and update the `About` action method of the `HomeController` to the following:

    ```
    public ActionResult About()
    {
        string time = String.Format("Current time: {0}", DateTime.Now.
        ToLongTimeString());
        return Content(time);
    }
    ```

7. Click the F5 button.

8. Navigate to the About Us page (see Figure 14B-2).

9. Stop debugging by closing the browser.

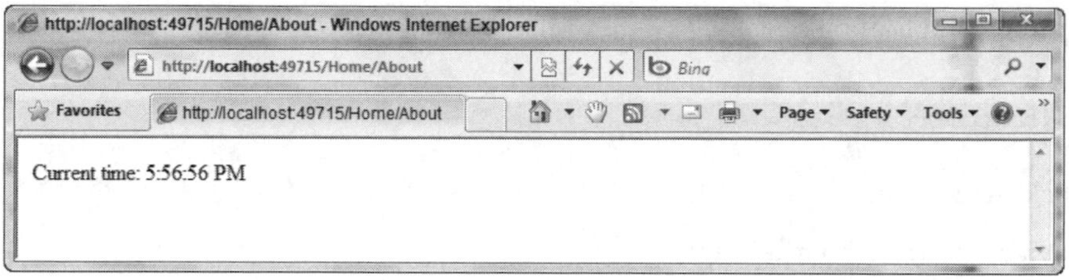

FIGURE 14B-2

Since the `About` action method does not return a view, only the string returned in the `ContentResult` is shown.

10. Update the `About` action method of the `HomeController` to the following:

```
public ActionResult About()
{
    throw new ApplicationException();
}
```

11. Click the F5 button.

12. Navigate to the About Us page (see Figure 14B-3).

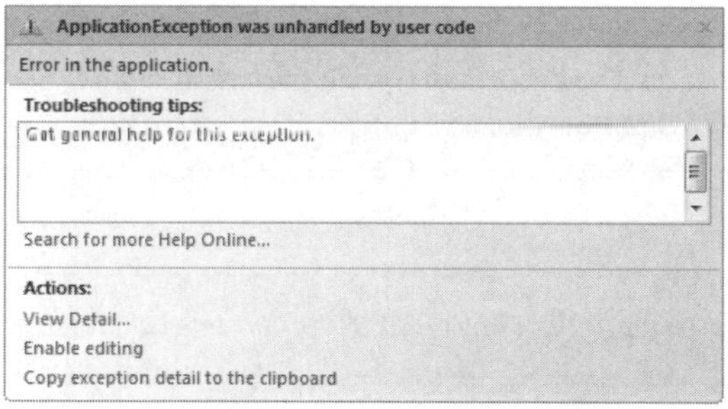

FIGURE 14B-3

The reason you see the unhandled exception, shown in Figure 14B-3, is that you are running in debug mode. Click Ctrl+F5 to run the application without debugging.

13. Click the F5 button to continue past the unhandled exception.

14. Stop debugging by closing the browser.

15. Open the application's root `web.config` file and add the following element to the `system.web` element.

```
<customErrors mode="On"/>
```

16. Click the F5 button.

17. Navigate to the About Us page.

18. Click the F5 button to continue (see Figure 14B-4).

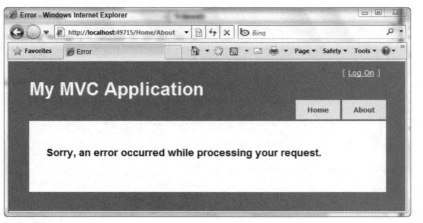

FIGURE 14B-4

 The reason that the user is redirected to the Error.aspx page is that the Home Controller *has been decorated with the* HandleErrorAttribute *attribute.*

Please select Lesson 14B on the DVD to view the video that accompanies this lesson.

15

URL Routing Overview

URL routing gives your application the ability to handle request URLs that do not map directly to specific files. Routing can be used to define URLs that are more meaningful to users and to improve the Search Engine Optimization (SEO) for your application. In this lesson I provide an overview of routing in ASP.NET 4. I cover the details for using routing in Web Forms and MVC in Lessons 15A and 15B, respectively.

Without URL routing, the URL for a page that lists recipes by category looks like this:

```
http://localhost/recipes/list.aspx?category=soup
```

With URL routing, the URL for the same page looks like this:

```
http://localhost/recipes/category/soup
```

This new URL is both easier for people to use and for search engines to index. Also, this new URL does not expose the file structure of your web application to the users.

To enable routing in your application, your application must have at least one route registered in the global `RouteTable`. The global `RouteTable` is defined in the `Global.asax` file and is initialized during the `Application_Start` method in the `Global.asax.cs` file.

Each route is a member of the `Route` class. The `Route` class is used to specify how routing is processed in your web application. You need to create a `Route` object for each unique URL pattern that your application needs to handle. These are the properties of the `Route` class:

- ➤ URL
- ➤ Defaults
- ➤ Constraints
- ➤ DataTokens
- ➤ RouteHandler

The URL property designates the URL pattern that the route will use. For example, if the following URL is used to return all of the recipes that were added on a particular day:

```
http://localhost/recipes/2010/4/15
```

this URL matches the following pattern:

```
recipes/{year}/{month}/{day}
```

Each route URL consists of several placeholders that are each delimited by curly brackets. The preceding example has three placeholders: year, month, and day. Each placeholder maps to a URL parameter.

The URL pattern can also contain literal values and more than one placeholder can be in each segment of the URL as long as they are separated by a literal value. Also, if you want to match additional segments you can create a catch-all segment by marking the last segment with an asterisk (*).

The following table shows some valid URL patterns with examples of matching URLs.

URL Pattern	Matching URL
/recipes/{year}/{month}/{day}	/recipes/2010/4/15
/recipes/{year}/{month}/{day}	/recipes/soup/cold/2010
/recipes/{year}/{month}/{day}	/recipes/one/two/three
/recipes/{table}/List.aspx	/recipes/categories/List.aspx
/recipes/{controller}/{action}/{id}	/recipes/view/soup/2
/recipes/{language}-{country}	/recipes/en-us
/recipes/{category}/{*values}	/recipes/soup/cold/2010

When a request comes into your web application, the request URL is parsed into a RouteValue Dictionary where the URL placeholders are the keys and the subsections of the URL are the values. The following table shows how the /recipes/{one}/{two}/{three} URL pattern will convert the specified URL into a RouteValueDictionary.

URL	RouteValueDictionary
/recipes/2010/4/15	{one} = 2010 {two} = 4 {three} = 15
/recipes/soup/list/2010	{one} = soup {two} = list {three} = 2010
/recipes/category/edit/12	{one} = category {two} = edit {three} = 12

Because the URL pattern that you are matching in the preceding table has three segments, all of the URLs that are matched against it must also have three segments. If you want a URL pattern to be able to match URLs that have fewer segments, use the Defaults property of the Route class to define the default values of the missing segments. The following code sets the Defaults property of the route named MyRoute to allow the third segment to be blank:

```
((Route)routes["MyRoute"]).Defaults = new RouteValueDictionary { { "three",
"" } };
```

The Constraints property of the Route class is used to specify constraints for the values of a segment. Regular expressions can be used to define the constraints. The following code sets the Constraints property of the route named MyRoute to only allow 4-digit numbers in the third segment of the URL:

```
((Route)routes["MyRoute"]).Constraints =
    new RouteValueDictionary { { "three", @"\d{4}" } };
```

The DataTokens property of the Route class is used to store values that are associated with the route, but are not used in the route-matching process. The DataTokens can be read by the page (ASP.NET Web Form) or controller (ASP.NET MVC) to which the URL is routed. The following code sets the DataTokens property of the route named MyRoute:

```
(Route)routes["MyRoute"]).DataTokens =
    new RouteValueDictionary { { "format", "long" } };
```

The values of the DataTokens can be accessed via the DataTokens collection of the RouteData method:

```
string format = RouteData.DataTokens["format"].ToString();
```

The final property of the Route class is the RouteHandler. For web applications that use the ASP.NET Web Forms framework the default RouteHandler is the WebFormRouteHandler, and for web applications that use the ASP.NET MVC framework the default RouteHandler is the MVCRouteHandler. Of course, you can write your own custom RouteHandler.

By default, routing does not handle the following two types of requests:

1. The URL matches a physical page on the web server.

2. The URL pattern has been explicitly disabled by using the Ignore method of the RouteCollection class.

Quite often, the RouteCollection will include more than one route. In that case, the order in which the routes have been added to the RouteCollection is very important. Route matching is attempted from the first route in order until the last route. For example, if the URL pattern matches the first route, that is the route that is used. If the URL pattern does not match the first route, the next route is tried. Therefore, if you are not careful with how you use default values, you may define a route that is never used.

15A

URL Routing in Web Forms

URL Routing was first introduced in the ASP.NET MVC framework and was later added to the ASP.NET Web Forms framework. In this lesson I show you how to enable and use routing in an ASP.NET Web Forms framework web application.

Only the MVC templates and the ASP.NET Dynamic Data templates have routing enabled by default. The ASP.NET Web Application template that I have been using in all of my examples does not have routing enabled by default. These are the four steps that must be completed to add routing to a web application that was created using a template that does not have routing enabled:

1.   Add a reference to the System.Web.Routing assembly (see Figure 15A-1).

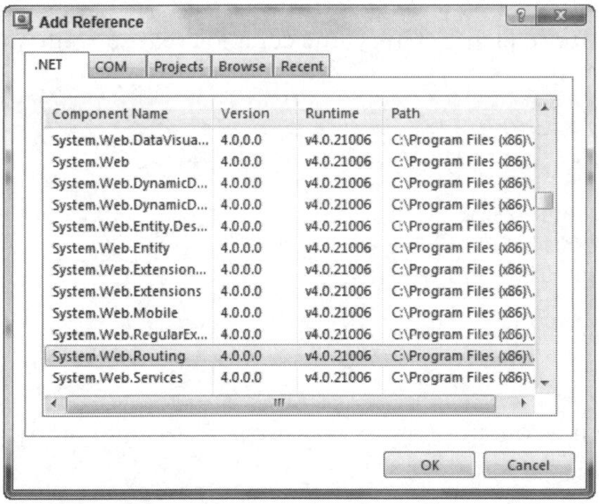

FIGURE 15A-1

2.   Add the following using statement to the Global.asax.cs file:

```
using System.Web.Routing;
```

3. Add the following `RegisterRoutes` method to the `Global.asax.cs` file:

```
void RegisterRoutes(RouteCollection routes)
{

)
```

4. Add the following line to the `Application_Start` method in the `Global.asax.cs` file:

```
RegisterRoutes(RouteTable.Routes);
```

Now you can start using routing in your ASP.NET Web Forms application.

ASP.NET Web Forms uses the `MapPageRoute` method of the `RouteCollection` class to define new routes. The `MapPageRoute` method can include the following parameters:

➤ **routeName** — This is a string representing the name of the route.

➤ **routeUrl** — This is a string that contains the URL pattern for the route.

➤ **physicalFile** — This is a string with the physical URL of the page.

➤ **checkPhysicalUrlAccessDefaults** — This is a Boolean that indicates whether the system should verify that the user has authority to access the page. The default value is True.

➤ **defaults** — This is a `RouteValueDictionary` containing the default values for the route.

➤ **constraints** — This is a `RouteValueDictionary` containing the constraints for the route.

➤ **dataTokens** — This is a `RouteValueDictionary` containing the data tokens for the route.

Only the route's name, URL, and physical file are required. This is the code to create a route in the `RegisterRoutes` method:

```
void RegisterRoutes(RouteCollection routes)
{
    routes.MapPageRoute(
        "Recipes",                  // Route Name
        "recipes/{category}",       // Route URL
        "~/List.aspx"               // Physical File
         );
    }
)
```

Figure 15A-2 shows a page that uses the following route:

```
http://localhost/recipes/soup
```

The page to which the route directs the user has access to the parameters of the route via the `Page.RouteData` property. The following code reads the category parameter of the preceding URL:

```
Page.RouteData.Values["category"]
```

The `Page.GetRouteURL` method is used to look up a route based on the name of the route and any parameter values. The following code will return a URL value of "/recipes/sandwich":

```
Page.GetRouteUrl("Recipes", new {category = "sandwich"})
```

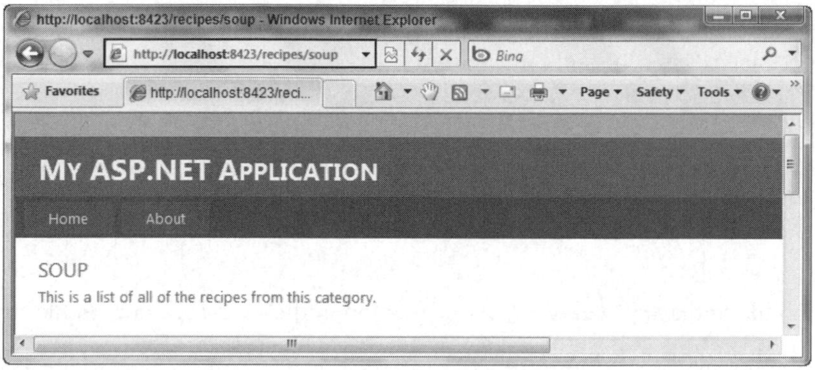

FIGURE 15A-2

The `Response.RedirectToRoute` method is used to redirect users to a route. Just like the `Page.GetRouteURL` method it takes the route name and any parameter values and redirects the user to the appropriate, routing-friendly URL.

TRY IT

In this lesson you enable and use routing.

Lesson Requirements

None.

Hints

None.

Step-by-Step

1. Open Microsoft Visual Web Developer 2010 Express.

2. Select New Project from the File menu.

3. Select **Visual C#** on the left side of the dialog box.

4. Select the **ASP.NET Web Application** template.

5. Enter **Lesson15a** in the Name field and **c:\ASPNETTrainer** in the Location field.

6. Click the OK button.

7. Right-click References in the Solution Explorer and select Add Reference to open the Add Reference dialog box. Click the .NET tab, select the **System.Web.Routing** component, and click the OK button.

8. Add the following `using` statement to the `Global.asax.cs` file:

```
using System.Web.Routing;
```

9. Add the following method to the `Global.asax.cs` file:

```
void RegisterRoutes(RouteCollection routes)
{
    routes.MapPageRoute(
        "Recipes",                // Route Name
        "recipes/{category}",     // Route URL
        "~/Recipes.aspx"          // Physical File
        );
}
```

10. Add the following line to the `Application_Start` method in the `Global.asax.cs` file.

```
RegisterRoutes(RouteTable.Routes);
```

11. Right-click the name of the project in the Solution Explorer window and select New Item from the Add menu to open the Add New Item dialog box. Select the **Web Form using Master Page** template, enter **Recipes.aspx** for the Name, and click the Add button. Select **Site.Master** as the Master Page and click the OK button.

12. Set the `Title` property of the `@Page` directive to **Recipes** on the `Recipes.aspx` page.

13. Add the following markup to the `Content2` control on the `Recipes.aspx` page:

```
<h1><asp:Literal ID="LiteralCategory" runat="server"/></h1>
 This is a list of all of the recipes from this category.
```

14. Add the following code to the `Page_Load` event of the `Recipes.aspx.cs` page:

```
this.LiteralCategory.Text = Page.RouteData.Values["category"].ToString();
```

15. Click the Ctrl+F5 button combination (see Figure 15A-3).

16. Replace Recipes.aspx in the address with **recipes/soup** (see Figure 15A-4).

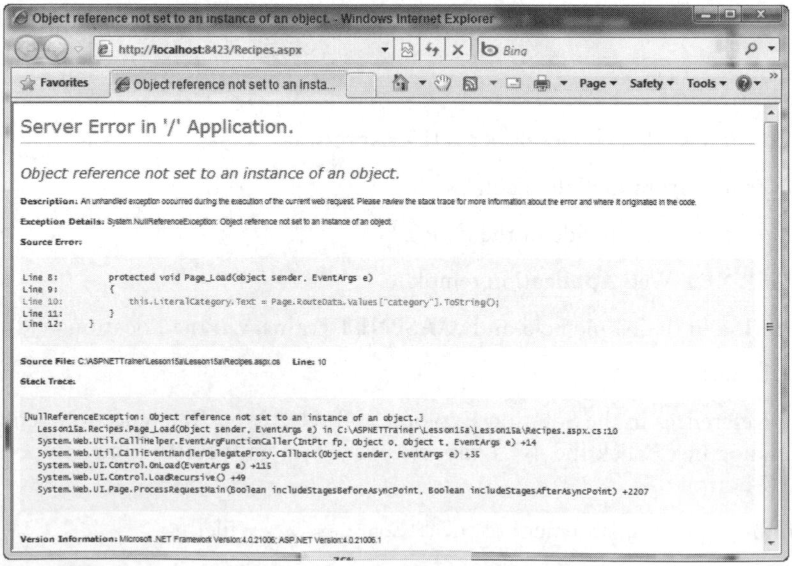

FIGURE 15A-3

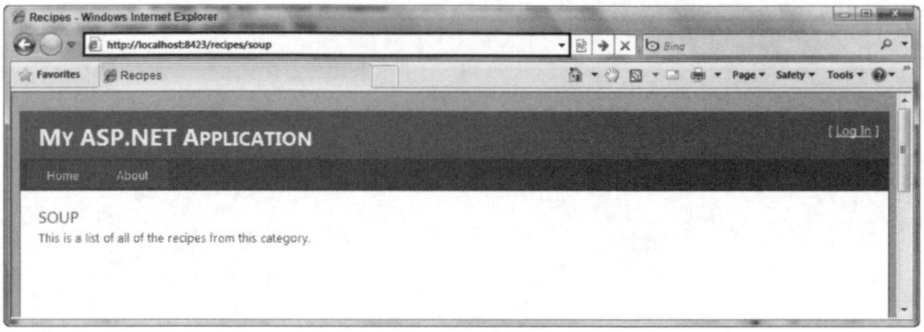

FIGURE 15A-4

 Please select Lesson 15A on the DVD to view the video that accompanies this lesson.

15B

URL Routing in MVC

As you learned in Lesson 8B, URL routing is a critical component of any ASP.NET MVC application. Routes are used to map incoming browser requests to their relevant controller action methods. In this lesson I show you how routing is used in an ASP.NET MVC web application, and I show you how to add a custom route.

When you create a new application using the ASP.NET MVC 2 Web Application template, a default `RegisterRoutes` method is created in the `Global.asax` page. This is the code in the default `RegisterRoutes` method:

```
public static void RegisterRoutes(RouteCollection routes)
{
    routes.IgnoreRoute("{resource}.axd/{*pathInfo}");

    routes.MapRoute(
        "Default",                      // Route name
        "{controller}/{action}/{id}",   // URL
        new { controller = "Home",
              action = "Index",
              id = UrlParameter.Optional}  // Defaults
    );
}
```

The first line of the `RegisterRoutes` method includes code to ignore any routes that include a file with the `.axd` file extension. You can use the `routes.IgnoreRoute` method to have routing ignore any files in your application.

An ASP.NET MVC web application uses the `MapRoute` method of the `RouteCollection` class to define new routes. The `MapRoute` method can include the following parameters:

➤ **name** — This is a string representing the name of the route. This is required.

➤ **url** — This is a string that contains the URL pattern for the route. This is required.

➤ **defaults** — This is an object containing the default values for the route.

➤ **constraints** — This is an object containing the constraints for the route.

➤ **namespaces** — This is a string array of the namespaces for the application.

The default route provided in an MVC application is the following:

```
{controller}/{action}/{id}
```

The first parameter maps to the controller. The second parameter maps to the action method of the controller and the third parameter is the string that is passed to the action method. Because the default route includes default values for each of the segments, only one route is required to handle all of the possible URL patterns.

The following table shows how different URLs will be handled based on the default route.

URL	Parameter Values
/home/about	controller = HomeController
	action method = About
	id = ""
/home	controller = HomeController
	action method = Index
	id = ""
/	controller = HomeController
	action method = Index
	id = ""

Because the default route handles URLs with any number of segments, it is possible to create an MVC application without adding any custom routes. However, imagine that your application allows users to view recipes by the month and year they were entered. Assume that this is the URL pattern that you would like to use:

```
/archive/{month}/{year}
```

If the user enters /archive/10/2010, the default route will assign the following parameter values:

> controller = ArchiveController
>
> action method = 10
>
> id = 2010

However, this is not your intent. You want this URL pattern to use the `HomeController` and the `Archive` action method. In this case you should add a new route. This is the code for a new route that includes both default values and constraint values:

```
routes.MapRoute(
    "RecipeArchive",
    "archive/{month}/{year}",
    new { controller = "Home",
          action = "Archive",
          month = "1",
          year = DateTime.Now.Year },
    new { month = @"\d{1,2}",
          year = @"\d{4}" }
);
```

If the month is not included in the URL pattern submitted by the request, January will be used as the default value. If the year is not submitted by the request, the current year will be used as the default value. Finally, if the month is not either one or two digits and the year is not four digits this route will not be applied.

> *Any new routes that you add must be placed above the Default rule or they will be ignored.*

If I add the following action method to the `HomeController`:

```
public string Archive(int month, int year)
{
    string message = string.Format("You have requested the archive for {0}/{1}.",
        month, year);
    return message;
}
```

Figure 15B-1 shows the page that will be rendered if I navigate to archive/10/2010.

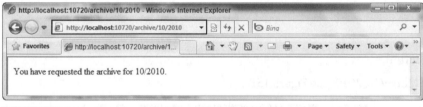

FIGURE 15B-1

TRY IT

In this lesson you add a custom route and create a new action method to consume the parameters that are returned from the new route.

Lesson Requirements

None.

Hints

None.

Step-by-Step

1. Open Microsoft Visual Web Developer 2010 Express.

2. Select New Project from the File menu.

3. Select **Visual C#** on the left side of the dialog box.

4. Select the **ASP.NET MVC 2 Web Application** template.

5. Enter **Lesson15b** in the Name field and **c:\ASPNETTrainer** in the Location field.

6. Open the `Global.asax.cs` file and add the following route to the `RegisterRoutes` method:

```
routes.MapRoute(
    "RecipeArchive",
    "archive/{month}/{year}",
    new { controller = "Home",
          action = "Archive",
          month = "1",
          year = DateTime.Now.Year },
    new { month = @"\d{1,2}",
          year = @"\d{4}" }
);
```

7. Add the following action method to the `HomeController`:

```
public string Archive(int month, int year)
{
    string message = String.Format("You have requested the archive for
        {0}/{1}.", month, year);
    return message;
}
```

8. Click the F5 button.

9. Navigate to **archive/10/2010** (see Figure 15B-2).

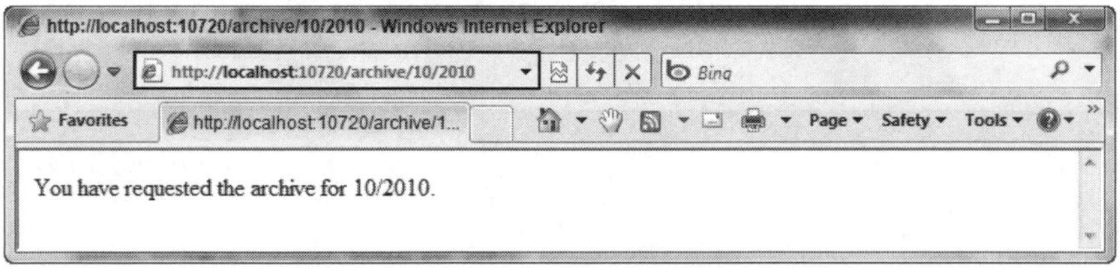

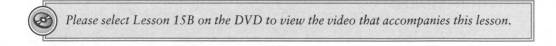

FIGURE 15B-2

Please select Lesson 15B on the DVD to view the video that accompanies this lesson.

SECTION VI
Validating User Input

16A

Validation Controls in Web Forms

Your web application must verify that all of the data entered by users is valid. This once formidable task has been made easier by the validation controls that are included with the ASP.NET Web Forms framework. In this lesson I show you how to use the various validation controls.

The validation controls are located on the Validation tab of the Toolbox. These are the validation controls:

➤ **CompareValidator** — This control is used to perform a data type check and to compare the values of two different controls.

➤ **CustomValidator** — This control is used to perform custom validation. I cover the CustomValidator in Lesson 17A.

➤ **RangeValidator** — This control is used to check that a given value is between two values.

➤ **RegularExpressionValidator** — This control is used to compare a value against a regular expression. It is used to validate the formats of such things as email addresses and phone numbers.

➤ **RequiredFieldValidator** — This control is used to ensure that a value has been entered.

➤ **ValidationSummary** — This control displays a list of all of the validation errors on the page.

All of the validation controls (except `ValidationSummary`) use the following properties:

➤ **ControlToValidate** — This is the ID of the control being validated. It is required.

➤ **Display** — This property designates how the control is displayed. It has three possible settings: None, Static, and Dynamic. Static is the default. I show you an example that uses a combination of these settings later in this lesson.

➤ **ErrorMessage** — This is the text that is displayed in the `ValidationSummary` when validation fails. Also, if the `Text` property is blank, this is the text that is displayed in the validation
control if validation fails.

➤ **IsValid** — This property indicates whether the value is valid.

➤ **SetFocusOnError** — This property specifies whether focus should be set to the
`ControlToValidate` if validation fails. The default value is false. If multiple controls fail
validation, the first control is given focus.

➤ **Text** — This is the text that is displayed in the control when validation fails. As I already
mentioned, if this property is blank, the `ErrorMessage` is displayed in the control.

➤ **ValidationGroup** — This designates the validation group to which the control belongs.

REQUIREDFIELDVALIDATOR

The most commonly used validation control is the `RequiredFieldValidator`. This is the markup
for a sample `RequiredFieldValidator`:

```
<asp:RequiredFieldValidator ID="RequiredFieldValidatorName" runat="server"
    ControlToValidate="TextBoxName" ErrorMessage="(Required)"/>
```

Figure 16A-1 shows a page, after the Submit button has been
clicked, that uses the preceding `RequiredFieldValidator`.

Because the control identified by the `ControlToValidate`
property was blank at the time the page was submitted, the
`RequiredFieldValidator` is displaying its error message. By
default, the text that is displayed in the validator control is not
formatted. If you want to format it, use the `CssClass` property
of the validation control. This is the cascading style sheet (CSS)
rule to change the color of the text to red:

FIGURE 16A-1

```
.validator
{
    color: Red;
}
```

This is the updated `RequiredFieldValidator` that uses the preceding CSS rule:

```
<asp:RequiredFieldValidator ID="RequiredFieldValidatorName" runat="server"
    ControlToValidate="TextBoxName" ErrorMessage="(Required)"
    CssClass="validator" />
```

The `RequiredFieldValidator` has one property that is unique: `InitialValue`. By default, the
`RequiredFieldValidator` assumes the initial value of the control being validated is blank, but there
are many times when this may not be the case. For example, if the `RequiredFieldValidator` is being
used to validate a drop-down list, the `InitialValue` property must be used.

COMPAREVALIDATOR

The CompareValidator serves three purposes. It can be used to verify that a value is of a certain data type, to compare the value to a fixed value, or to compare the value against the value in another control. These are the properties that are unique to the CompareValidator:

➤ **ControlToCompare** — This property specifies the control to compare to the control that is specified by the ControlToValidate property. By default, this property is blank.

➤ **Operator** — This property specifies the comparison operation to use. These are the options for the Operator property: Equal, NotEqual, GreaterThan, GreaterThanEqual, LessThan, LessThanEqual, and DataTypeCheck.

➤ **Type** — This is the data type that the value is converted to before being compared. If the value cannot be converted to this data type, validation fails. These are the options for the Type property: String, Integer, Double, Date and Currency.

➤ **ValueToCompare** — This property specifies the value to compare to the value of the control that is specified by the ControlToValidate property. By default, this property is blank.

Figure 16A-2 shows a page with four fields. On this page all of the fields are required. Therefore, I have added a RequiredFieldValidator for each of the fields on the page.

FIGURE 16A-2

This is the CompareValidator to verify that an integer greater than or equal to zero is entered in the Age field:

```
<asp:CompareValidator ID="CompareValidatorAge" runat="server"
    ControlToValidate="TextBoxAge" ErrorMessage="(Invalid Data)"
    CssClass="validator" ValueToCompare="0" Type="Integer"
    Operator="GreaterThanEqual" />
```

If I add the CompareValidator after the existing RequiredFieldValidator for the Age field and I enter text in the Age field, Figure 16A-3 shows the results.

Because "Test" is not an integer value, the CompareValidator fails and the value of its ErrorMessage property is displayed. However, there is a great deal of space before the text. The space is due to the fact that there is a RequiredFieldValidator before the CompareValidator. By default, the value of the `Display` property for all of the validation controls is Static. That means that all of the space needed to display the text is reserved in the UI just in case the error message needs to be displayed. The `Display` property can also be set to None or Dynamic. Setting the `Display` property to None hides the text. Setting the `Display` property to Dynamic dynamically adds space to the page to display the text if validation fails.

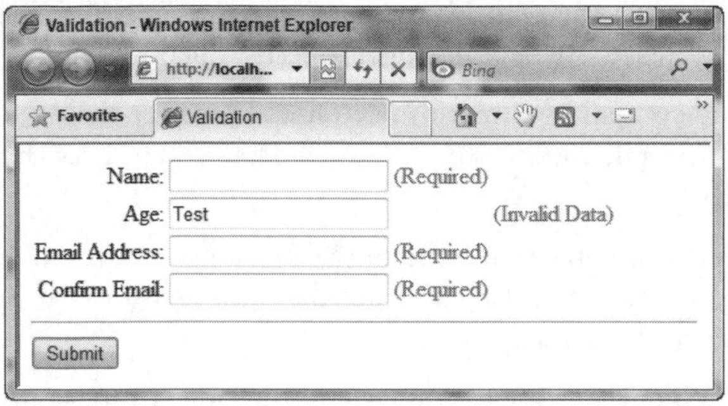

FIGURE 16A-3

Figure 16A-4 shows the same page with the `Display` property for the `RequiredFieldValidator` set to Dynamic.

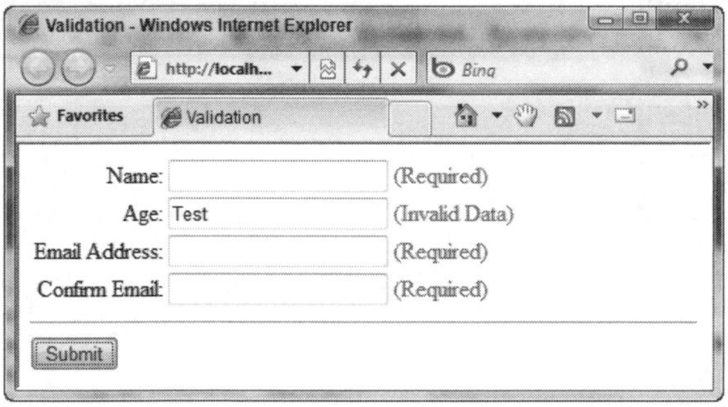

FIGURE 16A-4

The `CompareValidator` can also be used to compare the values in two fields. This is the `CompareValidator` to compare the values of the Email Address and the Confirm Email fields:

```
<asp:CompareValidator ID="CompareValidator1" runat="server"
    ControlToValidate="TextBoxConfirmEmail" ErrorMessage="(Compare Failed)"
    CssClass="validator" ControlToCompare="TextBoxEmail" />
```

Figure 16A-5 shows the page with the `CompareValidator` applied to the email addresses.

> The `CompareValidator` *is not triggered unless there is a value in the input field specified by its* `ControlToValidate` *property. In order to ensure that the* `CompareValidator` *is triggered, use the* `RequiredFieldValidator` *in conjunction with the* `CompareValidator`.

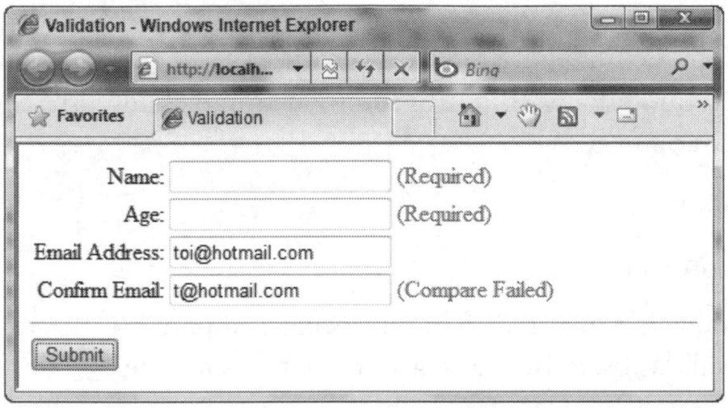

FIGURE 16A-5

REGULAREXPRESSIONVALIDATOR

The RegularExpressionValidator control is used to compare the value against a regular expression. A regular expression is a string of characters used to define a pattern of characters. This is a regular expression for an email address: ^\w+@[a-zA-Z_]+?\.[a-zA-Z]{2,3}$.

The RegularExpressionValidator only has one property that is unique to it: the Validation Expression property. The ValidationExpression property is a string that contains the regular expression used for the comparison. This is a RegularExpressionValidator that validates an email address:

```
<asp:RegularExpressionValidator ID="RegularExpressionValidator1" runat="server"
    ControlToValidate="TextBoxEmail"
    ValidationExpression="^\w+@[a-zA-Z_]+?\.[a-zA-Z]{2,3}$"
    ErrorMessage="(Invalid Format)" CssClass="validator" />
```

Figure 16A-6 shows the page with a RegularExpressionValidator applied to the Email Address field.

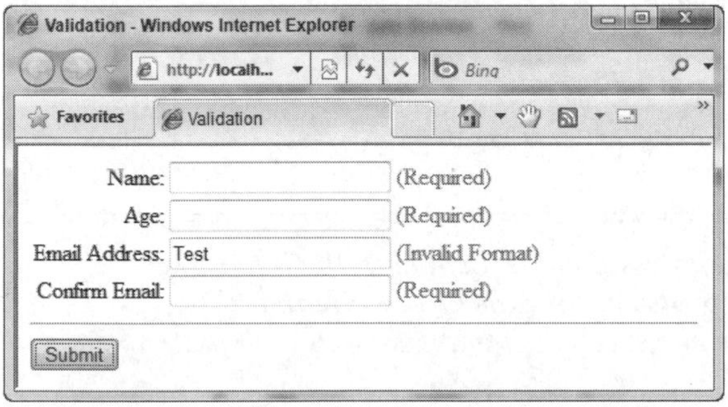

FIGURE 16A-6

> The RegularExpressionValidator *is not triggered unless there is a value in the* input field specified by its ControlToValidate *property. In order to ensure that* the RegularExpressionValidator *is triggered, use the* RequiredFieldValidator *in conjunction with the* RegularExpressionValidator.

RANGEVALIDATOR

The `RangeValidator` is used to verify that a value falls within a predefined range. These are the properties that are unique to the `RangeValidator`:

➤ **MinimumValue** — This is the minimum value.

➤ **MaximumValue** — This is the maximum value.

➤ **Type** — This is the data type that the value is converted to before being compared. If the value cannot be converted to this data type, validation fails. These are the options for the `Type` property: String, Integer, Double, Date and Currency.

In the earlier example I used a `CompareValidator` to ensure that the value entered into the Age field was a positive integer. I can use the `RangeValidator` to ensure that the value entered into the Age is within a certain range. For example, 200 should not be allowed in the field because no one lives that long. This is the `RangeValidator` to ensure that the value entered into the Age field is an integer between 0 and 110, inclusive:

```
<asp:RangeValidator ID="RangeValidator1" runat="server" CssClass="validator"
    ControlToValidate="TextBoxAge" MinimumValue="0" MaximumValue="110"
    Type="Integer" ErrorMessage="(Invalid Data)" />
```

Figure 16A-7 shows the page with the `RangeValidator` applied to the Age field.

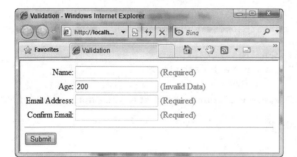

FIGURE 16A-7

> ⊗ *The* `RangeValidator` *is not triggered unless there is a value in the input filed specified by its* `ControlToValidate` *property. In order to ensure that the* `RangeValidator` *is triggered, use the* `RequiredFieldValidator` *in conjunction with the* `RangeValidator`*.*

VALIDATIONSUMMARY

The `ValidationSummary` control displays a list of all of the validation errors in one location. This is the markup for a sample `ValidationSummary`:

```
<asp:ValidationSummary ID="ValidationSummary1" runat="server" />
```

Figure 16A-8 shows the page with a ValidationSummary placed at the top of it.

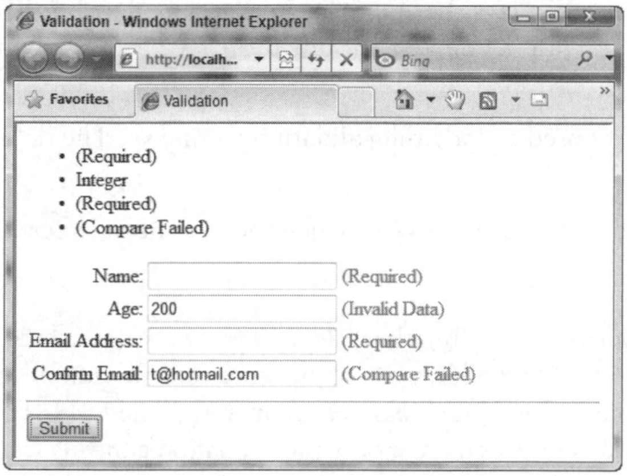

FIGURE 16A-8

The ValidationSummary shown in Figure 16A-8 is not very helpful. The validation controls should all be rewritten to use the Text property to indicate the information that should appear in the validation control and the ErrorMessage property to indicate the information that should appear in the ValidationSummary. Figure 16A-9 shows a more useful validation summary.

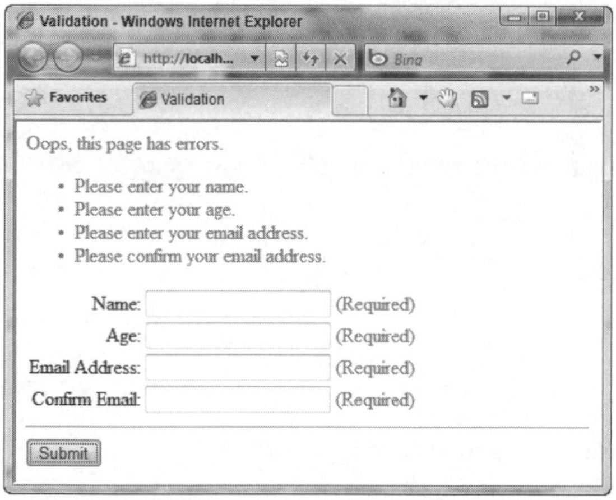

FIGURE 16A-9

This is the markup for the ValidationSummary shown in Figure 16A-9:

```
<asp:ValidationSummary ID="ValidationSummary1" runat="server" CssClass="validator"
    HeaderText="Oops, this page has errors." />
```

These are the properties that are unique to the ValidationSummary control:

➤ **DisplayMode** — This property specifies how the error messages will be formatted. These are the options for the DisplayMode property: BulletList, List and SingleParagraph. The default is BulletList and I personally always use the BulletList.

➤ **HeaderText** — This property specifies text to be used as a header above the error messages.

➤ **ShowMessageBox** — This Boolean property displays the summary in a popup alert box. The default is false. I recommend that you stick with the default for this property because popup boxes can be quite annoying.

➤ **ShowSummary** — This Boolean property is used to hide the validation summary. The default is true.

➤ **ValidationGroup** — This designates the group of controls for which the `ValidationSummary` displays error messages.

You may have noticed that all of the validation controls, including the `ValidationSummary`, include a `ValidationGroup` property. The `ValidationGroup` property allows you to group certain validation controls together. For example, a `Button` control also has a `ValidationGroup` property. If the `Validation Group` property for a button and a group of validation controls match, only the validation controls from the same `ValidationGroup` will be triggered when that button is clicked.

There are times when you may want to submit a form without triggering validation. For example, I do not want the `Cancel` button on the form shown in Figure 16A-10 to trigger validation. In that case, I set the `CausesValidation` property of the button to false.

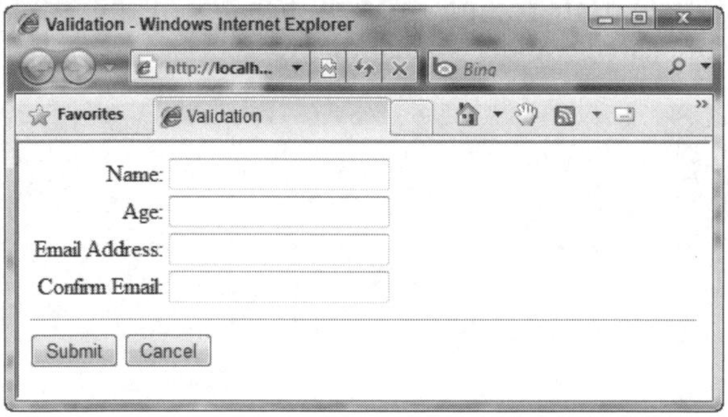

FIGURE 16A-10

This is the markup for the `Cancel` button.

```
<asp:Button ID="ButtonCancel" runat="server" Text="Cancel"
    CausesValidation="False" />
```

> *The* `Button`, `LinkButton` *and* `ImageButton` *controls all include the* `CausesValidation` *property.*

Validation controls perform validation on both the client and the server. The client-side validation is performed using JavaScript. If the browser does not have JavaScript enabled, the validation is only performed on the server. The validation controls always perform server-side validation. However, on the server-side, if one or more of the validation controls is not valid, no exceptions are thrown. Instead, you must check the `IsValid` property of the page to ensure that the `IsValid` property of each of the validation controls is true. The `Page.IsValid` property must be checked after a call to the `Page .Validate` method to ensure that all of the appropriate validation controls have been triggered. This is code that shows how to use the `Page.IsValid` property:

```csharp
protected void ButtonSubmit_Click(object sender, EventArgs e)
{
    Page.Validate();
    if (Page.IsValid)
    {
        // Do Something
    }
}
```

TRY IT

In this lesson you create a page with a number of validation controls, including a validation summary.

Lesson Requirements

None.

Hints

➤ Set the `Display` property for the validator to Dynamic to prevent the UI from reserving room for the error message.

➤ When using a `ValidationSummary` control make sure that the text in the `ErrorMessage` property and the `Text` property are different.

Step-By-Step

1. Open Microsoft Visual Web Developer 2010 Express.

2. Select New Project from the File menu.

3. Select **Visual C#** on the left side of the dialog box.

4. Select the **ASP.NET Empty Web Application** template.

5. Enter **Lesson16a** in the Name field and **c:\ASPNETTrainer** in the Location field. Click the OK button.

6. Right-click the name of the project in the Solution Explorer window and select New Item from the Add menu to open the Add New Item dialog box. Select the **Web Form** template, enter **CreateAccount.aspx** for the Name, and click the Add button.

7. Set the `title` element of the `CreateAccount.aspx` page to **Create Account**.

8. Add the following markup to the `div` element on the `CreateAccount.aspx` page:

```
<p>
    User Name:<br />
    <asp:TextBox ID="TextBoxUserName" runat="server" />
</p>
<p>
    Password:<br />
    <asp:TextBox ID="TextBoxPassword" runat="server" TextMode="Password" />
</p>
<p>
    Confirm Password:<br />
    <asp:TextBox ID="TextBoxConfirmPassword" runat="server" TextMode="Password"
/>
</p>
<hr />
<asp:Button ID="ButtonCreateAccount" runat="server" Text="Create Account" />
```

9. Add the following `RequiredFieldValidator` for the `TextBoxUserName` control:

```
<asp:RequiredFieldValidator ID="RequiredFieldValidatorUserName" runat="server"
    ControlToValidate="TextBoxUserName"
    ErrorMessage="Please enter your user name." Text="!" />
```

10. Add the following `RequiredFieldValidator` for the `TextBoxPassword` control:

```
<asp:RequiredFieldValidator ID="RequiredFieldValidatorPassword" runat="server"
    ControlToValidate="TextBoxPassword"
    ErrorMessage="Please enter your password." Text="!" />
```

11. Add the following `RequiredFieldValidator` for the `TextBoxConfirmPassword` control:

```
<asp:RequiredFieldValidator ID="RequiredFieldValidatorConfirmPassword"
    runat="server" ControlToValidate="TextBoxConfirmPassword"
    ErrorMessage="Please confirm your password." Text="!" Display="Dynamic"/>
```

> The `Display` *property of the preceding validation control is set to Dynamic so that space is not reserved for the error message.*

12. Add the following `CompareValidator` for the `TextBoxConfirmPassword` control:

```
<asp:CompareValidator ID="CompareValidatorPassword" runat="server"
    ErrorMessage="Please verify that the two passwords match." Text="!"
    ControlToValidate="TextBoxConfirmPassword"
    ControlToCompare="TextBoxPassword" />
```

13. Click the F5 button.

14. Click the Create Account button (see Figure 16A-11).

15. Stop debugging by closing the browser.

16. Add a `ValidationSummary` control to the page by dragging it from the Toolbox.

FIGURE 16A-11

17. Verify that the code in the CreateAccount.aspx page matches the following:

```
<%@ Page Language="C#" AutoEventWireup="true" CodeBehind="CreateAccount.aspx.cs"
    Inherits="Lesson16a.CreateAccount" %>

<!DOCTYPE html PUBLIC "-//W3C//DTD XHTML 1.0 Transitional//EN"
    "http://www.w3.org/TR/xhtml1/DTD/xhtml1-transitional.dtd">
<html xmlns="http://www.w3.org/1999/xhtml">
<head runat="server">
    <title>Create Account</title>
</head>
<body>
    <form id="form1" runat="server">
    <div>
        <p>
            User Name:
            <br />
            <asp:TextBox runat="server" ID="TextBoxUserName" />
            <asp:RequiredFieldValidator ID="RequiredFieldValidatorUserName"
                runat="server" ControlToValidate="TextBoxUserName"
                ErrorMessage="Please enter your user name." Text="!" />
        </p>
        <p>
            Password:
            <br />
            <asp:TextBox runat="server" ID="TextBoxPassword"
                TextMode="Password" />
            <asp:RequiredFieldValidator ID="RequiredFieldValidatorPassword"
                runat="server" ControlToValidate="TextBoxPassword"
                ErrorMessage="Please enter your password." Text="!" />
        </p>
        <p>
            Confirm Password:
            <br />
            <asp:TextBox runat="server" ID="TextBoxConfirmPassword"
                TextMode="Password" />
            <asp:RequiredFieldValidator ID="RequiredFieldValidatorConfirmPassword"
                runat="server"
```

```
                    ControlToValidate="TextBoxConfirmPassword"
                    ErrorMessage="Please confirm your password." Text="!"
                    Display="Dynamic" />
                <asp:CompareValidator ID="CompareValidatorPassword" runat="server"
                    ErrorMessage="Please verify that the two passwords match."
                    Text="!" ControlToValidate="TextBoxConfirmPassword"
                    ControlToCompare="TextBoxPassword" />
            </p>
            <hr />
            <asp:Button ID="ButtonCreateAccount" runat="server"
                Text="Create Account" />
            <asp:ValidationSummary ID="ValidationSummary1" runat="server" />
        </div>
        </form>
    </body>
    </html>
```

18. Press the F5 button.

19. Enter some text in the Password field and click the Create Account button (see Figure 16A-12).

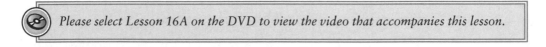

FIGURE 16A-12

Please select Lesson 16A on the DVD to view the video that accompanies this lesson.

16B

Validation Helpers in MVC

Your web application must verify that all of the data entered by users is valid. This once formidable task has been made easier by a special class of HTML helpers that support validating input from an HTML form. Most of these special HTML helpers are members of the `Validation Extensions` class. In this lesson I show you how to use the validation helpers provided by the ASP.NET MVC framework.

VALIDATION HELPERS

These are the validation helpers that are included as part of the ASP.NET MVC framework:

➤ **Html.EnableClientValidation()** — This method enables client-side validation.

➤ **Html.Validate()** — This method retrieves the validation metadata for the given model and applies each rule.

➤ **Html.ValidateFor()** — This method retrieves the validation metadata for the given strongly-typed object and applies each rule.

➤ **Html.ValidationMessage()** — This method displays the error message if an error exists for a given field.

➤ **Html.ValidationMessageFor()** — This method displays all of the error messages associated with a strongly-typed object.

➤ **Html.ValidationSummary()** — This method returns a bulleted list of all of the errors in the `ModelStateDictionary` object.

> To enable client-side validation, you must add this line of code
>
> ```
> <% Html.EnableClientValidation(); %>
> ```
>
> *before*
>
> ```
> <% using (Html.BeginForm()) {%>
> ```
>
> *and your page must refer to the following three files from the Scripts folder:*
>
> ```
> <script src="../../Scripts/jquery-1.3.2.js"
>     type="text/javascript" />
> <script src="../../Scripts/jquery.validate.js"
>     type="text/javascript" />
> <script src="../../Scripts/MicrosoftMvcJQueryValidation.js"
>     type="text/javascript" />
> ```

MODEL BINDING

The `ModelStateDictionary` represents the state of an attempt to bind data from a model to an action method. This is the model I use for this lesson:

```
namespace Lesson16b.Models
{
    public class Contact
    {
        public string Name { get; set; }
        public int Age { get; set; }
        public string EmailAddress { get; set; }
        public string ConfirmEmailAddress { get; set; }
    }
}
```

The simplest way to create a Create view for the `Contact` model is to use the Add View dialog box shown in Figure 16B-1.

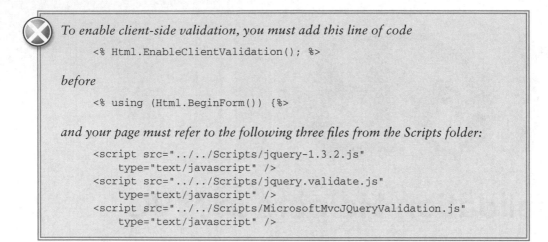

FIGURE 16B-1

This is the resulting markup:

```
<%@ Page Title="" Language="C#" MasterPageFile="~/Views/Shared/Site.Master"
    Inherits="System.Web.Mvc.ViewPage<Lesson16b.Models.Contact>" %>

<asp:Content ID="Content1" ContentPlaceHolderID="TitleContent" runat="server">
    Create
</asp:Content>

<asp:Content ID="Content2" ContentPlaceHolderID="MainContent" runat="server">

    <h2>Create</h2>

    <% using (Html.BeginForm()) {%>
        <%: Html.ValidationSummary(true) %>

        <fieldset>
            <legend>Fields</legend>

            <div class="editor-label">
                <%: Html.LabelFor(model => model.Name) %>
            </div>
            <div class="editor-field">
                <%: Html.TextBoxFor(model => model.Name) %>
                <%: Html.ValidationMessageFor(model => model.Name) %>
            </div>

            <div class="editor-label">
                <%: Html.LabelFor(model => model.Age) %>
            </div>
            <div class="editor-field">
                <%: Html.TextBoxFor(model => model.Age) %>
                <%: Html.ValidationMessageFor(model => model.Age) %>
            </div>

            <div class="editor-label">
                <%: Html.LabelFor(model => model.EmailAddress) %>
            </div>
            <div class="editor-field">
                <%: Html.TextBoxFor(model => model.EmailAddress) %>
                <%: Html.ValidationMessageFor(model => model.EmailAddress) %>
            </div>

            <div class="editor-label">
                <%: Html.LabelFor(model => model.ConfirmEmailAddress) %>
            </div>
            <div class="editor-field">
                <%: Html.TextBoxFor(model => model.ConfirmEmailAddress) %>
                <%: Html.ValidationMessageFor(model => model.ConfirmEmailAddress) %>
            </div>

            <p>
                <input type="submit" value="Create" />
            </p>
```

```
        </fieldset>

    <% } %>

    <div>
        <%: Html.ActionLink("Back to List", "Index") %>
    </div>

</asp:Content>
```

Validation errors are passed from a controller to a view by passing the `ModelStateDictionary`. Both the view and the controller have a `ModelState` property to access the `ModelStateDictionary`. `ModelState` has the following properties:

➤ **Errors** — This property contains all of the errors that occurred during model binding. The view can add errors to the `ModelState` using the `AddModelError` method.

➤ **Value** — This property contains the original values of the fields.

 Model binding is when the data from the incoming request is bound to the fields in the model.

This is the `Create` action method for the controller:

```
//
// GET: /Contact/Create

public ActionResult Create()
{
    return View();
}

//
// POST: /Contact/Create

[HttpPost]
public ActionResult Create(Models.Contact contact)
{
    // All of the fields are required.
    if (String.IsNullOrEmpty(contact.Name))
        ModelState.AddModelError("Name", "Please enter your name.");

    if (String.IsNullOrEmpty(contact.EmailAddress))
        ModelState.AddModelError("EmailAddress",
            "Please enter your email address.");

    if (String.IsNullOrEmpty(contact.ConfirmEmailAddress))
        ModelState.AddModelError("ConfirmEmailAddress",
            "Please confirm your email address.");

    try
```

```
        {
            if (ModelState.IsValid)
            {
                // TODO: Add insert logic here
                return RedirectToAction("Index");
            }
            else
            {
                return View(contact);
            };
        }
        catch
        {
            return View(contact);
        }
    }
```

The preceding `Create` action method uses the `AddModelError` method to add error messages to the `ModelState`. It confirms that values were entered for the Name, EmailAddress, and ConfirmEmailAddress fields. However, it does not need to confirm that the Age field is not blank because age is defined to be an integer and as such does not accept `null` values. Therefore, an error will automatically be added to the `ModelState` if the model binding process tries to bind a `null` value to the Age field.

Figure 16B-2 shows the page that is rendered when the Create button is clicked while the form is still blank.

FIGURE 16B-2

The automatic error message that is generated for the Age field does not match the format of the other error messages. This is the code to replace the automatically generated error message:

```
if (ModelState["Age"].Value.AttemptedValue.ToString().Length == 0)
{
    ModelState["Age"].Errors.Clear();
    ModelState.AddModelError("Age", "Please enter your age.");
}
```

The original error message has to be cleared from the ModelState before adding the new error message. If you do not clear the original error message, both error messages will appear in the validation summary.

This is the code to add some additional validation:

```
// Age must be between 0 and 110
if ((contact.Age <0) || (contact.Age > 110))
    ModelState.AddModelError("Age", "Age must be between 0 and 110.");

// EmailAddress and ConfirmEmailAddress must match
if (contact.EmailAddress != contact.ConfirmEmailAddress)
    ModelState.AddModelError("ConfirmEmailAddress",
        "Please verify that the email addresses match.");
```

Figure 16B-3 shows the page that is rendered when invalid data is entered in both the Age field and the ConfirmEmailAddress field before clicking the Create button.

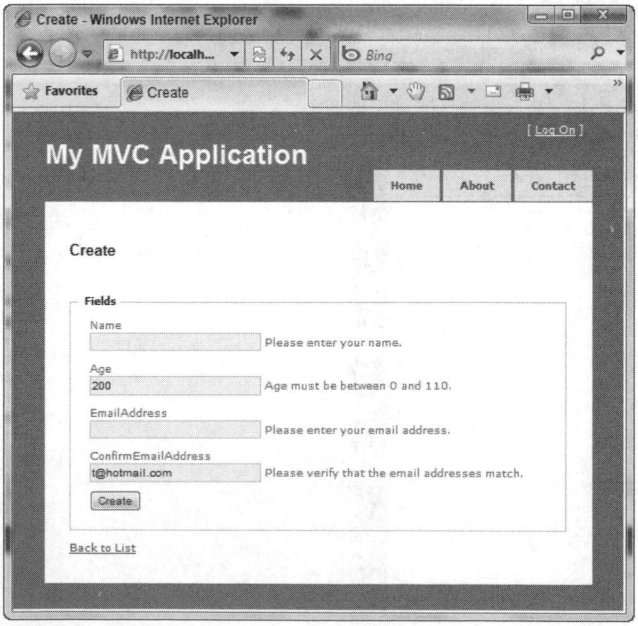

FIGURE 16B-3

> *I do not recommend that you add your validation logic to the controller. Instead, you should add it to your model. I show you how to add your validation logic to your model in Lesson 17B.*

VALIDATION SUMMARY

The `ValidationSummary` method returns a bulleted list of validation messages from the `ModelState Dictionary` object. This is the code to add a summary of the validation errors to the page:

```
<%= Html.ValidationSummary("Create was unsuccessful. Please correct the errors and
    try again.") %>
```

This sample `ValidationSummary` includes a message that will be included before the bulleted list of error messages. The message is not required. Figure 16B-4 shows the page that is rendered with the preceding validation summary added to the top of the page.

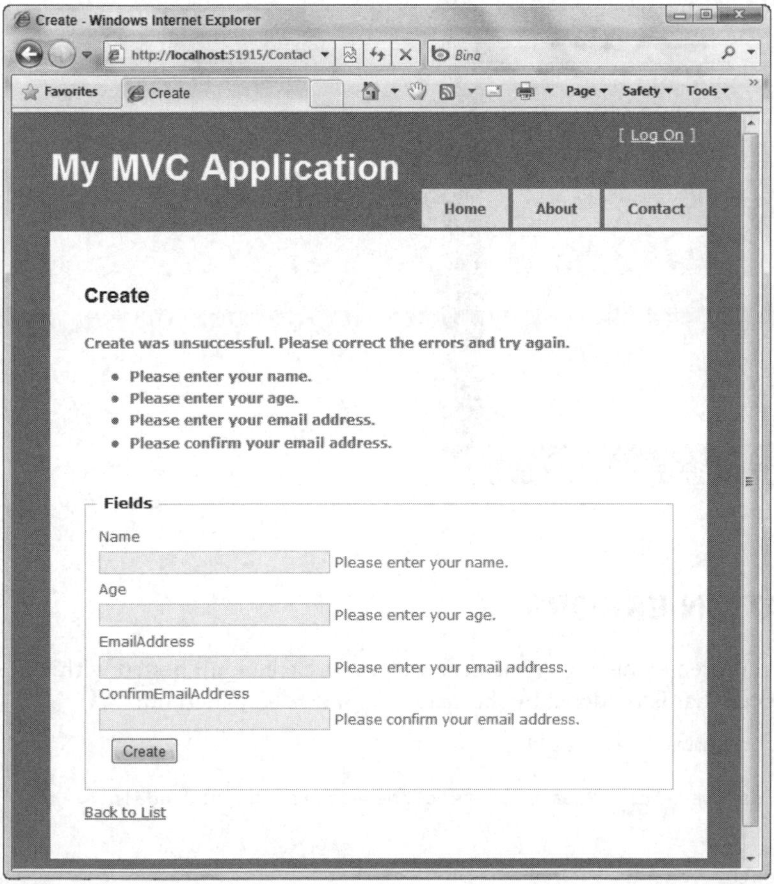

FIGURE 16B-4

In Figure 16B-4 the text used in the validation messages and in the validation summary are identical. When using the `ValidationSummary` method, you should modify the text that appears in the error messages so that they are not the same as the text that appears in the summary. This is an updated `ValidationMessageFor` method for the Name field that uses an asterisk in place of the error message as the text for the message:

```
<%= Html.ValidationMessageFor(model => model.Name, "*") %>
```

The complete error message will still be displayed in the `validation summary`. Figure 16B-5 shows the form after all of the fields have had their error text set to an asterisk.

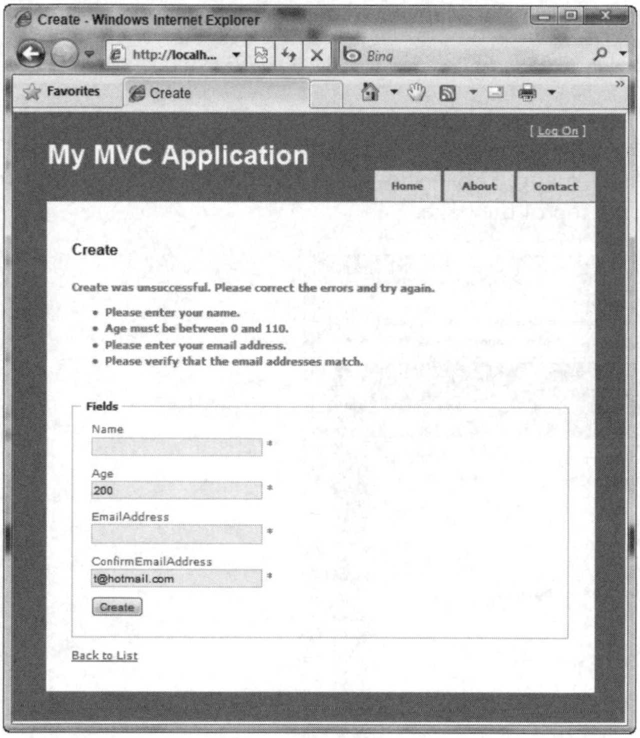

FIGURE 16B-5

RENDERING VALIDATION ERRORS

The validation summary is rendered using a `span` element and an `ul` element all nested within a `div` element. This is sample markup that is rendered by the `ValidationSummary` method:

```
<div class="validation-summary-errors">
    <span>
        Create was unsuccessful. Please correct the errors and try again.
    </span>
<ul>
        <li>Please enter your name.</li>
        <li>Age must be between 0 and 110.</li>
```

```
            <li>Please enter your email address.</li>
            <li>Please verify that the email addresses match.</li>
        </ul>
    </div>
```

The `div` element uses the `validation-summary-errors` class defined in the `Site.css` file located in the Content folder to style its content. This is how the CSS rule that renders all of the text using a bold, red font is defined:

```
.validation-summary-errors
{
    font-weight: bold;
    color: #ff0000;
}
```

The validation messages are rendered using a `span` element. This is the markup that is rendered for the Name field's validation message:

```
<span class="field-validation-error">*</span>
```

This is how the `field-validation-error` CSS rule that renders all of the text using a red font is defined:

```
.field-validation-error
{
    color: #ff0000;
}
```

If the field is invalid, the `input` element has the `input-validation-error` class applied to it in order to change the background color of the element. This is the markup that is rendered for the Name field:

```
<input class="input-validation-error" id="Name" name="Name" type="text" value="" />
```

This is how the `input-validation-error` CSS rule that changes the background color to light red is defined:

```
.input-validation-error
{
    border: 1px solid #ff0000;
    background-color: #ffeeee;
}
```

> *You can modify any of the styles defined in the* `Site.css` *file.*

TRY IT

In this lesson you use the validation helpers to provide both server-side and client-side validation on a web page.

Lesson Requirements

None.

Hints

None.

Step-by-Step

1. Open Microsoft Visual Web Developer 2010 Express.

2. Select New Project from the File menu.

3. Select **Visual C#** on the left side of the dialog box.

4. Select the **ASP.NET MVC 2 Web Application** template.

5. Enter **Lesson16b** in the Name field and **c:\ASPNETTrainer** in the Location field. Click the OK button.

6. Right-click the Models folder and select Class from the Add menu to create a class named **User.cs**.

7. Update the code for the `User.cs` class to the following:

    ```
    namespace Lesson16b.Models
    {
        public class User
        {
            public string UserName { get; set; }
            public string Password { get; set; }
            public string ConfirmPassword { get; set; }
        }
    }
    ```

8. Build the project by selecting Build Lesson16b from the Build menu.

9. Right-click the Views folder and select New Folder from the Add menu to add a subfolder named **User**.

10. Right-click the User folder and select View from the Add menu to open the Add View dialog box (see Figure 16B-6). Set the View name to **Create,** check the `Create a strongly-type view` checkbox, and select **Lesson16b.Models.User** as the View data class and **Create** as the View content. Make sure the `Select master page` checkbox is checked and click the Add button.

11. Replace the HTML helper that renders a `TextBox` with the HTML helper that renders a password for the Password field:

    ```
    <%= Html.PasswordFor(model => model.Password) %>
    ```

12. Replace the HTML helper that renders a `TextBox` with the HTML helper that renders a password for the ConfirmPassword field:

    ```
    <%= Html.PasswordFor(model => model.ConfirmPassword) %>
    ```

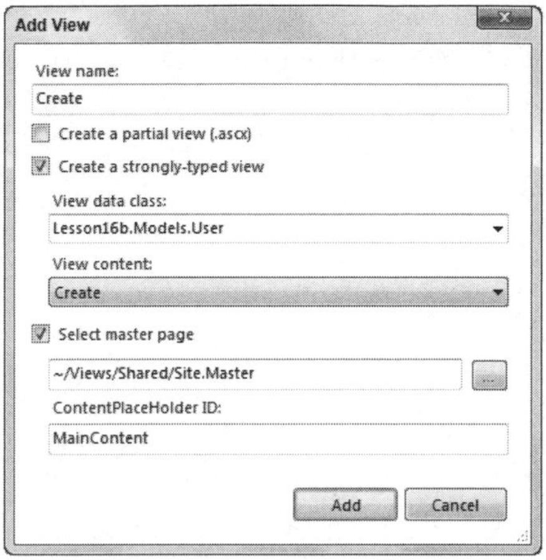

FIGURE 16B-6

13. Right-click the Controllers folder, select Controller from the Add menu, enter **UserController** for the name of the controller, check the Add action methods for Create, Update, Delete, and Details scenarios checkbox, and click the Add button (see Figure 16B-7).

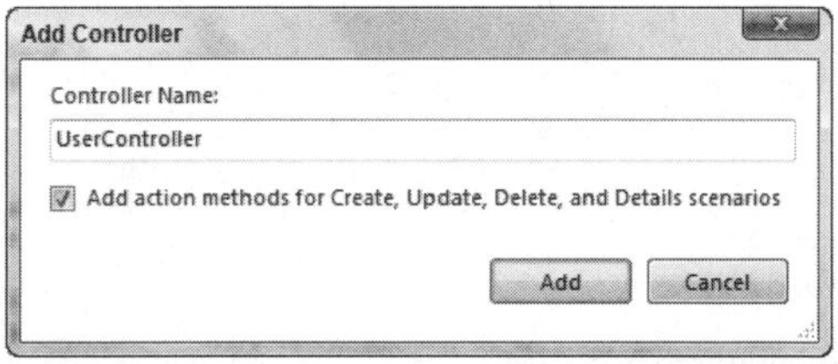

FIGURE 16B-7

14. Update the `Create` action item that accepts a POST that is in the `UserController` to the following:

```
[HttpPost]
public ActionResult Create(Models.User user)
{
    // All of the fields are required.
    if (String.IsNullOrEmpty(user.UserName))
        ModelState.AddModelError("UserName", "Please enter your user name.");

    if (String.IsNullOrEmpty(user.Password))
        ModelState.AddModelError("Password", "Please enter your password");

    if (String.IsNullOrEmpty(user.ConfirmPassword))
        ModelState.AddModelError("ConfirmPassword",
            "Please confirm your password.");

    // Password must match ConfirmPassword.
    if (user.Password != user.ConfirmPassword)
```

```
            ModelState.AddModelError("ConfirmPassword",
                "Please verify that the passwords match.");

        try
        {
            if (ModelState.IsValid)
            {
                // TODO: Add insert logic here
                return RedirectToAction("Index");
            }
            else
            {
                return View(user);
            };
        }
        catch
        {
            return View(user);
        }
    }
```

15. Open the `Site.Master` file that is located in the Shared subfolder of the Views folder. Add the following `li` element to the unordered list that is used to render the menu:

```
<li><%: Html.ActionLink("User", "Create", "User")%></li>
```

16. Click the F5 button.

17. Click the User tab.

18. Click the Create button (see Figure 16B-8).

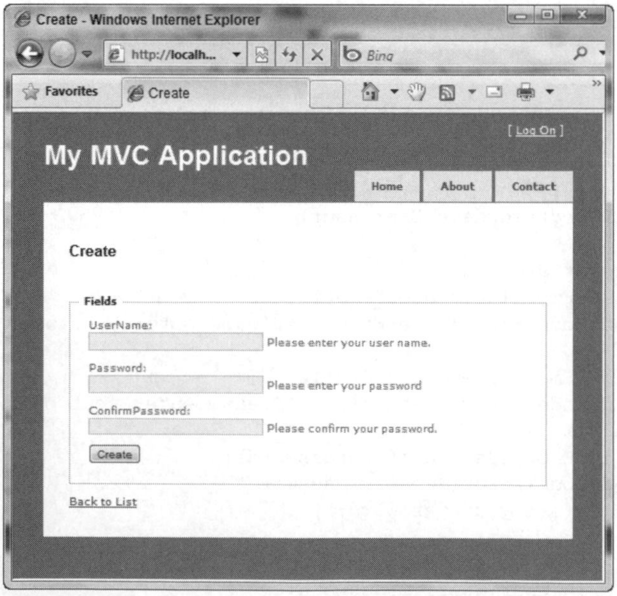

FIGURE 16B-8

19. Stop debugging by closing the browser.

20. Add the following line of code before the BeginForm method of the Create view to enable client-side validation:

```
<% Html.EnableClientValidation(); %>
```

21. Add the following references to the head element of the Site.Master file:

```
<script src="../../Scripts/MicrosoftAjax.js" type="text/javascript"></script>
<script src="../../Scripts/MicrosoftMvcAjax.js" type="text/javascript"></script>
<script src="../../Scripts/MicrosoftMvcValidation.js"
    type="text/javascript"></script>
```

22. Click the F5 button.

23. Click the User tab.

24. Click the Create button.

> *Since the model used for this lesson does not include any validation logic, the validation messages are being generated from the Create action method. In Lesson 17B I show you how to add validation logic to your model.*

> *Please select Lesson 16B on the DVD to view the video that accompanies this lesson.*

17A

Custom Validators in Web Forms

In Lesson 16A I showed you how to use all of the standard validation controls. Sometimes, you will find that none of the standard validation controls perform the exact type of validation that you need. In this lesson I show you how to create and use a CustomValidator control.

The CustomValidator control uses all of the same properties as the standard validation controls, plus two very unique properties. These are the unique properties of the CustomValidator:

➤ **ClientValidationFunction** — This is the name of the client-side script used to perform validation on the client. This property is not required.

➤ **ValidateEmptyText** — This Boolean property is used to trigger validation when the value of input field specified by the ControlToValidate property is empty. The default value is false.

Another unique feature of the CustomValidator is that the ControlToValidate property is not required. If the ControlToValidate property is left blank, the CustomValidator is always triggered on postback, unless it belongs to a different ValidationGroup from the control that triggered the postback.

The CustomValidator has one unique event:

➤ **ServerValidate** — This event is raised when the custom validation is performed on the server. This is required.

This is the markup for a CustomValidator:

```
<asp:CustomValidator ID="CustomValidator1" runat="server"
    ErrorMessage="CustomValidator"
    OnServerValidate="CustomValidator1_ServerValidate" />
```

Notice that the OnServerValidate method points to the ServerValidate event that it triggers. This is an empty ServerValidate event handler:

```
protected void CustomValidator1_ServerValidate(object source,
    ServerValidateEventArgs args)
{

}
```

These are the properties of the `ServerValidateEventArgs` class:

➤ **IsValid** — This Boolean property is used to indicate whether validation has succeeded.

➤ **Value** — This is the value to validate. If the `ControlToValidate` property is blank on the CustomValidator, this is empty.

Figure 17A-1 shows a page with a group of checkboxes.

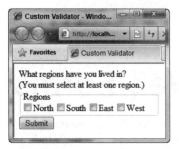

FIGURE 17A-1

I need to validate that at least one of the checkboxes has been checked. Because none of the standard validation controls will work, I need to use a `CustomValidator`. This is the markup for the `CustomValidator`:

```
<asp:CustomValidator ID="CustomValidatorRegion" runat="server"
    ErrorMessage="Please select at least one region."
    OnServerValidate="CustomValidatorRegion_ServerValidate" Display="Dynamic" />
```

This is the code to handle the `ServerValidate` event:

```
protected void CustomValidatorRegion_ServerValidate(object source,
    ServerValidateEventArgs args)
{
    if (!CheckBoxNorth.Checked && !CheckBoxSouth.Checked && !CheckBoxEast.Checked
        && !CheckBoxWest.Checked)
    {
        args.IsValid = false;
    }
    else
    {
        args.IsValid = true;
    };
}
```

Figure 17A-2 shows the page with the `CustomValidator`.

FIGURE 17A-2

This CustomValidator always requires a complete roundtrip to the server because I have not defined any client-side code. This is the updated markup for the CustomValidator to enable client-side validation:

```
<asp:CustomValidator ID="CustomValidatorRegion" runat="server"
    ErrorMessage="Please select at least one region."
    OnServerValidate="CustomValidatorRegion_ServerValidate" Display="Dynamic"
    ClientValidationFunction="regionsValidate" />
```

The ClientValidationFunction points to the regionsValidate function, which is a JavaScript function. JavaScript is covered in Lesson 23. This is the regionsValidate JavaScript function:

```
function regionsValidate(source, args)
{
    if (!document.getElementById("CheckBoxNorth").checked &&
        !document.getElementById("CheckBoxSouth").checked &&
        !document.getElementById("CheckBoxEast").checked &&
        !document.getElementById("CheckBoxWest").checked)
        args.IsValid = false;
}
```

TRY IT

In this lesson you use a CustomValidator to add customized validation logic that runs on both the server and the client.

Lesson Requirements

None.

Hints

➤   Add client-side validation to your CustomValidator to enhance the validation process by checking the user's input on the client before it is sent to the server.

Step-by-Step

1. Open Microsoft Visual Web Developer 2010 Express.

2. Select New Project from the File menu.

3. Select **Visual C#** on the left side of the dialog box.

4. Select the **ASP.NET Empty Web Application** template.

5. Enter **Lesson17a** in the Name field and **c:\ASPNETTrainer** in the Location field. Click the OK button.

6. Right-click the name of the project in the Solution Explorer window and select New Item from the Add menu to open the Add New Item dialog box. Select the **Web Form** template, enter **EvenNumber.aspx** for the Name, and click the Add button.

7. Set the `title` element of the `EvenNumber.aspx` page to **Even Number**.

8. Add the following markup to the `EvenNumber.aspx` page:

```
What is your favorite even number?
<asp:TextBox ID="TextBoxEvenNumber" runat="server" Columns="5" MaxLength="5" />
<hr />
<asp:Button ID="ButtonSubmit" runat="server" Text="Submit" />
```

9. Add a `CustomValidator` named **CustomValidatorEvenNumber** after the `ButtonSubmit` control with the following markup:

```
<asp:CustomValidator ID="CustomValidatorEvenNumber" runat="server"
    ErrorMessage="Please enter an EVEN number."
    ControlToValidate="TextBoxEvenNumber" ValidateEmptyText="True" />
```

10. View the `EvenNumber.aspx` page in Design view and double-click the `CustomValidator` to automatically generate the `ServerValidate` event handler.

11. Update the event handler code to the following:

```
protected void CustomValidatorEvenNumber_ServerValidate(object source,
    ServerValidateEventArgs args)
{
    try
    {
        if ((int.Parse(args.Value) % 2) == 0)
        {
            args.IsValid = true;
        }
        else
        {
            args.IsValid = false;
        };
    }
    catch (Exception)
    {
        args.IsValid = false;
    };
}
```

12. Click the F5 button.

13. Enter an odd number and click the Submit button (see Figure 17A-3).

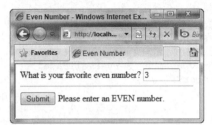

FIGURE 17A-3

14. Stop debugging by closing the browser.

15. Add the following markup to the `<head>` element of the `EvenNumber.aspx` page:

```
<script type="text/javascript">
    function evenNumberValidate(source, arg) {
        if ((arg.Value % 2) == 0)
            { arg.IsValid = true; }
        else
            { arg.IsValid = false; };
    }
</script>
```

16. Update the `ClientValidationFunction` property of the `CustomValidator` to reference the new client-side code:

```
ClientValidationFunction="evenNumberValidate"
```

17. Verify that the code in the EvenNumber.aspx page matches the following:

```
<%@ Page Language="C#" AutoEventWireup="true" CodeBehind="EvenNumber.aspx.cs"
    Inherits="Lesson17a.EvenNumber" %>

<!DOCTYPE html PUBLIC "-//W3C//DTD XHTML 1.0 Transitional//EN"
    "http://www.w3.org/TR/xhtml1/DTD/xhtml1-transitional.dtd">
<html xmlns="http://www.w3.org/1999/xhtml">
<head runat="server">
    <title>Even Number</title>
    <script type="text/javascript">
        function evenNumberValidate(source, arg) {
            if ((arg.Value % 2) == 0)
            { arg.IsValid = true; }
            else
            { arg.IsValid = false; };
        }
    </script>
</head>
<body>
    <form id="form1" runat="server">
    <div>
```

```
What is your favorite even number?
<asp:TextBox ID="TextBoxEvenNumber" runat="server" Columns="5"
    MaxLength="5" />
<hr />
<asp:Button ID="ButtonSubmit" runat="server" Text="Submit" />
<asp:CustomValidator ID="CustomValidatorEvenNumber" runat="server"
    ErrorMessage="Please enter an EVEN number."
    ControlToValidate="TextBoxEvenNumber" ValidateEmptyText="True"
    OnServerValidate="CustomValidatorEvenNumber_ServerValidate"
    ClientValidationFunction="evenNumberValidate" />
    </div>
    </form>
</body>
</html>
```

18. Click the F5 button.

19. Enter an odd number and click the Submit button. Notice that validation now occurs on the client.

Please select Lesson 17A on the DVD to view the video that accompanies this lesson.

17B

Data Annotation Validators in MVC

In Lesson 16B you saw how to add custom validation code to the controller. However, it is a much better practice **not** to include validation logic in the controller. One way to add simple data validation to your application without adding code to the controller is to use Data Annotation validators. In this lesson I show you how to annotate your model using Data Annotation validators.

To use Data Annotation validators you must add the following using statement to the code on your page:

```
using System.ComponentModel.DataAnnotations;
```

These are the validation attributes that are included in the DataAnnotations namespace:

- ➤ **CustomValidation** — This attribute is used to specify a custom validation method at run time.

- ➤ **Range** — This attribute is used to define the valid range for the value.

- ➤ **RegularExpression** — This attribute is used to provide the regular expression with which the value is compared.

- ➤ **Required** — This attribute is used to indicate that a value is required.

- ➤ **StringLength** — This attribute can be used to specify both the minimum and maximum number of characters for the value.

The DataAnnotations namespace provides a large number of attribute classes. I am only demonstrating the validation attribute classes in this lesson.

This is the model I use for this lesson:

```
using System.ComponentModel.DataAnnotations;

namespace Lesson17b.Models
{
    public class Contact
    {
        [Required]
        public string Name { get; set; }

        [Required]
        [Range(0, 110)]
        public int Age { get; set; }

        [Required]
        [RegularExpression("^\\w+@[a-zA-Z_]+?\\.[a-zA-Z]{2,3}$")]
        public string EmailAddress { get; set; }
    }
}
```

The simplest way to create a Create view for the `Contact` model is to use the Add View dialog box shown in Figure 17B-1.

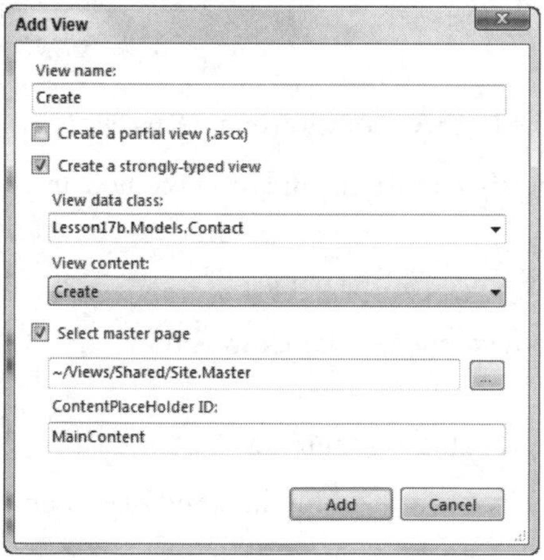

FIGURE 17B-1

This is the resulting markup:

```
<%@ Page Title="" Language="C#" MasterPageFile="~/Views/Shared/Site.Master"
    Inherits="System.Web.Mvc.ViewPage<Lesson17b.Models.Contact>" %>

<asp:Content ID="Content1" ContentPlaceHolderID="TitleContent" runat="server">
    Create
</asp:Content>
<asp:Content ID="Content2" ContentPlaceHolderID="MainContent" runat="server">
    <h2>Create</h2>
    <% using (Html.BeginForm()){%>
```

```
    <%: Html.ValidationSummary(true) %>
    <fieldset>
        <legend>Fields</legend>
        <div class="editor-label">
            <%: Html.LabelFor(model => model.Name) %>
        </div>
        <div class="editor-field">
            <%: Html.TextBoxFor(model => model.Name) %>
            <%: Html.ValidationMessageFor(model => model.Name) %>
        </div> Html.ValidationMessageFor(model => model.Name)
        <div class="editor-label">
            <%: Html.LabelFor(model => model.Age) %>
        </div>
        <div class="editor-field">
            <%: Html.TextBoxFor(model => model.Age) %>
            <%: Html.ValidationMessageFor(model => model.Age) %>
        </div>
        <div class="editor-label">
            <%: Html.LabelFor(model => model.EmailAddress) %>
        </div>
        <div class="editor-field">
            <%: Html.TextBoxFor(model => model.EmailAddress) %>
            <%: Html.ValidationMessageFor(model => model.EmailAddress) %>
        </div>
        <p>
            <input type="submit" value="Create" />
        </p>
    </fieldset>
    <% } %>
    <div>
        <%: Html.ActionLink("Back to List", "Index") %>
    </div>
</asp:Content>
```

This is the Create action method for the controller:

```
//
// GET: /Contact/Create

public ActionResult Create()
{
    return View();
}

//
// POST: /Contact/Create

[HttpPost]
public ActionResult Create(Models.Contact contact)
{
    try
    {
        if (ModelState.IsValid)
        {
            // TODO: Add insert logic here
```

```
            return RedirectToAction("Index");
        }
        else
        {
            return View(contact);
        }
    }
    catch
    {
        return View(contact);
    }
}
```

Figure 17B-2 shows the page that is rendered when the Create button is clicked before any data has been entered.

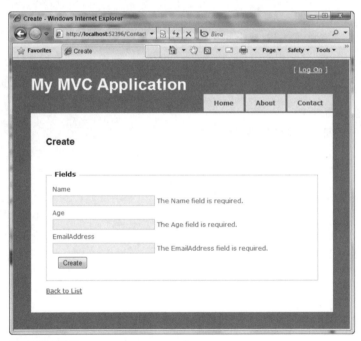

FIGURE 17B-2

Figure 17B-3 shows the page that is rendered if invalid data is entered in the Age and EmailAddress fields before the Create button is clicked.

The error message for the Age field is user friendly, but the error message for the EmailAddress field is just plain scary. The best way to update the error message is on the model. This is the updated EmailAddress model:

```
[Required]
[RegularExpression("^\\w+@[a-zA-Z_]+?\\.[a-zA-Z]{2,3}$",
    ErrorMessage="The EmailAddress is not valid.")]
public string EmailAddress { get; set; }
```

FIGURE 17B-3

Figure 17B-4 shows the page that is rendered using the updated model.

FIGURE 17B-4

In the preceding example the `ValidationMessageFor` method only includes one error message. Therefore, if you add a `ValidationSummary` to the page that shows all of the errors, the list of errors next to each field and the list of errors rendered by the `ValidationSummary` will be identical. The following code shows how to add a second string to the `ValidationMessageFor` method that will display next to the field in the event of a validation error.

```
<%: Html.ValidationMessageFor(model => model.Name, "*") %>
```

Figure 17B-5 shows the page that is rendered using the updated `ValidationMessageFor` method.

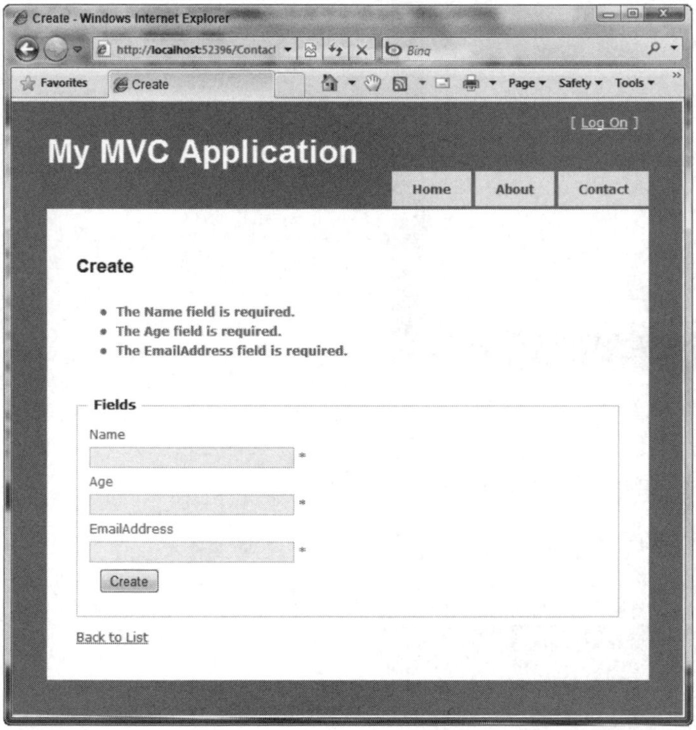

FIGURE 17B-5

TRY IT

In this lesson you use Data Annotation validators to add validation to a web application.

Lesson Requirements

None.

Hints

None.

Step-by-Step

1. Open Microsoft Visual Web Developer 2010 Express.

2. Select New Project from the File menu.

3. Select **Visual C#** on the left side of the dialog box.

4. Select the **ASP.NET MVC 2 Web Application** template.

5. Enter **Lesson17b** in the Name field and **c:\ASPNETTrainer** in the Location field. Click the OK button.

6. Right-click the Models folder and select Class from the Add menu to create a class named **Contact.cs**.

7. Update the code for the `Contact.cs` class to the following:

```csharp
using System.ComponentModel.DataAnnotations;

namespace Lesson17b.Models
{
    public class Contact
    {
        [Required]
        public string Name { get; set; }

        [Required]
        [Range(0, 110)]
        public int Age { get; set; }

        [Required]
        [RegularExpression("^\\w+@[a-zA-Z_]+?\\.[a-zA-Z]{2,3}$",
            ErrorMessage="The EmailAddress is not valid.")]
        public string EmailAddress { get; set; }
    }
}
```

8. Select Build Lesson17b from the Build menu to build the project.

9. Right-click the Views folder and select New Folder from the Add menu to add a subfolder named **Contact**.

10. Right-click the Contact folder and select View from the Add menu to open the Add View dialog box (see Figure 17B-6). Set the View name to **Create**, check the `Create a strongly-typed view` checkbox, and select **Lesson17b.Models.Contact** as the View data class and **Create** as the View content. Click the Add button.

FIGURE 17B-6

11. Right-click the Controllers folder, select Controller from the add menu, enter **ContactController** for the name of the controller, check the `Add action methods for Create, Update, Delete, and Details scenarios` checkbox, and click the Add button (see Figure 17B-7).

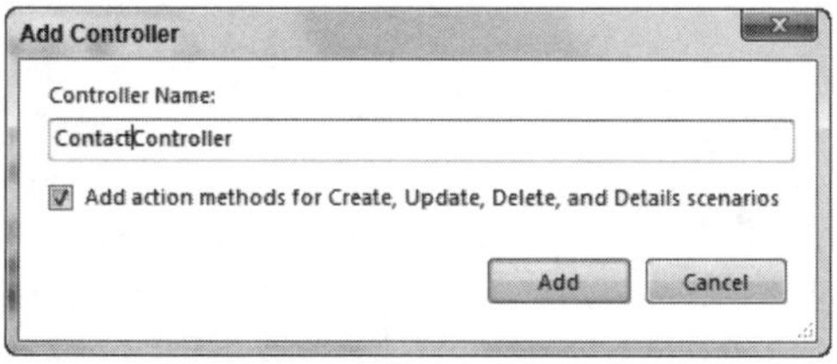

FIGURE 17B-7

12. Update the `Create` action method that accepts a POST to the following:

```
[HttpPost]
 public ActionResult Create(Models.Contact contact)
{
    try
    {
        if (ModelState.IsValid)
        {
            // TODO: Add insert logic here
            return RedirectToAction("Index");
        }
        else
        {
            return View(contact);
        }
    }
    catch
    {
```

```
            return View(contact);
        }
    }
```

13. Add the following menu item to the Site.Master file:

```
<li><%= Html.ActionLink("Contact", "Create", "Contact")%></li>
```

14. Click the F5 button.

15. Click the Contact tab.

16. Click the Create button (see Figure 17B-8).

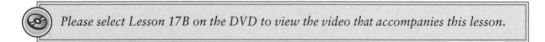

FIGURE 17B-8

Please select Lesson 17B on the DVD to view the video that accompanies this lesson.

SECTION VII
Reading and Displaying Data

18

Using the ADO.NET Entity Framework

Most web applications are used to collect, manipulate and share information. To do that, they need a way to manage data easily. The ADO.NET Entity Framework is Microsoft's recommended data access technology. With the ADO.NET Entity Framework your application uses a conceptual data model, called the Entity Data Model, to manage the data. In this lesson I show you how to create an Entity Data Model (EDM) and how to manage data using the EDM.

In this lesson I use a simple SQL Server database with the following four tables:

➤ **Category Table** — Contains the categories for the recipes.

➤ **Recipe Table** — Contains the recipes.

➤ **Ingredients Table** — Contains the ingredients for each recipe.

➤ **Tools Table** — Contains the tools for each recipe.

Figure 18-1 shows the database diagram for the database.

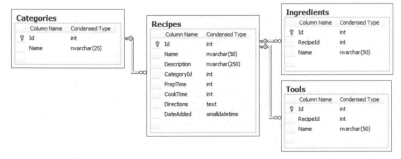

FIGURE 18-1

CREATING A SQL SERVER DATABASE

In this lesson I show you how to use the Entity Data Model Wizard to create an Entity Data Model from an existing database. However, if the database does not exist, you can create it from within the Microsoft Visual Web Developer 2010 Express IDE by following these steps:

1. Create an App_Data folder, if your application does not already have one. To create an App_Data folder, right-click the name of your project on the Solution Explorer window and select Add ▷ Add ASP.NET Folder ▷ App_Data from the menu.

2. Create the SQL Server database. To create a SQL Server database, right-click the App_Data folder and select New Item from the Add window to open the Add New Item dialog box (Figure 18-2). On the Add New Item dialog box, select the SQL Server Database template, enter a name for the database, and click the Add button.

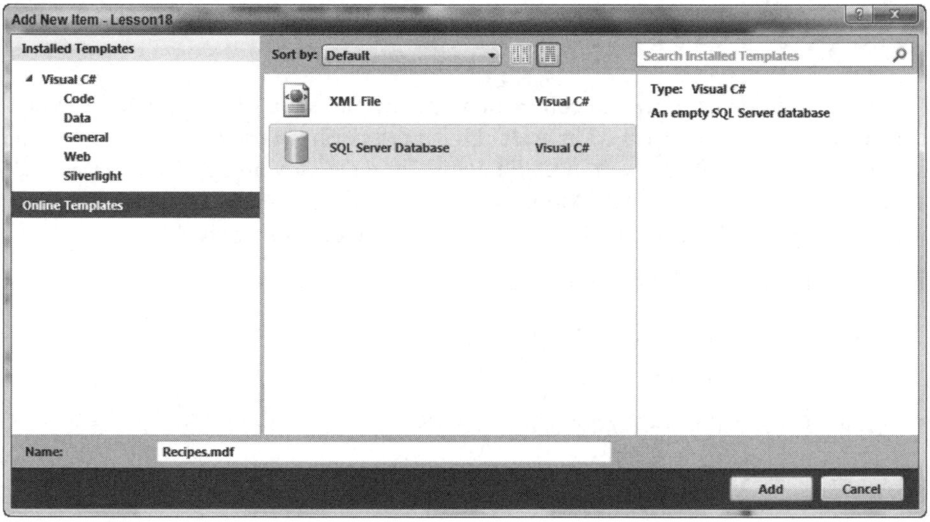

FIGURE 18-2

3. Add tables to the new SQL Server database. To edit the structure of your new database, right-click the MDF file in the Solution Explorer window to open the Database Explorer window shown in Figure 18-3.

To add a new table using the Database Explorer window, right-click the Tables folder and select Add New Table. To edit an existing table, double-click the name of the table. Figure 18-4 shows the Categories table in edit mode.

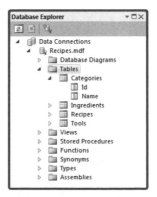

FIGURE 18-3

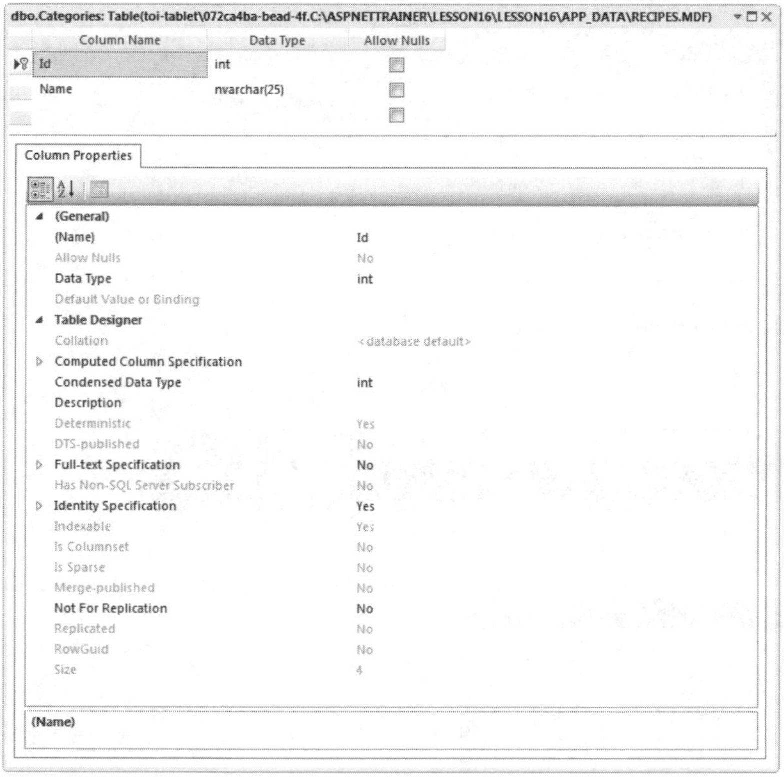

FIGURE 18-4

CREATING AN ENTITY DATA MODEL

To open the Entity Data Model Wizard, right-click a folder in the Solution Explorer window and select New Item from the Add menu to open the Add New Item dialog box shown in Figure 18-5. Click Data to display only the Data templates, select the ADO.NET Entity Data Model template, enter a name for the new model, and click the Add button.

Figure 18-6 shows the first page of the Entity Data Model Wizard. To create an Entity Data Model from an existing database, select the **Generate from database** option and click the Next button.

The second page of the Entity Data Model Wizard is used to select the data connection (see Figure 18-7). After you have selected your data connection, click the Next button.

The last page of the Entity Data Model Wizard is used to select the database objects that you want to include in the Entity Data Model (see Figure 18-8). Check the `Pluralize or singularize generated object names` checkbox to have the wizard adjust the names of the objects automatically. Also, leave the `Include foreign key columns in the model` checkbox checked. After you have selected the objects to include in the new EDM and entered a name for the Model Namespace, click the Finish button.

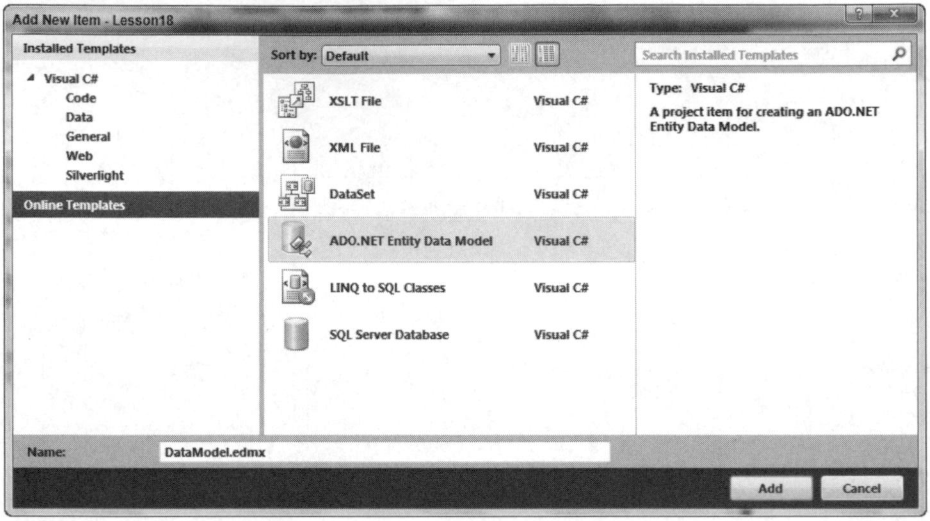

FIGURE 18-5

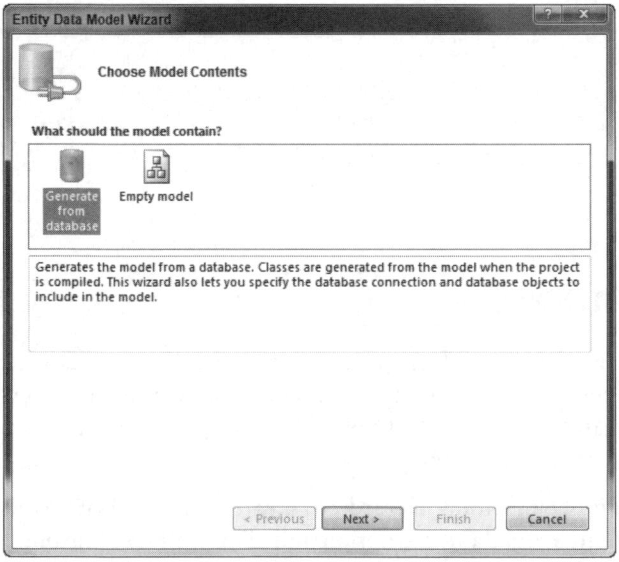

FIGURE 18-6

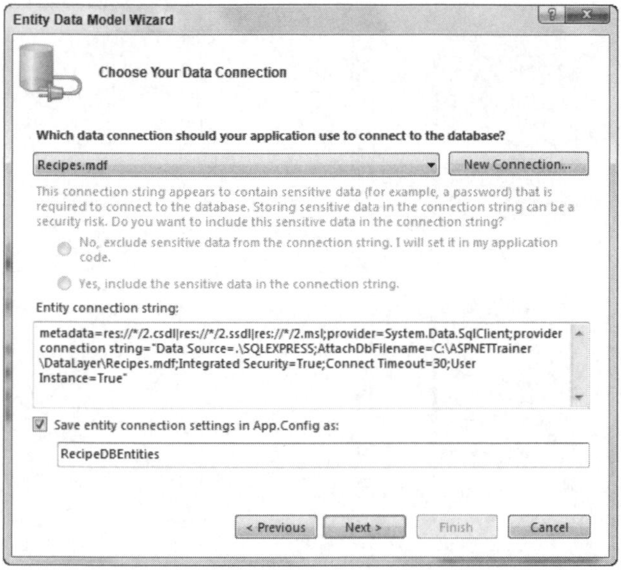

FIGURE 18-7

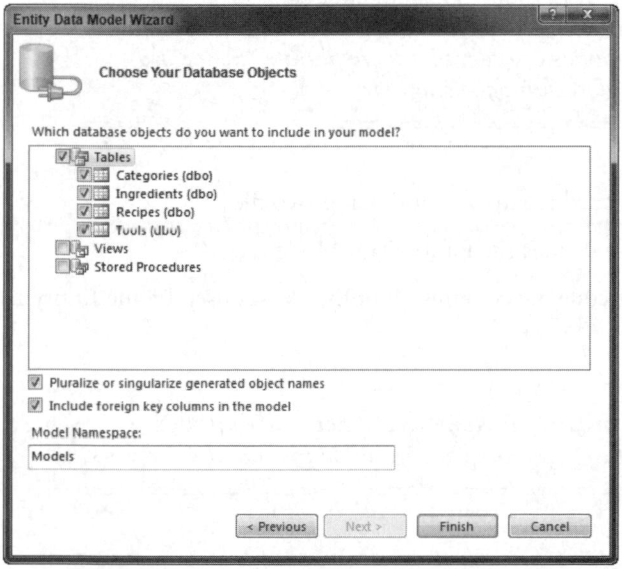

FIGURE 18-8

After the Entity Data Model Wizard finishes running, the ADO.NET Entity Designer opens to show the EDM that was created (see Figure 18-9.)

Each entity in the ADO.NET Entity Designer corresponds to a class. Whenever you modify an entity in the designer and save the changes, the ADO.NET Entity Framework automatically regenerates all of the classes.

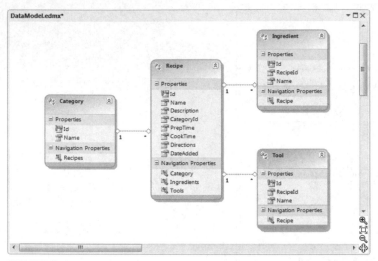

FIGURE 18-9

 Because I checked the `Pluralize or singularize generated object names` *checkbox in the wizard, the names of the objects in the generated Entity Data Model are singular although the names of the tables were plural. The wizard applies English language rules to determine the singular.*

In my example, the Entity Data Model Wizard created the following two files:

➤ `DataModel.edmx` — This XML file defines the Entity Data Model.

➤ `DataModel.Designer.cs` — This code file contains all of the classes used by the Entity Data Model.

Do not edit the `Designer.cs` *file because anytime you update the Entity Data Model the classes in this file will be regenerated and you will lose all of your edits.*

LINQ TO ENTITIES

Language-Integrated Query (LINQ) is a set of features that provides standard, easily-learned patterns for querying and updating data. LINQ to Entities is used to read and update the data in an Entity Data Model. With LINQ to Entities you can create strongly-typed queries against your EDM by using LINQ expressions.

A LINQ expression is a query expressed in query syntax. A LINQ expression begins with a `from` clause and ends with a `select` or `group` clause. Between the first `from` cause and the last `select` or `group` clause, it can contain one or more `where`, `orderby`, `join`, `let` and even additional `from` clauses.

With LINQ to Entities it is easy to perform the familiar CRUD operations on the data:

- ➤ Create
- ➤ Read
- ➤ Update
- ➤ Delete

The context object provides the data source for a LINQ expression. This is the definition of the context object used in all of the following CRUD examples:

```
RecipeDBEntities _entity = new RecipeDBEntities();
```

This is the LINQ to Entities code to read all of the categories from the `Category` object sorted in ascending order:

```
var categoryList = (from c in _entity.Categories
                    orderby c.Name
                    select c);
```

This is the LINQ to Entities code to read the name of the category with `Id = 2`:

```
var categoryName = (from c in _entity.Categories
                    where c.Id == 2
                    select c.Name).First();
```

This is the LINQ to Entities code to create a new category:

```
var categoryToAdd = new Models.Category();
categoryToAdd.Name = "Casserole";

_entity.Categories.AddObject(categoryToAdd);
_entity.SaveChanges();
```

This is the LINQ to Entities code to change the name of an existing category:

```
var categoryToUpdate = (from c in _entity.Categories
                        where c.Name == "Casserole"
                        select c).FirstOrDefault();

categoryToUpdate.Name = "Casseroles";
_entity.SaveChanges();
```

This is the LINQ to Entities code to delete a category:

```
var categoryToDelete = (from c in _entity.Categories
                        where c.Name == "Casserole"
                        select c).First();

_entity.Categories.DeleteObject(categoryToDelete);
_entity.SaveChanges();
```

The purpose of this very brief introduction to LINQ to Entities is to provide you with the LINQ expressions that you will use in the upcoming Lessons. However, there is much more that LINQ to Entities can do.

TRY IT

In this lesson you create the DataLayer project for use in the upcoming lessons. You use the Entity Data Model Wizard to create the Entity Data Model used by the DataLayer project.

Lesson Requirements

➤ The recipes.mdf file.

Hints

None.

Step-by-Step

1. Create a subfolder named **DataLayer** under the c:\ASPNETTrainer folder.

2. Copy the recipes.mdf file into the DataLayer folder and make sure the recipes.mdf file is not read-only.

Right-click the name of the file and select Properties to change the read-only setting.

3. Open Microsoft Visual Web Developer 2010 Express.

4. Select New Project from the File menu.

5. Select **Visual C#** on the left side of the dialog box.

6. Select the **Class Library** template.

7. Enter **DataLayer** in the Name field and **c:\ASPNETTrainer** in the Location field.

8. Click the OK button (see Figure 18-10).

9. Delete the Class1.cs file by right-clicking it and selecting Delete from the menu.

10. Right-click the name of the project in the Solution Explorer window and select New Item from the Add menu to open the Add New Item dialog box. Click **Data** to display only the Data templates, select the **ADO.NET Entity Data Model** template, enter **DataModel.edmx** for the name of the new model, and click the Add button to open the Entity Data Model Wizard.

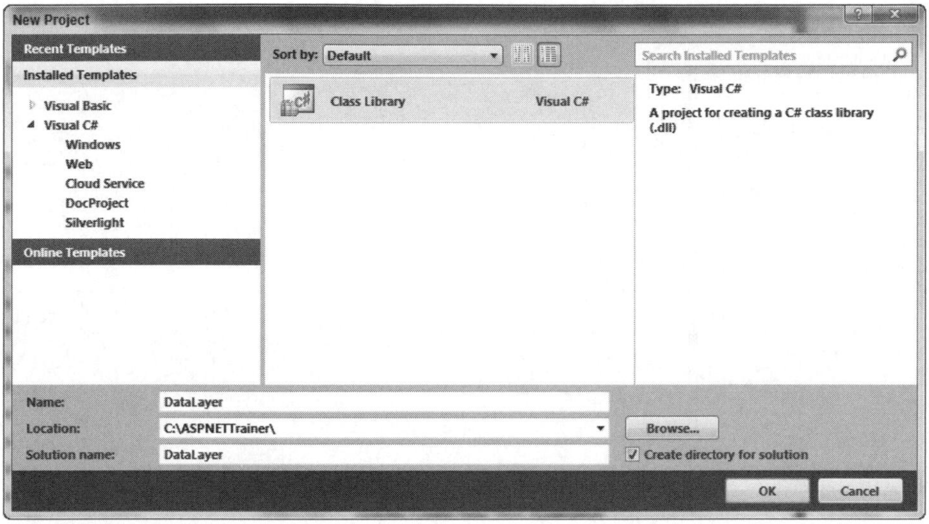

FIGURE 18-10

11. Select **Generate from database** and click the Next button.

12. Click the New Connection button to open the Connection Properties dialog box.

13. Click the Change button to open the Choose Data Source dialog box. Select **Microsoft SQL Server Database File from the Data Source** list box, and click the Continue button (see Figure 18-11) to return to the Connection Properties dialog box.

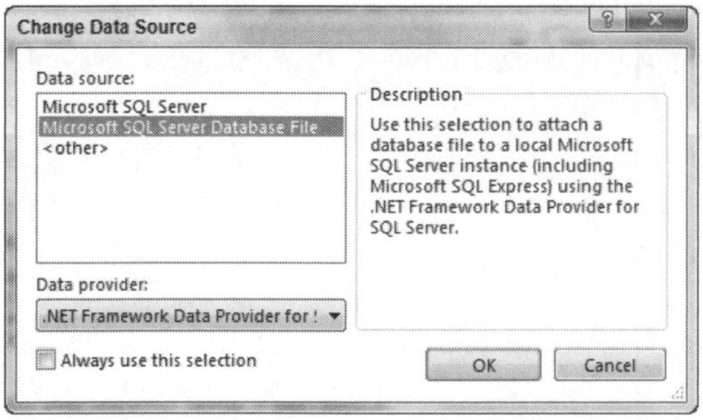

FIGURE 18-11

14. On the Connection Properties dialog box click the Browse button to navigate to the `recipes.mdf` file. Select the `recipes.mdf` file and click the Open button (see Figure 18-12).

15. Click the OK button to close the Connection Properties dialog box and return to the Entity Data Model Wizard.

16. Change the name of the entity to **RecipeDBEntities** and click the Next button (see Figure 18-13).

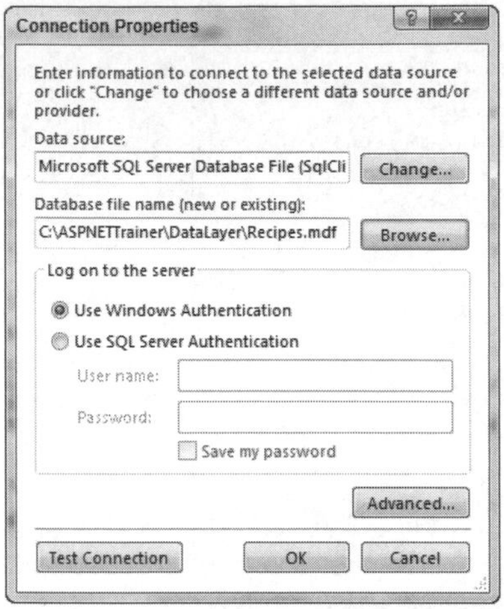

FIGURE 18-12

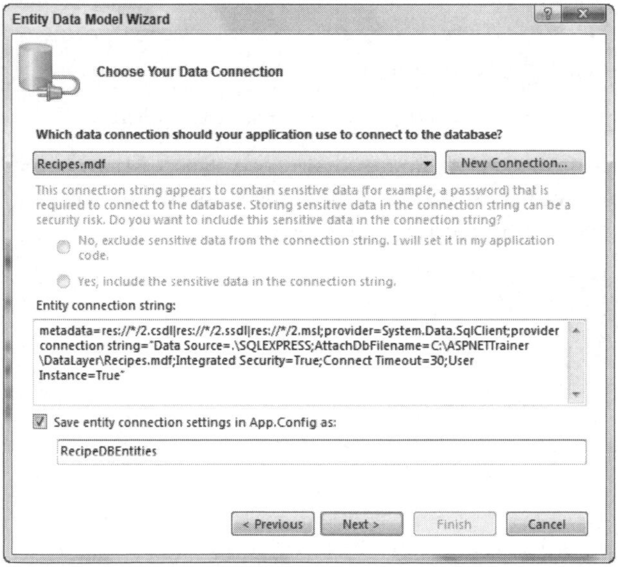

FIGURE 18-13

> *It is very important that you name the new entity model **RecipeDBEntities** because you use it in Lesson 19A, Lesson 20A and Lesson 20B.*

17. Click the No button on the dialog box that asks if you want to copy the database into the project (see Figure 18-14).

FIGURE 18-14

18. Select all of the tables, check the `Pluralize or singularize generated object names` checkbox, check the `Include foreign key columns in the model` checkbox, enter **Models** for the Model namespace, and click the Finish button (see Figure 18-15).

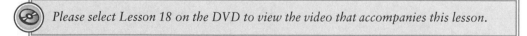

FIGURE 18-15

19. Select Build DataLayer from the Build menu to create the assembly (DLL) for this project.

Please select Lesson 18 on the DVD to view the video that accompanies this lesson.

19A

Displaying Data in Web Forms

Many web applications display data from a database. In this lesson I show you how to use the DataLayer that you created in the previous lesson to display data in an ASP.NET Web Forms application.

REFERRING TO THE DATA LAYER

To use the DataLayer from the previous lesson you must first add a reference to the assembly. You can do this a couple of ways:

1. Add the DataLayer project to the current solution and add a reference to the DataLayer project.

2. Add a reference to the DataLayer assembly (DLL).

Either way, you need to add the connection string to the web.config file. This is the connection string from Lesson 18:

```
<add name="RecipeDBEntities" connectionString=
    "metadata=res://*/DataModel.csdl|res:
//*/DataModel.ssdl|res://*/DataModel.msl;provider=System.Data.SqlClient;provider
connection string=&quot;DataSource=.\SQLEXPRESS;
AttachDbFilename=C:\ASPNETTrainer\DataLayer\Recipes.mdf;IntegratedSecurity=True;
Connect Timeout=30;User Instance=True;MultipleActiveResultSets=True&quot;"
providerName="System.Data.EntityClient" />
```

So far, I have shown you how to display data by setting the text property of the server control to the value, as shown in the following example:

```
MyTextBox.Text = value
```

Now I show you how to use some of the many data bound server controls provided by Microsoft Visual Web Developer 2010 Express.

LIST CONTROLS

List controls are used to display a simple list of items. These are the list controls found on the General tab of the Toolbox:

➤ **BulletedList** — This control displays a bulleted list of items.

➤ **CheckBoxList** — This control displays a group of checkboxes.

➤ **DropDownList** — This control displays a drop-down list of items.

➤ **ListBox** — This control displays a list box.

➤ **RadioButtonList** — This control displays a group of radio buttons.

Figure 19A-1 shows an example of each type of list control.

FIGURE 19A-1

This is the code to bind a `BulletedList` named BulletedListCategories to a list of categories programmatically:

```
DataLayer.RecipeDBEntities _entity = new DataLayer.RecipeDBEntities();

var categories = from c in _entity.Categories
                 orderby c.Name
                 select c;

BulletedListCategories.DataSource = categories;
BulletedListCategories.DataValueField = "Id";
BulletedListCategories.DataTextField = "Name";
BulletedListCategories.DataBind();
```

Because all of the list controls inherit from the `ListControl` class all of them bind to data using the same technique as the `BulletedList`. These are the properties that must be set before the `DataBind` method for the list control can be called.

➤ **DataSource** — This is the object that contains the data.

➤ **DataValueField** — This is a string that specifies the name of the field, in the `DataSource`, to use as the *value* for each item in the list.

➤ **DataTextField** — This is a string that specifies the name of the field, in the `DataSource`, to use as the *text* for each item in the list.

List controls provide a means for the user to select one or more items from a list. These are the list control properties for determining which items the user has selected:

➤ **SelectedIndex** — This is the index of the item that has been selected. The index is zero-based.

➤ **SelectedItem** — This is the `ListItem` that has been selected. The `ListItem` includes both the name and the value of the selected item.

➤ **SelectedValue** — This is the value of the item that has been selected.

Figure 19A-2 shows a drop-down list with a selected item.

FIGURE 19A-2

> *These properties do not need to be set programmatically. You can set them directly in the markup for the control. This example sets both the* `DataValueField` *and the* `DataTextField` *properties:*
>
> ```
> <asp:BulletedList ID="BulletedListCategories" runat="server"
>     DataValueField="Id" DataTextField="Name" />
> ```

This is the code to determine the text of the selected item for a drop-down list named `DropDownListCategory`:

```
DropDownListCategory.SelectedItem.Text;
```

By default, the drop-down list does not include a blank item at the top. If you want your drop-down list to include a blank item, you must add one. This is the code to add a blank item to the top of a drop-down list named `DropDownListCategory`:

```
DropDownListCategory.Items.Insert(0, new ListItem("", "-1"));
```

TABULAR CONTROLS

Tabular controls are used to display records either in an HTML table or via a template. These are the tabular controls found on the Data tab of the Toolbox:

➤ **DataList** — This control is used to display a group of records in an HTML table by using a template. This control has a handy property called `RepeatColumns` that is used to designate how many columns to repeat in each row.

➤ **DetailsView** — This control is used to display a single record in an HTML table. Each row of the table is used to display one field of the record. This control is usually used in conjunction with the `GridView`.

➤ **FormView** — This control is used to display a single record using a template.

➤ **GridView** — This control is used to display a group of records using an HTML table. This control supports sorting, paging, and editing. Lesson 20A is dedicated to the `GridView`.

➤ **ListView** — This control is used to display a group of records using a template. This control supports sorting, paging, and editing.

➤ **Repeater** — This control is used to display a group of records using a template.

Figure 19A-3 shows examples of the `GridView`, `DetailsView`, and `DataList` controls.

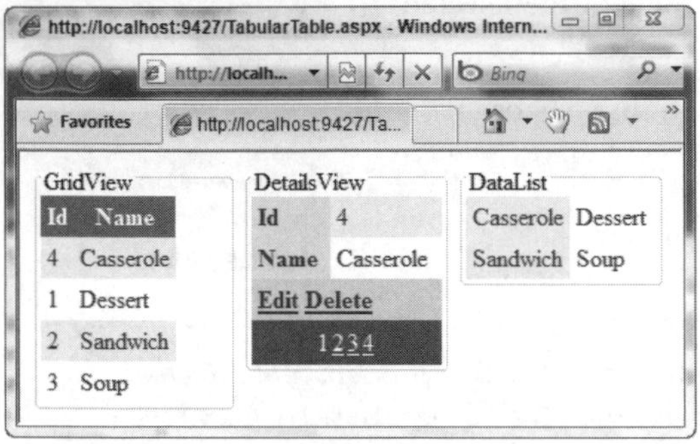

FIGURE 19A-3

The `DataList`, `FormView`, `ListView`, and `Repeater` all require you to use templates. The `DetailsView` and the `GridView` do not require templates, but they support them. This is a list of the various templates:

➤ **ItemTemplate** — This template defines the content of each item.

➤ **AlternatingItemTemplate** — This template defines the content of alternating items. If this template is not included, the `ItemTemplate` is used.

➤ **SeparatorTemplate** — This template defines the content that is rendered between items.

➤ **HeaderTemplate** — This template defines the content of the header.

➤ **FooterTemplate** — This template defines the content of the footer.

The `Repeater` server control is the most versatile of the data bound controls. It allows you to display the data anyway you choose. This is an example of a simple `Repeater`:

```
<asp:Repeater ID="RepeaterCategory" runat="server">
    <ItemTemplate>
        The unique ID for <%# Eval("Name") %> is <%# Eval("Id") %>.
    </ItemTemplate>
    <SeparatorTemplate>
        <br />
    </SeparatorTemplate>
</asp:Repeater>
```

In this example I am using a `<br />` element in the `SeparatorTemplate` in order to force a line break between each item.

The important things to notice about the preceding `ItemTemplate` are the `DataBinding` expressions:

```
<%# Eval("Name") %>
<%# Eval("Id") %>.
```

The first DataBinding expression displays the Name of the category and the second DataBinding expression displays the Id of the category.

Figure 19A-4 shows how the Repeater renders on the page.

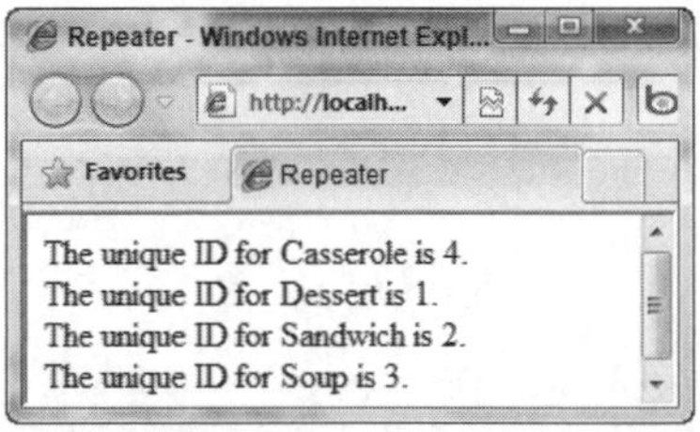

FIGURE 19A-4

Following is the code I used to bind the data to the RepeaterCategory control:

```
DataLayer.RecipeDBEntities _entity = new DataLayer.RecipeDBEntities();

var categories = from c in _entity.Categories
                 orderby c.Name
                 select c;

RepeaterCategory.DataSource = categories;
RepeaterCategory.DataBind();
```

NESTING CONTROLS

You can nest tabular controls. Also, you can nest list controls within tabular controls. The following markup shows how to include multiple BulletedList controls within a FormView control:

```
<%@ Page Language="C#" AutoEventWireup="true" CodeBehind="Recipe.aspx.cs"
    Inherits="Lesson19a.Recipe" %>

<!DOCTYPE html PUBLIC "-//W3C//DTD XHTML 1.0 Transitional//EN"
    "http://www.w3.org/TR/xhtml1/DTD/xhtml1-transitional.dtd">
<html xmlns="http://www.w3.org/1999/xhtml">
<head runat="server">
    <title>Recipe</title>
    <link href="Styles/StyleSheet.css" rel="stylesheet" type="text/css" />
</head>
<body>
    <form id="form1" runat="server">
    <div class="header">
        <img src="/images/SuperEasyRecipesLogo.gif" alt="Super Easy Recipes" />
    </div>
    <asp:FormView ID="FormView1" runat="server" RenderOuterTable="False">
        <ItemTemplate>
            <div class="sidebar">
                <h2>Tools</h2>
                <asp:BulletedList ID="BulletedListTools" runat="server"
                    BulletStyle="Numbered" />
            </div>
            <div class="content">
```

```
                        <h1><%# Eval("Name") %></h1>
                        <table>
                            <tr>
                                <td>Prep Time:</td>
                                <td>Cook Time:</td>
                                <td>Ready In:</td>
                            </tr>
                            <tr>
                                <td>
                                    <%# Eval("PrepTime") %> Min
                                </td>
                                <td>
                                    <%# Eval("CookTime") %> Min
                                </td>
                                <td>
                                    <%# (int)Eval("PrepTime")+(int)Eval("CookTime") %> Min
                                </td>
                            </tr>
                        </table>
                        <h2>Ingredients</h2>
                        <asp:BulletedList ID="BulletedListIngredients" runat="server" />
                        <h2>Directions</h2>
                        <%#Eval("Directions") %>
                    </div>
                </ItemTemplate>
            </asp:FormView>
            </form>
    </body>
    </html>
```

This is the code:

```
using System;
using System.Linq;
using System.Web.UI.WebControls;

namespace Lesson19a
{
    public partial class Recipe : System.Web.UI.Page
    {
        DataLayer.RecipeDBEntities _entity = new DataLayer.RecipeDBEntities();

        protected void Page_Load(object sender, EventArgs e)
        {
            var recipe = from r in _entity.Recipes
                         where r.Id == 1
                         select r;

            FormView1.DataSource = recipe;
            FormView1.DataBind();

            BulletedList bulletedListTools =
                (BulletedList)FormView1.FindControl("BulletedListTools");
            bulletedListTools.DataSource = from t in recipe.First().Tools
                                           select t.Name;
            bulletedListTools.DataBind();

            BulletedList bulletedListIngredients =
```

```
            (BulletedList)FormView1.FindControl("BulletedListIngredients");
        bulletedListIngredients.DataSource =
            from i in recipe.First().Ingredients
            select i.Name;
        bulletedListIngredients.DataBind();
        }
    }
}
```

Figure 19A-5 shows the page that is rendered, assuming that the cascading style sheet (CSS) from Lesson 3 is used.

FIGURE 19A-5

TRY IT

In this lesson you use the `DataLayer` that you created in Lesson 18 to display data in an ASP.NET Web Forms application.

Lesson Requirements

➤ The `DataLayer.dll` created in Lesson 18.

➤ The `recipes.mdf` file used in Lesson 18.

➤ The `ConnectionString.txt` file.

Hints

None.

Step-by-Step

1. Verify that the recipes.mdf file is in a folder named c:\ASPNETTrainer\DataLayer and that the file is not read-only.

2. Open Microsoft Visual Web Developer 2010 Express.

3. Select New Project from the File menu.

4. Select **Visual C#** on the left side of the dialog box.

5. Select the **ASP.NET Web Application** template.

6. Enter **Lesson19a** in the Name field and **c:\ASPNETTrainer** in the Location field. Click the OK button.

7. Right-click References in the Solution Explorer window and select Add Reference to open the Add Reference dialog box. Select the .NET tab, select the **System .Data.Entity** Component Name, and click the OK button (see Figure 19A-6).

FIGURE 19A-6

8. Right-click References in the Solution Explorer window and select Add Reference to open the Add Reference dialog box. Select the Browse tab, browse to the `DataLayer.dll` file, and click the OK button.

> The `DataLayer.dll` *is located in the following folder:*
>
>   c:\ASPNETTrainer\DataLayer\DataLayer\bin\Debug

9. Open the ConnectionString.txt and copy the text to add the following connection string to the list of connection strings in the `web.config` file:

```
<add name="RecipeDBEntities" connectionString=
    "metadata=res://*/DataModel.csdl|res:
//*/DataModel.ssdl|res://*/DataModel.msl;provider=System.Data.SqlClient;provider
connection string=&quot;DataSource=.\SQLEXPRESS;
AttachDbFilename=C:\ASPNETTrainer\DataLayer\Recipes.mdf;IntegratedSecurity=True;
Connect Timeout=30;User Instance=True;MultipleActiveResultSets=True&quot;"
providerName="System.Data.EntityClient" />
```

> *This connection string assumes that the* `recipes.mdf` *file is in the* `C:\ASPNETTrainer\` `DataLayer` *folder. If it is in a different folder, you will need to update the path to the* `recipes.mdf` *file.*

10. Right-click the name of the project in the Solution Explorer window and select New Item from the Add menu to open the Add New Item dialog box. Select the **Web Form using Master Page** template, enter **Category.aspx** for the Name, and click the Add button. Select Site.Master as the Master Page and click the OK button.

11. Update the `Title` attribute of the `@Page` directive to **Category**.

12. Add the following markup to the `MainContent` on the `Category.aspx` page:

```
<asp:CheckBoxList ID="CheckBoxListCategory" runat="server" RepeatColumns="2" />
<asp:Button ID="ButtonCategory" runat="server" Text="Select Category"
    OnClick="ButtonCategory_Click" />
<hr />
<asp:Literal ID="LiteralCount" runat="server" />
```

13. Add the following code to the `Page_Load` event of the `Category.aspx.cs` file:

```
DataLayer.RecipeDBEntities _entity = new DataLayer.RecipeDBEntities();

var categories = from c in _entity.Categories
                 orderby c.Name
                 select c;

CheckBoxListCategory.DataSource = categories;
CheckBoxListCategory.DataValueField = "Id";
CheckBoxListCategory.DataTextField = "Name";
CheckBoxListCategory.DataBind();
```

14. Add the following code to the `Category.aspx.cs` file:

```
protected void ButtonCategory_Click(object sender, EventArgs e)
{
    int count = 0;
    foreach (ListItem item in CheckBoxListCategory.Items)
    {
        if (item.Selected)
        {
            count = count + 1;
        }
    };

    LiteralCount.Text = String.Format("You have selected {0} items.",
        count.ToString());
}
```

15. Add the following menu item to the `Site.Master` file:

```
<asp:MenuItem NavigateUrl="~/Category.aspx" Text="Category"/>
```

16. Click the F5 button.

17. Navigate to the Category tab.

18. Select a couple checkboxes and click the Select Category button.

19. Zero items have been marked as selected because the `Page_Load` event is being called on the postback. Update the `Page_Load` code to the following:

```
protected void Page_Load(object sender, EventArgs e)
{
    if (!Page.IsPostBack)
    {
        var categories = from c in _entity.Categories
                         orderby c.Name
                         select c;

        CheckBoxListCategory.DataSource = categories;
        CheckBoxListCategory.DataValueField = "Id";
        CheckBoxListCategory.DataTextField = "Name";
        CheckBoxListCategory.DataBind();
    }
}
```

20. Click the F5 button.

21. Navigate to the Category tab.

22. Select a few checkboxes and click the Select Category button (see Figure 19A-7).

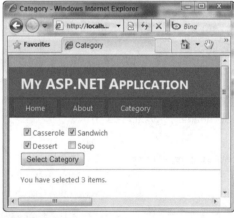

FIGURE 19A-7

 Please select Lesson 19A on the DVD to view the video that accompanies this lesson.

19B

Displaying Data in MVC

Most web applications display data from a database. In this lesson I show you how to use the DataLayer that you created in the previous lesson to display data in an ASP.NET MVC application.

REFERRING TO THE DATALAYER

To use the DataLayer from the previous lesson you must first add a reference to the assembly. You can do this a couple of ways:

1. Add the DataLayer project to the current solution and add a reference to the DataLayer project.

2. Add a reference directly to the DataLayer assembly (DLL).

Either way, you need to add the connection string to the web.config file. This is the connection string from Lesson 18:

```
<add name="RecipeDBEntities" connectionString=
    "metadata=res://*/DataModel.csdl|res:
//*/DataModel.ssdl|res://*/DataModel.msl;provider=System.Data.SqlClient;provider
connection string=&quot;DataSource=.\SQLEXPRESS;
AttachDbFilename=C:\ASPNETTrainer\DataLayer\Recipes.mdf;IntegratedSecurity=True;
Connect Timeout=30;User Instance=True;MultipleActiveResultSets=True&quot;"
providerName="System.Data.EntityClient" />
```

This is the reference to the Entity Data Model that I use throughout this lesson:

```
RecipeDBEntities _entity = new RecipeDBEntities();
```

USING VIEWDATA

The `SelectList` class represents a list from which the user can select an item. In this case, the CategoryList will be used to populate a drop-down list. This is a `Select` action method that reads all of the records in the Category table, sorts them by Name, and returns them to the Select view using the `ViewData` object:

```
public ActionResult Select()
{
    var categories = from c in _entity.Categories
                     orderby c.Name
                     select c;

    ViewData["CategoryList"] = new SelectList(categories, "id", "Name");

    return View();
}
```

This is the markup for the view associated with the preceding action method:

```
<%@ Page Title="" Language="C#" MasterPageFile="~/Views/Shared/Site.Master"
    Inherits="System.Web.Mvc.ViewPage" %>

<asp:Content ID="Content1" ContentPlaceHolderID="TitleContent" runat="server">
    Select Category
</asp:Content>
<asp:Content ID="Content2" ContentPlaceHolderID="MainContent" runat="server">
    <% Html.BeginForm(); %>
        <h2>Select Category</h2>
        <%: Html.DropDownList("CategoryList") %>
        <input id="ButtonSubmit" type="submit" value="Submit" />
    <% Html.EndForm(); %>
</asp:Content>
```

Figure 19B-1 shows the page that is rendered.

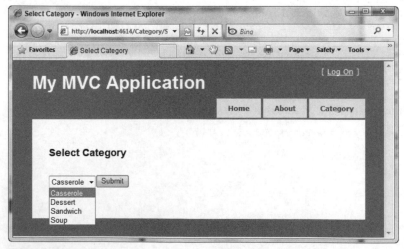

FIGURE 19B-1

When the user clicks the Submit button, the page is posted back to the `Select` action method. However, on the postback, I want to redirect the user to the Details view, so I need to add another `Select` action item that is only called during a postback.

The new action method will need an `AcceptVerbs` attribute to limit the `HttpVerbs` that are accepted. Also, the new action method needs a collection parameter of type `FormCollection`. The `FormCollection` class is a `NameValueCollection`. This is how you access items from a `NameValueCollection`:

```
string Id = collection["CategoryList"];
```

So where does "CategoryList" come from? It comes from the posting form's HTML value:

```
<%: Html.DropDownList("CategoryList") %>
```

This is the new `Select` action method that is only called during a postback:

```
[HttpPost]
public ActionResult Select(FormCollection collection)
{
    return RedirectToAction("Details", new { id = collection["CategoryList"] });
}
```

This is the `Details` action result that is called by the `RedirectToAction` method. It returns the details for a given category.

```
public ActionResult Details(int? id)
{
    if (!id.HasValue)
    {
        return RedirectToAction("Select");
    };

    var category = (from c in _entity.Categories
                    where c.Id == id
                    select c). FirstOrDefault();

    if (category == null)
    {
        category = new Category();
        category.Id = id.Value;
        category.Name = "Invalid Category ID";
    };

    ViewData["Id"] = category.Id;
    ViewData["Name"] = category.Name;

    return View();
}
```

This is markup for the Details view:

```
<%@ Page Title="" Language="C#" MasterPageFile="~/Views/Shared/Site.Master"
Inherits="System.Web.Mvc.ViewPage" %>

<asp:Content ID="Content1" ContentPlaceHolderID="TitleContent" runat="server">
```

```
            Category Details
        </asp:Content>
        <asp:Content ID="Content2" ContentPlaceHolderID="MainContent" runat="server">
            <h2>
                Category Details</h2>
            <table>
                <tr>
                    <th>Category ID</th>
                    <th>Category Name</th>
                </tr>
                <tr>
                    <td><%: ViewData["Id"] %></td>
                    <td><%: ViewData["Name"] %></td>
                </tr>
            </table>
        </asp:Content>
```

Figure 19B-2 shows the page that is rendered using this view with the preceding controller.

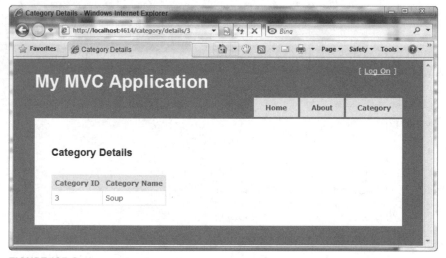

FIGURE 19B-2

USING STRONGLY-TYPED VIEWS

The code used to render this page used the ViewData object to pass the values from the controller to the view. In fact, a better way to pass the values is to use the Model. ASP.NET MVC makes it easy to do just that by providing the Add View dialog box shown in Figure 19B-3.

With the Add View dialog box you can select the data class from which you want the view to inherit. For example, if you check the Create a strongly typed view checkbox, select **DataLayer.Category** from the drop-down list of View data classes, select **Details** from the drop-down list of View contents, and click the Add button, this is the markup for the Details view that is automatically generated:

```
<%@ Page Title="" Language="C#" MasterPageFile="~/Views/Shared/Site.Master"
    Inherits="System.Web.Mvc.ViewPage<DataLayer.Category>" %>
```

```
<asp:Content ID="Content1" ContentPlaceHolderID="TitleContent" runat="server">
    Details
</asp:Content>

<asp:Content ID="Content2" ContentPlaceHolderID="MainContent" runat="server">

    <h2>Details</h2>

    <fieldset>
        <legend>Fields</legend>

        <div class="display-label">Id</div>
        <div class="display-field"><%: Model.Id %></div>

        <div class="display-label">Name</div>
        <div class="display-field"><%: Model.Name %></div>

    </fieldset>
    <p>
        <%: Html.ActionLink("Edit", "Edit", new { id=Model.Id }) %> |
        <%: Html.ActionLink("Back to List", "Index") %>
    </p>

</asp:Content>
```

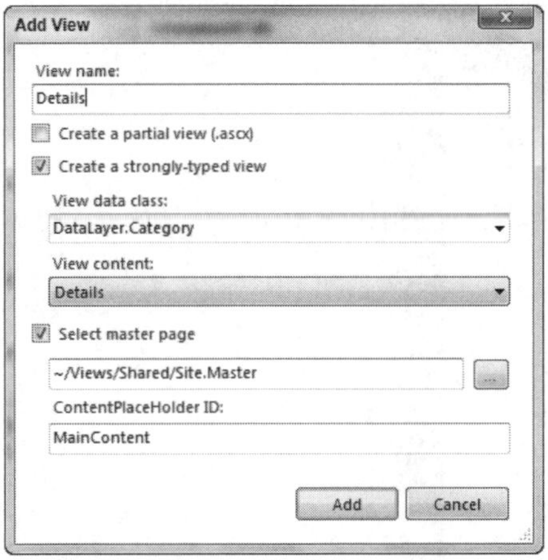

FIGURE 19B-3

The important thing to notice about this code is that this new view inherits from System.Web.Mvc.
ViewPage<DataLayer.Category> whereas the original version of this view inherited from simply
System.Web.Mvc.ViewPage. The DataLayer.Category object is the Model for this new view. As
such, the HTML helpers can refer to the strongly-typed properties of the model when they are displaying the data.

To use this new view, you need to update the Details actions method of the controller. This is the
updated code:

```
public ActionResult Details(int? id)
{
```

```
        if (!id.HasValue)
        {
            return RedirectToAction("Select");
        };

        var category = (from c in context.Categories
                        where c.Id == id
                        select c).FirstOrDefault();

        if (category == null)
        {
            category = new Category();
            category.Id = id.Value;
            category.Name = "Invalid Category ID";
        };

        return View(category);
    }
```

Figure 19B-4 shows the page that is rendered using the new view.

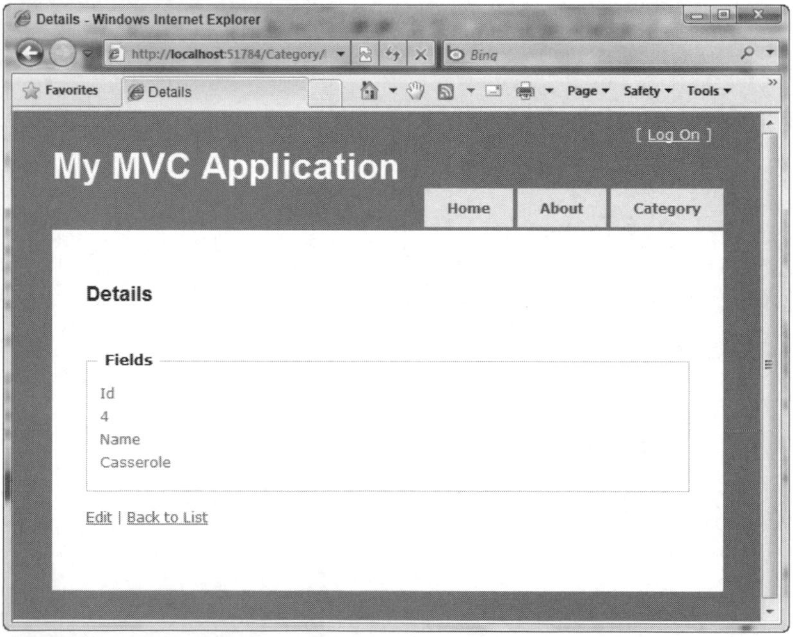

FIGURE 19B-4

If I combine everything I have shown you so far about displaying data with MVC I get the following markup for a view that displays one recipe:

```
<%@ Page Language="C#" Inherits="System.Web.Mvc.ViewPage<DataLayer.Recipe>" %>

<!DOCTYPE html PUBLIC "-//W3C//DTD XHTML 1.0 Transitional//EN"
```

```
        "http://www.w3.org/TR/xhtml1/DTD/xhtml1-transitional.dtd">

<html xmlns="http://www.w3.org/1999/xhtml" >
<head id="Head1" runat="server">
    <title>Recipe</title>
    <link href="/Content/StyleSheet.css" rel="stylesheet" type="text/css" />
</head>
<body>
    <div class="header">
        <img src="/images/SuperEasyRecipesLogo.gif" alt="Super Easy Recipes" />
    </div>
    <div class="sidebar">
        <h2>Tools</h2>
        <ol>
            <% foreach (var item in Model.Tools) { %>
                <li><%: item.Name %></li>
            <% } %>
        </ol>
    </div>
    <div class="content">
        <h1><%: Model.Name %></h1>
        <table>
            <tr>
                <td>Prep Time:</td>
                <td>Cook Time:</td>
                <td>Ready In:</td>
            </tr>
            <tr>
                <td><%: Model.PrepTime %> Min</td>
                <td><%: Model.CookTime %> Min</td>
                <td><%: Model.PrepTime + Model.CookTime %> Min</td>
            </tr>
        </table>
        <h2>Ingredients</h2>
        <ul>
            <% foreach (var item in Model.Ingredients) { %>
                <li><%: item.Name %></li>
            <% } %>
        </ul>
        <%: Model.Directions %>
    </div>
</body>
</html>
```

> *The ordered list that is used to display the list of tools can also be rendered using the
> HTML helper that you created in Lesson 10B.*

Figure 19B-5 shows the page that is rendered, assuming that the cascading style sheet (CSS) from
Lesson 3 is used.

FIGURE 19B-5

TRY IT

In this lesson you use the DataLayer that you created in Lesson 18 to display data in an ASP.NET MVC application.

Lesson Requirements

➤ The DataLayer.dll created in Lesson 18.

➤ The recipes.mdf file used in Lesson 18.

➤ The ConnectionString.txt file.

Hints

➤ Don't forget to check the Create a strongly typed view checkbox when you create the views.

Step-by-Step

1. Verify that the recipes.mdf file is in a folder named c:\ASPNETTrainer\DataLayer and that the file is not read-only.

2. Open Microsoft Visual Web Developer 2010 Express.

3. Select New Project from the File menu.

4. Select **Visual C#** on the left side of the dialog box.

5. Select the **ASP.NET MVC 2 Web Application** template.

6. Enter **Lesson19b** in the Name field and **c:\ASPNETTrainer** in the Location field. Click the OK button.

7. Right-click References in the Solution Explorer window and select Add Reference to open the Add Reference dialog box. Select the .NET tab, select the **System.Data.Entity** Component Name, and click the OK button (see Figure 19B-6).

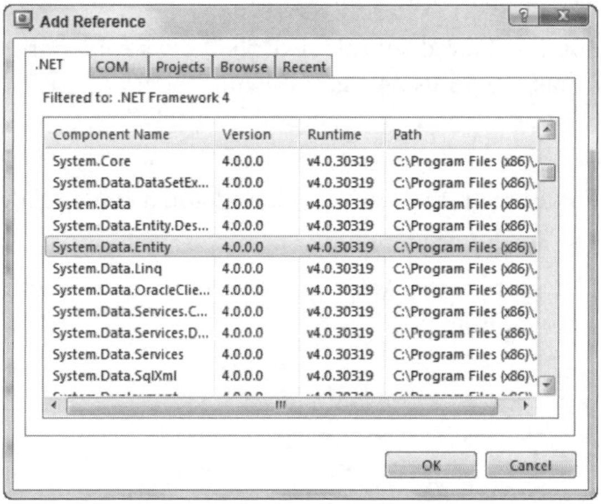

FIGURE 19B-6

8. Right-click References in the Solution Explorer window and select Add Reference to open the Add Reference dialog box. Select the Browse tab, browse to the `DataLayer.dll` file, and click the OK button.

> The `DataLayer.dll` *is located in the following folder:*
>
> `c:\ASPNETTrainer\DataLayer\DataLayer\bin\Debug`

9. Open the ConnectionString.txt and copy the text to add the following connection string to the list of connection strings in the `web.config` file:

```
<add name="RecipeDBEntities" connectionString=
    "metadata=res://*/DataModel.csdl|res:
//*/DataModel.ssdl|res://*/DataModel.msl;provider=System.Data.SqlClient;provider
connection string=&quot;DataSource=.\SQLEXPRESS;
AttachDbFilename=C:\ASPNETTrainer\DataLayer\Recipes.mdf;IntegratedSecurity=True;
Connect Timeout=30;User Instance=True;MultipleActiveResultSets=True&quot;"
providerName="System.Data.EntityClient" />
```

> *This connection string assumes that the* `recipes.mdf` *file is in the* `C:\ASPNETTrainer\` `DataLayer` *folder. If it is in a different folder, you will need to update the path to the* `recipes.mdf` *file.*

10. Add the following assembly into the `assemblies` element of the `web.config` file.

```
<add assembly="System.Data.Entity, Version=4.0.0.0, Culture=neutral,
    PublicKeyToken=b77A5c561934e089" />
```

11. Select Build Lesson 19b from the Build menu to build the application.

12. Open the `Site.Master` file that is located in the Shared subfolder of the Views folder and update the `Site.Master` file to add a new menu item using the following code:

```
<li><%: Html.ActionLink("Category", "Index", "Category")%></li>
```

13. Right-click the Views folder, select New Folder from the Add menu, and add a folder called **Category**.

14. Right-click the Category folder and select View from the Add menu to create a new strongly-typed view called **Index** using the settings shown in Figure 19B-7.

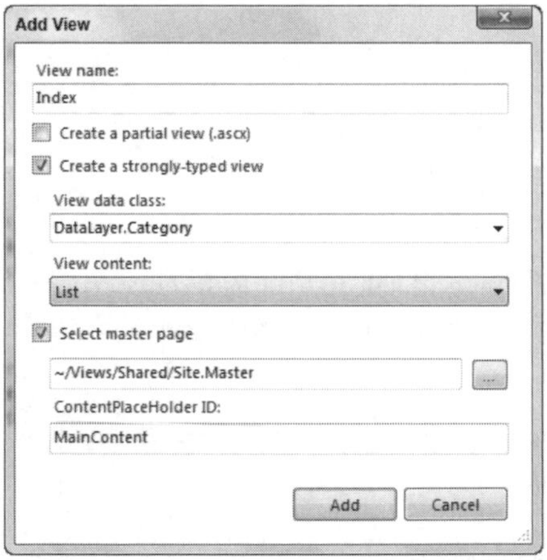

FIGURE 19B-7

15. Right-click the Category folder and select View from the Add menu to create a new strongly-typed view called **Details** using the settings shown in Figure 19B-8.

16. Right-click the Controllers folder, select Controller from the Add menu, and check the `Add action methods for Create, Update, Delete, and Details scenarios` checkbox to add a new controller named **CategoryController**. This adds the default scaffolding for the controller.

17. Add the following `using` statement to the top of the `CategoryController.cs` file:

```
using DataLayer;
```

18. Add the following reference to the `CategoryController`:

```
RecipeDBEntities _entity = new RecipeDBEntities();
```

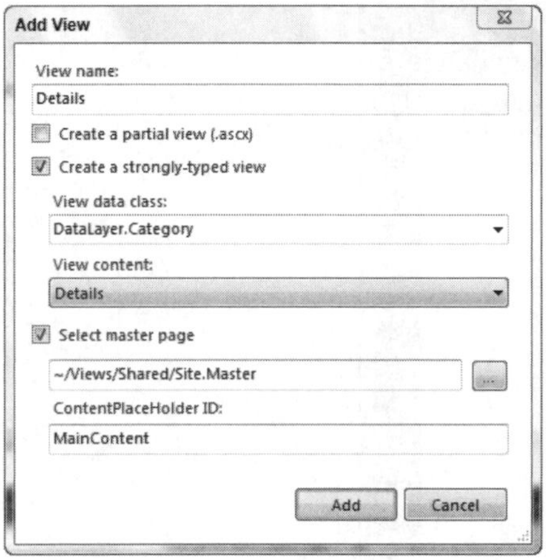

FIGURE 19B-8

19. Update the `Index` action item of the `CategoryController` to the following:

```
public ActionResult Index()
{
    var categories = from c in _entity.Categories
                     orderby c.Name
                     select c;
    return View(categories);
}
```

20. Update the `Details` action item of the `CategoryController` to the following:

```
public ActionResult Details(int id)
{
    var category = (from c in _entity.Categories
                    where c.Id == id
                    select c).FirstOrDefault();

    return View(category);
}
```

21. Click the F5 Button.

22. Click the Category tab (Figure 19B-9).

23. Click the Details link (see Figure 19B-10).

> *If you attempt to edit, delete or create a new category you will receive an unhandled exception because you have not yet created those views. You create the Edit, Delete and Create views in Lesson 20B.*

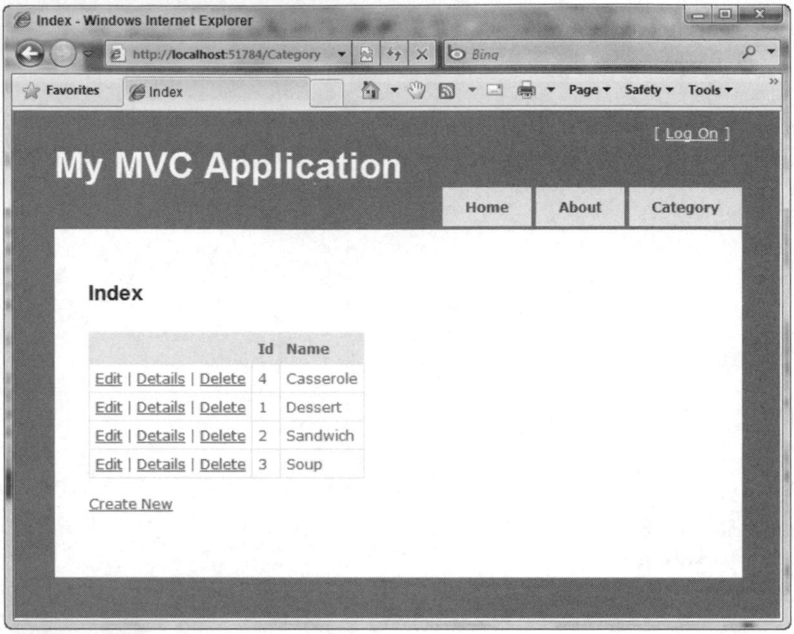

FIGURE 19B-9

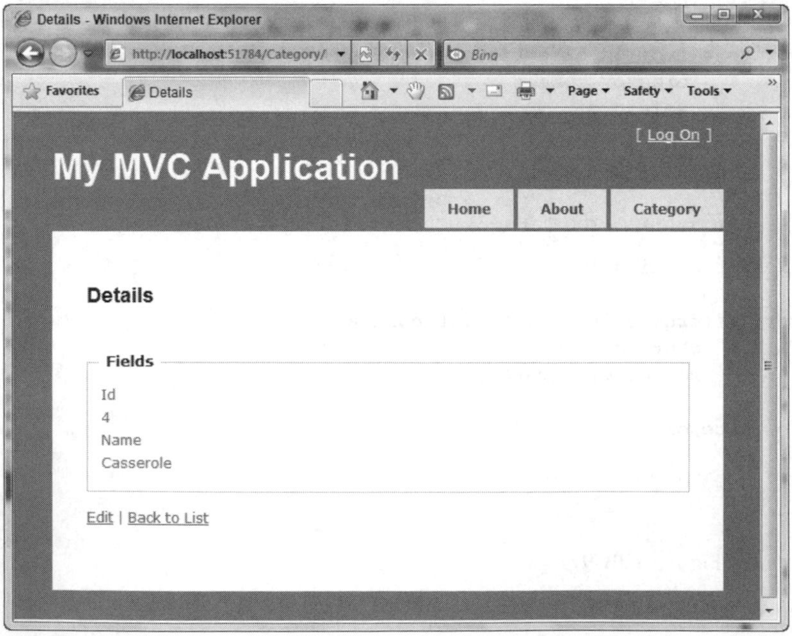

FIGURE 19B-10

 Please select Lesson 19B on the DVD to view the video that accompanies this lesson.

20A

Using GridView in Web Forms

The GridView control is one of the most useful yet complex server controls provided by Web Forms. Nothing like it exists in the MVC framework (unless you write your own). In this lesson I show you how to use the GridView control to display, select, sort, page, and edit data.

FORMATTING THE GRIDVIEW

For this lesson I have created the ADO.NET Entity Data Model shown in Figure 20A-1.

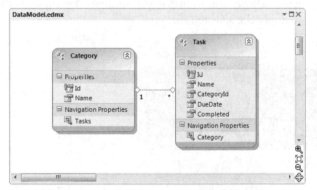

FIGURE 20A-1

This is the markup for a GridView named GridViewTasks:

```
<asp:GridView ID="GridViewTasks" runat="server"
    DataSourceID="EntityDataSourceTasks">
</asp:GridView>
```

 I cover the DataSourceID later in this lesson.

Figure 20A-2 shows the page that is rendered using the preceding GridView markup.

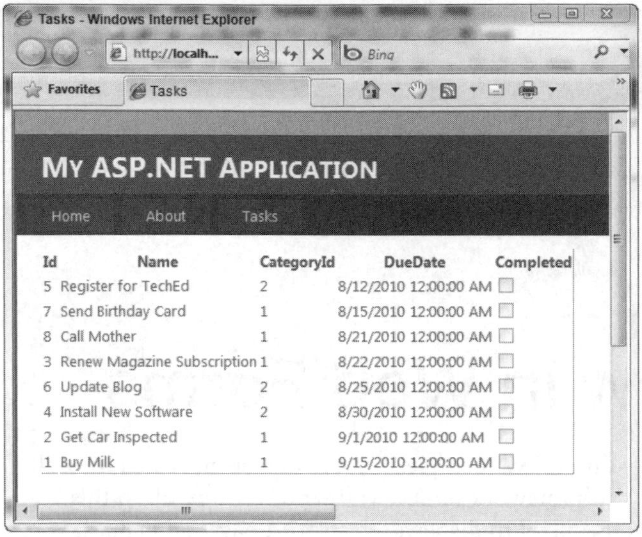

FIGURE 20A-2

The page shows a grid that lists all of the records in the table. However, the grid looks incredibly plain. The easiest way to jazz up the appearance of a `GridView` control is to select the AutoFormat option from the GridView Tasks smart tag (see Figure 20A-3) to open the AutoFormat dialog box (see Figure 20A-4). The AutoFormat dialog box allows you to preview a number of professionally designed formats. Click the Apply button to apply the selected format.

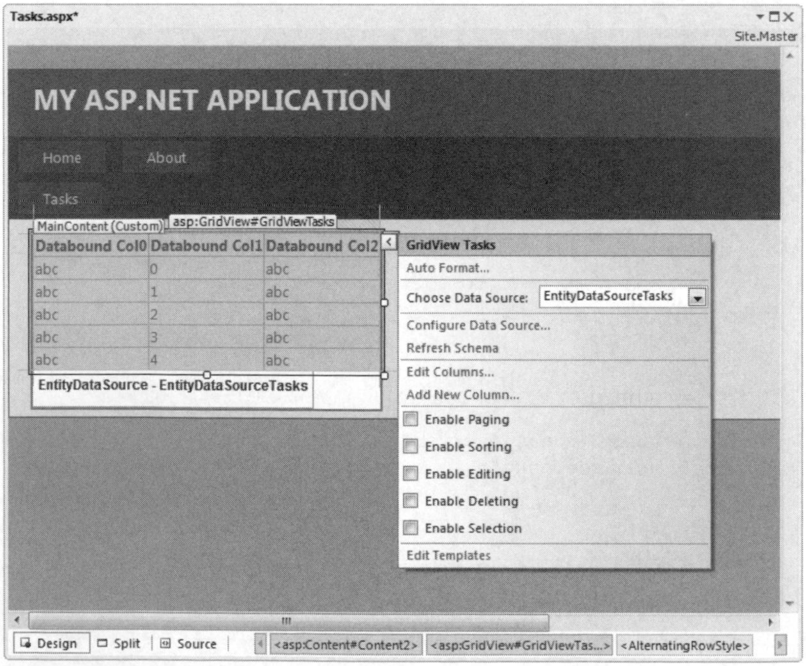

FIGURE 20A-3

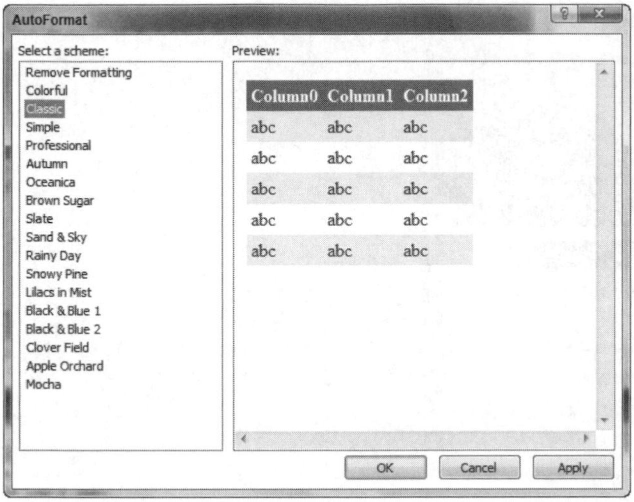

FIGURE 20A-4

This is the markup for the `GridView` after the Classic scheme has been applied:

```
<asp:GridView ID="GridViewTasks" runat="server"
    DataSourceID="EntityDataSourceTasks" CellPadding="4" ForeColor="#333333"
    GridLines="None">
    <AlternatingRowStyle BackColor="White" />
    <EditRowStyle BackColor="#2461BF" />
    <FooterStyle BackColor="#507CD1" Font-Bold="True" ForeColor="White" />
    <HeaderStyle BackColor="#507CD1" Font-Bold="True" ForeColor="White" />
    <PagerStyle BackColor="#2461BF" ForeColor="White" HorizontalAlign="Center" />
    <RowStyle BackColor="#EFF3FB" />
    <SelectedRowStyle BackColor="#D1DDF1" Font-Bold="True" ForeColor="#333333" />
    <SortedAscendingCellStyle BackColor="#F5F7FB" />
    <SortedAscendingHeaderStyle BackColor="#6D95E1" />
    <SortedDescendingCellStyle BackColor="#E9EBEF" />
    <SortedDescendingHeaderStyle BackColor="#4870BE" />
</asp:GridView>
```

Figure 20A-5 shows the page that is rendered after applying the Classic scheme to the `GridViewTasks`.

EDITING COLUMNS

The grid looks much better with the scheme applied. However, a number of problems exist with how the data is displayed:

1. The Id field is shown.

2. The DueDate field includes the time.

3. The CategoryId field is shown instead of the Category's name.

To correct these items, you need to select the Edit Columns option from the GridView Tasks smart tag to open the Fields dialog box shown in Figure 20A-6.

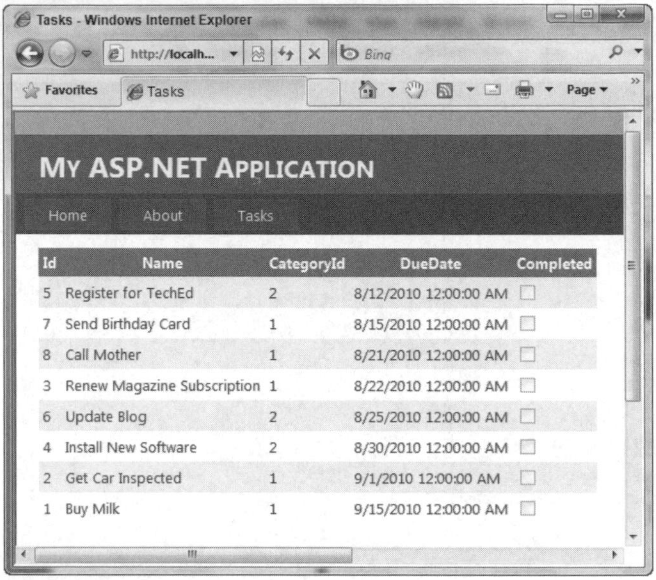

FIGURE 20A-5

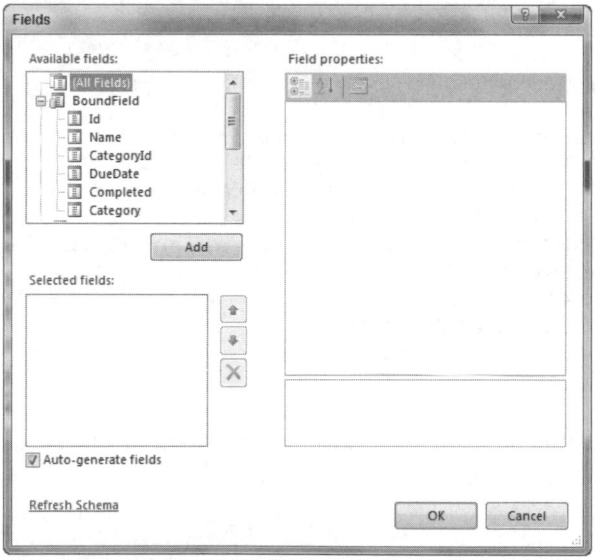

FIGURE 20A-6

Using the Fields dialog box, follow these steps:

1. In the Available fields list box under BoundField, select **Name** and click the Add button.

2. In the Available fields list box under BoundField, select **Category** and click the Add button.

3. In the Available fields list box under BoundField, select **DueDate** and click the Add button.

4. In the Available fields list box under CheckBoxField, select **Completed** and click the Add button.

5. Uncheck the Auto-generate fields checkbox.

6. In the Selected fields list box, select DueDate and update `ApplyFormatInEditMode` to True and `DataFormatString` to `{0:d}`(see Figure 20A-7).

> *If the Available fields list box does not include any bound fields, click the Refresh Schema link at the bottom of the Fields dialog box.*

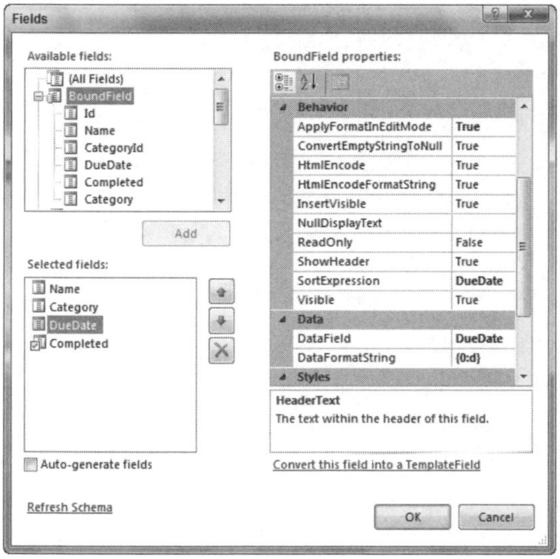

FIGURE 20A-7

Figure 20A-8 shows the page with the updated grid.

USING TEMPLATED FIELDS

Some things look better, but the Category field now says Lesson20a.Models.Category instead of the name of the category. To fix this issue, you need to once again select the Edit Columns option from the GridView Tasks smart tag to open the Fields dialog box. On the Fields dialog box, you need to select the Category field from the Selected fields list box and click the `Convert this field into a TemplateField` link at the bottom of the Fields dialog box.

In the new TemplateField, the data bound to the `Text` property needs to be updated from "Category" to "Category.Name." This is the updated category TemplateField:

```
<asp:TemplateField HeaderText="Category" SortExpression="Category.Name">
    <EditItemTemplate>
        <asp:TextBox ID="TextBox1" runat="server"
            Text='<%# Bind("Category.Name") %>'>
        </asp:TextBox>
```

```
        </EditItemTemplate>
        <ItemTemplate>
            <asp:Label ID="Label1" runat="server" Text='<%# Bind("Category.Name") %>'>
            </asp:Label>
        </ItemTemplate>
    </asp:TemplateField>
```

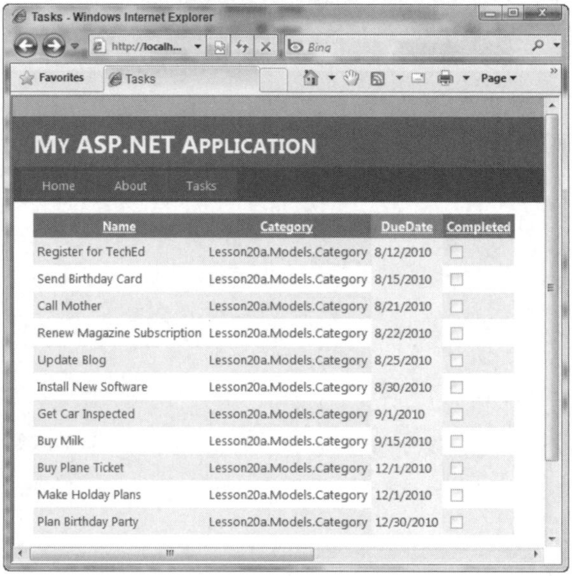

FIGURE 20A-8

Figure 20A-9 shows the page with the updated grid.

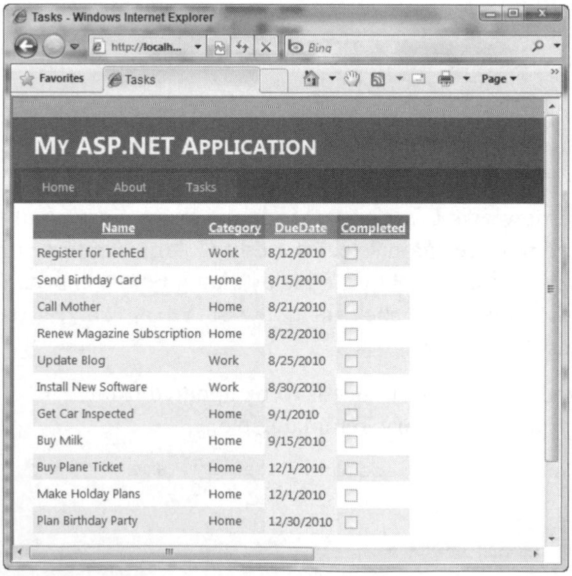

FIGURE 20A-9

To enable paging, sorting, editing, deleting, and selecting, open the GridView Tasks smart tag panel and click all of the checkboxes shown in Figure 20A-10.

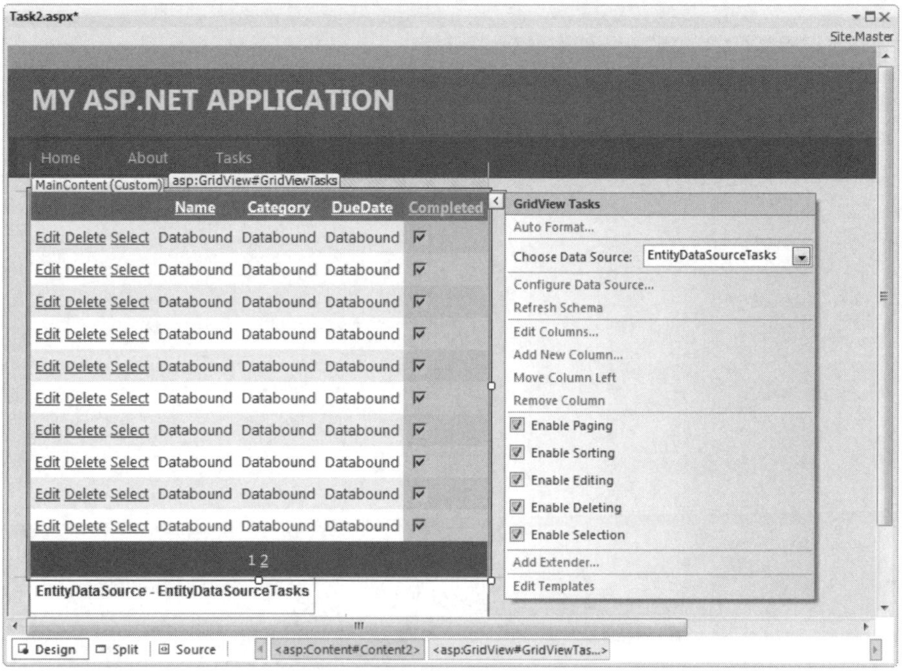

FIGURE 20A-10

Everything works, except the Category field should use a drop-down list instead of a textbox when the record is in edit mode. Select the Edit Templates option from the GridView Tasks smart tag to open the Template Editor and select **EditItemTemplate** from the Display drop-down list (see Figure 20A-11).

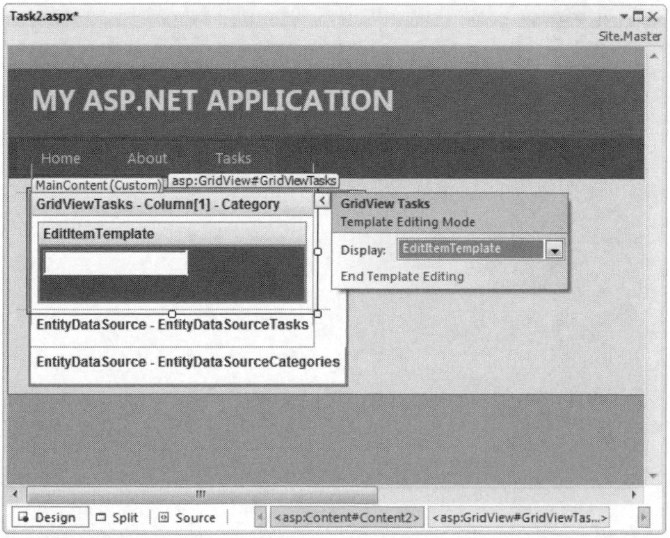

FIGURE 20A-11

Delete the `TextBox` from the EditItemTemplate and replace it with a `DropDownList`. Set the Data Source for the `DropDownList` to **EntityDataSourceCategories,** and set the display field to **Name** and the value field to **Id** using the Data Source Configuration Wizard shown in Figure 20A-12.

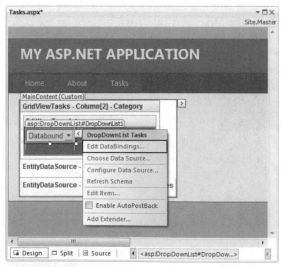

FIGURE 20A-12

Edit the DataBindings for the new `DropDownList` (see Figure 20A-13).

FIGURE 20A-13

Set the `SelectedValue` Bindable property to **Bind("CategoryId")** as shown in Figure 20A-14.

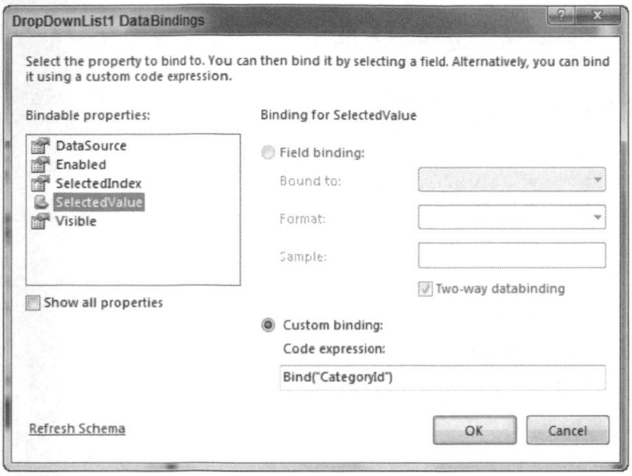

FIGURE 20A-14

Figure 20A-15 shows the final grid with everything working properly.

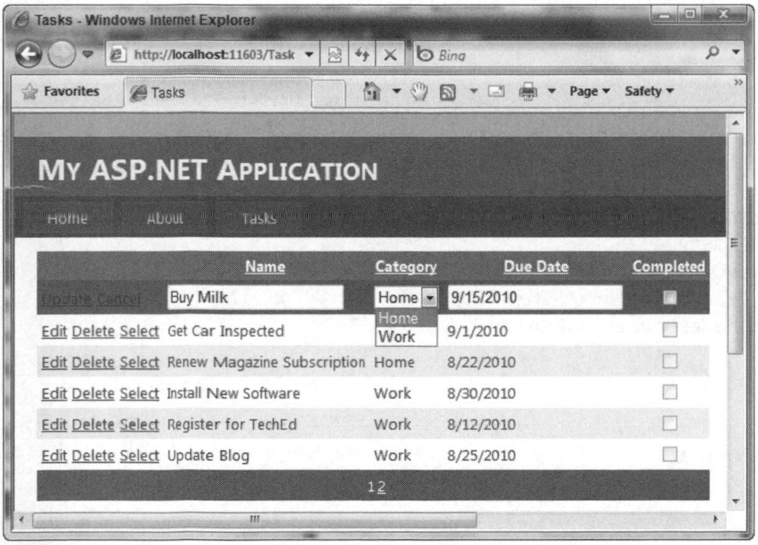

FIGURE 20A-15

This is the final markup for the grid:

```
<asp:GridView ID="GridViewTasks" runat="server" AutoGenerateColumns="False"
    CellPadding="4" ForeColor="#333333" GridLines="None"
    DataSourceID="EntityDataSourceTasks" DataKeyNames="Id" AllowSorting="True"
    AllowPaging="True">
    <AlternatingRowStyle BackColor="White" />
```

```
    <Columns>
        <asp:CommandField ShowDeleteButton="True" ShowEditButton="True"
            ShowSelectButton="True" />
        <asp:BoundField DataField="Name" HeaderText="Name"
            SortExpression="Name" />
        <asp:TemplateField HeaderText="Category" SortExpression="Category.Name">
            <EditItemTemplate>
                <asp:DropDownList ID="DropDownList1" runat="server"
                    DataSourceID="EntityDataSourceCategories"
                    DataTextField="Name" DataValueField="Id"
                    SelectedValue='<%# Bind("CategoryId") %>'>
                </asp:DropDownList>
            </EditItemTemplate>
            <ItemTemplate>
                <asp:Label ID="Label1" runat="server"
                    Text='<%# Bind("Category.Name") %>'>
                </asp:Label>
            </ItemTemplate>
        </asp:TemplateField>
        <asp:BoundField DataField="DueDate" DataFormatString="{0:d}"
            HeaderText="Due Date" SortExpression="DueDate"
            ApplyFormatInEditMode="True" />
        <asp:CheckBoxField DataField="Completed" HeaderText="Completed"
            SortExpression="Completed">
            <ItemStyle HorizontalAlign="Center" />
        </asp:CheckBoxField>
    </Columns>
    <EditRowStyle BackColor="#2461BF" />
    <FooterStyle BackColor="#507CD1" Font-Bold="True" ForeColor="White" />
    <HeaderStyle BackColor="#507CD1" Font-Bold="True" ForeColor="White" />
    <PagerStyle BackColor="#2461BF" ForeColor="White" HorizontalAlign="Center" />
    <RowStyle BackColor="#EFF3FB" />
    <SelectedRowStyle BackColor="#D1DDF1" Font-Bold="True" ForeColor="#333333" />
    <SortedAscendingCellStyle BackColor="#F5F7FB" />
    <SortedAscendingHeaderStyle BackColor="#6D95E1" />
    <SortedDescendingCellStyle BackColor="#E9EBEF" />
    <SortedDescendingHeaderStyle BackColor="#4870BE" />
</asp:GridView>
```

DATASOURCE CONTROLS

In this example I use the following two EntityDataSource controls:

```
<asp:EntityDataSource ID="EntityDataSourceTasks" runat="server"
    ConnectionString="name=TaskDBEntities" DefaultContainerName="TaskDBEntities"
    EnableDelete="True" EnableFlattening="False" EnableDelete="True"
    EnableUpdate="True" EntitySetName="Tasks" Include="Category">
</asp:EntityDataSource>
<asp:EntityDataSource ID="EntityDataSourceCategories" runat="server"
    ConnectionString="name=TaskDBEntities" DefaultContainerName="TaskDBEntities"
    EntitySetName="Categories">
</asp:EntityDataSource>
```

As you have seen, the EntityDataSource control made it simple to bind the GridView to an Entity Data Model. The ASP.NET 4 Framework provides seven different DataSource controls to represent different types of data. This is a list of the DataSource controls:

➤ **AccessDataSource** — Represents a Microsoft Access database.

➤ **EntityDataSource** — Represents an Entity Data Model.

➤ **LinqDataSource** — Represents a LINQ to SQL query.

➤ **ObjectDataSource** — Represents a business object.

➤ **SiteMapDataSource** — Represents Site Map.

➤ **SqlDataSource** — Represents a SQL relational database.

➤ **XmlDataSource** — Represents an XML document.

The DataSource controls are located on the Data tab of the Toolbox. The DataSourceID of a DataSource control is used to bind the data that the DataSource control represents to a data bound control. This is called declarative databinding. In the previous lesson I used programmatic databinding. Declarative databinding is easier to use than programmatic databinding, but you lose control of when the databinding occurs because it is handled by the framework instead of your code.

TRY IT

In this lesson you create a GridView that is bound to an Entity Data Model.

Lesson Requirements

➤ The tasks.mdf file.

Hints

➤ Verify that the tasks.mdf file is not read-only.

➤ The GridView is located on the Data tab of the Toolbox.

Step-by-Step

1. Open Microsoft Visual Web Developer 2010 Express.

2. Select New Project from the File menu.

3. Select **Visual C#** on the left side of the dialog box.

4. Select the **ASP.NET Web Application** template.

5. Enter **Lesson20a** in the Name field and **c:\ASPNETTrainer** in the Location field. Click the OK button.

6. Right-click the App_Data folder and select Existing Item from the Add menu. Navigate to the `tasks.mdf` file and click the Add button.

7. Right-click the name of the project in the Solution Explorer window and choose New Folder from the Add menu to add a new folder called **Models**.

8. Right-click the Models folder and select New Item from the Add menu to open the Add New Item dialog box. Click Data to display only the Data templates, select the **ADO.NET Entity Data Model** template, enter **DataModel.edmx** for the name of the new model, and click the Add button to open the Entity Data Model Wizard.

9. Select **Generate from database** and click the Next button.

10. Click the New Connection button and verify that the Data source field contains **Microsoft SQL Server Database File (SqlClient)**.

11. Click the Browse button to navigate to the `tasks.mdf` file. Select the `tasks.mdf` file and click the Open button.

12. Change the name of the entity to **TaskDBEntities** and click the Next button (see Figure 20A-16).

Choose Your Data Connection

Which data connection should your application use to connect to the database?

Tasks.mdf1 ▾ [New Connection...]

This connection string appears to contain sensitive data (for example, a password) that is required to connect to the database. Storing sensitive data in the connection string can be a security risk. Do you want to include this sensitive data in the connection string?

◉ No, exclude sensitive data from the connection string. I will set it in my application code.

○ Yes, include the sensitive data in the connection string.

Entity connection string:

```
metadata=res://*/Model.Model1.csdl|res://*/Model.Model1.ssdl|
res://*/Model.Model1.msl;provider=System.Data.SqlClient;provider connection
string="Data Source=.\SQLEXPRESS;AttachDbFilename=|DataDirectory|
\Tasks.mdf;Integrated Security=True;Connect Timeout=30;User Instance=True"
```

☑ Save entity connection settings in Web.Config as:

TaskDBEntities

[< Previous] [Next >] [Finish] [Cancel]

FIGURE 20A-16

13. Select all of the tables, check the `Pluralize or singularize generated object names` checkbox, check the `Include foreign key columns in the model` checkbox, enter **Models** for the Model namespace, and click the Finish button (see Figure 20A-17).

14. Select **Build Lesson20a** from the Build menu to build the application.

15. Right-click the name of the project in the Solution Explorer window and select New Item from the Add menu to open the Add New Item dialog box. Select the **Web Form using Master Page** template, enter **Tasks.aspx** for the Name, and click the Add button. Select **Site.Master** as the Master Page and click OK.

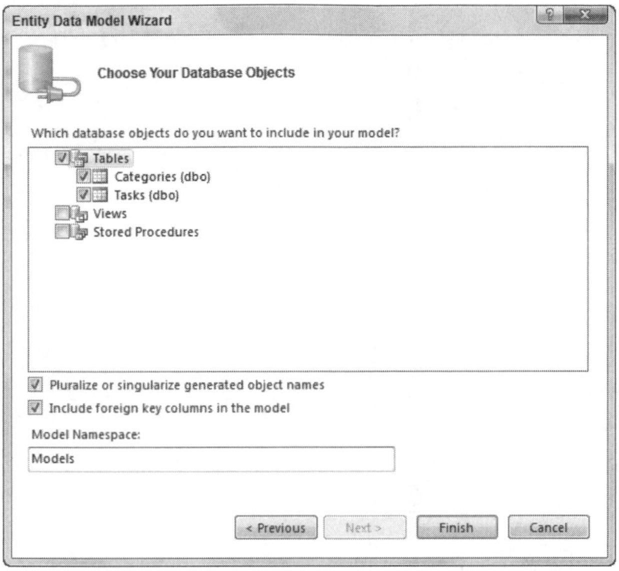

FIGURE 20A-17

16. Update the `Title` attribute of the `@Page` directive to **Tasks**.

17. Add a `GridView` server control to the `MainContent` control on `Tasks.aspx`.

18. Select **<New data source>** from the Choose Data Source drop-down list on the smart tag of the `GridView` to open the Data Source Configuration Wizard (see Figure 20A-18).

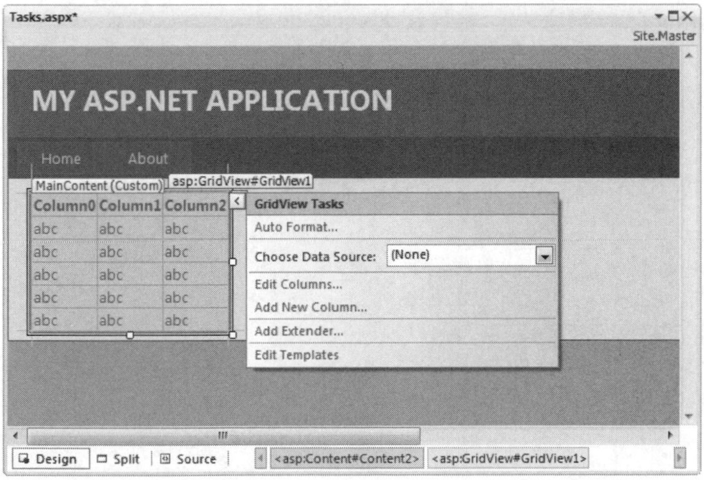

FIGURE 20A-18

19. Select **Entity** and specify **EntityDataSourceTasks** as the ID (see Figure 20A-19). Click the OK button to proceed to the next page.

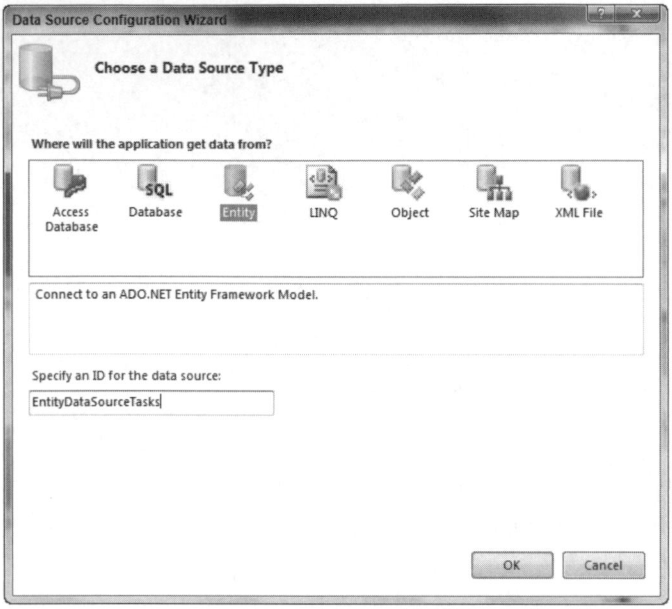

FIGURE 20A-19

20. Select **TaskDBEntities** as the Named Connection and **TaskDBEntities** as the DefaultContainerName (see Figure 20A-20). Click the OK button to proceed to the next page.

FIGURE 20A-20

21. Select **Tasks** as the EntitySetName and click the checkboxes next to Name and Completed (see Figure 20A-21). Click the Finish button to complete the wizard.

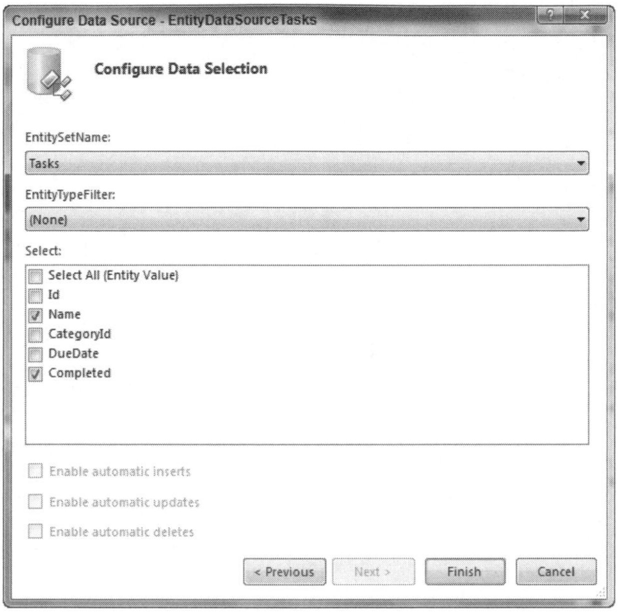

FIGURE 20A-21

22. Select the AutoFormat option from the GridView Tasks smart tag and apply the Classic scheme.

23. Press the F5 button (see Figure 20A-22).

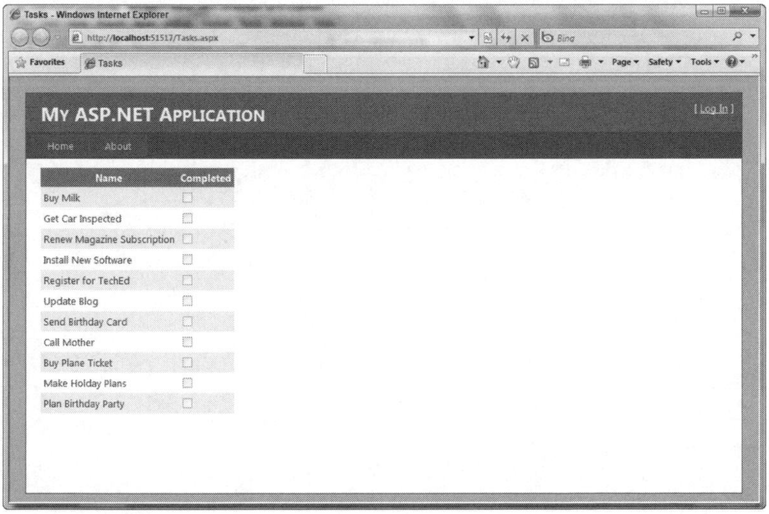

FIGURE 20A-22

Please select Lesson 20A on the DVD to view the video that accompanies this lesson.

20B

Managing Data in MVC

In lesson 19B I showed you how to display data using the ASP.NET MVC framework. In this lesson I show you how to create a new record, update a record, and delete a record using the Entity Data Model that was created in Lesson 18.

ADDING RECORDS

This is the default scaffolding that ASP.NET MVC provides for the Create action method:

```
//
// GET: /Category/Create

public ActionResult Create()
{
    return View();
}


//
// POST: /Category/Create

[HttpPost]
public ActionResult Create(FormCollection collection)
{
    try
    {
        // TODO: Add insert logic here

        return RedirectToAction("Index");
    }
    catch
    {
        return View();
    }
}
```

The action method that accepts a GET does not need to be modified; however, the action method that accepts a POST is incomplete.

In this example, I am assuming the Create View is a strongly-typed view of type `System.Web.Mvc.ViewPage<DataLayer.Category>`. In that case, the first thing I need to do is to change the type of the parameter that is used by the action method from `FormCollection` to `Category`. By doing this the framework does the model binding for me. If I leave the data type as `FormCollection`, I need to either loop through all of the objects on the form manually to update the model or use the `UpdateModel` method of the controller to update the model.

```
var category = new DataLayer.Category();
category.Name = collection["Name"];
...
```

It is much better to let the system try to bind the data to a strongly-typed object. When the system attempts to bind the data it not only looks in the FormCollection, but in the URI Query String and the route data as well. This is the order that it searches:

1. FormCollection

2. URI Query String

3. Values from RouteData

The only downside to letting the system attempt to do the model binding is that it may fail. To handle that case, you should call the `ModelState.IsValid` property, which is a property on the controller.

This is the updated version of the `Create` method that responds to an HTTP POST:

```
//
// POST: /Category/Create

[HttpPost]
public ActionResult Create(Category category)
{
    if (ModelState.IsValid)
    {
        try
        {
            _entity.AddToCategories(category);
            _entity.SaveChanges();

            return RedirectToAction("Index");
        }
        catch
        {
            return View(category);
        }
    };

    return View(category);
}
```

EDITING RECORDS

This is the default scaffolding that ASP.NET MVC provides for the `Edit` action method:

```
//
// GET: /Category/Edit/5

public ActionResult Edit(int id)
{
    return View();
}


//
// POST: /Category/Edit/5

[HttpPost]
public ActionResult Edit(int id, FormCollection collection)
{
    try
    {
        // TODO: Add update logic here

        return RedirectToAction("Index");
    }
    catch
    {
        return View();
    }
}
```

In this case I need to update both the action method that accepts a GET and the action method that accepts a POST. In both cases I need to look up the category that has an Id that matches the `id` that is the first parameter of the action method. This is the updated code:

```
//
// GET: /Category/Edit/5

public ActionResult Edit(int id)
{
    var category = (from c in _entity.Categories
                    where c.Id == id
                    select c).FirstOrDefault();

    if (category != null)
    {
        return View(category);
    };

    // if the category is not found, return to the Index view.
    return RedirectToAction("Index");
}

//
```

```
// POST: /Category/Edit/5

[HttpPost]
public ActionResult Edit(int id, FormCollection collection)
{
    var category = (from c in _entity.Categories
                    where c.Id == id
                    select c).FirstOrDefault();

    if (category != null)
    {
        try
        {
            UpdateModel(category, collection.ToValueProvider());
            _entity.SaveChanges();

            return RedirectToAction("Index");
        }
        catch
        {
            return View(category);
        }
    }

    // if the category is not found, return to the Index view.
    return RedirectToAction("Index");
}
```

The updated `Edit` action method that accepts a POST uses `UpdateModel` to update the category object by using the values returned in the FormCollection.

DELETING RECORDS

This is the default scaffolding that ASP.NET MVC provides for the `Delete` action method:

```
//
// GET: /Default1/Delete/5

public ActionResult Delete(int id)
{
    return View();
}

//
// POST: /Default1/Delete/5

[HttpPost]
public ActionResult Delete(int id, FormCollection collection)
{
    try
    {
        // TODO: Add delete logic here

        return RedirectToAction("Index");
```

```
        }
        catch
        {
            return View();
        }
    }
```

This is the updated code:

```
//
// GET: /Category/Delete/5

public ActionResult Delete(int id)
{
    var category = (from c in _entity.Categories
                    where c.Id == id
                    select c).FirstOrDefault();

    if (category != null)
    {
        return View(category);
    };

    // if the category is not found, return to the Index view.
    return RedirectToAction("Index");
}


//
// POST: /Category/Delete/5

[HttpPost]
public ActionResult Delete(int id, FormCollection collection)
{
    var category = (from c in _entity.Categories
                    where c.Id == id
                    select c).FirstOrDefault();

    if (category != null)
    {
        try
        {
            _entity.Categories.DeleteObject(category);
            _entity.SaveChanges();

            return RedirectToAction("Index");
        }
        catch
        {
            return View(category);
        }
    }

    // if the category is not found, return to the Index view.
    return RedirectToAction("Index");
}
```

TRY IT

In this lesson you add the ability to add, edit, and delete records on the project you worked on in Lesson 19B.

Lesson Requirements

➤ The project created in Lesson 19B.

Hints

➤ Don't forget to check the `Create a strongly typed view` checkbox when you create the views.

Step-by-Step

1. Open Microsoft Visual Web Developer 2010 Express.

2. Select Open Project from the File menu, navigate to the `Lesson19a.sln` file, and click the Open button.

3. Click the F5 button.

4. Navigate to the Category tab (see Figure 20B-1).

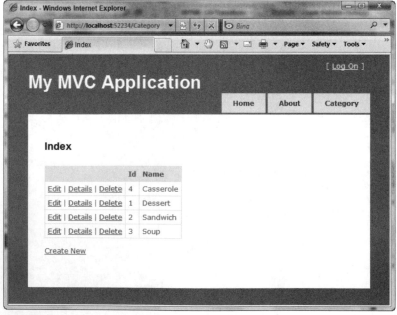

FIGURE 20B-1

5. Stop debugging by closing the browser.

6. Open the `CategoryController.cs` file.

7. Update the `Create` action method that accepts a POST to the following:

```
//
// POST: /Category/Create

[HttpPost]
public ActionResult Create(Category category)
{
    if (ModelState.IsValid)
    {
        try
        {
            _entity.AddToCategories(category);
            _entity.SaveChanges();

            return RedirectToAction("Index");
        }
        catch
        {
            return View(category);
        }
    };

    return View(category);
}
```

8. Right-click anywhere in the updated action item to open the Add View dialog box.

9. Use the Add View dialog box to add a strongly-typed view named **Create** as shown in Figure 20B-2.

FIGURE 20B-2

10. Delete the following markup from the Create view:

```
<div class="editor-label">
    <%: Html.LabelFor(model => model.Id) %>
```

```
</div>
<div class="editor-field">
    <%: Html.TextBoxFor(model => model.Id) %>
    <%: Html.ValidationMessageFor(model => model.Id) %>
</div>
```

> *Since the Id field will be generated automatically by the system, you do not need to enter it on the Create view.*

11. Click the F5 button.

12. Navigate to the Category tab and click the Create New link to open the Create page shown in Figure 20B-3.

FIGURE 20B-3

13. Enter **Test** in the Name field and click the Create button.

14. Stop debugging by closing the browser.

15. Update the Edit action methods to the following:

```
//
// GET: /Category/Edit/5

public ActionResult Edit(int id)
{
    var category = (from c in _entity.Categories
```

```
                    where c.Id == id
                    select c).FirstOrDefault();

        if (category != null)
        {
            return View(category);
        };

         return RedirectToAction("Index");
    }

    //
    // POST: /Category/Edit/5

    [AcceptVerbs(HttpVerbs.Post)]
    public ActionResult Edit(int id, FormCollection collection)
    {
        var category = (from c in _entity.Categories
                        where c.Id == id
                        select c).FirstOrDefault();

        if (category != null)
        {
            try
            {
                UpdateModel(category, collection.ToValueProvider());
                _entity.SaveChanges();

                 return RedirectToAction("Index");
            }
            catch
            {
                 return View(category);
            }
        }

        return RedirectToAction("Index");
    }
```

16. Right-click anywhere in the updated action item to open the Add View dialog box.

17. Use the Add View dialog box to add a strongly-typed view named **Edit** as shown in Figure 20B-4.

18. Replace the TextBox that is used to display the Id field by deleting the following code:

```
<%: Html.TextBoxFor(model => model.Id) %>
```

19. And adding this code:

```
<%: Model.Id  %>
```

20. Press the F5 button.

21. Navigate to the Category tab and click the Edit link next to the first category to open the Edit view shown in Figure 20B-5.

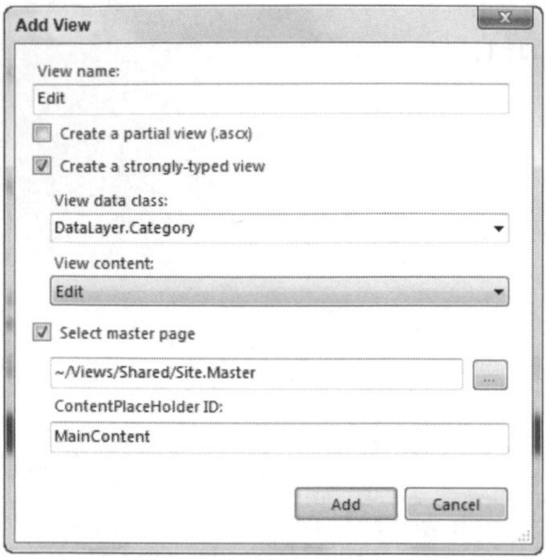

Add View

View name:

Edit

☐ Create a partial view (.ascx)

☑ Create a strongly-typed view

View data class:

DataLayer.Category ▼

View content:

Edit ▼

☑ Select master page

~/Views/Shared/Site.Master   [...]

ContentPlaceHolder ID:

MainContent

[Add]   [Cancel]

FIGURE 20B-4

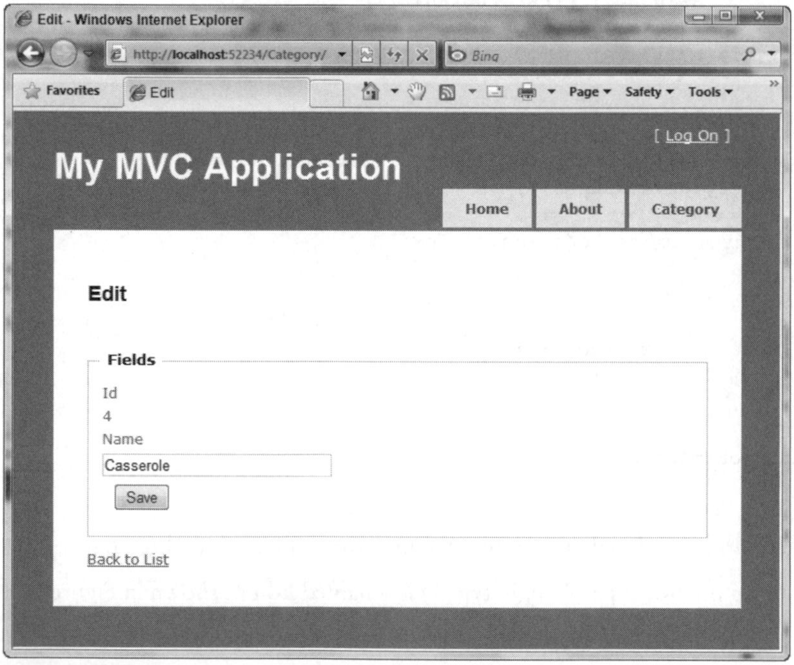

Edit - Windows Internet Explorer

http://**localhost**:52234/Category/ ▼   b Bing

☆ Favorites   Edit   Page ▼ Safety ▼ Tools ▼

[Log On]

My MVC Application

| Home | About | Category |

Edit

┌─ Fields ──
│ Id
│ 4
│ Name
│ [Casserole   ]
│
│ [Save]
└───

Back to List

FIGURE 20B-5

22.   Stop debugging by closing the browser.

23.   Update the Delete action method to the following:

```
//
// GET: /Category/Delete/5

public ActionResult Delete(int id)
```

```
    {
        var category = (from c in _entity.Categories
                        where c.Id == id
                        select c).FirstOrDefault();

        if (category != null)
        {
            return View(category);
        };

        return RedirectToAction("Index");
    }

    //
    // POST: /Category/Delete/5

    [HttpPost]
    public ActionResult Delete(int id, FormCollection collection)
    {
        var category = (from c in _entity.Categories
                        where c.Id == id
                        select c).FirstOrDefault();

        if (category != null)
        {
            try
            {
                _entity.Categories.DeleteObject(category);
                _entity.SaveChanges();

                return RedirectToAction("Index");
            }
            catch
            {
                return View(category);
            }
        }

        return RedirectToAction("Index");
    }
```

24. Right-click anywhere in the updated action item to open the Add View dialog box.

25. Use the Add View dialog box to add a strongly-typed view named **Delete** as shown in Figure 20B-6.

26. Click the F5 button.

27. Navigate to the Category tab and click the **Delete** link next to the Test category to open the Delete view shown in Figure 20B-7.

28. Click the Delete button.

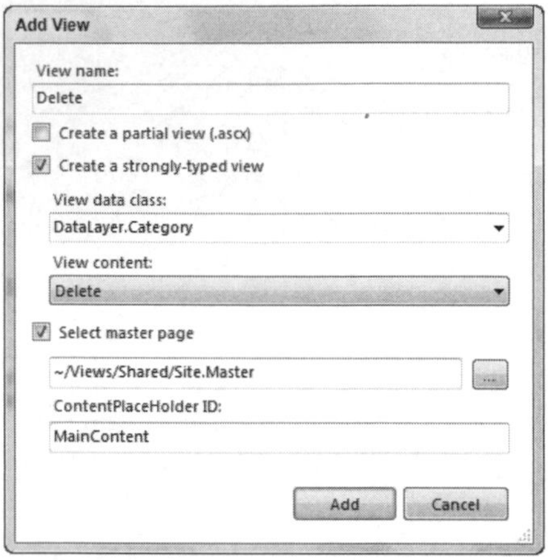

Add View

View name:

Delete

☐ Create a partial view (.ascx)

☑ Create a strongly-typed view

View data class:

DataLayer.Category

View content:

Delete

☑ Select master page

~/Views/Shared/Site.Master

ContentPlaceHolder ID:

MainContent

[Add]   [Cancel]

FIGURE 20B-6

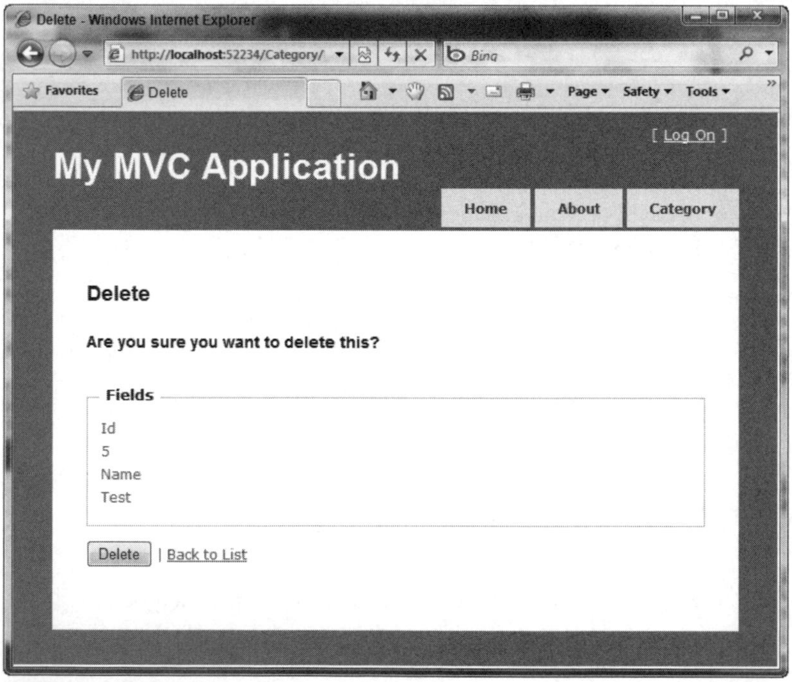

My MVC Application

[Log On]

Home   About   Category

Delete

Are you sure you want to delete this?

Fields

Id
5
Name
Test

[Delete] | Back to List

FIGURE 20B-7

Please select Lesson 20B on the DVD to view the video that accompanies this lesson.

SECTION VIII
Managing Data

21A

Dynamic Data in Web Forms

Dynamic Data is a framework that enables you to create a fully functional data-driven web application in only five minutes. In the previous lessons I have shown you how to extend the simple sample application that Microsoft Visual Web Developer 2010 Express creates when you use the ASP.NET Web Application template. In this lesson I show you how to create a data-driven application that uses the Dynamic Data framework.

Microsoft Visual Web Developer 2010 Express provides two different templates for creating applications that use Dynamic Data:

➤ **ASP.NET Dynamic Data Entities Web Application** — This template uses an Entity Data Model to access the data.

➤ **ASP.NET Dynamic Data Linq to SQL Web Application** — This template uses LINQ to SQL to access the data.

THE DYNAMIC DATA ENTITIES WEB APPLICATION TEMPLATE

In this lesson I use the ASP.NET Dynamic Data Entities Web Application template. Unlike with the other templates that I have demonstrated in this book, you cannot immediately run a new web application that uses the Dynamic Data framework. Instead, you must do two things before the application can run:

1. Add an Entity Data Model.

2. Update the `Global.asax` file.

Figure 21A-1 shows the Entity Data Model (EDM) that I use in this lesson. This is the same model I used in Lesson 20A.

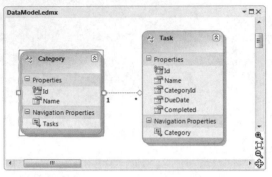

FIGURE 21A-1

The namespace for the EDM is Models and the entity container is TaskDBEntities.

Now, I need to update the `Global.asax` file. The default `Global.asax` file contains a `RegisterRoutes` method that is called during the `Application_Start` event and has most of its contents commented out. This is the code in the default `RegisterRoutes` method:

```
public static void RegisterRoutes(RouteCollection routes)
{
    //                    IMPORTANT: DATA MODEL REGISTRATION
    // Uncomment this line to register an ADO.NET Entity Framework model for
    // ASP.NET Dynamic Data.
    // Set ScaffoldAllTables = true only if you are sure that you want all tables
    // in the data model to support a scaffold (i.e. templates) view. To control
    // scaffolding for individual tables, create a partial class for the table and
    // apply the [ScaffoldTable(true)] attribute to the partial class.
    // Note: Make sure that you change "YourDataContextType" to the name of the
    // data context class in your application.
    //DefaultModel.RegisterContext(typeof(YourDataContextType), new
    //    ContextConfiguration() { ScaffoldAllTables = false });

    // The following statement supports separate-page mode, where the List,
    // Detail, Insert, and Update tasks are performed by using separate pages. To
    // enable this mode, uncomment the following route definition, and comment
    // out the route definitions in the combined-page mode section that follows.
    routes.Add(new DynamicDataRoute("{table}/{action}.aspx")
    {
        Constraints = new RouteValueDictionary(
            new { action = "List|Details|Edit|Insert" }
        ),
        Model = DefaultModel
    });

    // The following statements support combined-page mode, where the List, Detail,
    // Insert, and Update tasks are performed by using the same page. To enable
    // this mode, uncomment the following routes and comment out the route
    // definition in the separate-page mode section above.
    //routes.Add(new DynamicDataRoute("{table}/ListDetails.aspx") {
    //    Action = PageAction.List,
```

```
    //     ViewName = "ListDetails",
    //     Model = DefaultModel
    //});

    //routes.Add(new DynamicDataRoute("{table}/ListDetails.aspx") {
    //     Action = PageAction.Details,
    //     ViewName = "ListDetails",
    //     Model = DefaultModel
    //});
}
```

> 🖉 Dynamic Data uses URL routing to match HTTP requests with the appropriate page template and data. Lesson 15 covers URL routing.

According to the comments in the `Global.asax` file, the following line of code must be uncommented and updated in order to run the application:

```
//DefaultModel.RegisterContext(typeof(YourDataContextType), new
//     ContextConfiguration() { ScaffoldAllTables = false });
```

This is the updated code that uses my EDM:

```
DefaultModel.RegisterContext(typeof(Models.TaskDBEntities),
    new ContextConfiguration() { ScaffoldAllTables = true });
```

Figure 21A-2 shows the home page of my new application.

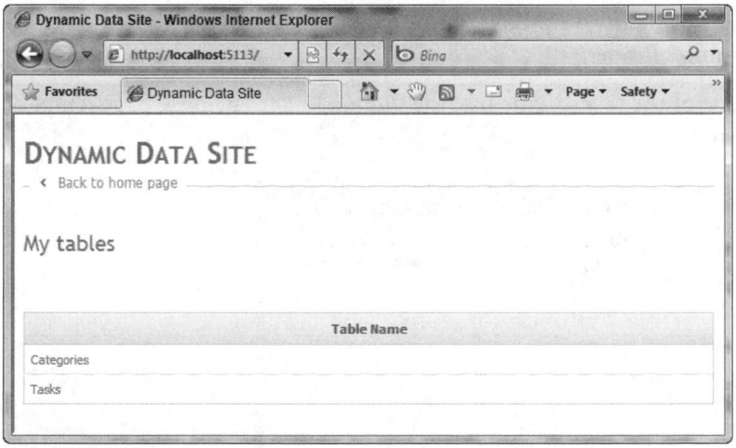

FIGURE 21A-2

As you can see, since I have changed the value of `ScaffoldAllTables` to true, all of the tables are included on the home page. If I click Tasks, the `Tasks/List.aspx` page template shown in Figure 21A-3 is rendered.

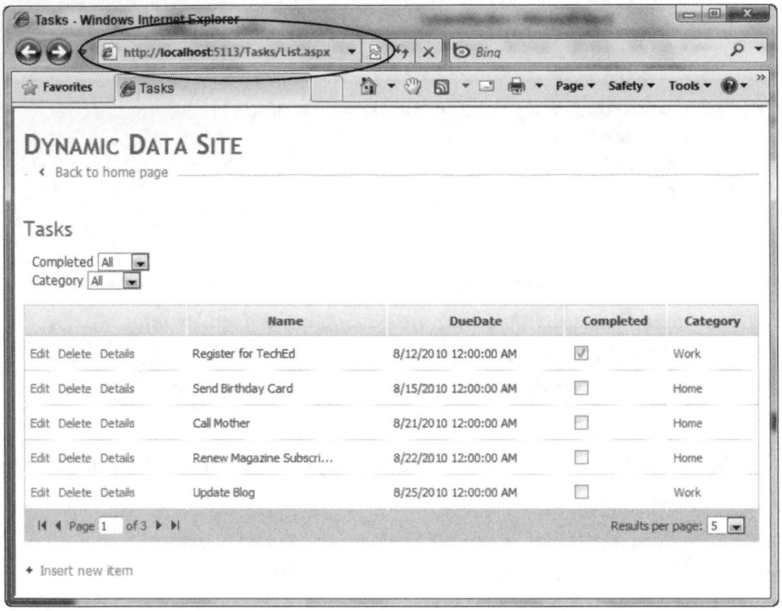

FIGURE 21A-3

PAGE TEMPLATES

On the `Lists.aspx` page template, paging is automatically enabled. I can edit, delete, and insert new items. I can also filter the items by using the drop-down lists at the top of the page. Finally, I can sort each column by clicking the column's header.

If I click the `Details` link for one of the tasks in the list, the `Tasks/Details.aspx` page template shown in Figure 21A-4 is rendered.

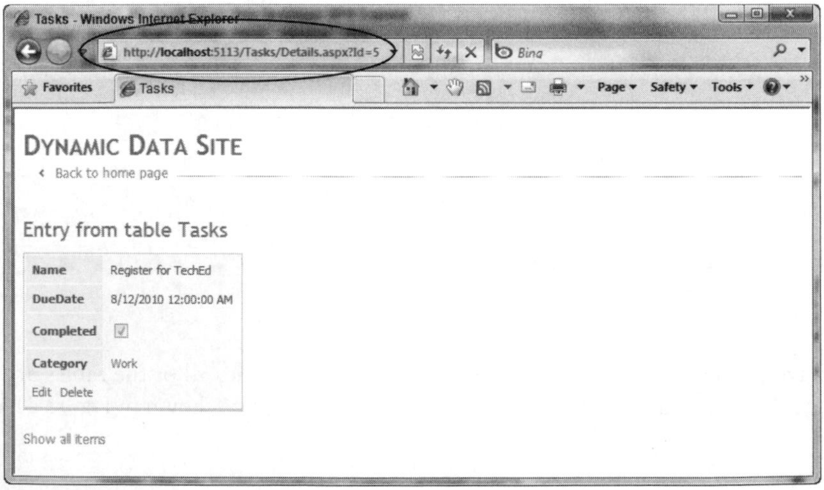

FIGURE 21A-4

> *The Dynamic Data framework is smart enough to hide the Id field for the table. In fact, by default, the Dynamic Data framework will not display a foreign key field or a field that is automatically generated by the database.*

If I click the Edit link, I see the Tasks/Edits.aspx page template (Figure 21A-5), which allows me to edit all of the fields in the table except for the Id field.

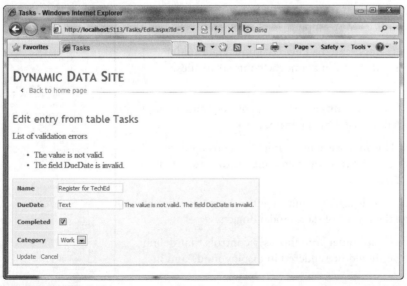

FIGURE 21A-5

One of the nice features of Dynamic Data is that it uses your underlying data model to validate the data. For example, if I try to enter a text string in the DueDate field it automatically returns an error (see Figure 21A-6).

FIGURE 21A-6

For completeness, if I return to the `Tasks/Lists.aspx` page template and click the `Add New Item` link, the page shown in Figure 21A-7 is rendered.

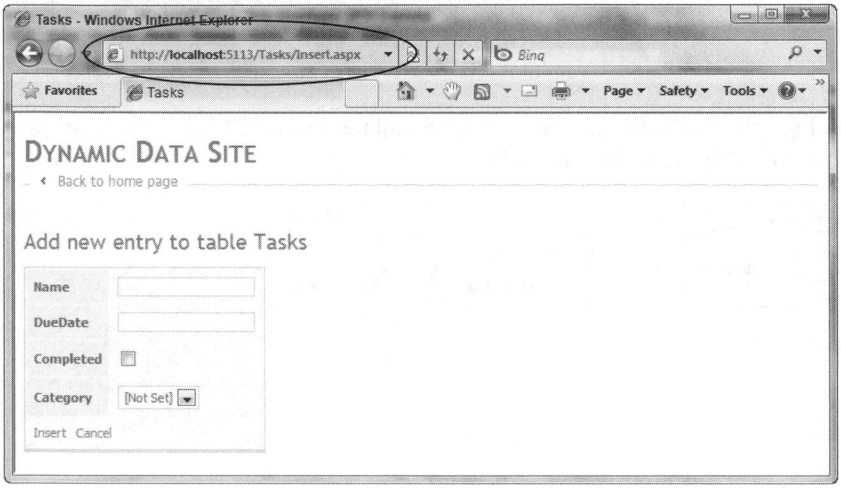

FIGURE 21A-7

The amazing thing about the Dynamic Data framework is that by default all of the tables use the same page templates — `Lists.aspx`, `Edit.aspx`, `Insert.aspx`, and `Details.aspx` — to manage their data. It accomplishes this by using URL routing.

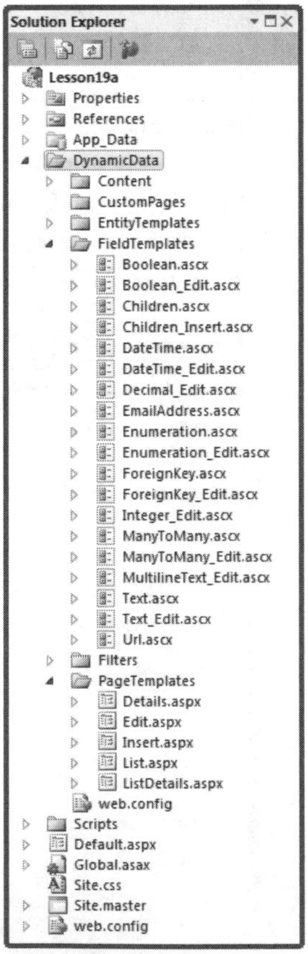

DYNAMIC DATA FOLDER STRUCTURE

The Solution Explorer window shown in Figure 21A-8 shows most of the files and folders that are created when you create a web application using the Dynamic Data Entities Web Application template.

As you can see the template has created a new Dynamic Data folder with six subfolders. This is information about the contents of these subfolders:

➤ **Content** — This folder contains an images subfolder and a couple of user controls that are used by the framework.

➤ **Custom Pages** — This folder is empty. It is the repository for your custom page templates. I cover creating custom page templates in Lesson 22A.

➤ **Entity Templates** — This folder contains entity templates that are used to customize the layout of data model objects.

➤ **Field Templates** — This folder contains user controls that define how each data type should be rendered in display mode and in edit mode.

FIGURE 21A-8

➤ **Filters** — This folder contains user controls used to filter data.

➤ **Page Templates** — This folder contains the page templates that dynamically create the UI to display and edit data. By default it contains the `Details.aspx`, `Edit.aspx`, `Insert.aspx`, `List.aspx` and `ListDetails.aspx` page templates.

> *The* `ListDetails.aspx` *page is not used with the default URL route that is defined in the* `Global.asax` *file. You must edit the* `RegisterRoutes` *method in the* `Global.asax` *file in order to use it. The* `ListDetails` *page template is an all-in-one; that is, it can be used for all actions: List, Insert, Details, and Edit.*

In practice, you rarely want to allow users to edit *all* of the tables in your Entity Data Model. To include only certain tables in the scaffolding provided by the Dynamic Data framework, you need to modify the code in the `RegisterRoutes` method to set `ScaffoldAllTables` to `false`. This is the updated code to set `ScaffoldAllTables` to `false`:

```
DefaultModel.RegisterContext(typeof(Models.TaskDBEntities),
    new ContextConfiguration() { ScaffoldAllTables = false });
```

PARTIAL CLASSES

If you set `ScaffoldAllTables` to `false` you need to designate individually which tables should be included. You do this by creating a partial class that is decorated with `[ScaffoldTable(true)]`. This is the code to enable scaffolding on the Tasks table:

```
using System.ComponentModel.DataAnnotations;

namespace Lesson21a.Models
{
    public class Partials
    {
        [ScaffoldTable(true)]
        public partial class Task
        {
        }
    }
}
```

Likewise, there are times when you do not want to expose every field in a table. You can control which fields are displayed by using the `ScaffoldColumnAttribute`. This is the code that hides the Completed field:

```
using System.ComponentModel.DataAnnotations;

namespace Lesson21a.Models
{
    [MetadataType(typeof(Task_MetaData))]
    public partial class Task
    {
```

```
    }

    [ScaffoldTable(true)]
    public class Task_MetaData
    {
        [ScaffoldColumn(false)]
        public object Completed;
    }
}
```

To apply the `ScaffoldColumnAttribute` I had to create a `Task_MetaData` class. I can also use the `Task_MetaData` class to modify the display name and the format of the DueDate field. This is the updated code:

```
using System.ComponentModel.DataAnnotations;

namespace Lesson21a.Models
{
    [MetadataType(typeof(Task_MetaData))]
    public partial class Task
    {
    }

    [ScaffoldTable(true)]
    public class Task_MetaData
    {
        [ScaffoldColumn(false)]
        public object Completed;

        [Display(Name="Due Date")]
        [DisplayFormat(DataFormatString="{0:d}")]
        public object DueDate;
    }
}
```

Figure 21A-9 shows the updated page.

TRY IT

In this lesson you build a fully functional web application, using the Dynamic Data framework, in only five minutes, and with only one line of code to modify.

Lesson Requirements

➤   The `tasks.mdf` file.

Hints

➤   Verify that the `tasks.mdf` file is not read-only.

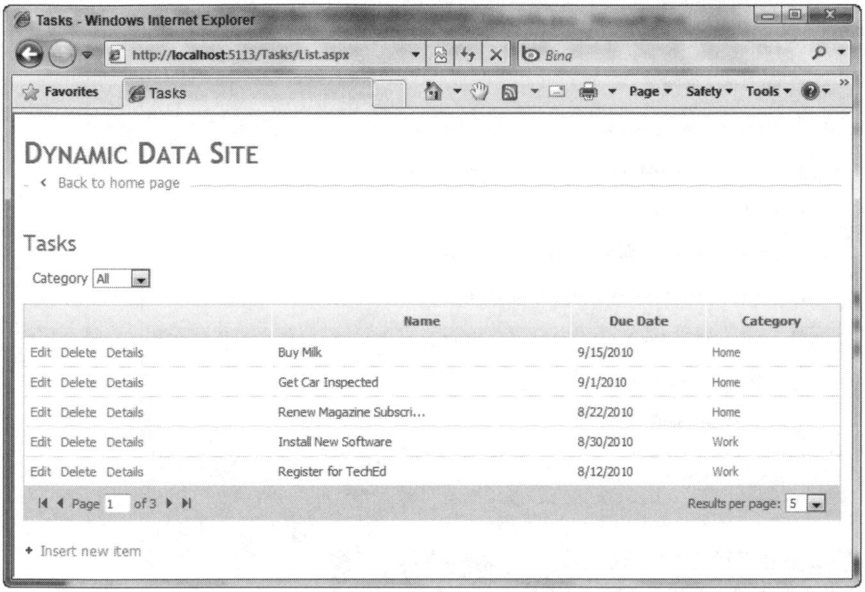

FIGURE 21A-9

Step-by-Step

1. Open Microsoft Visual Web Developer 2010 Express.

2. Select New Project from the File menu.

3. Select **Visual C#** on the left side of the dialog box.

4. Select the **ASP.NET Dynamic Data Entities Web Application** template (see Figure 21A-10).

5. Enter **Lesson21a** in the Name field and **c:\ASPNETTrainer** in the Location field. Click the Add button.

6. Right-click the App_Data folder and select Existing Item from the Add menu. Navigate to the `tasks.mdf` file and click the Add button.

7. Right-click the name of the project in the Solution Explorer window and choose New Folder from the Add menu to add a new folder called **Models**.

8. Right-click Models folder and select Add New from the Add menu to open the Add New Item dialog box. Click Data to display only the Data templates, select the **ADO.NET Entity Data Model** template, enter **DataModel.edmx** for the name of the new model, and click the Add button to open the Entity Data Model Wizard.

9. Select **Generate from database** and click the Next button.

10. Click the New Connection button to open the Connection Properties dialog box.

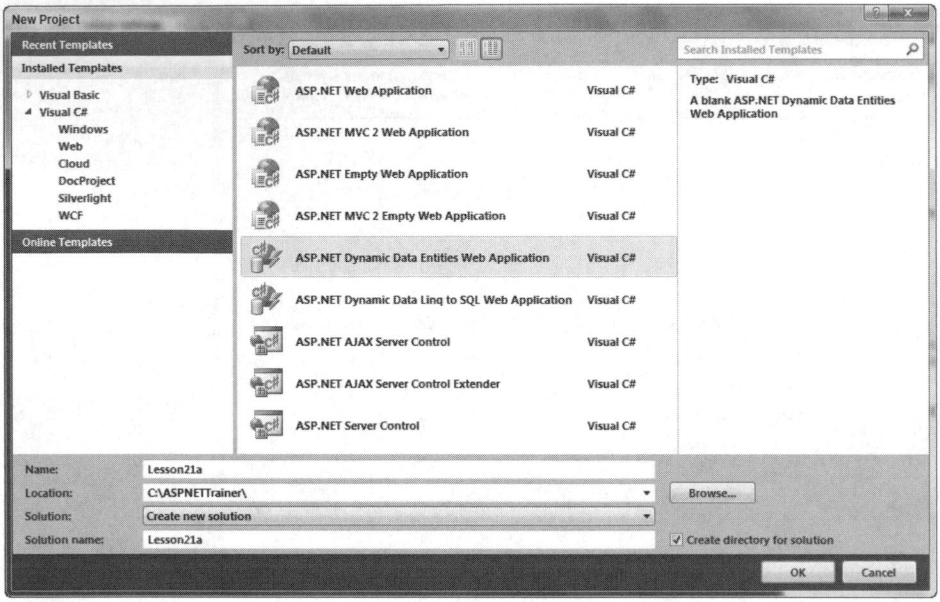

FIGURE 21A-10

11. Click the Change button, select Microsoft SQL Server Database File from the Data Source list box, and click the OK button.

12. Click the Browse button to navigate to the `tasks.mdf` file. Select the `tasks.mdf` file and click the Open button.

13. Click the OK button to close the Connection Properties dialog box.

14. Change the name of the entity to **TaskDBEntities** and click the Next button.

15. Select all of the tables, check the `Pluralize or singularize generated object names` checkbox, check the `Include foreign key columns in the model` checkbox, enter **Models** for the Model namespace, and click the Finish button.

> For more detailed information on how to create an Entity Data Model, see Lesson 18.

16. Right-click the `Default.aspx` file and select Set As Start Page from the menu.

17. Add this code to the top of the `RegisterRoutes` method in the `Global.asax` file:

```
DefaultModel.RegisterContext(typeof(Models.TaskDBEntities), new
ContextConfiguration() { ScaffoldAllTables = true });
```

18. Click the F5 button.

19. Click the OK button to enable debugging.

20. Add, edit and delete a task.

 Please select Lesson 21A on the DVD to view the video that accompanies this lesson.

21B

Display Templates in MVC

Display templates are templated helpers that enable you to build a user interface based on your data model. In this lesson I show you how to use display templates to display the data in your model.

Here are the three helper methods in the `DisplayExtensions` class:

➤ **Display**() — This helper returns HTML markup for a particular property in the model where the property is identified via a string expression.

➤ **DisplayFor**() — This helper also returns HTML markup for a particular property in the model. However, with this helper, the property is identified via a strongly-typed expression.

➤ **DisplayForModel**() — This helper returns HTML markup for all of the simple properties in the model.

> *The expression* `DisplayFor(model => model)` *is equivalent to* `DisplayForModel()`.

THE DISPLAYFORMODEL HELPER

Figure 21B-1 shows the Entity Data Model (EDM) that I use in this lesson.

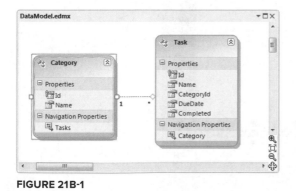

FIGURE 21B-1

This is the `Details` action method:

```
//
// GET: /Task/Details/5

public ActionResult Details(int id = 1)
{
    var task = (from t in _entity.Tasks
                where t.Id == id
                select t).FirstOrDefault();

    return View(task);
}
```

In the preceding action method I have set the default value of the `id` parameter to `1`. This is the View that uses the `DisplayForModel` helper:

```
<%@ Page Title="" Language="C#" MasterPageFile="~/Views/Shared/Site.Master"
    Inherits="System.Web.Mvc.ViewPage<Lesson21b.Models.Task>" %>

<asp:Content ID="Content1" ContentPlaceHolderID="TitleContent" runat="server">
    Details
</asp:Content>
<asp:Content ID="Content2" ContentPlaceHolderID="MainContent" runat="server">
    <h2>Details</h2>
    <%: Html.DisplayForModel() %>
</asp:Content>
```

Figure 21B-2 shows the page that is rendered.

FIGURE 21B-2

The page shown in Figure 21B-2 shows most of the properties and their values, however, although the CategoryID property is shown, the Category property is missing. This is because the DisplayForModel helper method renders HTML markup only for the simple properties of the model. I show you how to include the Category information later in this lesson.

Another problem with the page shown in Figure 21B-2 is that the DueDate field displays both the date and time when it should only display the date. The format of the DueDate field can be controlled by using data annotations. This is the code to properly format the DueDate field:

```
using System.ComponentModel.DataAnnotations;

namespace Lesson21b.Models
{
    [MetadataType(typeof(Task_MetaData))]
    public partial class Task
    {}

    public class Task_MetaData
    {
        [DisplayFormat(DataFormatString="{0:d}")]
        public object DueDate;
    }
}
```

> *Because the* DueDate *property is already defined in the* Task *class I cannot redefine it, so, I have to create a new class called* Task_MetaData *in order to make changes to the* DueDate *property.*

Figure 21B-3 shows the page with the correctly formatted DueDate field.

As you can see, the default formatting that is provided is not very pleasing to the eye. This is the rendered markup that is used to display the data:

```
<h2>Details</h2>
<div class="display-label">Id</div>
<div class="display-field">1</div>
<div class="display-label">Name</div>
<div class="display-field">Buy Milk</div>
<div class="display-label">CategoryId</div>
<div class="display-field">1</div>
<div class="display-label">DueDate</div>
<div class="display-field">9/15/2010</div>
<div class="display-label">Completed</div>
<div class="display-field">
    <input class="check-box" disabled="disabled" type="checkbox" />
</div>
```

FIGURE 21B-3

Because by default, all of the labels use the `display-label` class and all of the values use the `display-field` class, the output that is rendered can be readily formatted via a cascading style sheet. Figure 21B-4 shows the page that is rendered by using the following style rule:

```
.display-label
{
    margin: 0px 10px 0px 0px;
    font-weight: bold;
    float: left;
    display: inline;
}
```

FIGURE 21B-4

CUSTOM DISPLAY TEMPLATES

This updated page is a little better. However, custom display templates can be used to further fine-tune the output. Custom display templates are stored in a DisplayTemplates subfolder of the Views folder. They can be either regular view pages or view user controls (`.aspx` or `.ascx`). The system looks for an appropriate display template in the following locations:

➤ ~/Views/ControllerName/DisplayTemplates/TemplateName

➤ ~/Views/Shared/DisplayTemplates/TemplateName

The TemplateName is determined by looking at the ModelMetadata and the property's data type. This is the order in which template names are searched:

1. TemplateHint from ModelMetadata

2. DataTypeName from ModelMetadata

3. Name of the type

4. String: if the object is not complex

5. Object: if the object is complex

To create a custom display template that uses a table to format all of the fields in a complex object, I need to create an `Object.ascx` file. This is the markup for a file named `Object.ascx` that I have placed in the Views/Shared/DisplayTemplates folder:

```
<%@ Control Language="C#" Inherits="System.Web.Mvc.ViewUserControl" %>
<table>
    <% foreach (var prop in ViewData.ModelMetadata.Properties) {%>
    <tr>
        <td><strong><%: prop.PropertyName %></strong></td>
        <td><%: Html.Display(prop.PropertyName) %></td>
    </tr>
    <% } %>
</table>
```

Figure 21B-5 shows the page that is rendered.

At this point you are asking yourself two questions:

1. What is ModelMetadata?

2. Why is the completed field being rendered with a checkbox?

The `ModelMetadata` class is a container for common metadata. It is constructed from the attributes of the `System.ComponentModel` and the `System.ComponentModel.DataAnnotations` namespaces. These are the properties of the `ModelMetadata` class:

➤ `AdditionalValues`

➤ `ContainerType`

➤ `ConvertEmptyStringToNull`

➤ `DataTypeName`

➤ Description

➤ DisplayFormatString

➤ DisplayName

➤ EditFormatString

➤ HideSurroundingHtml

➤ IsComplexType

➤ IsNullableValueType

➤ IsReadOnly

➤ IsRequired

➤ Model

➤ ModelType

➤ NullDisplayText

➤ Properties

➤ PropertyName

➤ ShortDisplayName

➤ ShowForDisplay

➤ ShowForEdit

➤ SimpleDisplayText

➤ TemplateHint

➤ Watermark

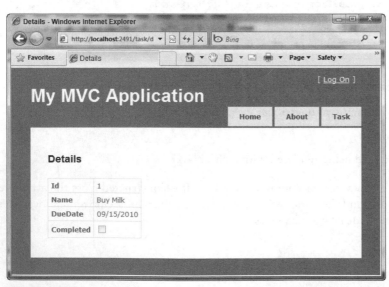

FIGURE 21B-5

The `ModelMetadata` class also has a number of helper methods. This is a list of the most useful ones:

➤ **FromLambdaExpression** — This method returns the `ModelMetadata` for the model identified by the expression.

➤ **FromStringExpression** — This method returns the `ModelMetadata` for the model identified by the expression.

➤ **GetDisplayName** — This method returns the display name of the model. If the `DisplayName` is `null`, it returns the `PropertyName`. If the `PropertyName` is `null`, it returns the `ModelType.Name`.

➤ **GetValidators** — This method returns the validators for the model.

The reason that the Completed field is rendered with a checkbox is that the ASP.NET MVC framework includes a number of built-in display templates. This is a list of the built-in display templates:

➤ **Boolean** — This template renders a disabled checkbox. The checkbox is disabled because it is a display template.

➤ **Decimal** — This template renders a number with two decimal places unless a DataFormatString has been applied to the property.

➤ **EmailAddress** — This template renders a mailto link.

➤ **HiddenInput** — This template renders a hidden object.

➤ **Html** — This template renders the HTML.

➤ **Object** — This template renders a complex object.

➤ **String** — This template renders text.

➤ **Text** — This template renders text. It has the same implementation as String.

➤ **Url** — This template renders a link.

Any of the built-in display templates can be replaced with a custom display template. Also, additional display templates can be added. To replace the checkbox with a custom display template for Boolean type objects, add a `Boolean.ascx` page to the Views/Shared/DisplayTemplates folder. This is the markup for a Boolean display template that replaces the checkbox with some text:

```
<%@ Control Language="C#" Inherits="System.Web.Mvc.ViewUserControl" %>
<% if (Convert.ToBoolean(ViewData.Model))
    { %>
Good Job!
<% }
    else
    { %>
:-<
<% }; %>
```

Figure 21B-6 shows the page that is rendered.

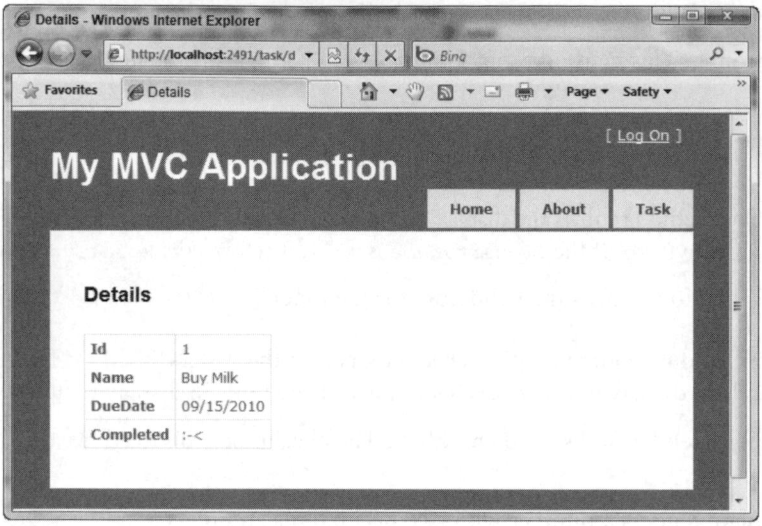

FIGURE 21B-6

So far, I have shown you how to create a generic display template to handle any complex object. However, as you might expect, you can also create a display template for a particular complex object. This is the markup for the `Task.ascx` file that functions as a display template for the Task object:

```
<%@ Control Language="C#"
    Inherits="System.Web.Mvc.ViewUserControl<Lesson21b.Models.Task>" %>
<fieldset>
    <legend>Fields</legend>
    <p>
        Id: <%: Html.DisplayFor(t => Model.Id) %>
    </p>
    <p>
        Name: <%: Html.DisplayFor(t => Model.Name)%>
    </p>
    <p>
        Category: <%: Html.DisplayFor(t => Model.Category)%>
    </p>
    <p>
        DueDate: <%: Html.DisplayFor(t => Model.DueDate)%>
    </p>
    <p>
        Completed: <%: Html.DisplayFor(t => Model.Completed)%>
    </p>
</fieldset>
```

The `Task.ascx` file is in the Views/Shared/DisplayTemplates folder. Figure 21B-7 shows the page that is rendered.

TRY IT

In this lesson you use the built-in display templates to display the information found in a simple model.

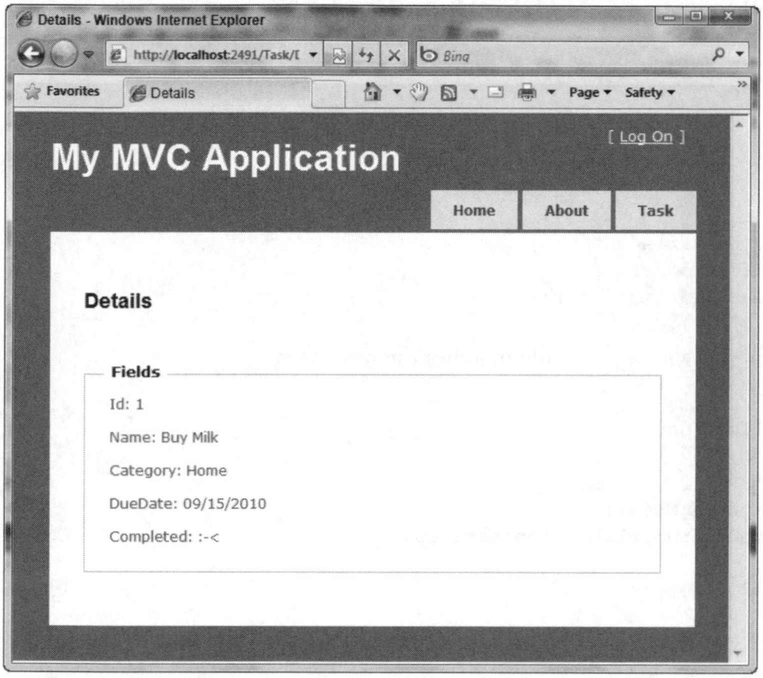

FIGURE 21B-7

Lesson Requirements

None.

Hints

None.

Step-by-Step

1. Open Microsoft Visual Web Developer 2010 Express.

2. Select New Project from the File menu.

3. Select **Visual C#** on the left side of the dialog box.

4. Select the **ASP.NET MVC 2 Web Application** template.

5. Enter **Lesson21b** in the Name field and **c:\ASPNETTrainer** in the Location field. Click the Add button.

6. Right-click the Models folder and select Class from the Add menu to create a class named **Contact.cs**.

7. Add the following using statements to the Contact.cs file:

```
using System.ComponentModel;
using System.ComponentModel.DataAnnotations;
```

8. Add the following code to the Contact class:

```
[Required]
public string Name { get; set; }

[Required]
public int Age { get; set; }

[Required]
[DataType(DataType.EmailAddress)]
[DisplayName("Email Address")]
public string EmailAddress { get; set; }
```

9. Verify that the code in the Contact.cs file matches the following:

```
using System;
using System.Collections.Generic;
using System.Linq;
using System.Web;
using System.ComponentModel;
using System.ComponentModel.DataAnnotations;

namespace Lesson21b.Models
{
    public class Contact
    {
        [Required]
        public string Name { get; set; }

        [Required]
        public int Age { get; set; }

        [DataType(DataType.EmailAddress)]
        [DisplayName("Email Address")]
        public string EmailAddress { get; set; }
    }
}
```

10. Select Build Lesson21b from the Build menu and wait for the build process to complete.

11. Right-click the Views folder and select New Folder from the Add menu to add a subfolder named **Contact**.

12. Right-click the Contact folder and select View from the Add menu to open the Add View dialog box (see Figure 21B-8). Set the View name to **Details**, check the Create a strongly-typed view checkbox, select **Lesson21b.Models.Contact** as the View data class and **Empty** as the View content. Click the Add button.

13. Add the following line to the MainContent content placeholder:

```
<%: Html.DisplayForModel() %>
```

14. Right-click the Controllers folder, select Controller from the Add menu, enter **ContactController** for the name of the controller, check the Add action methods for Create, Update, Delete, and Details scenarios checkbox, and click the Add button.

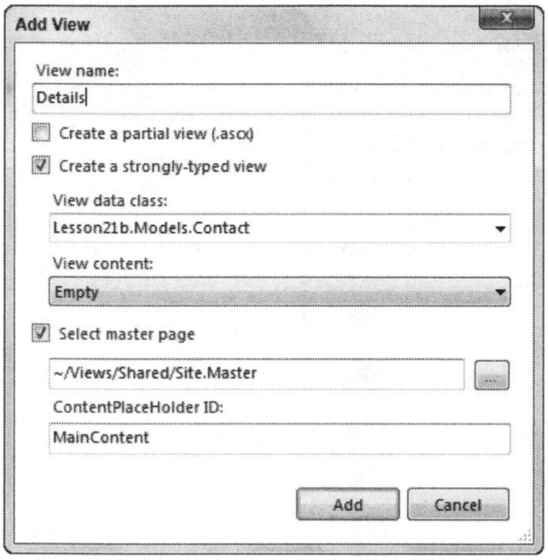

FIGURE 21B-8

15. Update the `Details` action method to the following:

```
//
// GET: /Contact/Details/5

public ActionResult Details(int id)
{
    Models.Contact contact = new Models.Contact();
    contact.Name = "John Smith";
    contact.Age = 32;
    contact.EmailAddress = "jsmith@hotmail.com";
    return View(contact);
}
```

16. Click the F5 button and navigate to the page shown in Figure 21B-9 by adding **contact/details/1** to the browser's address bar.

The email address is rendered as a link because the default display template for email address is being used.

17. Stop debugging by closing the browser.

18. Add the following rule to the bottom of the `Site.css` file that is located in the Content folder:

```
/* DisplayForModel
   ----------------------------------------------------------------------*/
.display-label
{
    margin: 0px 10px 0px 0px;
    font-weight: bold;
    float: left;
    display: inline;
}
```

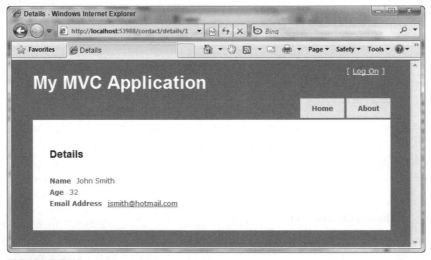

FIGURE 21B-9

19. Click the F5 button and navigate to the page shown in Figure 21B-10 by adding **contact/details/1** to the browser's address bar.

FIGURE 21B-10

Please select Lesson 21B on the DVD to view the video that accompanies this lesson.

22A

Dynamic Data Templates in Web Forms

In Lesson 21A you created a fully functional data-driven application by writing only one line of code. The Dynamic Data framework uses templates to provide the default views for data. It uses entity templates, field templates, and page templates. In this lesson I show you how to customize a page template and how to create a new field template.

PAGE TEMPLATES

The Dynamic Data framework uses five page templates. All of the page templates are just regular ASPX pages. They are:

➤ **Details.aspx** — This page displays the data from a single row of the table.

➤ **Edit.aspx** — This page allows you to edit the data from a single row of the table.

➤ **Insert.aspx** — This page allows you to insert a row into the table.

➤ **List.aspx** — This page lists all of the rows in the table using a `GridView` control.

➤ **ListDetails.aspx** — This page lists all of the rows in the table using a `GridView` control and allows you to edit and insert rows using a `DetailsView` control.

CUSTOM PAGE TEMPLATES

If you make a change to any of the pages in the PageTemplates folder, it will have a global effect on your application. Figure 22A-1 shows the default `List.aspx` page template.

As you can see the `GridView` that is used on the default `List.aspx` page template is not formatted to show alternating rows in a different color. This is the code to have alternating rows of a `GridView` appear yellow:

```
<AlternatingRowStyle BackColor="#FFFF99" />
```

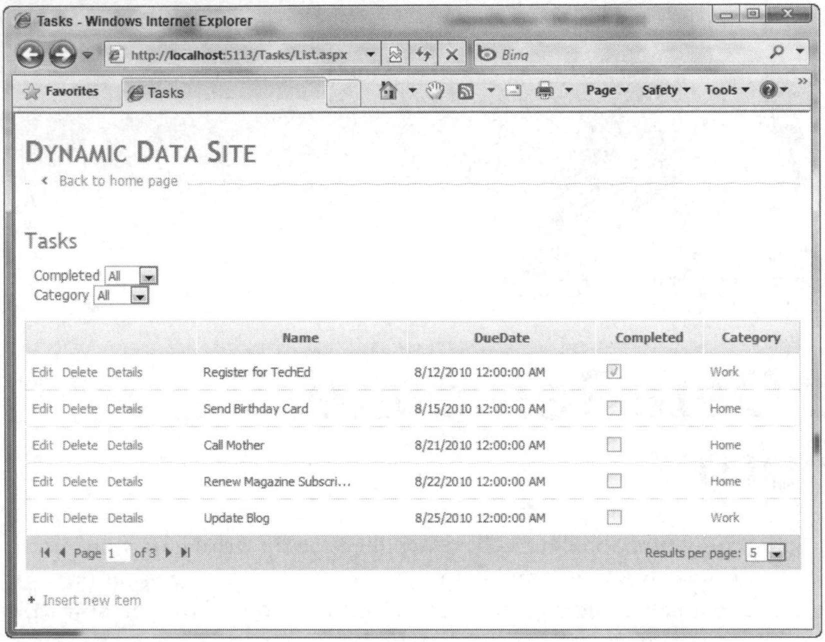

FIGURE 22A-1

If I add the preceding markup to the GridView in the List.aspx page template, all of the tables that use the default List.aspx page template will use the new alternating row style (see Figure 22A-2).

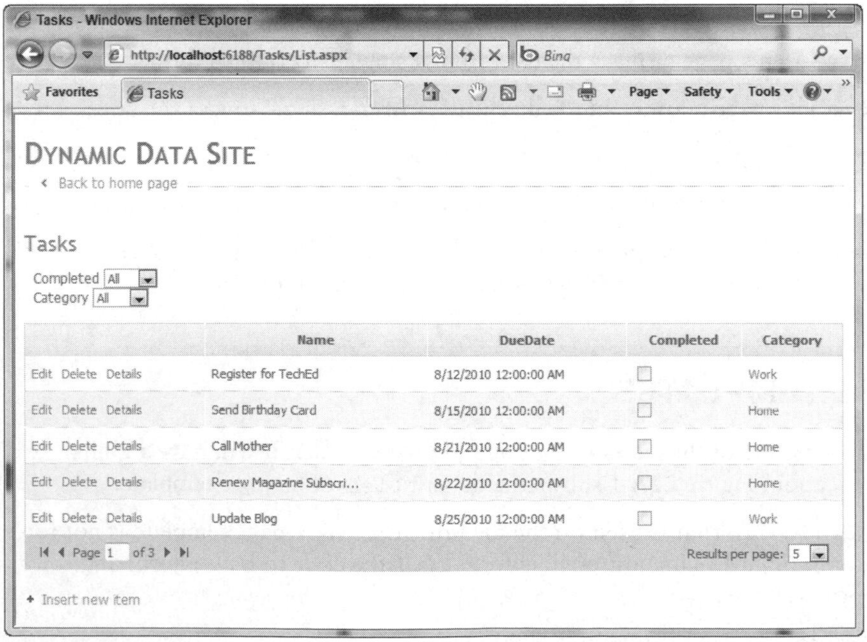

FIGURE 22A-2

If you need to change one or more of the page templates for a particular table, you can do that by using the CustomPages folder. These are the steps to create a custom `List.aspx` page template for the Task table:

1. Create a subfolder under the CustomPages folder named Task.

2. Copy the `List.aspx` page template from the PageTemplates folder into the new Task folder.

3. Update the `List.aspx` page template that is located in the Task folder.

FIELD TEMPLATES

The Dynamic Data framework uses field templates to render individual data fields. Field templates are user controls that are associated with each data type. These are the field templates that are included as part of the Dynamic Data framework:

➤ **Boolean.ascx** — This renders a disabled `CheckBox` control.

➤ **Boolean_Edit.ascx** — This renders an enabled `CheckBox` control.

➤ **Children.ascx** — This renders a link to the relationship page.

➤ **Children_Insert.ascx** — This is blank. The reason that this is blank is that in insert mode the relationships are not yet defined.

➤ **DateTime.ascx** — This renders a `Literal` control.

➤ **DateTime_Edit.ascx** — This renders a `TextBox` control and a `CompareValidator` control. The `CompareValidator` control is used to ensure that the value entered is a `DateTime`.

➤ **Decimal_Edit.ascx** — This renders a `TextBox` control and a `CompareValidator` control. The `CompareValidator` control is used to ensure that the value entered is a Decimal.

➤ **EmailAddress.ascx** — This renders a mailto link.

➤ **Enumeration.ascx** — This renders a `Literal` control.

➤ **Enumeration_Edit.ascx** — This renders a `DropDownList` control.

➤ **ForeignKey.ascx** — This renders a link to the relationship page.

➤ **ForeignKey_Edit.ascx** — This renders a `DropDownList` control.

➤ **Integer_Edit.ascx** — This renders a `TextBox` control and a `CompareValidator` control. The `CompareValidator` control is used to ensure that the value entered is an Integer.

➤ **ManyToMany.ascx** — This renders a `Repeater` control that contains a link to each item.

➤ **ManyToMany_Edit.ascx** — This renders a `CheckBoxList` control.

➤ **MultilineText_Edit.ascx** — This renders a `TextBox` with the `TextMode` property set to `MultiLine`.

➤ **Text.ascx** — This renders a `Literal` control.

➤ **Text_Edit.ascx** — This renders a `TextBox` with the `TextMode` property set to `SingleLine`.

➤ **Url.ascx** — This renders a link.

You probably noticed that there are three types of field templates; display, edit, and insert. The names of the edit templates end with "_Edit" and the names of the insert templates end with "_Insert". The various types of templates are associated with the mode that the control is in. There are three modes: display, edit, and insert.

If the control is in insert mode, Dynamic Data looks for an appropriate "_Insert" field template. If it cannot find an appropriate "_Insert" field template, it looks for an appropriate "_Edit" field template. If it cannot find an appropriate "_Edit" field template, it defaults to the display template.

Likewise, if the control is in edit mode, Dynamic Data looks for an appropriate "_Edit" field template. If it cannot find an appropriate "_Edit" field template, it defaults to the display template.

The appropriate field template is determined by the data type of the field unless a UIHint property has been defined for the field. I show you an example that uses the UIHint property later in this lesson.

By default, some data types, such as Decimal and Integer, do not have a field template defined for their display mode. They use the Text field template. Any simple data type that does not have a display field template defined uses its fallback data type. The fallback data type for Float and Double is Decimal. The fallback data type for Int16, Byte, and Long is Integer. The fallback type for Char, Integer, Decimal, GUID, DateTime, DateTimeOffset, and TimeSpan is String.

Now, look at some of the markup used by the field templates. The markup used by the field templates that are used to display Boolean values is quite simple. This is the markup in the Boolean.ascx file:

```
<%@ Control Language="C#" CodeBehind="Boolean.ascx.cs"
    Inherits="Lesson22a.BooleanField" %>

<asp:CheckBox runat="server" ID="CheckBox1" Enabled="false" />
```

This is the code:

```
using System;
using System.Web.UI;

namespace Lesson22a
{
    public partial class BooleanField :
        System.Web.DynamicData.FieldTemplateUserControl
    {
        protected override void OnDataBinding(EventArgs e)
        {
            base.OnDataBinding(e);

            object val = FieldValue;
            if (val != null)
                CheckBox1.Checked = (bool)val;
        }

        public override Control DataControl
        {
            get
            {
                return CheckBox1;
            }
        }
    }
}
```

This is the markup in the `Boolean_Edit.ascx` file:

```
<%@ Control Language="C#" CodeBehind="Boolean_Edit.ascx.cs"
    Inherits="Lesson22a.Boolean_EditField" %>

<asp:CheckBox runat="server" ID="CheckBox1" />
```

This is the code:

```csharp
using System;
using System.Collections.Specialized;
using System.Web.UI;

namespace Lesson22a
{
    public partial class Boolean_EditField :
        System.Web.DynamicData.FieldTemplateUserControl
    {
        protected override void OnDataBinding(EventArgs e)
        {
            base.OnDataBinding(e);

            object val = FieldValue;
            if (val != null)
                CheckBox1.Checked = (bool)val;
        }

        protected override void ExtractValues(IOrderedDictionary dictionary)
        {
            dictionary[Column.Name] = CheckBox1.Checked;
        }

        public override Control DataControl
        {
            get
            {
                return CheckBox1;
            }
        }

    }
}
```

CUSTOM FIELD TEMPLATES

To add a new field template, all you have to do is add it to the list of files in the FieldTemplates folder. This is the markup for a new field template called MessageBoolean:

```
<%@ Control Language="C#" AutoEventWireup="true"
    CodeBehind="MessageBoolean.ascx.cs"
    Inherits="Lesson22a.DynamicData.FieldTemplates.MessageBooleanField" %>

<asp:Literal runat="server" ID="Literal1" Text="<%# FieldValueString %>" />
```

Instead of returning a `CheckBox`, the MessageBoolean field template returns a `Literal`. This is the code used by the MessageBoolean field template:

```
using System;
using System.Web.UI;

namespace Lesson22a.DynamicData.FieldTemplates
{
    public partial class MessageBooleanField :
        System.Web.DynamicData.FieldTemplateUserControl
    {
        public override string FieldValueString
        {
            get
            {
                string message = ":-<";

                object value = FieldValue;
                if  ((Boolean)value)
                    message = "Good Job!";

                return message;
            }
        }

        public override Control DataControl
        {
            get
            {
                return Literal1;
            }
        }
    }
}
```

To apply the new MessageBoolean field template to the Completed field of a Task, I need to add a `UIHint` to the Completed field. The `UIHint` property is used to specify the name of the field template to use. This is the updated code:

```
using System.ComponentModel.DataAnnotations;

namespace Lesson22a.Model
{
    [MetadataType(typeof(Task_MetaData))]
    public partial class Task
    {
    }

    [ScaffoldTable(true)]
    public class Task_MetaData
    {
        [UIHint("MessageBoolean")]
        public object Completed;

        [Display(Name = "Due Date")]
```

```
            [DisplayFormat(DataFormatString = "{0:d}")]
            public object DueDate;
        }
    }
```

Figure 22A-3 shows the updated page that is rendered.

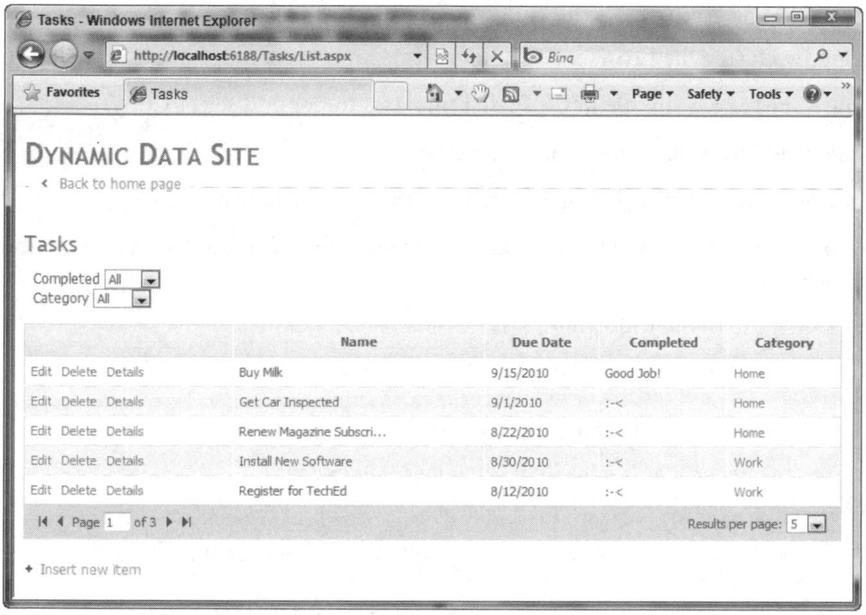

FIGURE 22A-3

TRY IT

In this lesson you modify a page template and add a new field template.

Lesson Requirements

➤   The project created in Lesson 21A.

Hints

None.

Step-by-Step

1.   Open Microsoft Visual Web Developer 2010 Express.

2.   Select Open Project from the File menu, navigate to Lesson21a.sln, and click the Open button.

3. Open the `List.aspx` file in the PageTemplates subfolder of the DynamicData folder and add the following markup to the bottom of the `GridView` to set the color of alternating rows to yellow:

```
<AlternatingRowStyle BackColor="#FFFF99" />
```

4. Click the F5 button.

5. Click the Tasks link.

6. Stop debugging by closing the browser.

7. Right-click the `DateTime.ascx` file in the FieldTemplates folder and select Copy.

8. Right-click the FieldTemplates folder and select Paste.

9. Right-click the new file and click Rename to rename the file to **DueDate.ascx**.

10. Open `DueDate.ascx` and change DateTimeField to **DueDateField** in the `Inherits` attribute of the @Page directive.

11. Replace the `Literal` with the following `Label`:

```
<asp:Label runat="server" ID="Label1" Text="<%# FieldValueString %>" />
```

12. Verify that the markup in the DueDate.ascx file matches the following:

```
<%@ Control Language="C#" CodeBehind="DueDate.ascx.cs"
    Inherits="Lesson21a.DueDateField" %>

<asp:Label runat="server" ID="Label1" Text="<%# FieldValueString %>" />
```

13. Open the `DueDate.ascx.cs` file and change DateTimeField to **DueDateField.**

14. Replace Literal1 with **Label1.**

15. Add the following code to the `DueDateField` class to change the color of any past due items to red:

```
protected override void OnDataBinding(EventArgs e)
{
    base.OnDataBinding(e);

    object val = FieldValue;
    if (DateTime.Compare((DateTime)val,DateTime.Now)< 0)
        Label1.ForeColor = System.Drawing.Color.Red;
}
```

16. Verify that the code in the `DueDate.ascx.cs` matches the following:

```
using System;
using System.Collections.Specialized;
using System.ComponentModel.DataAnnotations;
using System.Web.DynamicData;
using System.Web;
using System.Web.UI;
using System.Web.UI.WebControls;

namespace Lesson21a
```

```
    {
        public partial class DueDateField : System.Web.DynamicData.
FieldTemplateUserControl
        {
            public override Control DataControl
            {
                get
                {
                    return Label1;
                }
            }

            protected override void OnDataBinding(EventArgs e)
            {
                base.OnDataBinding(e);

                object val = FieldValue;
                if (DateTime.Compare((DateTime)val, DateTime.Now) < 0)
                    Label1.ForeColor = System.Drawing.Color.Red;
            }
        }
    }
}
```

17. Right-click the Models folder and select Class from the Add menu to add a new class named **Models.cs**.

18. Delete the following code from the `Models.cs` file:

```
public class Models
{
}
```

19. Add the following using statement to the top of the `Models.cs` file:

```
using System.ComponentModel.DataAnnotations;
```

20. Add the following code to the `Models.cs` file:

```
[MetadataType(typeof(Task_MetaData))]
public partial class Task
{}

public class Task_MetaData
{
    [UIHint("DueDate")]
    [Display(Name = "Due Date")]
    [DisplayFormat(DataFormatString = "{0:d}")]
    public object DueDate;
}
```

21. Verify that the code in the `Models.cs` file matches the following:

```
using System;
using System.Collections.Generic;
using System.Linq;
using System.Web;
```

```
using System.ComponentModel.DataAnnotations;

namespace Lesson21a.Models
{
    [MetadataType(typeof(Task_MetaData))]
    public partial class Task
    {
    }

    public class Task_MetaData
    {
        [UIHint("DueDate")]
        [Display(Name = "Due Date")]
        [DisplayFormat(DataFormatString = "{0:d}")]
        public object DueDate;
    }
}
```

22. Click the F5 button.

23. Click the Tasks link (see Figure 22A-4).

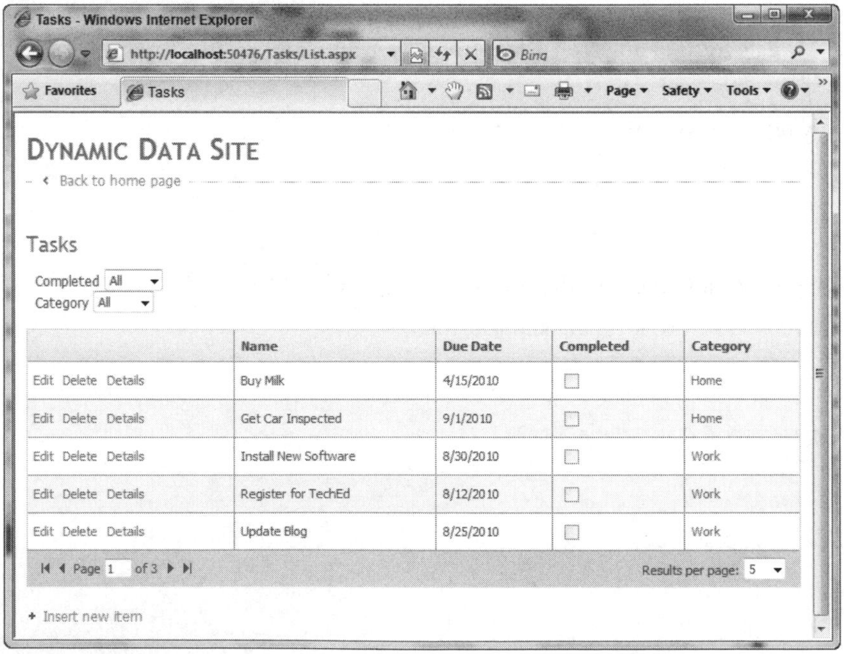

FIGURE 22A-4

24. Add, edit and delete a task.

Please select Lesson 22A on the DVD to view the video that accompanies this lesson.

22B

Editor Templates in MVC

Editor templates are structured helpers that enable you to build a user interface based on your data model. In this lesson I show you how to use the editor templates to edit the data in your model.

Here are the three helper methods in the `EditorExtensions` class:

- ➤ **Editor**() — This helper returns the HTML input markup for a particular property in the model where the property is identified via a string expression.

- ➤ **EditorFor**() — This helper also returns the HTML input markup for a particular property in the model. However, with this helper, the property is identified via a strongly-typed expression.

- ➤ **EditorModelFor**() — This helper returns the HTML input markup for all of the simple properties in the model.

> *The expression* `EditorFor(model => model)` *is equivalent to* `EditorForModel()`.

THE EDITORFORMODEL HELPER

Figure 22B-1 shows the Entity Data Model (EDM) that I use in this lesson.

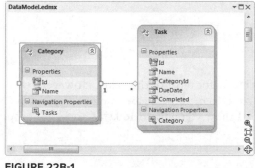

FIGURE 22B-1

These are the `Create` action methods:

```
//
// GET: /Task/Create

public ActionResult Create()
{
    Models.Task task = new Models.Task();
    return View(task);
}
//
// POST: /Task/Create

[HttpPost]
public ActionResult Create(Models.Task task)
{
    if (ModelState.IsValid)
    {
        try
        {
            // TODO: Add insert logic here
            return RedirectToAction("Index");
        }
        catch
        {
            return View(task);
        }
    }
    return View(task);
}
```

This is the View that uses the `EditorForModel` helper:

```
<%@ Page Title="" Language="C#" MasterPageFile="~/Views/Shared/Site.Master"
    Inherits="System.Web.Mvc.ViewPage<Lesson21b.Models.Task>" %>

<asp:Content ID="Content1" ContentPlaceHolderID="TitleContent" runat="server">
    Create
</asp:Content>
<asp:Content ID="Content2" ContentPlaceHolderID="MainContent" runat="server">
    <h2>Create</h2>
    <% using (Html.BeginForm()) {%>
        <%: Html.EditorForModel() %>
        <input type="submit" value="Create" />
    <% } %>
</asp:Content>
```

Figure 22B-2 shows the page that is rendered.

The page shown in Figure 22B-2 provides input elements for most of the fields. However, the `Category` property is missing. This is because the `EditorForModel` helper method renders HTML markup only for the simple properties of the model. I show you how to add the `Category` property later in this lesson.

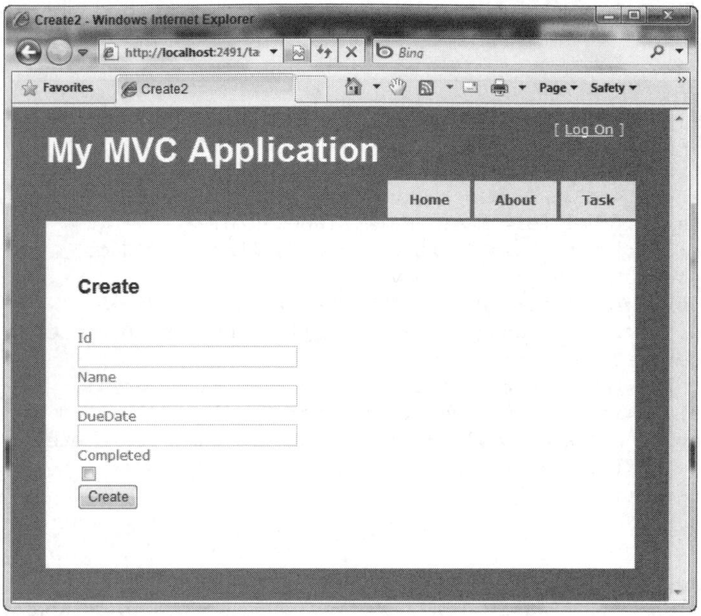

FIGURE 22B-2

A great feature of this page is that validation is enabled automatically by the inclusion of validation helpers on the page. When I click the Create button, without entering any text, Figure 22B-3 shows the page that is rendered.

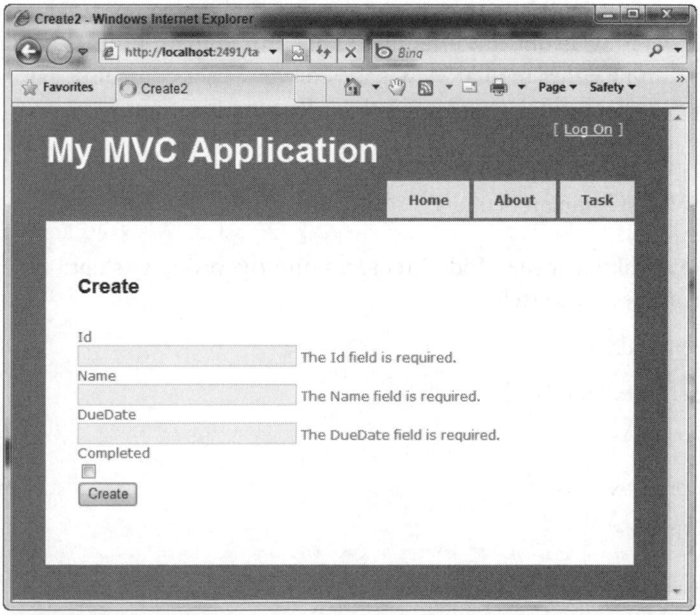

FIGURE 22B-3

This is the markup that is rendered automatically by the `EditorModelFor` helper method when there are no errors on the page:

```
<h2>Create</h2>
<form action="/task/create" method="post">
    <div class="editor-label"><label for="Id">Id</label></div>
    <div class="editor-field"><input class="text-box single-line" id="Id" name="Id"
       type="text" value="" /> </div>
    <div class="editor-label"><label for="Name">Name</label></div>
    <div class="editor-field"><input class="text-box single-line" id="Name"
       name="Name" type="text" value="" /> </div>
    <div class="editor-label"><label for="DueDate">DueDate</label></div>
    <div class="editor-field"><input class="text-box single-line" id="DueDate"
       name="DueDate" type="text" value="" /> </div>
    <div class="editor-label"><label for="Completed">Completed</label></div>
    <div class="editor-field"><input class="check-box" id="Completed"
       name="Completed" type="checkbox" value="true" /><input name="Completed"
       type="hidden" value="false" /> </div>
    <input type="submit" value="Create" />
</form>
```

As you can see, the labels use the `editor-label` class and the input objects use the `editor-field` class. When there are errors on the page, the `input-validation-error` class is used to display the textboxes in red and the `field-validation-error` class is used to display the error messages. The rules for these styles are defined in the `Site.css` file that is located in the Content folder.

CUSTOM EDITOR TEMPLATES

The default page that is provided is pretty good. However, custom editor templates can be used to further fine-tune the HTML that is rendered. Custom editor templates are stored in an EditorTemplates subfolder of the Views folder. They can be either regular view pages or view user controls (`.aspx` or `.ascx`). The system looks for an appropriate editor template in the following locations:

➤ ~/Views/ControllerName/EditorTemplates/TemplateName

➤ ~/Views/Shared/EditorTemplates/TemplateName

The TemplateName is determined by looking at the ModelMetadata and the property's data type. This is the order in which template names are searched:

1. TemplateHint from ModelMetadata

2. DataTypeName from ModelMetadata

3. Name of the type

4. String: if the object is not complex

5. Object: if the object is complex

For more information about the `ModelMetadata` *class, please refer to Lesson 21B.*

Most of the input objects that are rendered are just regular textboxes. However, the Completed field renders a checkbox. The reason for that is that the ASP.NET MVC framework has a number of built-in editor templates. This is a list of the built-in editor templates that are provided by the framework:

➤ **Boolean** — This template renders a checkbox by calling `Html.CheckBox()`.

➤ **Decimal** — This template renders a textbox by calling `Html.Textbox()`.

➤ **HiddenInput** — This template renders a hidden value by calling `Html.Hidden()`.

➤ **MultilineText** — This template renders a multiline textbox by calling `Html.TextArea()`.

➤ **Object** — This template renders all of the simple properties and the validation for those properties using the default Object editor template.

➤ **Password** — This template renders a password textbox by calling `Html.Password()`.

➤ **String** — This template renders a textbox by calling `Html.Textbox()`.

Any of the built-in editor templates can be replaced with a custom editor template. Also, additional editor templates can be added. To add a new editor template for Category type objects, add a `Category.ascx` page to the Views/Shared/EditorTemplates folder. This is the code that provides a dropdown list to select the appropriate category:

```
<%@ Control Language="C#" Inherits="System.Web.Mvc.ViewUserControl" %>
<%: Html.DropDownList("", new SelectList(new[] {"Home", "Work"}))%>
```

The preceding code hardcoded the values used for the drop-down list. This is the code that provides a drop-down list that reads its values from the database:

```
<%@ Control Language="C#" Inherits="System.Web.Mvc.ViewUserControl" %>
<%: Html.DropDownList("",
    new SelectList((IEnumerable)ViewData["Categories"], "Id", "Name"))%>
```

The `Create` action method needs to be updated to return the `ViewData["Categories"]` object. This is the code to return the `ViewData["Categories"]` object:

```
ViewData["Categories"] = from c in _entity.Categories
                            select c;
```

This is the markup for the Task custom editor named `Task.ascx`:

```
<%@ Control Language="C#"
    Inherits="System.Web.Mvc.ViewUserControl<Lesson21b.Models.Task>" %>

<p>
<label for="Name">Name:</label>
<%: Html.EditorFor(t => Model.Name) %>
<%: Html.ValidationMessageFor(t => Model.Name) %>
</p>
<p>
<label for="Category">Category:</label>
<%: Html.EditorFor(t => Model.Category) %>
<%: Html.ValidationMessageFor(t => Model.Category) %>
</p>
<p>
```

```
<label for="DueDate">DueDate:</label>
<%: Html.EditorFor(t => Model.DueDate)%>
<%: Html.ValidationMessageFor(t => Model.DueDate)%>
</p>
<p>
<label for="Completed">Completed:</label>
<%: Html.EditorFor(t => Model.Completed) %>
<%: Html.ValidationMessageFor(t => Model.Completed) %>
</p>
```

Figure 22B-4 shows the page that is rendered when the `Task.ascx` file in placed in the Views/Shared/EditorTemplates folder.

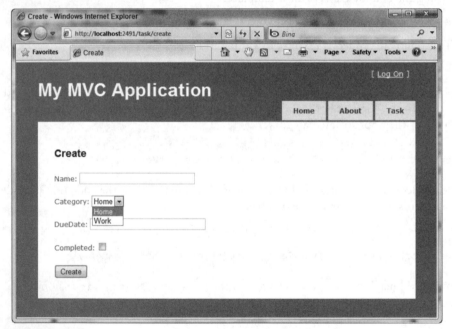

FIGURE 22B-4

TRY IT

In this lesson you use the built-in editor templates to edit the information in a simple model.

Lesson Requirements

➤ The project created in Lesson 21B.

Hints

None.

Step-by-Step

1. Open Microsoft Visual Web Developer 2010 Express.

2. Select Open Project from the File menu, navigate to Lesson21b.sln, and click the Open button.

3. Right-click the Contact folder and select View from the Add menu to open the Add View dialog box (see Figure 22B-5). Set the View name to **Create**, check the `Create a strongly-typed view` checkbox, select **Lesson21b.Models.Contact** as the View data class and **Empty** as the View content. Click the Add button.

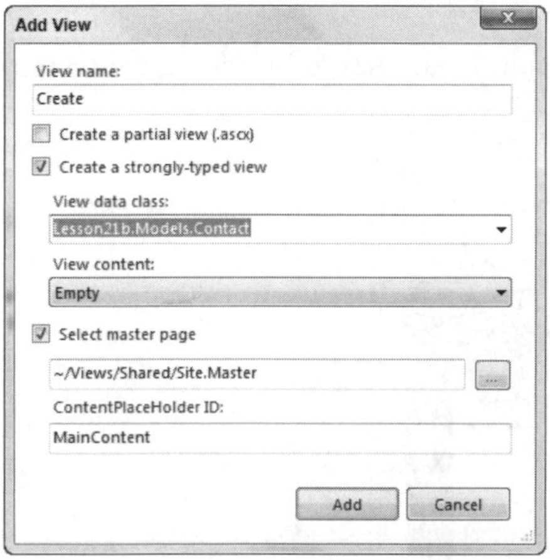

FIGURE 22B-5

4. Add the following code to the `MainContent` content placeholder:

```
<% using (Html.BeginForm()) {%>
    <%: Html.EditorForModel() %>
    <input type="submit" value="Create" />
<% } %>
```

5. Open the `ContactController.cs` file.

6. Update the `Create` action method that responds to an HTTP POST to the following:

```
//
// POST: /Contact/Create

[HttpPost]
public ActionResult Create(Models.Contact contact)
{
```

```
            if (ModelState.IsValid)
            {
                try
                {
                    // TODO: Add insert logic here

                    return RedirectToAction("Index");
                }
                catch
                {
                    return View(contact);
                }
            }

            return View(contact);
    }
```

7. Click the F5 button and navigate to the page shown in Figure 22B-6 by adding **contact/create** to the browser's address bar.

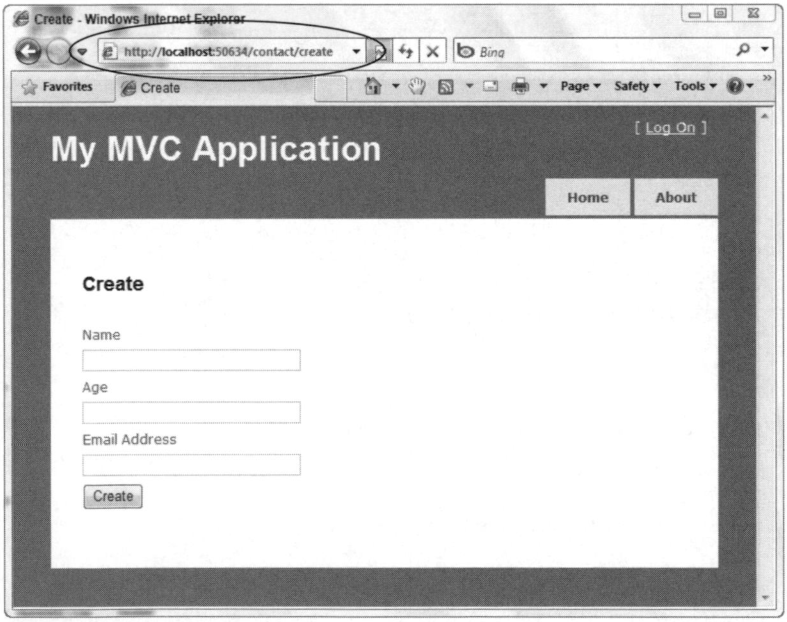

FIGURE 22B-6

8. Click the Create button (see Figure 22B-7).

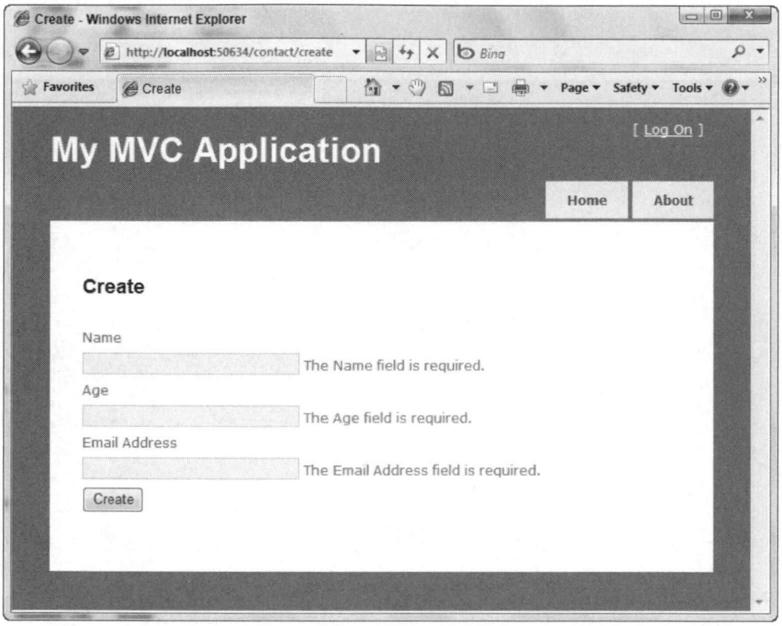

FIGURE 22B-7

Please select Lesson 22B on the DVD to view the video that accompanies this lesson.

SECTION IX
Client-side Programming

JavaScript

So far you have learned about server-side programming. With server-side programming all of the processing takes place on the server and has to be sent over the Internet to the browser; the browser is the client. With JavaScript, it is possible to do client-side programming to take advantage of the processing power of the computer that is running the browser. In this lesson I teach you how to use JavaScript and introduce you to jQuery, one of the most popular JavaScript libraries.

JavaScript was developed by Netscape back in 1995. Due to its name, many people assume that JavaScript is related to Java; however, it has nothing to do with Java. It is a dynamic, object-oriented language that has many similarities to C#, such as case-sensitivity and syntax.

HOW TO USE JAVASCRIPT

This is a sample of an HTML page that includes JavaScript:

```
<!DOCTYPE html PUBLIC "-//W3C//DTD XHTML 1.0 Transitional//EN"
    "http://www.w3.org/TR/xhtml1/DTD/xhtml1-transitional.dtd">
<html xmlns="http://www.w3.org/1999/xhtml">
<head>
    <title>Hello World</title>
</head>
<body>
    <input id="SubmitButton" type="submit" value="Click Me" onclick="Hello()"
        />

    <script type="text/javascript">
        // Displays Hello World in a popup box.
        function Hello() {
            alert("Hello World");
        }
    </script>
</body>
</html>
```

Figure 23-1 shows the page that is rendered by using the preceding code.

When the Click Me button in Figure 23-1 is clicked, the popup box shown in Figure 23-2 is rendered.

In the example, the JavaScript code is the code within the `<script>` tag. The `<script>` tag can be placed anywhere within the HTML document; however, its location has an impact on when the JavaScript is executed. If the `<script>` tag is placed within the `head` element of the HTML page, it will not be executed until it is explicitly called. Conversely, if the `<script>` tag is placed within the `body` element of the HTML page, it will be executed while the page is loading. Therefore, if you need your JavaScript to be executed after the page has loaded, place it at the bottom of the body section of the page.

FIGURE 23-1

JavaScript does not need to be included directly in the page; you can attach an external JavaScript file instead. This is the code to refer to an external JavaScript file that is located in the Scripts folder:

FIGURE 23-2

```
<script src="../Scripts/jquery-1.4.1.js" type="text/javascript" />
```

JAVASCRIPT SYNTAX

As I mentioned earlier, JavaScript uses much of the same syntax as C#. It concludes each statement with a semicolon and places blocks of code between curly brackets just like C#. It also includes `if`, `switch`, `while`, `for`, `break`, `return`, `throw`, and `try-catch-finally` statements that are similar to those used by C#.

This is the format of an `if...else` statement:

```
if (condition) {
    // something happens
} else {
    // something different happens
};
```

This is the format of a `switch` statement:

```
switch (n) {
    case 1:
        // do something
        break;
    case 2:
        // do something
        break;
    default:
        // do something
};
```

This is the format of a `while` loop:

```
while (condition) {
    //  something happens
};
```

This is the format of a `try...catch` statement:

```
try {
    // do something
} catch (err) {
    // handle error
}
```

As you can see, JavaScript looks very similar to C#. Nevertheless, there is one very important difference between them. Whereas all of the variables in C# are strongly typed, the variables in JavaScript are weakly typed. This means that the following code is perfectly acceptable in JavaScript:

```
var x = 3;
var y = "text";
var z = true;
x = x + y + z;
```

A secondary difference between JavaScript and C# is how arrays are handled. In JavaScript an array can include any mix of values and it allows you to refer to elements using a string value. These are all examples of valid arrays:

```
var days = ["Monday", "Tuesday", "Wednesday", "Thursday", "Friday"];
var numbers = [1, 2, 3, 4, 5, 6, 7, 8, 9, 10];
var preferences = [123, "Main", false]
```

Because arrays are zero-based, this is the code to access the second value of the `days` array:

```
days[1]
```

However, since JavaScript allows you to refer to an array element using a string value, you can also access the second value of the `days` array by using the following code:

```
days["1"]
```

DOCUMENT OBJECT MODEL

When a browser loads an HTML page, it creates a model of that page known as the Document Object Model (DOM). The DOM provides a structured object-oriented representation of all of the elements and content on the page. You can use the DOM not only to locate items on the page, but also to manipulate items on the page. The DOM is not JavaScript; it is a standard from the World Wide Web Consortium (W3C) that most browsers have adopted.

To understand the DOM better, take a look at this simple page:

```
<head>
    <title>Document Object Model</title>
</head>
<body>
    <h1>
        Heading</h1>
    <div id="content">
        <p>
            This is my <strong>important</strong> content.
        </p>
    </div>
    <div id="footer">
        <p class="gray">
            This is my footer.
        </p>
    </div>
</body>
</html>
```

Figure 23-3 shows the relationship between the tags on the page.

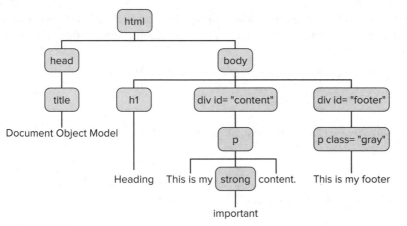

FIGURE 23-3

The relationship between the tags resembles a tree. The `<html>` tag is the root of the tree and the other tags are the branches. When you understand the DOM of the page, you can easily select an element, add new content, show and hide content, modify a tag's attributes, and handle events. Nevertheless, the details of working with the DOM can be quite tedious.

This is code to "walk" the DOM:

```
function walkTheDOM(node) {
    document.writeln(node);
        node = node.firstChild;
        while (node) {
            walkTheDOM(node);
```

```
            node = node.nextSibling;
        }
    }
```

The preceding function uses recursion to traverse the DOM from a given node. To walk the DOM from the `<div>` tag that has its `id` attribute set to `footer`, use this code:

```
walkTheDOM(document.getElementById("footer"));
```

This is the text that is written out to the page:

```
[object HTMLDivElement]
[object HTMLParagraphElement]
[object Text]
```

JQUERY

A JavaScript library is a collection of JavaScript code that provides functions to make your life easier by handling common tasks. One of the most popular JavaScript libraries is jQuery: an open source JavaScript library that simplifies interactions between the DOM and JavaScript. According to the jQuery web site, `www.jquery.com`:

> *jQuery is a fast and concise JavaScript Library that simplifies HTML document traversing, event handling, animating, and Ajax interactions for rapid web development. jQuery is designed to change the way that you write JavaScript.*

You are probably wondering how you can get a copy of jQuery. Not to worry, jQuery is so popular that Microsoft has decided to include it with Visual Studio 2010. In fact, three versions of two different jQuery files are included.

- ➤ `jquery-1.4.1`
  - ➤ `jquery-1.4.1-vsdoc.js`
  - ➤ `jquery-1.4.1.js`
  - ➤ `jquery-1.4.1.min.js`
- ➤ `jquery.validate`
  - ➤ `jquery.validate-vsdoc.js`
  - ➤ `jquery.validate.js`
  - ➤ `jquery.validate.min.js`

The files that include `vsdoc` in their names are versions that support Visual Studio IntelliSense. The files that include `min` in their names have been minimized by removing comments, white space, and new lines. For example, the `jquery-1.4.1.js` file is 164 KB whereas the `jquery-1.4.1.min.js` file is only 70 KB. You should use the `min` version of the files on your production web sites.

> You should not use the vsdoc files at run time inside the browser. They are
> intended to be used only for design-time IntelliSense.

Microsoft Ajax Content Delivery Network

You do not have to include the jQuery files in your application because Microsoft provides a free
service called the Microsoft Ajax Content Delivery Network (CDN). By using this service, your
application can refer to JavaScript simply by including the following tag:

```
<script src="http://ajax.microsoft.com/ajax/jquery/jquery-1.4.1.js"
    type="text/javascript" />
```

Using the Microsoft Ajax CDN can significantly improve how your application performs. The contents of the Microsoft Ajax CDN are cached on servers around the world so that when the browser
requests a file, it is automatically served by the server that is closest to the user. These are the advantages of using the Microsoft Ajax CDN:

➤ The request is processed much faster.

➤ You do not have to pay for the bandwidth of the file — Microsoft pays.

➤ The script is cached by the user's browser, so, if another web site has already requested the
file, it is already in the browser's cache.

jQuery Selectors

You can use jQuery to access any element in the DOM. jQuery offers a number of selectors that you
can use to select an element or a group of elements. The following table shows how to use some of
the selectors:

Selector	Example	Result
#id	$("#content")	This code selects the div element with id="content".
element	$("div")	This code selects all of the div elements.
.class	$(".gray")	This code selects all of the elements where class="gray".

All of the selectors can return an array of elements. Following is a list of some of the commonly used
filters that can be used with the selectors:

➤ Basic filters:

   ➤ **:first** — This filter matches the first selected element.

   ➤ **:last** — This filter matches the last selected element.

   ➤ **:not(selector)** — This filter removes all of the elements matching the selector.

   ➤ **:even** — This filter matches the even elements.

➤ **:odd** — This filter matches the odd elements.

➤ **:header** — This filter matches all header elements; for example, h1.

➤ **:animated** — This filter matches all elements that are currently being animated.

➤ Content filters:

➤ **:contains(text)** — This filter matches the elements that contain the given text.

➤ **:empty** — This filter matches all of the empty elements.

➤ Visibility filters:

➤ **:hidden** — This filter matches all the hidden elements.

➤ **:visible** — This filter matches all the visible elements.

➤ Attribute filters:

➤ **[attribute]** — This filter matches the elements with the given attribute.

➤ **[attribute=value]** — This filter matches the elements with a given attribute of the specified value.

> *This list of filters is by no means complete. There are many more, including filters to select certain types of input elements and buttons. Please refer to the jQuery web site,* www.jquery.com, *for a complete list.*

The following code selects the first div from the page:

```
$("div:first")
```

The following code updates the contents of the first div to **New Content**:

```
$("div:first").text("New Content");
```

jQuery Attributes

In the preceding code the text attribute is used to update the contents of the element. This is a list of some of the attributes provided by jQuery:

➤ **attr(key, value)** — This attribute is used to set a particular attribute to the given value.

➤ **addClass(class)** — This attribute is used to add the specified class.

➤ **removeClass(class)** — This attribute is used to remove the specified class.

➤ **toggleClass(class)** — This attribute is used to add or remove the specified class based on whether or not it is present.

➤ **html(value)** — This attribute sets the innerHTML to the specified value.

➤ **text(value)** — This attribute sets the text contents to the specified value.

The following two JavaScript statements update the contents of the first div element to **New Content** and add a class named **important**:

```
$("div:first").text("New Content")
$("div:first").addClass("important");
```

These two statements can be replaced with the following statement that "chains" the methods together:

```
$("div:first").text("New Content").addClass("important");
```

> *It is much faster to "chain" the methods together. This allows the system to search for the element only once.*

jQuery Effects

Using jQuery it is easy to add animation effects to your web page. This is a partial list of some of the effects provided by jQuery:

➤ **show()** — This effect displays all of the elements.

➤ **hide()** — This effect hides all of the elements.

➤ **toggle()** — This effect displays the hidden elements and hides the others.

➤ **slideDown(speed, callback)** — This effect reveals the elements by adjusting their height. The value of speed can be slow, medium, or fast, or speed can be a numeric value representing the number of milliseconds. An optional callback can be fired after completion.

➤ **slideUp(speed, callback)** — This effect hides the elements by adjusting their height. The value of speed can be slow, medium, or fast, or speed can be a numeric value representing the number of milliseconds. An optional callback can be fired after completion.

jQuery Event Helpers

Another valuable type of function that jQuery provides is event helpers. This is a partial list of the event helpers provided by jQuery:

➤ **click()** — This event function triggers the click of each matched element.

➤ **mouseout()** — This event function triggers the mouseout of each matched element.

➤ **mouseover()** — This event function triggers the mouseover of each matched element.

➤ **submit()** — This event function triggers the submit of each matched element.

FIGURE 23-4

To use jQuery on your page, you must add a reference to the jQuery file that you want to use. The following code displays the number of list items that are on the page, as shown in Figure 23-4:

```
<!DOCTYPE html PUBLIC "-//W3C//DTD XHTML 1.0 Transitional//EN"
    "http://www.w3.org/TR/xhtml1/DTD/xhtml1-transitional.dtd">

<html xmlns="http://www.w3.org/1999/xhtml">
<head>
    <title>Movies</title>
    <script src="http://ajax.microsoft.com/ajax/jquery/jquery-1.4.1.js"
        type="text/javascript" >
    </script>
</head>
<body>
    <h1>
        Movies</h1>
    <ul>
        <li>Avatar</li>
        <li>The Blind Side</li>
        <li>District 9</li>
        <li>An Education</li>
        <li>The Hurt Locker</li>
        <li>Inglourious Basterds</li>
        <li>Precious</li>
        <li>A Serious Man</li>
        <li>Up</li>
        <li>Up in the Air</li>
    </ul>
    <script type="text/javascript">
        alert("List items: " + $("li").size());
    </script>
</body>
</html>
```

In the preceding example, the `<script>` tag that is at the bottom of the body element contains the jQuery statement. If you move the `<script>` tag to the top of the body element, Figure 23-5 shows the new results.

The incorrect results are returned because the DOM has not yet been loaded. To have jQuery wait for the DOM to load, jQuery provides the `ready()` method. This is the updated `<script>` tag that uses the `ready()` method:

FIGURE 23-5

```
<script type="text/javascript">
    $(document).ready(function () {
        alert("List items: " + $("li").size());
    });
</script>
```

TRY IT

In this lesson you use jQuery to manipulate an HTML document.

Lesson Requirements

➤ The `Oscars.htm` file.

Hints

➤ Use Ctrl+Shift+W to view the current page in the browser.

Step-by-Step

1. Open Microsoft Visual Web Developer 2010 Express.

2. Click **New Web Site**.

3. Select **Visual C#**.

4. Select **ASP.NET Empty Web Site** from the list of installed templates.

5. Type **c:\ASPNETTrainer\Lesson23** for the Web Location property and click the OK button.

6. Select Add Existing Item from the Web site menu, navigate to the `Oscars.htm` file, select it, and click the Add button.

7. Open the `Oscars.htm` file and add the following reference to the jQuery file, that is hosted by the Microsoft Ajax Content Delivery Network (CDN), to the bottom of the `head` element:

```
<script src="http://ajax.microsoft.com/ajax/jquery/jquery-1.4.1.js"
    type="text/javascript"></script>
```

> *If you do not have access to the Internet, you can find the file on your hard drive in the following folder:* C:\Program Files (x86)\Microsoft Visual Studio 10.0\ Common7\IDE\VWDExpress\ProjectTemplates\CSharp\Web\1033\MvcWebApplication ProjectTemplatev2.0.cs.zip\Scripts.

8. Add the following `script element` to the bottom of the `body` element:

```
<script type="text/javascript">
</script>
```

9. Add the following code to the `script` element that you have just added:

```
alert("List Items: " + $("li").size());
```

10. Save the `Oscars.htm` file. Right-click the page and select View in Browser.

11. Click the OK button (see Figure 23-6).

12. Close the browser.

FIGURE 23-6

13. Replace the code in the script element with the following code:

```
$("ul").slideUp(5000);
```

14. Save the Oscars.htm file. Right-click the page and select View in Browser.

15. Close the browser.

16. Add the following style rule to the head element:

```
<style type="text/css">
    .yellow
    {
        background-color: Yellow;
    }
</style>
```

17. Add the following code to the script element at the bottom of the body element to turn the background color of every other list item yellow:

```
$("li:even").addClass("yellow");
```

18. Save the Oscars.htm file. Right-click the page and select View in Browser.

19. Close the browser.

20. Replace the code in the script element with the following code to remove the list of directors and to change the background color of all of the list items with the word "Air" in them:

```
$("#director").remove();
$("li:contains(Up)").addClass("yellow");
```

21. Add the following checkbox to the top of the body element:

```
Hide All? <input id="hide" type="checkbox"/>
```

22. Add the following markup to the script element to bind a function to the click event of the checkbox:

```
$("#hide").click(function () {
    $("ul").slideUp(5000);
});
```

23. Save the Oscars.htm file. Right-click the page and select View in Browser.

24. Click the checkbox.

Please select Lesson 23 on the DVD to view the video that accompanies this lesson.

24A

Using the AJAX Extensions in Web Forms

When a typical ASP.NET page needs to be refreshed from the server, it triggers a complete page refresh. The result is a slight delay and a flicker of the page. Wouldn't it be great if your page had the ability to submit only the section that needed to be updated, and it subsequently only needed to refresh that section? The AJAX Extensions in the ASP.NET Web Forms framework gives your web pages the ability to perform partial page updates. In this lesson I teach you how to use all of the controls included as part of the AJAX Extensions.

Ajax stands for **A**synchronous **J**avaScript **a**nd **X**ML. It enables your client-side web pages to exchange information with the server by using asynchronous calls. To do this, it uses both JavaScript and XML and can require a great deal of code. Because of the complexity involved in programming Ajax, a number of popular Ajax libraries have been developed. In fact, Microsoft includes an Ajax library as part of the ASP.NET 4 framework. The AJAX Extensions are server-side controls that use the Ajax library that is shipped with ASP.NET 4.

AJAX EXTENSIONS CONTROLS

The controls that are included in the AJAX Extensions are located in the AJAX Extensions tab of the Toolbox. Figure 24A-1 shows the list of AJAX Extensions.

This is information about each of the controls:

> **ScriptManager** — This control manages the ASP.NET Ajax script libraries. This control is required. However, there can be only one `ScriptManager` on a page.

> **ScriptManagerProxy** — This control is used by pages that are nested inside of pages that already have a `ScriptManager`. Because each page must have one and only one `ScriptManager`, this control is provided to enable the nested pages to use the AJAX Extensions. This control is required for nested pages.

FIGURE 24A-1

➤ **Timer** — This control performs postbacks at defined intervals. It works with the UpdatePanel.

➤ **UpdatePanel** — This control enables portions of the page to be refreshed without doing a postback of the entire page.

➤ **UpdateProgress** — This control provides visual feedback on the status of the update. It works with the UpdatePanel.

To use the AJAX Extensions the page must include a ScriptManager and an UpdatePanel. This is the markup for a sample page that includes both a ScriptManager and an UpdatePanel:

```
<%@ Page Language="C#" AutoEventWireup="true" CodeBehind="UpdatePanel.aspx.cs"
    Inherits="Lesson24a.UpdatePanel" %>

<!DOCTYPE html PUBLIC "-//W3C//DTD XHTML 1.0 Transitional//EN"
    "http://www.w3.org/TR/xhtml1/DTD/xhtml1-transitional.dtd">
<html xmlns="http://www.w3.org/1999/xhtml">
<head>
    <title>Update Panel</title>
</head>
<body>
    <form id="form1" runat="server">

    <asp:ScriptManager ID="ScriptManager1" runat="server" />

    Time Page Rendered:
    <asp:Literal ID="LiteralTimeRendered" runat="server" />

    <asp:UpdatePanel ID="UpdatePanel1" runat="server">
       <ContentTemplate>
           Time Page Updated:
           <asp:Literal ID="LiteralTimeUpdated" runat="server" />
           <br /><br />
           <asp:Button ID="ButtonUpdate" runat="server" Text="Update Time" />
       </ContentTemplate>
    </asp:UpdatePanel>

    </form>
</body>
</html>
```

> ⊗ *All of the content of the* UpdatePanel *must be included within a* ContentTemplate *element.*

Figure 24A-2 shows the page that is rendered using the preceding code.

The Time Page Rendered field shows the original time that the page was rendered. The Time Page Updated field is updated every time the Update Time button is clicked. Because this page is using an UpdatePanel and the Update Time button is within the UpdatePanel, only the contents of the UpdatePanel are refreshed when the button is clicked.

Time Page Rendered: 1:33:08 PM
Time Page Updated: 1:33:16 PM

Update Time

FIGURE 24A-2

UpdatePanel Control

These are the properties of the UpdatePanel control:

➤ **ChildrenAsTriggers** — This Boolean property determines whether the controls within the UpdatePanel can trigger a refresh of the UpdatePanel. The default is true.

➤ **Triggers** — This property is used to allow controls that are not within the UpdatePanel to trigger a refresh of the UpdatePanel. It is also used to allow controls that are within the UpdatePanel to trigger a refresh of the UpdatePanel when ChildrenAsTriggers has been set to false.

➤ **RenderMode** — This property is used to determine how the UpdatePanel will be rendered. It can be rendered as a block element using a <div> tag, or as an inline element using a <span> tag. The default is block.

➤ **UpdateMode** — This property determines when the UpdatePanel will be refreshed. It can be set to either Always or Conditional. The default is Always.

By using the Triggers property, a control that is not within the UpdatePanel can refresh the UpdatePanel. This is code that uses the Triggers property to identify the control that will refresh the UpdatePanel:

```
<%@ Page Language="C#" AutoEventWireup="true" CodeBehind="Trigger.aspx.cs"
    Inherits="Lesson24a.Trigger" %>

<!DOCTYPE html PUBLIC "-//W3C//DTD XHTML 1.0 Transitional//EN"
    "http://www.w3.org/TR/xhtml1/DTD/xhtml1-transitional.dtd">
<html xmlns="http://www.w3.org/1999/xhtml">
<head>
    <title>Trigger</title>
</head>
<body>
    <form id="form1" runat="server">

    <asp:ScriptManager ID="ScriptManager1" runat="server" />

    Time Page Rendered:
    <asp:Literal ID="LiteralTimeRendered" runat="server" />

    <asp:UpdatePanel ID="UpdatePanel1" runat="server">
        <ContentTemplate>
            Time Page Updated: 
            <asp:Literal ID="LiteralTimeUpdated" runat="server" />
        </ContentTemplate>
        <Triggers>
            <asp:AsyncPostBackTrigger ControlID="ButtonTrigger" />
        </Triggers>
    </asp:UpdatePanel>

    <br />
    <asp:Button ID="ButtonTrigger" runat="server" Text="Trigger" />

    </form>
</body>
</html>
```

Figure 24A-3 shows the page that is rendered using the preceding code.

On this page, the `UpdatePanel` is refreshed every time the Trigger button is clicked. There are two types of triggers: AsyncPostBackTriggers and PostBackTriggers.

> ➤ **AsyncPostBackTrigger** — This type of trigger is used to identify controls that can trigger a refresh to the contents of the `UpdatePanel`.

FIGURE 24A-3

> ➤ **PostBackTrigger** — This type of trigger is used to allow a control within the `UpdatePanel` to force a full page postback.

UpdateProgress Control

The `UpdateProgress` control is used to give visual feedback to the user. It is not required, but is recommended for updates that take more than a few seconds. This is sample markup for an `UpdateProgress` control:

```
<asp:UpdateProgress ID="UpdateProgress1" runat="server"
    AssociatedUpdatePanelID="UpdatePanel1" DisplayAfter="100">
    <ProgressTemplate>
        <img src="PleaseWait.gif" alt="Please Wait" />
    </ProgressTemplate>
</asp:UpdateProgress>
```

The `UpdateProgress` control includes a `ProgressTemplate`. The `ProgressTemplate` contains all of the markup that will be displayed to the user. Usually, an animated image is displayed to convey to users that they are waiting for a process to finish. The `UpdateProgress` control can be located anywhere on the page including within the `UpdatePanel`.

These are the properties of the `UpdateProgress` control:

> ➤ **AssociatedUpdatePanelID** — This property designates the `UpdatePanel` that is associated with the `UpdateProgress` control.

> ➤ **DisplayAfter** — This property determines the number of milliseconds that the control waits before it displays its contents. The default is 500 milliseconds.

Timer Control

The `Timer` control is the final control in the group of AJAX Extensions controls. It is used to fire a `Tick` event at a given interval. This is sample markup for a `Timer` control:

```
<asp:Timer ID="Timer1" runat="server" Interval="100" ontick="Timer1_Tick" >
</asp:Timer>
```

The `Timer` control has the following properties:

> ➤ **Enabled** — This Boolean property determines whether the timer is enabled. The default is true.

> ➤ **Interval** — This property determines the number of milliseconds between `Tick` events. The default is one minute.

This is sample code for the event that is triggered by the `ontick` event of the timer:

```
protected void Timer1_Tick(object sender, EventArgs e)
{
    this.LiteralTimeUpdated.Text = DateTime.Now.ToLongTimeString();
}
```

TRY IT

In this lesson you use all of the controls in the group of AJAX Extensions controls to create a page that uses partial postbacks.

Lesson Requirements

➤ The `PleaseWait.gif` file.

Hints

➤ Use the UpdatePanelTrigger Collection Editor to manage the triggers associated with a particular `UpdatePanel`. The UpdatePanelTrigger Collection Editor is accessed via the `Triggers` property of the `UpdatePanel` while in Design view.

Step-by-Step

1. Open Microsoft Visual Web Developer 2010 Express.

2. Select New Project from the File menu.

3. Select **Visual C#** on the left side of the dialog box.

4. Select the **ASP.NET Web Application** template.

5. Enter **Lesson24a** in the Name field and **c:\ASPNETTrainer** in the Location field. Click the OK button.

6. Add a `ScriptManager` to the `Site.Master` page by adding the following markup to the top of the `form` element:

```
<asp:ScriptManager ID="ScriptManager1" runat="server">
</asp:ScriptManager>
```

7. Right-click the name of the project in the Solution Explorer window and select New Item from the Add menu to open the Add New Item dialog box. Select the **Web Form using Master Page** template, enter **Ajax.aspx** for the Name, and click the Add button. Select **Site. Master** as the master page and click the OK button.

8. Add a `ScriptManagerProxy` to the `Ajax.aspx` page by adding the following code to the `MainContent` content control:

```
<asp:ScriptManagerProxy ID="ScriptManagerProxy1" runat="server">
</asp:ScriptManagerProxy>
```

9.   Add the following code below the `ScriptManagerProxy`:

```
Time Page Rendered:
<asp:Literal ID="LiteralTimeRendered" runat="server" />
```

10.   Add an `UpdatePanel` to the page using the following code:

```
<asp:UpdatePanel ID="UpdatePanel1" runat="server">
</asp:UpdatePanel>
```

11.   Add the following content to the `UpdatePanel`:

```
<ContentTemplate>
    Time Page Updated:
    <asp:Literal ID="LiteralTimeUpdated" runat="server" />
    <br /><br />
    <asp:Button ID="ButtonUpdate" runat="server" Text="Update Time"
        OnClick="ButtonUpdate_Click" />
</ContentTemplate>
```

12.   Update the `Ajax.aspx.cs` page to the following:

```csharp
using System;
using System.Collections.Generic;
using System.Linq;
using System.Web;
using System.Web.UI;
using System.Web.UI.WebControls;

namespace Lesson24a
{
    public partial class Ajax : System.Web.UI.Page
    {
        protected void Page_Load(object sender, EventArgs e)
        {
            if (!IsPostBack)
            {
                this.LiteralTimeRendered.Text =
                    DateTime.Now.ToLongTimeString();
                this.LiteralTimeUpdated.Text =
                    DateTime.Now.ToLongTimeString();
            }
        }

        protected void ButtonUpdate_Click(object sender, EventArgs e)
        {
            this.LiteralTimeUpdated.Text = DateTime.Now.ToLongTimeString();
        }
    }
}
```

13.   Click the F5 button.

14. Click the Update Time button.

> *Because you are using an* UpdatePanel, *the page does not flicker when you click the Update Time button.*

15. Stop debugging by closing the browser.

16. Right-click the name of the project and select New Folder from the Add menu to add a folder named **images**.

17. Right-click the images folder, select Existing Item from the Add menu, navigate to the PleaseWait.gif file, select it, and click the Add button.

18. Add an UpdateProgress control, after the UpdatePanel control on the Ajax.aspx page, using the following markup:

```
<asp:UpdateProgress ID="UpdateProgress1" runat="server"
    AssociatedUpdatePanelID="UpdatePanel1" DisplayAfter="1000">
</asp:UpdateProgress>
```

19. Add the following ProgressTemplate to the UpdateProgress controls:

```
<ProgressTemplate>
    <img src="images/PleaseWait.gif" alt="" /> Please Wait…
</ProgressTemplate>
```

20. Add the following code to the top of the ButtonUpdate_Click event in the Ajax.aspx.cs file to ensure that the ProgressTemplate is shown:

```
System.Threading.Thread.Sleep(3000);
```

21. Click the F5 button.

22. Click the Update Time button (see Figure 24A-4).

23. Stop debugging by closing the browser.

24. Add a Timer control after the UpdateProgress control on the Ajax.aspx page by using the following markup:

```
<asp:Timer ID="Timer1" runat="server" Interval="1000" ontick="Timer1_Tick">
</asp:Timer>
```

25. Add the following code to the Ajax.aspx.cs page:

```
protected void Timer1_Tick(object sender, EventArgs e)
{
    this.LiteralTimeUpdated.Text = DateTime.Now.ToLongTimeString();
}
```

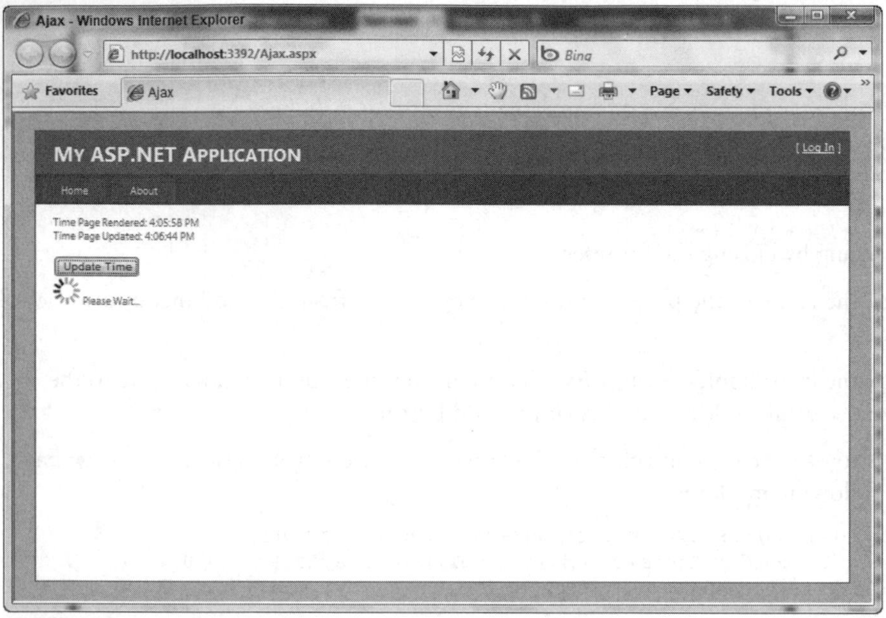

FIGURE 24A-4

26. Add a trigger to the `UpdatePanel` to allow the `Tick` event of the `Timer` control to refresh the `UpdatePanel` by adding the following markup to the `UpdatePanel`:

```
<Triggers>
    <asp:AsyncPostBackTrigger ControlID="Timer1" EventName="Tick" />
</Triggers>
```

> *If you had added the* `Timer` *control directly to the* `UpdatePanel`, *you would not need to update the* `Triggers` *property of the* `UpdatePanel`.

27. Verify that the markup in the Ajax.aspx page matches the following:

```
<%@ Page Title="" Language="C#" MasterPageFile="~/Site.Master"
AutoEventWireup="true"
    CodeBehind="Ajax.aspx.cs" Inherits="Lesson24a.Ajax" %>

<asp:Content ID="Content1" ContentPlaceHolderID="HeadContent" runat="server">
</asp:Content>
<asp:Content ID="Content2" ContentPlaceHolderID="MainContent" runat="server">
    <asp:ScriptManagerProxy ID="ScriptManagerProxy1" runat="server">
    </asp:ScriptManagerProxy>
    Time Page Rendered:
    <asp:Literal ID="LiteralTimeRendered" runat="server" />
    <asp:UpdatePanel ID="UpdatePanel1" runat="server">
        <ContentTemplate>
```

```
             Time Page Updated:
             <asp:Literal ID="LiteralTimeUpdated" runat="server" />
             <br />
             <br />
             <asp:Button ID="ButtonUpdate" runat="server" Text="Update Time"
                 OnClick="ButtonUpdate_Click" />
         </ContentTemplate>
         <Triggers>
             <asp:AsyncPostBackTrigger ControlID="Timer1" EventName="Tick" />
         </Triggers>
     </asp:UpdatePanel>
     <asp:UpdateProgress ID="UpdateProgress1" runat="server"
         AssociatedUpdatePanelID="UpdatePanel1" DisplayAfter="1000">
         <ProgressTemplate>
             <img src="images/PleaseWait.gif" alt="" />
             Please Wait…
         </ProgressTemplate>
     </asp:UpdateProgress>
     <asp:Timer ID="Timer1" runat="server" Interval="1000"
         OnTick="Timer1_Tick">
     </asp:Timer>
 </asp:Content>
```

28. Click the F5 button and watch the timer control automatically update the time.

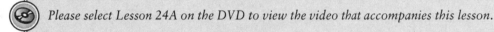

Please select Lesson 24A on the DVD to view the video that accompanies this lesson.

24B

Using the Ajax Helpers in MVC

When a typical ASP.NET page needs to be refreshed from the server, it triggers a complete page refresh. The result is a slight delay and a flicker of the page. Wouldn't it be great if your page had to ability to submit only the section that needed to be updated, and it subsequently only needed to refresh that section? The Ajax helpers in the ASP.NET MVC framework give your web pages the ability to perform partial page updates. In this lesson I teach you how to use the Ajax helpers.

Ajax stands for **A**synchronous **J**avaScript **a**nd **X**ML. It enables your client-side web pages to exchange information with the server by using asynchronous calls. To do this, it uses both JavaScript and XML and can require a great deal of code. Because of the complexity involved in programming, a number of popular Ajax libraries have been developed. In fact, Microsoft includes an Ajax library as part of the ASP.NET 4 framework.

Whenever you create a new MVC project using an MVC template, the Scripts folder is automatically populated with both jQuery and Ajax scripts as shown in Figure 24B-1.

FIGURE 24B-1

Before you can use the Ajax helpers you must include the following libraries in your page:

➤   MicrosoftAjax.js

➤   MicrosoftMvcAjax.js

The Scripts folder includes two versions of each of these libraries. The debug versions should be used during development because they return more detailed error messages. However, you should use the regular versions of these files in production because they are much smaller than the debug versions.

> *The Microsoft Ajax Content Delivery Network (CDN) discussed in Lesson 23 can be used to distribute the ASP.NET Ajax Library.*

This is a list of the Ajax helpers included in the ASP.NET MVC framework:

➤ **Ajax.ActionLink()** — This helper creates a link to the specified action method. The action method is invoked asynchronously using JavaScript when the link is clicked.

➤ **Ajax.BeginForm()** — This helper is used to designate the beginning of a form that will be submitted asynchronously using JavaScript.

➤ **Ajax.BeginRouteForm()** — This helper is also used to designate the beginning of a form that will be submitted asynchronously using JavaScript. The difference between `BeginForm` and `BeginRouteForm` is that `BeginRouteForm` includes the `Route` as one of its parameters.

➤ **Ajax.GlobalizationScript()** — This helper is used to define the culture information.

➤ **Ajax.RouteLink()** — This helper creates a link using the specified route. The request is made asynchronously using JavaScript when the link is clicked.

The following code creates a link with the text "Update Time" that calls the `CurrentTime` action method using the information supplied by the `AjaxOptions` parameter:

```
<%: Ajax.ActionLink("Update Time",
                    "CurrentTime",
                    new AjaxOptions { UpdateTargetId="time" }
)%>
```

In this case, there is only one item supplied by the `AjaxOptions parameter`. The `UpdateTargetId` is set to `time`. That means that the results returned by the `CurrentTime` action method will be used to update the element with `id` equal to `"time"`.

This is the `CurrentTime` action method:

```
public string CurrentTime()
{
    return DateTime.Now.ToLongTimeString();
}
```

This is the view:

```
<%@ Page Language="C#" MasterPageFile="~/Views/Shared/Site.Master"
    Inherits="System.Web.Mvc.ViewPage" %>
<asp:Content ID="aboutTitle" ContentPlaceHolderID="TitleContent" runat="server">
    Action Link
</asp:Content>

<asp:Content ID="aboutContent" ContentPlaceHolderID="MainContent" runat="server">
    <script src="../../Scripts/MicrosoftAjax.debug.js" type="text/javascript">
    </script>
    <script src="../../Scripts/MicrosoftMvcAjax.debug.js"
```

```
              type="text/javascript">
    </script>
    <h2>Action Link</h2>
    Time Page Rendered: <%: DateTime.Now.ToLongTimeString() %>
    <br />
    Time Page Updated: <span id="time" />
    <br /><br />
    <%: Ajax.ActionLink("Update Time",
                        "CurrentTime",
                        new AjaxOptions { UpdateTargetId="time" } )%>
</asp:Content>
```

> *The view contains links to both of the Microsoft Ajax libraries. However, if most of your pages use the Microsoft Ajax libraries you should add them to the Master Page instead of adding them to every page.*

Figure 24B-2 shows the page that is rendered.

Whenever the Update Time link is clicked, the time is updated asynchronously. The only information on the page that is refreshed is the time.

All of the Ajax helpers use the `AjaxOptions` class. The `AjaxOptions` class has the following properties:

FIGURE 24B-2

➤ **Confirm** — This property contains the message displayed in a confirmation window before a request is submitted. A confirmation window appears only if this property is not empty.

➤ **HttpMethod** — This property contains the HTTP request method. It can be either GET or POST. The default value is POST.

➤ **InsertionMode** — This property contains the insertion mode. The insertion mode can be InsertAfter, InsertBefore, or Replace. The default value is Replace.

➤ **LoadingElementId** — This property contains the id of the HTML element that should be displayed while the Ajax function is loading.

➤ **OnBegin** — This property contains the name of the JavaScript function to call before the page is updated.

➤ **OnComplete** — This property contains the name of the JavaScript function to call after the response data has been instantiated but before the page has been updated.

➤ **OnFailure** — This property contains the name of the JavaScript function to call if the update fails. Because the default behavior of the Ajax helpers is to fail silently, you must use this property to communicate to the user that the update has failed.

➤ **OnSuccess** — This property contains the name of the JavaScript function to call after the update succeeds.

➤ **UpdateTargetId** — This property contains the id of the DOM element to update.

➤ **Url** — This property contains the URL to which to make the request.

The `Ajax.BeginForm` helper is used to submit an entire form asynchronously using JavaScript and it is simple to use. All you need to do is to replace `Html.BeginForm` with `Ajax.BeginForm` and add the `AjaxOptions` parameter. This is the code to use the `Ajax.BeginForm` helper:

```
<% using (Ajax.BeginForm(new AjaxOptions { Confirm="Are you sure?" })) {%>
    ...
<% } %>
```

In this example the confirmation window shown in Figure 24B-3 is displayed before the page is updated.

FIGURE 24B-3

 In this example, the page is updated only if the user clicks the OK button in the confirmation window.

TRY IT

In this lesson you use the `Ajax.BeginForm` helper and a partial view to asynchronously submit a form using JavaScript.

Lesson Requirements

➤ The `PleaseWait.gif` file.

Hints

➤ Add the references to the JavaScript libraries by dragging them from the Scripts folder directly onto the form.

Step-by-Step

1. Open Microsoft Visual Web Developer 2010 Express.

2. Select New Project from the File menu.

3. Select **Visual C#** on the left side of the dialog box.

4. Select the **ASP.NET MVC 2 Web Application** template.

5. Enter **Lesson24b** in the Name field and **c:\ASPNETTrainer** in the Location field. Click the OK button.

6. Right-click the Content folder and select New Folder from the Add menu to add a subfolder named **images**.

7. Right-click the images folder, select Existing Item from the Add menu, navigate to the `PleaseWait.gif` file, select it, and click the Add button.

8. Right-click the Models folder and select Class from the Add menu to create a class named **Time.cs**.

9. Update the code for the `Time.cs` class to the following:

```
using System;
using System.Collections.Generic;
using System.Linq;
using System.Web;

namespace Lesson24b.Models
{
    public class Time
    {
        public DateTime CurrentTime { get; set; }
    }

    public class Timestamps : List<Time>
    {}
}
```

10. Select Build Lesson24b from the Build menu and wait for the build process to complete.

11. Right-click the Views folder and select New Folder from the Add menu to add a subfolder named **Time**.

12. Right-click the Time folder, and select View from the Add menu to open the Add View dialog box (see Figure 24B-4). Set the View name to **Index**, check the `Create a strongly-typed view` checkbox, select **Lesson24b.Models.Timestamps** as the View data class and **Empty** as the View content Click the Add button.

13. Delete the following markup from the `MainContent` content control of the `Index.aspx` page:

```
<h2>Index</h2>
```

FIGURE 24B-4

14. Add the following references to the Index.aspx page:

```
<script src="../../Scripts/MicrosoftAjax.debug.js" type="text/javascript">
</script>
<script src="../../Scripts/MicrosoftMvcAjax.debug.js" type="text/javascript">
</script>
```

15. Add the following code to the Index.aspx page:

```
<% using (Ajax.BeginForm("Create",
                        new AjaxOptions { UpdateTargetId = "timestamps",
                                          LoadingElementId="pleaseWait" }))
   { %>

        <input id="AddTimestamp" type="submit" value="Add Timestamp" />
<% } %>
```

16. The following code will update the timestamp object when the Add Timestamp button is clicked. Add the following div element to the Index.aspx page:

```
<div id="timestamps">
    <% Html.RenderPartial("Timestamps"); %>
</div>
```

17. Add the following div element to the Index.aspx page:

```
<div id="pleaseWait" style="display:none">
    <img src="../../Content/images/PleaseWait.gif" alt="" /> Please Wait…
</div>
```

18. Right-click the Time folder, and select View from the Add menu to open the Add View dialog box (see Figure 24B-5). Set the View name to **Timestamps,** check the Create a partial view checkbox, check the `Create a strongly-typed view` checkbox, select **Lesson24b .Models.Timestamps** as the View data class and **Empty** as the View content. Click the Add button.

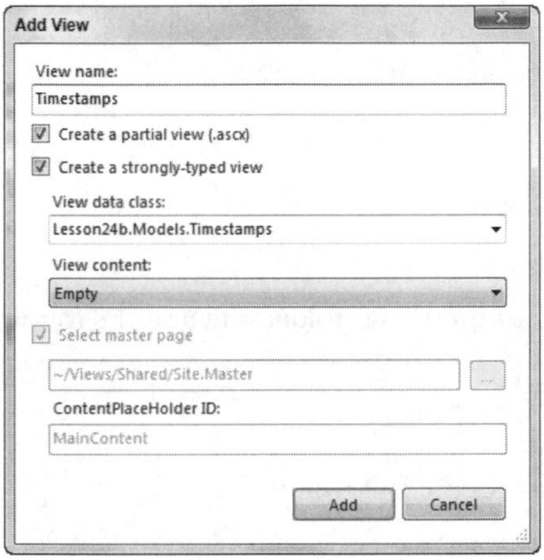

FIGURE 24B-5

19. Add the following code to the `Timestamps.ascx` file:

```
<h2>Timestamps</h2>
<% foreach (var item in Model) { %>
    <%= String.Format("{0:T}", item.CurrentTime) %>
    <br />
<% } %>
```

20. Right-click the Controllers folder, enter **TimeController** for the name of the controller, do not check the `Add action methods for Create, Update, Delete and Details scenarios` checkbox, and click the Add button.

21. Add the following code to the top of the `TimeController` class:

```
private Lesson24b.Models.Timestamps timestamps =
    new Lesson24b.Models.Timestamps();
```

22. Update the `Index` action method of the `TimeController` class to the following:

```
public ActionResult Index()
{
    Session["Timestamps"] = timestamps;
    return View(timestamps);
}
```

23. Add the following `Create` action method to the `TimeController` class:

```
[HttpPost]
public PartialViewResult Create()
{
```

```
            // This sleep is added to force the loading element to display.
            // It is not required.
            System.Threading.Thread.Sleep(3000);

            timestamps = (Lesson24b.Models.Timestamps)Session["Timestamps"];

            Lesson24b.Models.Time time = new Lesson24b.Models.Time();
            time.CurrentTime = DateTime.Now;
            timestamps.Add(time);

            return PartialView("Timestamps", timestamps);
        }
```

24.   Open the `Site.Master` file in the Shared subfolder of the Views folder and add the following
menu item to the `menu`:

```
<li><%= Html.ActionLink("Time", "Index", "Time")%></li>
```

25.   Verify that the markup on the Index.aspx page matches the following:

```
<%@ Page Title="" Language="C#" MasterPageFile="~/Views/Shared/Site.Master"
    Inherits="System.Web.Mvc.ViewPage<Lesson24b.Models.Timestamps>" %>

<asp:Content ID="Content1" ContentPlaceHolderID="TitleContent" runat="server">
    Index
</asp:Content>

<asp:Content ID="Content2" ContentPlaceHolderID="MainContent" runat="server">
<script src="../../Scripts/MicrosoftAjax.debug.js" type="text/javascript">
</script>
<script src="../../Scripts/MicrosoftMvcAjax.debug.js" type="text/javascript">
</script>

<% using (Ajax.BeginForm("Create",
                         new AjaxOptions { UpdateTargetId = "timestamps",
                                           LoadingElementId="pleaseWait" }))
    { %>

        <input id="AddTimestamp" type="submit" value="Add Timestamp" />
<% } %>
<div id="timestamps">
    <% Html.RenderPartial("Timestamps"); %>
</div>
<div id="pleaseWait" style="display:none">
    <img src="../../Content/images/PleaseWait.gif" alt="" /> Please Wait…
</div>

</asp:Content>
```

26.   Click the F5 button and navigate to the Time tab (see Figure 24B-6).

27.   Click the Add Timestamp button six times (see Figure 24B-7).

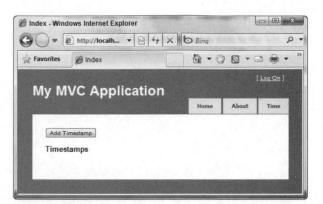

FIGURE 24B-6

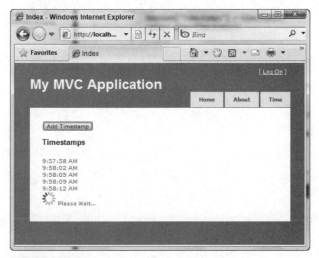

FIGURE 24B-7

 Please select Lesson 24B on the DVD to view the video that accompanies this lesson.

25A

Using jQuery for Ajax in Web Forms

In Lesson 23 you learned about using JavaScript to perform client-side programming. In that lesson you were introduced to the jQuery script library. In Lesson 24A you learned how to use the AJAX Extensions provided by the ASP.NET Web Forms framework. In this lesson I teach you how to use the Ajax tools provided by jQuery.

AJAX METHODS

These are the Ajax methods that jQuery provides:

- ➤ **$.ajax** — This method performs an Ajax request. All of the other methods in this list are shortcuts that use this method.

- ➤ **$.get** — This method loads HTML using an HTTP GET request.

- ➤ **$.getJSON** — This method loads JSON-encoded data using an HTTP GET request.

- ➤ **$.getScript** — This method loads a JavaScript file using an HTTP GET request and executes it.

- ➤ **.load** — This method loads HTML into the specified element.

- ➤ **$.post** — This method loads HTML using an HTTP POST request.

> *JSON stands for JavaScript Object Notation. It is a format used to represent simple data structures and objects in a lightweight, text-based, human-readable format.*

The simplest way to fetch data asynchronously from the server is to use the `.load` method. The `.load` method can be used to replace the `UpdatePanel` server control that was introduced in Lesson 24A. These are the parameters of the `.load` method:

➤ **url** — This is a string that contains the URL to which the request is sent. This is the only required parameter.

➤ **data** — This is a string that contains any data that needs to be sent to the URL.

➤ **complete** — This is the function that is called when the request completes.

The `.load` method uses a `GET` method to fetch data from the server, unless the data provided is provided as an object. In that case, the `.load` method uses a `POST` method. This is the markup for a page that uses the `.load` method:

```
<%@ Page Language="C#" AutoEventWireup="true" CodeBehind="Time.aspx.cs"
    Inherits="Lesson25a.Time" %>

<!DOCTYPE html PUBLIC "-//W3C//DTD XHTML 1.0 Transitional//EN"
    "http://www.w3.org/TR/xhtml1/DTD/xhtml1-transitional.dtd">
<html xmlns="http://www.w3.org/1999/xhtml">
<head runat="server">
    <title>Load Method</title>
    <script src="http://ajax.microsoft.com/ajax/jquery/jquery-1.3.2.js"
        type="text/javascript">
    </script>
</head>
<body>
    <form id="form1" runat="server">
    Time Page Rendered:
    <asp:Literal ID="LiteralTimeRendered" runat="server" />
    <br />
    Time Page Updated:
    <span id="currentTime">
        <asp:Literal ID="LiteralTimeUpdated" runat="server" />
    </span>
    <br /> <br />
    <input id="SubmitUpdate" type="button" value="Update Time" />
    </form>

    <script type="text/javascript">
        // By default cache is true.
        $.ajaxSetup({
            cache: false
        });

        $("#SubmitUpdate").click(function () {
            $("#currentTime").load("CurrentTime.aspx");
        });

    </script>
</body>
</html>
```

The preceding code loads the HTML that is returned by the CurrentTime.aspx page into the span element with id equal to "currentTime". The CurrentTime.aspx page returns a string that represents the current time. This is the code used in the CurrentTime.aspx.cs file:

```
protected void Page_Load(object sender, EventArgs e)
{
    Response.Write(DateTime.Now.ToLongTimeString());
}
```

> *By default, the pages are cached on the server. You must set the cache to false to have the click function update the page each time the button is clicked.*

Figure 25A-1 shows the page that is rendered using the preceding code.

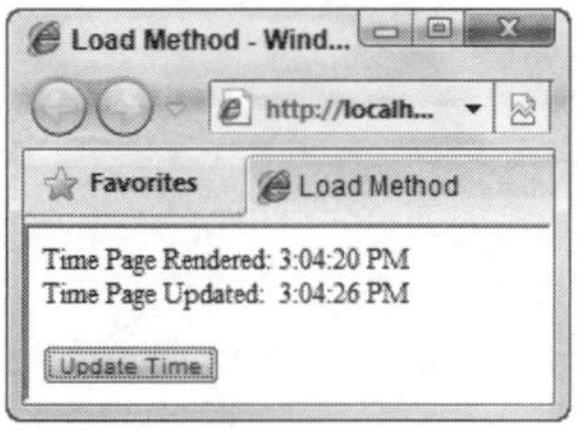

FIGURE 25A-1

The Time Page Rendered field shows the original time when the page was rendered. The Time Page Updated field is updated every time the Update Time button is clicked. Because this page is being updated asynchronously using the .load method, only the Page Uploaded field is updated when the Update Time button is clicked.

The ajaxSetup method is used to configure the default Ajax request. This is the JavaScript code to set default values for the URL, cache, type of request, and the password and username to be used in response to an HTTP access authentication request:

```
$.ajaxSetup({
    url: currenttime.aspx, // Default is the current page.
    cache: false,          // Default is true.
    type: "POST",          // Default is "Get".
    password: "secret",
    username: "jwright"
});
```

AJAX EVENT HANDLERS

jQuery provides a number of global Ajax event handlers:

➤   ajaxComplete

➤   ajaxError

➤   ajaxSend

➤ ajaxStart

➤ ajaxStop

➤ ajaxSuccess

This is the JavaScript code to show and hide a progress indicator:

```
$("#wait").ajaxStart(function () {
    $(this).show();
});

$("#wait").ajaxStop(function () {
    $(this).hide();
});
```

This is the element that the preceding code is toggling:

```
<div id="wait" style="display: none">
    <img src="images/PleaseWait.gif" alt="" /> Please Wait…
</div>
```

TRY IT

In this lesson you use jQuery to create the same page that you created in Lesson 24A.

Lesson Requirements

➤ The PleaseWait.gif file.

Hints

None.

Step-by-Step

1. Open Microsoft Visual Web Developer 2010 Express.

2. Select New Project from the File menu.

3. Select **Visual C#** on the left side of the dialog box.

4. Select the **ASP.NET Web Application** template.

5. Enter **Lesson25a** in the Name field and **c:\ASPNETTrainer** in the Location field. Click the OK button.

6. Open the Site.Master file.

7. Add a reference to the jQuery library by adding the following code into the head element:

```
<script src="http://ajax.microsoft.com/ajax/jquery/jquery-1.4.1.js"
    type="text/javascript">
</script>
```

8. Right-click the name of the project in the Solution Explorer window and select New Item from the Add menu to open the Add New Item dialog box. Select the **Web Form using Master Page** template, enter **Ajax.aspx** for the Name, and click the Add button. Select **Site. Master** as the Master Page and click OK.

9. Update the `title` attribute of the `@Page` directive to **Ajax**, and right-click the `Ajax.aspx` page and select Set As Start Page from the menu.

10. Add the following markup to the `MainContent` content control:

```
Time Page Rendered:
<asp:Literal ID="LiteralTimeRendered" runat="server" />
<br />
Time Page Updated: 
<span id="currentTime">
    <asp:Literal ID="LiteralTimeUpdated" runat="server" />
</span>
<br /><br />
<input id="SubmitUpdate" type="button" value="Update Time" />
```

11. Add the following `script` element to the page:

```
<script type="text/javascript">
    $.ajaxSetup({
        cache: false
    });

    $("#SubmitUpdate").click(function () {
        $("#currentTime").load("CurrentTime.aspx");
    });
</script>
```

12. Add the following code to the `Page_Load` event of the `Ajax.aspx.cs` file:

```
this.LiteralTimeRendered.Text = DateTime.Now.ToLongTimeString();
this.LiteralTimeUpdated.Text = DateTime.Now.ToLongTimeString();
```

13. Right-click the name of the project in the Solution Explorer window and select New Item from the Add menu to open the Add New Item dialog box. Select the **Web Form** template, enter **CurrentTime.aspx** for the Name, and click the Add button.

14. Delete all of the markup except for the `@Page` directive.

15. Add the following code to the `Page_Load` event of the `CurrentTime.aspx.cs` file:

```
Response.Write(DateTime.Now.ToLongTimeString());
```

16. Click the F5 button.

17. Click the Update Time button (see Figure 25A-2).

18. Stop debugging by closing the browser.

19. Right-click the name of the project and select New Folder from the Add menu to add a folder named **images**.

20. Right-click the images folder, select Existing Item from the Add menu, navigate to the `PleaseWait.gif` file, select it, and click the Add button.

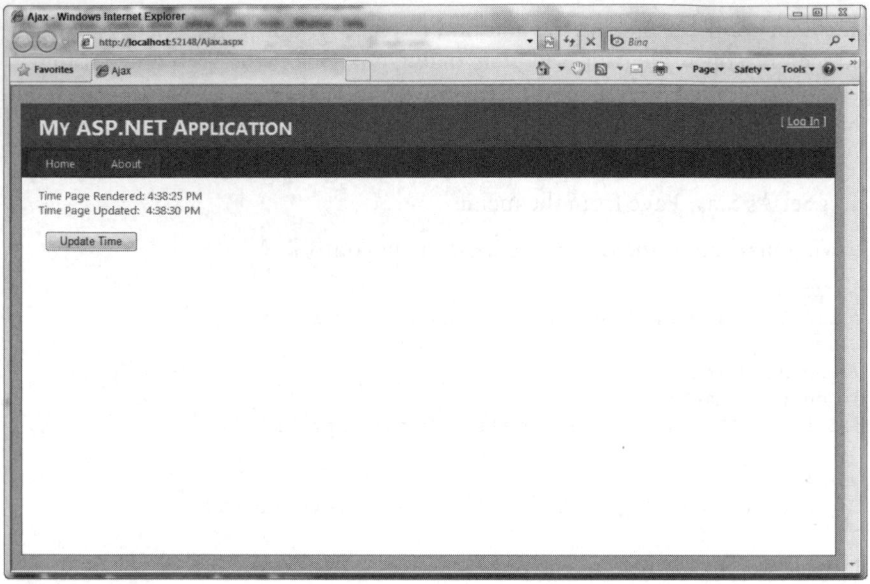

FIGURE 25A-2

21. Add the following markup to the `Ajax.aspx` file above the `script` element:

```
<div id="wait" style="display: none">
    <img src="images/PleaseWait.gif" alt="" /> Please Wait...
</div>
```

22. Add the following JavaScript to the `Ajax.aspx` file at the bottom of the `script` element:

```
$("#wait").ajaxStart(function () {
    $(this).show();
});

$("#wait").ajaxStop(function () {
    $(this).hide();
});
```

23. Add the following code to the `Page_Load` event of the `CurrentTime.aspx.cs` file.

```
System.Threading.Thread.Sleep(3000);
```

24. Click the F5 button.

25. Click the Update Time button (see Figure 25A-3).

26. Stop debugging by closing the browser.

27. Add the following code to the bottom of the `script` element in the Ajax.aspx file.

```
window.setInterval('$("#currentTime").load("CurrentTime.aspx")', 5000);
```

28. Click the F5 button and watch the time get automatically updated.

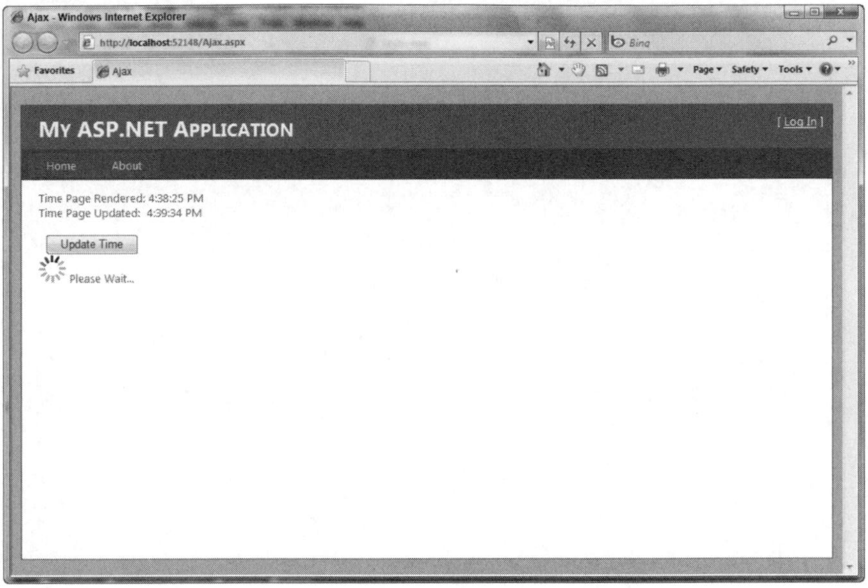

FIGURE 25A-3

Please select Lesson 25A on the DVD to view the video that accompanies this lesson.

Using jQuery for Ajax in MVC

In Lesson 23 you learned about using JavaScript to perform client-side programming. In that lesson you were introduced to the jQuery script library. In Lesson 24B you learned how to use the Ajax helpers provided by the ASP.NET MVC framework. In this lesson I teach you how to use the Ajax tools provided by jQuery.

AJAX METHODS

These are the Ajax methods that jQuery provides:

- ➤ **$.ajax** — This method performs an Ajax request. All of the other methods in this list are shortcuts that use this method.

- ➤ **$.get** — This method loads HTML using an HTTP GET request.

- ➤ **$.getJSON** — This method loads JSON-encoded data using an HTTP GET request.

- ➤ **$.getScript** — This method loads a JavaScript file using an HTTP GET request and executes it.

- ➤ **.load** — This method loads HTML into the specified element.

- ➤ **$.post** — This method loads HTML using an HTTP POST request.

> *JSON stands for JavaScript Object Notation. It is a format used to represent simple data structures and objects in a lightweight, text-based, human-readable format.*

The simplest way to fetch data asynchronously from the server is to use the `.load` method. These are the parameters of the `.load` method:

- ➤ **url** — This is a string that contains the URL to which the request is sent. This is the only required parameter.

➤ **data** — This is a string that contains any data that needs to be sent to the URL.

➤ **complete** — This is the function that is called when the request completes.

The `.load` method uses a GET method to fetch data from the server, unless the data provided is provided as an object. In that case, the `.load` method uses a POST method. The following view uses the `.load` method:

```
<%@ Page Language="C#" MasterPageFile="~/Views/Shared/Site.Master"
    Inherits="System.Web.Mvc.ViewPage" %>

<asp:Content ContentPlaceHolderID="TitleContent" runat="server">
    jQuery.load
</asp:Content>
<asp:Content ContentPlaceHolderID="MainContent" runat="server">
    <script src="../../Scripts/jquery-1.3.2.js" type="text/javascript"></script>

    <h2>jQuery.load</h2>
    Time Page Rendered:
    <%: DateTime.Now.ToLongTimeString() %>
    <br />
    Time Page Updated:
    <span id="time">
        <%: DateTime.Now.ToLongTimeString() %>
    </span>
    <br /><br />
    <div id="update" class="link">
        Update Time
    </div>

    <script type="text/javascript">
        $("#update").click(function () {
            $("#time").load("/Home/CurrentTime");
        });
    </script>
</asp:Content>
```

The preceding code loads the HTML that is returned by the /Home/CurrentTime route into the span element with the id equal to "time". This is the CurrentTime action method:

```
public PartialViewResult CurrentTime()
{
    ViewData["time"] = DateTime.Now.ToLongTimeString();
    return PartialView("CurrentTime");
}
```

The CurrentTime action method returns a PartialViewResult. This is the markup from the CurrentTime.ascx user control:

```
<%@ Control Language="C#" Inherits="System.Web.Mvc.ViewUserControl" %>
<%: ViewData["time"] %>
```

Figure 25B-1 shows the page that is rendered using the preceding code.

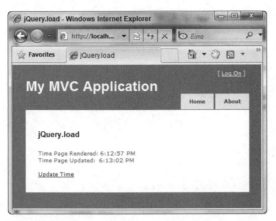

FIGURE 25B-1

The Time Page Rendered field shows the original time that the page was rendered. The Time Page Updated field is updated every time the Update Time link is clicked. Because this page is being updated asynchronously using the .load method, only the Page Uploaded field is updated when the Update Time link is clicked.

The ajaxSetup method is used to configure the default Ajax request. This is the JavaScript code to set default values for the URL, cache, type of request, and the password and username to be used in response to an HTTP access authentication request:

```
$.ajaxSetup({
    url: currenttime.aspx, // Default is the current page.
    cache: false,          // Default is true.
    type: "POST",          // Default is "Get".
    password: "secret",
    username: "jwright"
});
```

AJAX EVENT HANDLERS

jQuery provides a number of global Ajax event handlers:

➤   ajaxComplete

➤   ajaxError

➤   ajaxSend

➤   ajaxStart

➤   ajaxStop

➤   ajaxSuccess

This is the JavaScript code to show and hide a progress indicator:

```
$("#wait").ajaxStart(function () {
    $(this).show();
});

$("#wait").ajaxStop(function () {
    $(this).hide();
});
```

This is the element that the preceding code is toggling:

```
<div id="wait" style="display: none">
    <img src="images/PleaseWait.gif" alt="" /> Please Wait…
</div>
```

TRY IT

In this lesson you use jQuery to create the same page that you created in Lesson 24B.

Lesson Requirements

➤ The `PleaseWait.gif` file.

Hints

➤ Add a reference to the jQuery library by dragging it from the Scripts folder directly onto the form.

Step-by-Step

1. Open Microsoft Visual Web Developer 2010 Express.

2. Select New Project from the File menu.

3. Select **Visual C#** on the left side of the dialog box.

4. Select the **ASP.NET MVC 2 Web Application** template.

5. Enter **Lesson25b** in the Name field and **c:\ASPNETTrainer** in the Location field. Click the OK button.

6. Right-click the Content folder and select New Folder from the Add menu to add a subfolder named **images**.

7. Right-click the images folder, select Existing Item from the Add menu, navigate to the `PleaseWait.gif` file, select it, and click the Add button.

8. Right-click the Models folder and select Class from the Add menu to create a class named **Time.cs**.

9. Update the code for the `Time.cs` class to the following:

```
using System;
using System.Collections.Generic;

namespace Lesson25b.Models
{
    public class Time
    {
        public DateTime CurrentTime { get; set; }
    }

    public class Timestamps : List<Time>
    {}
}
```

10. Select Build Lesson25b from the Build menu and wait for the build process to complete.

11. Right-click the Views folder and select New Folder from the Add menu to add a subfolder named **Time**.

12. Right-click the Time folder and select View from the Add menu to open the Add View dialog box (see Figure 25B-2). Set the View name to **Index**, check the `Create a strongly-typed view` checkbox, select **Lesson25b.Models.Timestamps** as the View data class and **Empty** as the View content. Click the Add button.

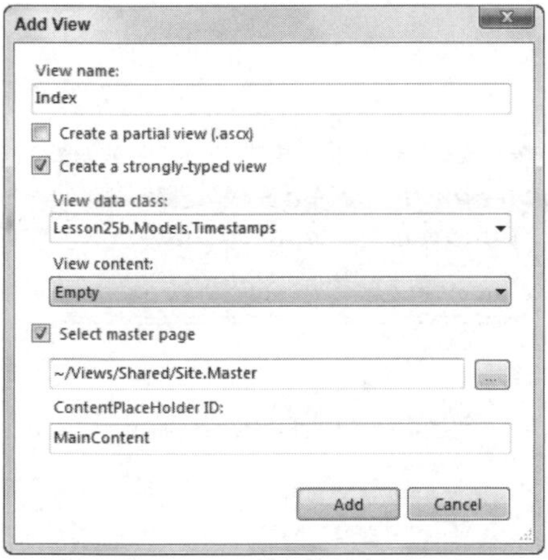

FIGURE 25B-2

13. Delete the following markup from the `MainContent` content control of the `Index.aspx` page:

```
<h2>Index</h2>
```

14. Add the following reference to the `MainContent` content control of the `Index.aspx` page:

```
<script src="../../Scripts/jquery-1.4.1.js" type="text/javascript"></script>
```

15. Add the following markup to the `Index.aspx` page:

```
<input id="AddTimestamp" type="button" value="Add Timestamp" />
<div id="Timestamps">
</div>

<div id="pleaseWait" style="display:none">
    <img src="../../Content/images/PleaseWait.gif" alt="" /> Please Wait…
</div>
```

16. Add the following JavaScript code to the `Index.aspx` page:

```
<script type="text/javascript">
    $.ajaxSetup({
        cache: false
    });

    $("#AddTimestamp").click(function () {
        $("#Timestamps").load("/Time/Timestamps");
    });

    $("#pleaseWait").ajaxStart(function () {
        $(this).show();
    });

    $("#pleaseWait").ajaxStop(function () {
        $(this).hide();
    });
</script>
```

> The `ajaxSetup` method is used to set the default values for future Ajax requests. Since the default value for cache is true, you must set it to false in order to prevent the browser from caching the page.

17. Right-click the Time folder and select View from the Add menu to open the Add View dialog box (see Figure 25B-3). Set the View name to **Timestamps,** check the `Create a partial view` checkbox, check the `Create a strongly-typed view` checkbox, select **Lesson25b.Models .Timestamps** as the View data class and **Empty** as the View content. Click the Add button.

FIGURE 25B-3

18. Add the following code to the `Timestamps.ascx` file:

```
<h2>Timestamps</h2>
<% foreach (var item in Model) { %>
    <%= String.Format("{0:T}", item.CurrentTime) %>
    <br />
<% } %>
```

19. Right-click the Controllers folder, enter **TimeController** for the name of the controller, do not check the `Add action methods for Create, Update, Delete, and Details scenarios` checkbox, and click the Add button.

20. Add the following code to the top of the `TimeController` class:

```
private Lesson25b.Models.Timestamps timestamps =
    new Lesson25b.Models.Timestamps();
```

21. Update the `Index` action method of the `TimeController` class to the following:

```
public ActionResult Index()
{
    Session["Timestamps"] = timestamps;
    return View(timestamps);
}
```

22. Add the following `Timestamps` action method to the `TimeController` class:

```
public PartialViewResult Timestamps()
{
    // This sleep is added to force the loading element to display.
    System.Threading.Thread.Sleep(3000);

    timestamps = (Lesson25b.Models.Timestamps)Session["Timestamps"];

    Lesson25b.Models.Time time = new Lesson25b.Models.Time();
    time.CurrentTime = DateTime.Now;
    timestamps.Add(time);

    return PartialView("Timestamps", timestamps);
}
```

23. Open the `Site.Master` file in the Shared subfolder of the Views folder and add the following menu item to the menu:

```
<li><%= Html.ActionLink("Time", "Index", "Time")%></li>
```

24. Click the F5 button and navigate to the Time tab (see Figure 25B-4).

25. Click the Add Timestamps button six times (see Figure 25B-5).

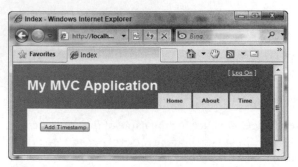

FIGURE 25B-4

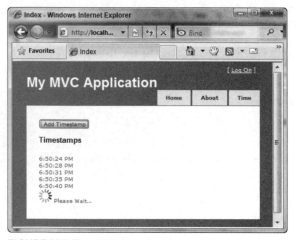

FIGURE 25B-5

Please select Lesson 25B on the DVD to view the video that accompanies this lesson.

SECTION X
Securing Your Application

26

Authentication

Security is an important component of many web sites that need to be able to verify whoever is accessing the information on the web site. Authentication refers to the process of identifying the users of your web site. It is the process of validating credentials, such as name and password, against some authority. The ASP.NET framework includes a couple of different ways to authenticate your users. Also, the framework includes a Membership provider that you can use to maintain a list of your users and a Role provider that you can use to associate users with roles. In this lesson you learn how to configure the two types of authentication providers and how to use both the Membership provider and the Role provider.

AUTHENTICATION PROVIDERS

These are the two types of authentication providers that ASP.NET provides:

➤ **Windows Authentication Provider** — This provider uses the authentication built into the Windows operating system to secure the application.

➤ **Forms Authentication Provider** — This provider uses a login form to secure the application. This is the default provider used by both Web Forms and MVC.

Authentication is configured by using the authentication element in the web.config file. This is the default value for the authentication element in a Web Forms application:

```
<configuration>
    …
    <system.web>
        …
        <authentication mode="Forms">
            <forms loginUrl="~/Account/Login.aspx" timeout="2880" />
        </authentication>
    </system.web>
</configuration>
```

This is the default value for the `authentication` element in an MVC application:

```
<configuration>
    ...
    <system.web>
        ...
        <authentication mode="Forms">
            <forms loginUrl="~/Account/LogOn" timeout="2880"/>
        </authentication>
    </system.web>
</configuration>
```

The valid values for the `mode` attribute are Forms, None, and Windows. In both of the default `web.config` files, the `loginUrl` is identified and the timeout is set to 2880 minutes. These configuration settings are made via the `forms` element of the `authentication` element. This is a list of the most frequently used attributes of the `forms` element:

➤ **cookieless** — This attribute specifies how cookies are used. The default is to use cookies if the browser supports them.

➤ **defaultUrl** — This attribute specifies the default URL or route to which the users are redirected after they have been authenticated.

➤ **loginUrl** — This attribute specifies the URL or route of the login page.

➤ **name** — This attribute specifies the name of the cookie used for authentication.

➤ **requireSSL** — This Boolean attribute specifies whether an SSL connection is required. The default value is false.

➤ **slidingExpiration** — This Boolean attribute specifies whether sliding expiration is enabled. The default is true.

➤ **timeout** — This attribute specifies the number of minutes before the cookie expires. If the `SlidingExpiration` attribute is set to true, the number of minutes until the cookie expires is reset every time that a request is received.

> *Secure Sockets Layer (SSL) is used to encrypt data that is sent between the server and the browser. To use SSL, you must install an SSL Certificate on your server. Web sites that use an SSL connection start with https:// instead of http://.*

MEMBERSHIP

The ASP.NET `Membership` class is used to validate users and manage their settings. This is a list of the methods of the `Membership` class:

➤ `CreateUser()`

➤ `DeleteUser()`

➤ FindUserByEmail()

➤ FindUserByName()

➤ GeneratePassword()

➤ GetAllUsers()

➤ GetNumberOfUsersOnline()

➤ GetUser()

➤ GetUserNameByEmail()

➤ UpdateUser()

➤ ValidateUser()

This is the syntax of the simplest CreateUser method:

```
public static MembershipUser CreateUser(
    string username,
    string password
)
```

This is the code to create a new user using a Web Form with two textboxes on it:

```
using System;
using System.Web.Security;

namespace Lesson26
{
    public partial class AddUser : System.Web.UI.Page
    {
        protected void ButtonAddUser_Click(object sender, EventArgs e)
        {
            MembershipUser user = Membership.CreateUser(TextBoxName.Text,
                                                TextBoxEmail.Text);
        }
    }
}
```

You can get and set a number of properties for each user. This is a list of the properties of the MembershipUser class:

➤ Comment

➤ CreationDate

➤ Email

➤ IsApproved

➤ IsLockedOut

➤ IsOnline

➤ LastActivityDate

➤   LastLockoutDate

➤   LastLoginDate

➤   LastPasswordChangedDate

➤   PasswordQuestion

➤   ProviderName

➤   ProviderUserKey

➤   UserName

Membership is configured in the `web.config` file. This is the default value for the `membership` element used by both Web Forms and MVC:

```
<configuration>
    ...
    <system.web>
        ...
        <membership>
            <providers>
                <clear/>
                <add name="AspNetSqlMembershipProvider"
                    type="System.Web.Security.SqlMembershipProvider"
                    connectionStringName="ApplicationServices"
                    enablePasswordRetrieval="false"
                    enablePasswordReset="true"
                    requiresQuestionAndAnswer="false"
                    requiresUniqueEmail="false"
                    maxInvalidPasswordAttempts="5"
                    minRequiredPasswordLength="6"
                    minRequiredNonalphanumericCharacters="0"
                    passwordAttemptWindow="10"
                    applicationName="/" />
            </providers>
        </membership>
    </system.web>
</configuration>
```

As you can see, `SqlMembershipProvider` is the default Membership provider. It stores membership information in the local ASPNETDB.mdf SQL Server Express database located in the App_Data folder. This is the complete list of attributes for the Membership provider:

➤ **applicationName** — This attribute specifies the name of the application.

➤ **description** — This attribute specifies a brief description of the provider.

➤ **enablePasswordReset** — This Boolean attribute specifies whether the passwords can be reset when using this provider.

➤ **enablePasswordRetrieval** — This Boolean attribute specifies whether the passwords can be retrieved by the users. If the passwords are hashed, they cannot be retrieved even if the value of this property is true.

➤ **maxInvalidPasswordAttempts** — This attribute specifies the number of invalid password attempts that are allowed before the user is locked out.

> ➤ **minRequiredNonAlphanumericCharacters** — This attribute specifies the minimum number of special characters that are required for a password to be valid.

> ➤ **name** — This attribute specifies the name of the provider.

> ➤ **passwordAttemptWindow** — This attribute specifies the number of minutes before a locked password is unlocked. The default is ten minutes.

> ➤ **passwordFormat** — This attribute specifies the format for storing passwords. The options are Clear, Encrypted, and Hashed.

> ➤ **passwordStrengthRegularExpression** — This attribute specifies the regular expression against which a password is evaluated.

> ➤ **requiresQuestionAndAnswer** — This Boolean attribute specifies whether users must answer a question in order to retrieve their password.

> ➤ **requiresUniqueEmail** — This Boolean attribute specifies whether each user must have a unique email address.

If you store your passwords in clear text, anyone with access to the Membership provider also has access to all of the passwords. Therefore you should always either encrypt or hash the passwords. Keep in mind that if you choose to hash the passwords, neither you nor an intruder will be able to retrieve them. Most web sites choose to hash their passwords because of the added security that hashing provides.

After a user has been authenticated, the `User` property is used to retrieve information about the user. This property contains the following properties:

> ➤ **Identity.AuthenticationType** — This property indicates the method that was used to authenticate the user.

> ➤ **Identity.IsAuthenticated** — This Boolean property indicates whether the user has been authenticated.

> ➤ **Identity.Name** — This property contains the user's name. If the user has not been authenticated, this property is blank.

The `User` property also contains the following method to determine whether a user is a member of a given role:

> ➤ `IsInRole()`

In the ASP.NET Web Forms framework, the `User` property is a property of the Page, whereas in ASP.NET MVC framework, the `User` property is a property of the Controller.

ROLES

The ASP.NET `Role` class is used to manage the roles to which users belong. This is a list of the methods of the `Role` class:

- ➤ `AddUsersToRole()`
- ➤ `AddUsersToRoles()`
- ➤ `AddUserToRole()`
- ➤ `AddUserToRoles()`
- ➤ `CreateRole()`
- ➤ `DeleteCookie()`
- ➤ `DeleteRole(String)`
- ➤ `DeleteRole(String, Boolean)`
- ➤ `FindUsersInRole()`
- ➤ `GetAllRoles()`
- ➤ `GetRolesForUser()()()`
- ➤ `GetRolesForUser(String)`
- ➤ `GetUsersInRole()`
- ➤ `IsUserInRole(String)`
- ➤ `IsUserInRole(String, String)`
- ➤ `RemoveUserFromRole()`
- ➤ `RemoveUserFromRoles()`
- ➤ `RemoveUsersFromRole()`
- ➤ `RemoveUsersFromRoles()`
- ➤ `RoleExists()`

This is the syntax of the `CreateRole` method:

```
CreateRole(
    string roleName
)
```

The Role Manager is configured in the `web.config` file. This is the default value for the `roleManager` element used by both Web Forms and MVC:

```
<roleManager enabled="false">
    <providers>
        <clear/>
        <add name="AspNetSqlRoleProvider"
```

```
        type="System.Web.Security.SqlRoleProvider"
        connectionStringName="ApplicationServices"
        applicationName="/" />
    <add name="AspNetWindowsTokenRoleProvider"
        type="System.Web.Security.WindowsTokenRoleProvider"
        applicationName="/" />
    </providers>
</roleManager>
```

The `AspNetSqlRoleProvider` is used to store role information in a SQL Server database, and the `AspNetWindowsTokenRoleProvider` is used when role information is stored in Microsoft Windows groups. You must enable Windows authentication in order to use the `AspNetWindowsTokenRoleProvider`.

> *By default, role management is disabled. You must enable role management in order to use it.*

ASP.NET WEB SITE ADMINISTRATION TOOL

So far, I have shown you how to work with both users and roles programmatically. Remember, you can also use the ASP.NET Web Site Administration Tool (WSAT) that was introduced in Lesson 5 to manage both users and roles. To open the WSAT from within a Web Project, select ASP.NET Configuration from the Project menu. Figure 26-1 shows the WSAT.

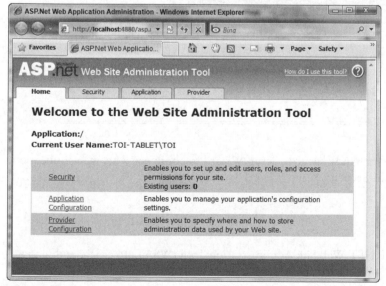

FIGURE 26-1

Figure 26-2 shows the Security tab of the WSAT. The Security tab can be used to create users, manage users, select the authentication type, enable and disable roles, create roles, manage roles, create access rules, and manage access rules.

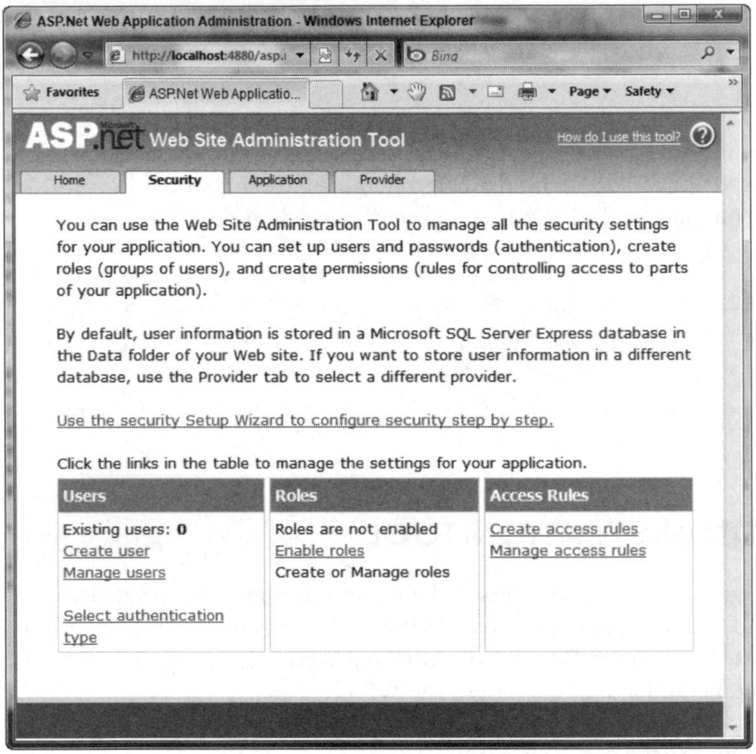

FIGURE 26-2

If the authentication type for the project is Windows, user management from within the WSAT is disabled.

The Security tab even includes a handy security Setup Wizard to configure your web application's security. Figure 26-3 shows the Security Setup Wizard.

TRY IT

In this lesson you use the ASP.NET Web Site Administration Tool (WSAT) to create and manage a user.

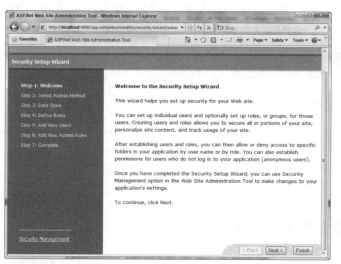

FIGURE 26-3

Lesson Requirements

None.

Hints

➤ Build your project before you open the ASP.NET Web Site Administration Tool.

Step-by-Step

1. Open Microsoft Visual Web Developer 2010 Express.

2. Select **New Project** from the File menu.

3. Select **Visual C#** on the left side of the dialog box.

4. Select either the **ASP.NET Web Application** template or the **ASP.NET MVC 2 Web Application** template.

5. Enter **Lesson26** in the Name field and **c:\ASPNETTrainer** in the Location field. Click the OK button.

6. Select Build Lesson26 from the Build menu and wait for the build process to complete.

7. Select ASP.NET Configuration from the Project menu to open the ASP.NET Web Site Administration Tool (WSAT).

8. Navigate to the Security tab of the WSAT.

9. Click the `Create user link` to view the Create user dialog (see Figure 26-4).

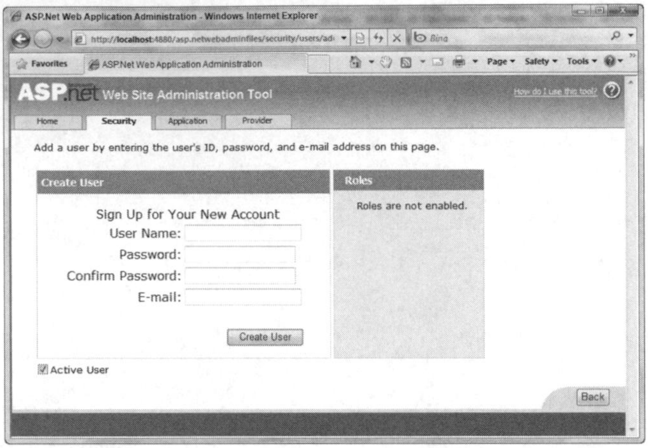

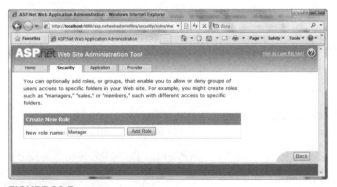

FIGURE 26-4

10. Enter information into the User Name, Password, Confirm Password, and E-mail fields and click the Create User button.

11. Click the Continue button.

12. Click the Back button.

13. Click the `Enable Roles` link.

14. Click the `Create or Manage roles` link.

15. Enter **Manager** for the new role's name and click the Add Role button (see Figure 26-5).

FIGURE 26-5

16. Click the Back button.

17. Click the `Manage users` link.

18. Click the `Edit roles` link next to the user.

19. Check the checkbox next to the Manager role (see Figure 26-6).

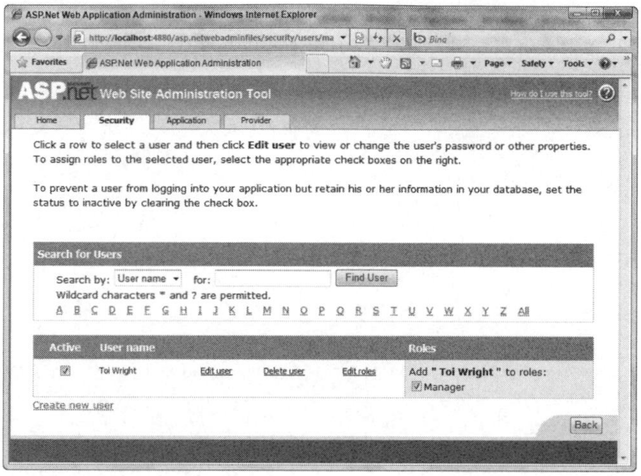

FIGURE 26-6

20. Close the WSAT.

21. Click the Show All Files button on the Solution Explorer to display the ASPNETDB.MDF file (Figure 26-7).

22. Open the App_Data folder and double-click the ASPNETDB.MDF file to open the Database Explorer.

23. Open the Tables folder, right-click the aspnet_Users table, and select Show Table Data to see the user that you created.

24. Open the Tables folder, right-click the aspnet_Membership table, and select Show Table Data to see more information about the user.

FIGURE 26-7

25. Open the Tables folder, right-click the aspnet_Roles table, and select Show Table Data to see the role that you created.

 Please select Lesson 26 on the DVD to view the video that accompanies this lesson.

27A

Create a Login Page in Web Forms

By default, applications that use the ASP.NET Web Forms framework use Forms authentication. If your application uses Forms authentication to authenticate users, you must create a login page. ASP.NET Web Forms includes seven Login server controls that both enable you to create a login page and to display status information without writing a single line of code. In this lesson I introduce you to the Login server controls.

The Login server controls are located in the Login tab of the Toolbox. Figure 27A-1 shows the Login server controls.

The Login server controls use the Membership provider defined in the `web.config` file to manage and authenticate users. The Membership provider was introduced in Lesson 26. Also, each of the Login server controls is fully customizable. This is a little information about each of the Login server controls:

FIGURE 27A-1

➤ **ChangePassword** — This control is a composite control that enables users to change their password.

➤ **CreateUserWizard** — This control is a templated composite control that allows users to create an account in your application.

➤ **Login** — This control is a composite control that allows users to log in to the application.

➤ **LoginName** — This control displays the user's name. If the user is not logged in, this control is not rendered.

➤ **LoginStatus** — This control displays either a login link or a logout link depending on whether or not the user is authenticated.

➤ **LoginView** — This control is a templated control that displays different information to the users depending on whether they are authenticated, by displaying the contents of either the `AnonymousTemplate` or the `LoggedInTemplate`.

➤ **PasswordRecovery** — This control is a composite control that enables users to recover their password. The password is sent to the user via email. Therefore, your server must be able to send email for the `PasswordRecovery` control to work.

LOGIN CONTROL

To create a login form, all you need is the `Login` control. This is the markup for the `Login` control:

```
<asp:Login ID="Login1" runat="server">
</asp:Login>
```

Figure 27A-2 shows the Design view of the `Login` control. As you can see, the Design view includes some labels, a couple of `TextBox` controls, and a `Checkbox` control. The `Login` control is a composite control that includes all of the common fields used to authenticate a user. By default, it uses the Membership provider defined in the `web.config` file to confirm the user's credentials. Therefore, you do not have to write any code in order to perform user authentication when you are using the `Login` control.

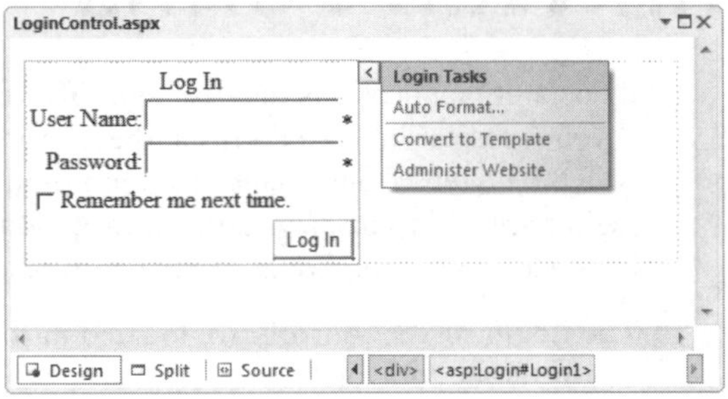

FIGURE 27A-2

You can choose from a number of attractive formats for the `Login` control by selecting Auto Format from the Login Task menu. Figure 27A-3 shows the AutoFormat dialog box.

The `Login` control has dozens of custom properties that can be used to fully customize it. This is just a handful of some of the various properties of the Login control:

➤ **CreateUserText** — This property contains the text of the link to the registration page.

➤ **CreateUserUrl** — This property designates the URL of the registration page.

➤ **DestinationPageUrl** — This property designates the URL to which the users are redirected after they log in.

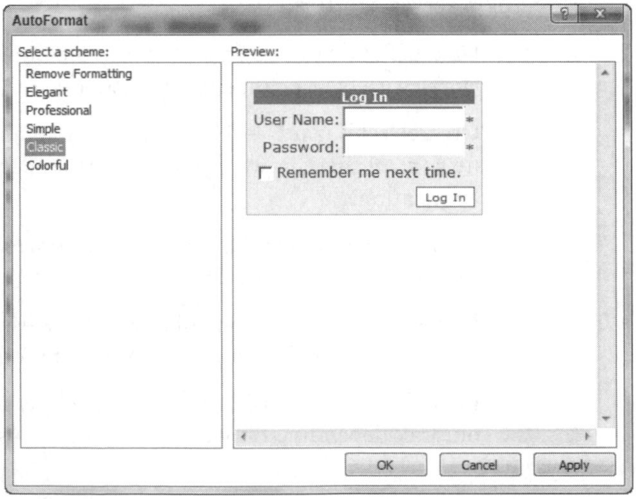

FIGURE 27A-3

➤ **DisplayRememberMe** — This Boolean property determines whether the Remember Me checkbox is displayed.

➤ **FailureAction** — This property designates the action that will occur after a failed login attempt.

➤ **FailureText** — This property contains the text that is displayed after a failed login attempt.

➤ **LoginButtonText** — This property contains the text for the login button.

➤ **PasswordLabelText** — This property contains the text for the password label.

➤ **UserNameLabelText** — This property contains the text for the username label.

In spite of the vast number of properties provided by the Login control, if you are unable to customize it to meet your specific needs, you can select Convert to Template from the Login Task menu to convert the control into a templated control. Once you have done so, you have complete control over the markup that is rendered. This is the markup for the default template:

```
<asp:Login ID="Login1" runat="server">
    <LayoutTemplate>
        <table cellpadding="1" cellspacing="0" style="border-collapse: collapse;">
            <tr>
                <td>
                    <table cellpadding="0">
                        <tr>
                            <td align="center" colspan="2">
                                Log In
                            </td>
                        </tr>
                        <tr>
                            <td align="right">
                                <asp:Label ID="UserNameLabel" runat="server"
                                    AssociatedControlID="UserName">
                                    User Name:
                                </asp:Label>
                            </td>
                            <td>
                                <asp:TextBox ID="UserName" runat="server">
                                </asp:TextBox>
                                <asp:RequiredFieldValidator ID="UserNameRequired"
                                    runat="server" ControlToValidate="UserName"
                                    ErrorMessage="User Name is required."
                                    ToolTip="User Name is required."
                                    ValidationGroup="Login1">
                                    *</asp:RequiredFieldValidator>
                            </td>
                        </tr>
                        <tr>
                            <td align="right">
                                <asp:Label ID="PasswordLabel" runat="server"
                                    AssociatedControlID="Password">
                                    Password:
                                </asp:Label>
                            </td>
```

```
                                 <td>
                                     <asp:TextBox ID="Password" runat="server"
                                         TextMode="Password"></asp:TextBox>
                                     <asp:RequiredFieldValidator ID="PasswordRequired"
                                         runat="server" ControlToValidate="Password"
                                         ErrorMessage="Password is required."
                                         ToolTip="Password is required."
                                         ValidationGroup="Login1">
                                         *</asp:RequiredFieldValidator>
                                 </td>
                             </tr>
                             <tr>
                                 <td colspan="2">
                                     <asp:CheckBox ID="RememberMe" runat="server"
                                         Text="Remember me next time." />
                                 </td>
                             </tr>
                             <tr>
                                 <td align="center" colspan="2" style="color: Red;">
                                     <asp:Literal ID="FailureText" runat="server"
                                         EnableViewState="False"></asp:Literal>
                                 </td>
                             </tr>
                             <tr>
                                 <td align="right" colspan="2">
                                     <asp:Button ID="LoginButton" runat="server"
                                         CommandName="Login" Text="Log In"
                                         ValidationGroup="Login1" />
                                 </td>
                             </tr>
                         </table>
                     </td>
                 </tr>
             </table>
         </LayoutTemplate>
     </asp:Login>
```

CHANGEPASSWORD CONTROL

Another popular control in the group of Login server controls is the `ChangePassword` control. The `ChangePassword` control allows users to change their own password. This is the markup for the ChangePassword control:

```
<asp:ChangePassword ID="ChangePassword1" runat="server">
</asp:ChangePassword>
```

Figure 27A-4 shows the Design view of the control.

The `ChangePassword` control is also a composite control. Like the `Login` control, it too is fully customizable via dozens of custom properties. Also, both an Auto Format option and a Convert to Template option are provided on the ChangePassword Task menu.

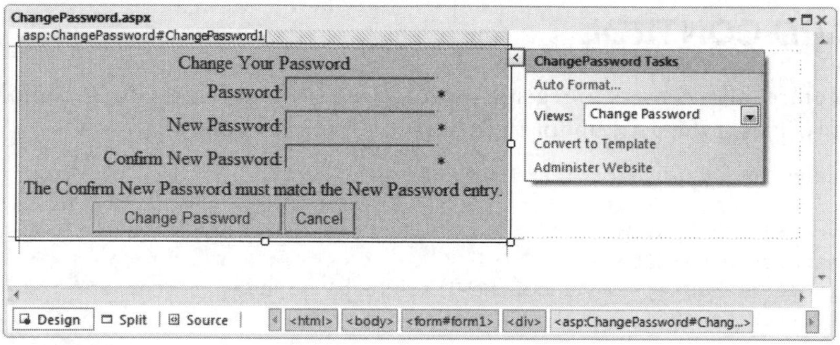

FIGURE 27A-4

PASSWORDRECOVERY CONTROL

Users occasionally forget their passwords. The PasswordRecovery control allows them to request that their password be sent to them via e-mail using the email address associated with their account.

> *If your application hashes the passwords before it stores them in the database, they are not retrievable. In that case, the PasswordRecovery control generates a new password that is then sent to the user.*

This is the markup for the PasswordRecovery control:

```
<asp:PasswordRecovery ID="PasswordRecovery1" runat="server">
</asp:PasswordRecovery>
```

Figure 27A-5 shows the Design view of the control.

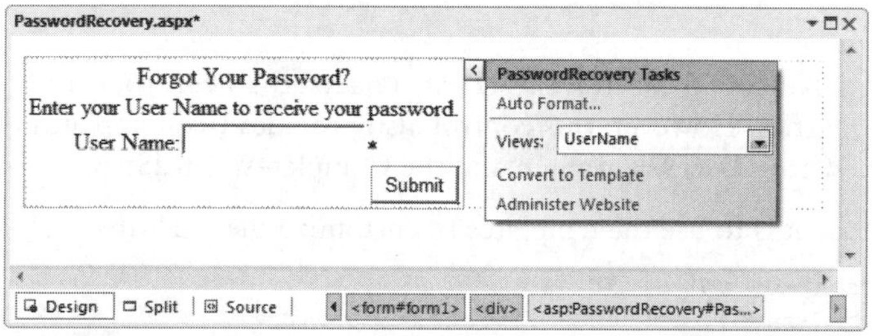

FIGURE 27A-5

The PasswordRecovery control is also a composite control. Like the Login control, it too is fully customizable via dozens of custom properties. Also, both an Auto Format option and a Convert to Template option are provided on the PasswordRecovery Task menu.

CREATEUSERWIZARD CONTROL

The `CreateUserWizard` control allows users to register on your web site and it is the most complex of the Login server controls. This is the markup for the `CreateUserWizard` control:

```
<asp:CreateUserWizard ID="CreateUserWizard1" runat="server">
    <WizardSteps>
        <asp:CreateUserWizardStep ID="CreateUserWizardStep1" runat="server">
        </asp:CreateUserWizardStep>
        <asp:CompleteWizardStep ID="CompleteWizardStep1" runat="server">
        </asp:CompleteWizardStep>
    </WizardSteps>
</asp:CreateUserWizard>
```

Figure 27A-6 shows the Design view of the control.

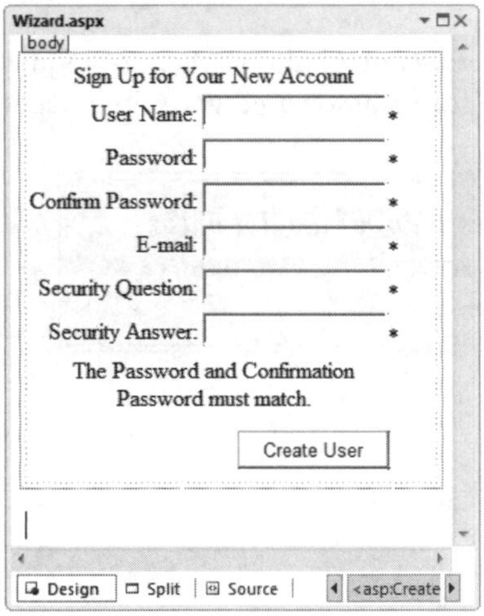

FIGURE 27A-6

Like the `Login` control and the `ChangePassword` control, the `CreateUserWizard` control is fully customizable by using its custom properties. However, this control also provides two templates that allow you to fully customize both the CreateUserWizardStep and the CompleteWizardStep.

The following example shows how easy it is to use the templates to customize the wizard:

```
<asp:createuserwizard id="CreateUserWizard1"
    oncreateduser="CreateUserWizard1_CreatedUser" runat="server">
    <wizardsteps>
        <asp:wizardstep ID="Wizardstep1" runat="server" steptype="Start"
            title="Identification">
            Create your account:<br />
            <table width="100%">
                <tr>
                    <td>
                        Email Address:</td>
                    <td>
                        <asp:textbox id="TextBoxEmail" runat="server" /></td>
```

```
                    </tr>
                    <tr>
                        <td>
                            Password:</td>
                        <td>
                            <asp:textbox id="TextBoxPassword" runat="server" /></td>
                    </tr>
                </table>
            </asp:wizardstep>
            <asp:createuserwizardstep ID="Createuserwizardstep1" runat="server"
                title="Sign Up for Your New Account">
            </asp:createuserwizardstep>
        </wizardsteps>
    </asp:createuserwizard>
```

Figure 27A-7 shows the Design view for the customized `CreateUserWizard` control.

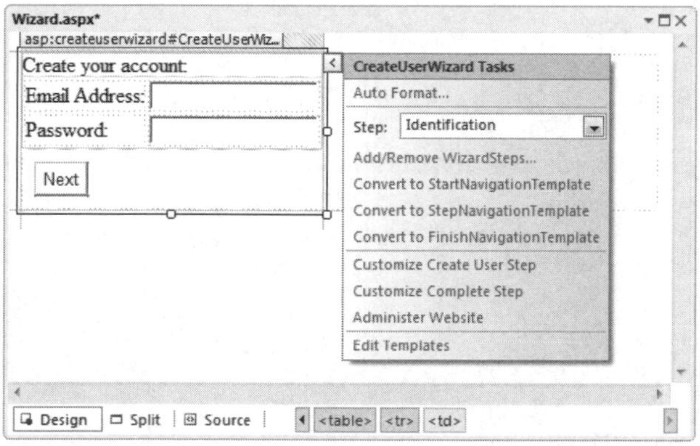

FIGURE 27A-7

Like the other templates, the `CreateUserWizard` control also provides an Auto Format option on its Tasks menu.

MORE LOGIN SERVER CONTROLS

Three Login controls display the status of the current user: the `LoginName` control, the `LoginStatus` control, and the `LoginView` control. Both the `LoginName` control and the `LoginStatus` control are very simple controls. They display the name of the current user and the login status of the current user, respectively. However, the `LoginView` control is much more complex than these two controls.

The `LoginView` control displays different information depending on whether the user has been authenticated by successfully logging in to the application. If the user has not yet been authenticated, he is considered an anonymous user. This is the markup for a sample `LoginView` control:

```
<asp:LoginView ID="HeadLoginView" runat="server" EnableViewState="false">
    <AnonymousTemplate>
        [ <a href="~/Account/Login.aspx" ID="HeadLoginStatus" runat="server">
            Log In</a> ]
    </AnonymousTemplate>
```

```
<LoggedInTemplate>
    Welcome
    <span class="bold"><asp:LoginName ID="HeadLoginName" runat="server" />
    </span>!
    [ <asp:LoginStatus ID="HeadLoginStatus" runat="server"
        LogoutAction="Redirect" LogoutText="Log Out" LogoutPageUrl="~/"/> ]
</LoggedInTemplate>
</asp:LoginView>
```

See Figure 27A-9 for an example of how this LoginView control renders information on the page for an authenticated user.

TRY IT

In this lesson you replace the default Login page that is provided in the ASP.NET Web Application template.

Lesson Requirements

None.

Hints

None.

Step-by-Step

1. Open Microsoft Visual Web Developer 2010 Express.

2. Select **New Project** from the File menu.

3. Select **Visual C#** on the left side of the dialog box.

4. Select the **ASP.NET Web Application** template.

5. Enter **Lesson27a** in the Name field and **c:\ASPNETTrainer** in the Location field. Click the OK button.

6. Press the F5 button.

7. Click the Log In link in the upper-right corner to navigate to the Login page.

8. Click the Register link to open the Registration page that is included as part of the template (see Figure 27A-8).

9. Complete all of the fields on the Registration page and click the Create User button.

10. Stop debugging by closing the browser.

11. Right-click the Login.aspx file in the Account folder and select Delete from the menu. Click the OK button to delete the file permanently.

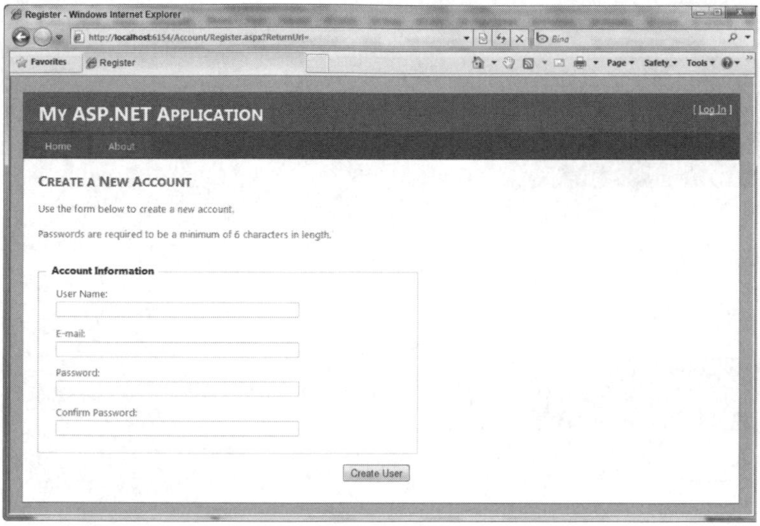

FIGURE 27A-8

12. Right-click the Account folder in the Solution Explorer window and select New Item from the Add menu to open the Add New Item dialog box. Select the **Web Form using Master Page** template, enter **MyLogin.aspx** for the Name, and click the Add button. Select **Site.Master** as the Master Page and click the OK button.

13. Update the `title` attribute of the `MyLogin.aspx` page to **MyLogin**.

14. Add a `Login` control to the `MainContent` content control on the `MyLogin.aspx` page by adding the following markup:

```
<asp:Login ID="Login1" runat="server">
</asp:Login>
```

15. View the `MyLogin.aspx` page in Design view.

16. Click on the `Login` control and select Auto Format from the Login Tasks smart tag (see Figure 27A-9) to open the AutoFormat dialog box.

17. Select the **Elegant** scheme and click the OK button.

18. Open the root `web.config` file for the application.

> *Verify that you have opened the root `web.config` file for the application and not the `web.config` file located in the Account folder.*

19. Update the `authentication` element in the `web.config` file to match the following:

```
<authentication mode="Forms">
    <forms loginUrl="~/Account/MyLogin.aspx" timeout="2880" />
</authentication>
```

FIGURE 27A-9

20. Update the AnonymousTemplate element of the LoginView control on the Site.Master page to reference the MyLogin.aspx file instead of the Login.aspx file.

21. Click the F5 button.

22. Click the Log In link in the upper-right corner to navigate to your new Login page.

23. Enter your User Name and Password and click the Log In button.

24. Notice that the LoginView in the upper-right corner now shows that you are logged in (see Figure 27A-10).

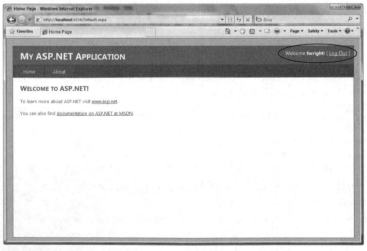

FIGURE 27A-10

Please select Lesson 27A on the DVD to view the video that accompanies this lesson.

Create a Login Page in MVC

By default, applications that use the ASP.NET MVC framework use Forms authentication. If your application uses Forms authentication to authenticate users, you must create a login page. In this lesson I show you how to both add users and how to authenticate those users by using the `AccountController` that is included as part of the ASP.NET MVC Web Application template.

As you have seen, the easiest way to add new users is to use the ASP.NET Web Site Administration Tool (WSAT) that was demonstrated in Lesson 26. However, unless your web site has only a few users, you will want to add a page to your site to allow new users either to register themselves or be registered by an administrator.

When you create a new project using the ASP.NET MVC Web Application template it includes an `AccountController` plus its associated models and views. It also defines two services:

➤   AccountMembershipService

➤   FormsAuthenticationService

The `AccountMembershipService` uses the `Membership` provider to store and validate usernames and passwords. For more information on the `Membership` provider, see Lesson 26. The `FormsAuthenticationService` uses the Forms Authentication system. It too was covered in Lesson 26. Figure 27B-1 shows the files that are included in the Solution Explorer.

FIGURE 27B-1

REGISTRATION PAGE

This is the model that is used for the Registration page:

```
[PropertiesMustMatch("Password", "ConfirmPassword", ErrorMessage = "The password
    and confirmation password do not match.")]
public class RegisterModel
{
    [Required]
    [DisplayName("User name")]
    public string UserName { get; set; }

    [Required]
    [DataType(DataType.EmailAddress)]
    [DisplayName("Email address")]
    public string Email { get; set; }

    [Required]
    [ValidatePasswordLength]
    [DataType(DataType.Password)]
    [DisplayName("Password")]
    public string Password { get; set; }

    [Required]
    [DataType(DataType.Password)]
    [DisplayName("Confirm password")]
    public string ConfirmPassword { get; set; }
}
```

This is the associated view:

```
<%@ Page Language="C#" MasterPageFile="~/Views/Shared/Site.Master"
    Inherits="System.Web.Mvc.ViewPage<Lesson27b.Models.RegisterModel>" %>

<asp:Content ID="registerTitle" ContentPlaceHolderID="TitleContent" runat="server">
    Register
</asp:Content>

<asp:Content ID="registerContent" ContentPlaceHolderID="MainContent"
    runat="server">
    <h2>Create a New Account</h2>
    <p>
        Use the form below to create a new account.
    </p>
    <p>
        Passwords are required to be a minimum of
        <%: ViewData["PasswordLength"] %> characters in length.
    </p>

    <% using (Html.BeginForm()) { %>
```

```
<%: Html.ValidationSummary(true,
    "Account creation was unsuccessful. Please correct the errors and
    try again.") %>
<div>
    <fieldset>
        <legend>Account Information</legend>

        <div class="editor-label">
            <%: Html.LabelFor(m => m.UserName) %>
        </div>
        <div class="editor-field">
            <%: Html.TextBoxFor(m => m.UserName) %>
            <%: Html.ValidationMessageFor(m => m.UserName) %>
        </div>

        <div class="editor-label">
            <%: Html.LabelFor(m => m.Email) %>
        </div>
        <div class="editor-field">
            <%: Html.TextBoxFor(m => m.Email) %>
            <%: Html.ValidationMessageFor(m => m.Email) %>
        </div>

        <div class="editor-label">
            <%: Html.LabelFor(m => m.Password) %>
        </div>
        <div class="editor-field">
            <%: Html.PasswordFor(m => m.Password) %>
            <%: Html.ValidationMessageFor(m => m.Password) %>
        </div>

        <div class="editor-label">
            <%: Html.LabelFor(m => m.ConfirmPassword) %>
        </div>
        <div class="editor-field">
            <%: Html.PasswordFor(m => m.ConfirmPassword) %>
            <%: Html.ValidationMessageFor(m => m.ConfirmPassword) %>
        </div>

        <p>
            <input type="submit" value="Register" />
        </p>
    </fieldset>
</div>
<% } %>
</asp:Content>
```

Figure 27B-2 shows the Registration page that is rendered.

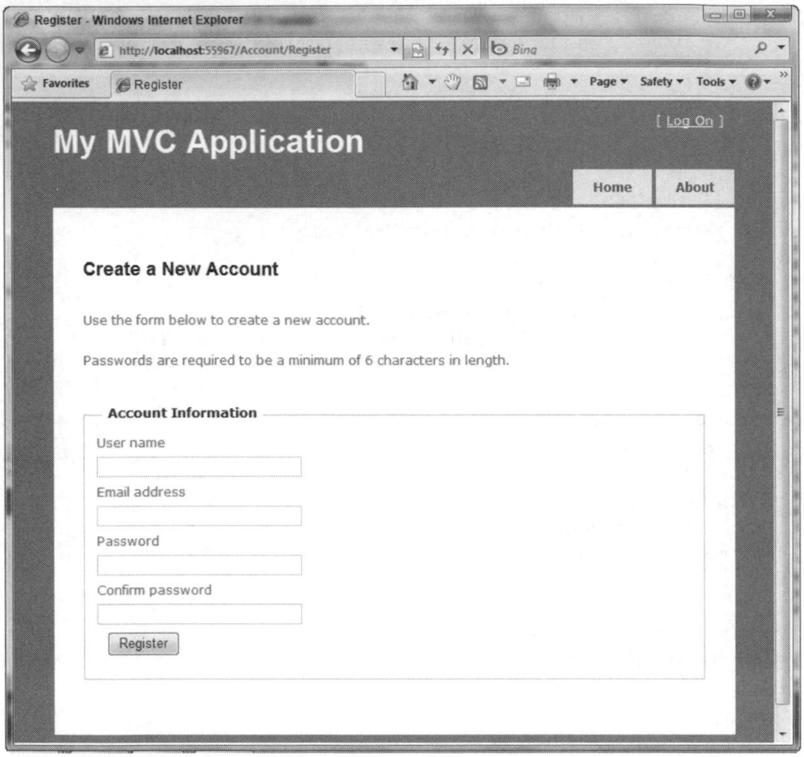

FIGURE 27B-2

The `AccountController` includes two `Register` action methods. The first action method handles direct requests for the Registration page and the other is for HTTP POST requests. These are the `Register` action methods that are included in the AccountController:

```
// ***************************************
// URL: /Account/Register
// ***************************************

public ActionResult Register()
{
    ViewData["PasswordLength"] = MembershipService.MinPasswordLength;
    return View();
}

[HttpPost]
public ActionResult Register(RegisterModel model)
{
    if (ModelState.IsValid)
    {
```

```
        // Attempt to register the user
        MembershipCreateStatus createStatus =
        MembershipService.CreateUser(model.UserName,
            model.Password, model.Email);

        if (createStatus == MembershipCreateStatus.Success)
        {
            FormsService.SignIn(model.UserName, false /* createPersistentCookie
*/);

            return RedirectToAction("Index", "Home");
        }
        else
        {
            ModelState.AddModelError("",
                AccountValidation.ErrorCodeToString(createStatus));
        }
    }

    // If we got this far, something failed, redisplay form
    ViewData["PasswordLength"] = MembershipService.MinPasswordLength;
    return View(model);
}
```

LOG ON PAGE

This is the model that is used for the Log On page:

```
public class LogOnModel
{
    [Required]
    [DisplayName("User name")]
    public string UserName { get; set; }

    [Required]
    [DataType(DataType.Password)]
    [DisplayName("Password")]
    public string Password { get; set; }

    [DisplayName("Remember me?")]
    public bool RememberMe { get; set; }
}
```

This is the associated view:

```
<%@ Page Language="C#" MasterPageFile="~/Views/Shared/Site.Master"
    Inherits="System.Web.Mvc.ViewPage<Lesson27b.Models.LogOnModel>" %>

<asp:Content ID="loginTitle" ContentPlaceHolderID="TitleContent" runat="server">
    Log On
```

```
    </asp:Content>

    <asp:Content ID="loginContent" ContentPlaceHolderID="MainContent" runat="server">
        <h2>Log On</h2>
        <p>
            Please enter your username and password.
            <%: Html.ActionLink("Register", "Register") %> if you don't have an
account.
        </p>

        <% using (Html.BeginForm()) { %>
            <%: Html.ValidationSummary(true,
                "Login was unsuccessful. Please correct the errors and try again.") %>
            <div>
                <fieldset>
                    <legend>Account Information</legend>

                    <div class="editor-label">
                        <%: Html.LabelFor(m => m.UserName) %>
                    </div>
                    <div class="editor-field">
                        <%: Html.TextBoxFor(m => m.UserName) %>
                        <%: Html.ValidationMessageFor(m => m.UserName) %>
                    </div>

                    <div class="editor-label">
                        <%: Html.LabelFor(m => m.Password) %>
                    </div>
                    <div class="editor-field">
                        <%: Html.PasswordFor(m => m.Password) %>
                        <%: Html.ValidationMessageFor(m => m.Password) %>
                    </div>

                    <div class="editor-label">
                        <%: Html.CheckBoxFor(m => m.RememberMe) %>
                        <%: Html.LabelFor(m => m.RememberMe) %>
                    </div>

                    <p>
                        <input type="submit" value="Log On" />
                    </p>
                </fieldset>
            </div>
        <% } %>
    </asp:Content>
```

Figure 27B-3 shows the page that is rendered.

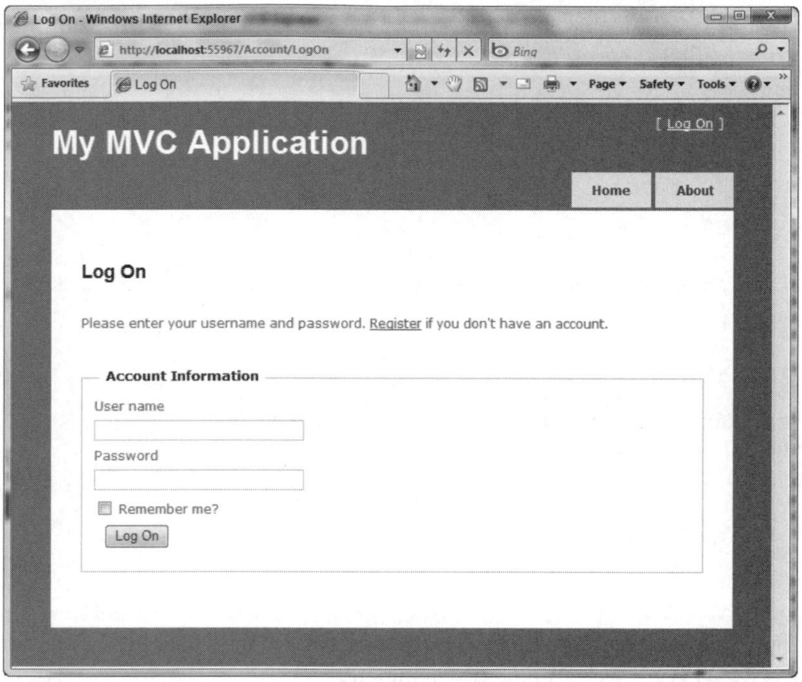

FIGURE 27B-3

The `AccountController` includes two `LogOn` action methods. The first action method handles direct requests for the Log On page and the other is for HTTP POST requests. These are the `LogOn` action methods included in the `AccountController`:

```
// ***************************************
// URL: /Account/LogOn
// ***************************************

public ActionResult LogOn()
{
    return View();
}

[HttpPost]
public ActionResult LogOn(LogOnModel model, string returnUrl)
{
    if (ModelState.IsValid)
    {
        if (MembershipService.ValidateUser(model.UserName, model.Password))
        {
            FormsService.SignIn(model.UserName, model.RememberMe);
            if (!String.IsNullOrEmpty(returnUrl))
```

```
        {
            return Redirect(returnUrl);
        }
        else
        {
            return RedirectToAction("Index", "Home");
        }
    }
    else
    {
        ModelState.AddModelError("", "The user name or password provided is
incorrect.");
    }
}

// If we got this far, something failed, redisplay form
return View(model);
}
```

TRY IT

In this lesson you use the Registration page, the Log On page, and the Change Password page that are included with the ASP.NET MVC 2 Web Application template.

Lesson Requirements

None.

Hints

None.

Step-by-Step

1. Open Microsoft Visual Web Developer 2010 Express.

2. Select **New Project** from the File menu.

3. Select **Visual C#** on the left side of the dialog box.

4. Select the **ASP.NET MVC 2 Web Application** template.

5. Enter **Lesson27b** in the Name field and **c:\ASPNETTrainer** in the Location field. Click the OK button.

6. Click the F5 button.

7. Click the Log On link.

8. Click the Register link.

9. Complete all of the fields and click the Register button.

10. Click the `Log Off` link.

11. Click the `Log On` link.

12. Enter your username and password and click the Log On button.

13. Stop debugging by closing the browser.

14. Open the Shared subfolder of the Views folder.

15. Double-click the `LogOnUserControl.ascx` file to open it.

16. Add the following ActionLink to the content that is displayed for authenticated users:

```
[ <%= Html.ActionLink("Change Password", "ChangePassword", "Account") %> ]
```

17. Click the F5 button.

18. Click the `Log On` link.

19. Enter your username and password and click the Log On button.

20. Click the `Change Password` link to open the Change Password page shown in Figure 27B-4.

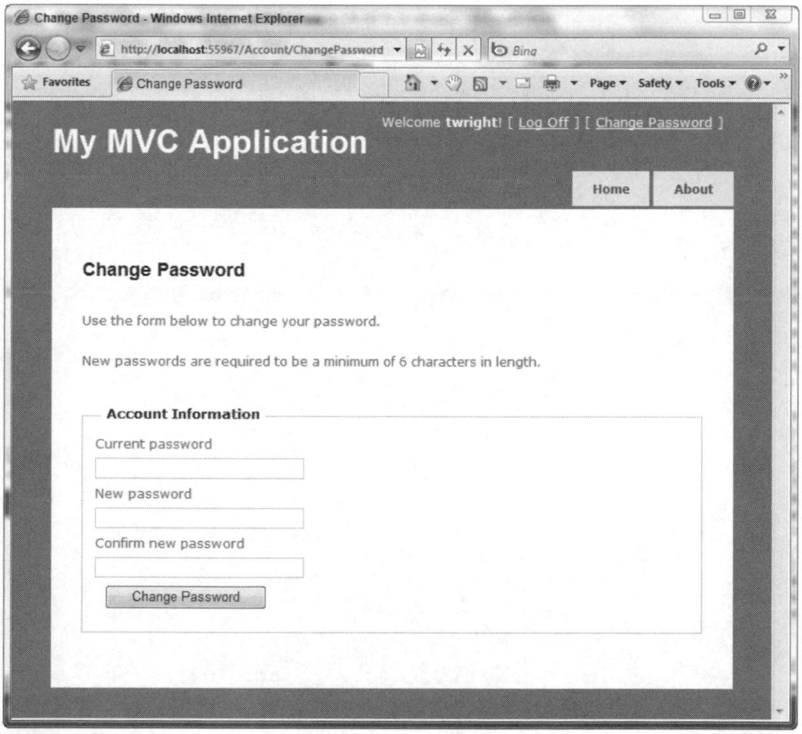

FIGURE 27B-4

Please select Lesson 27B on the DVD to view the video that accompanies this lesson.

28A

Authorization in Web Forms

Authorization refers to the process of determining what a user is authorized to do in your web application. In Lessons 26 and 27 you learned how to use various types of authentication to determine who the user is. In this lesson you learn how to control to which pages users have access.

AUTHORIZATION ELEMENT

Authorization works the same way regardless of how the user is authenticated. Authorization is configured by using the `authorization` element in the `web.config` file. If you place the following `authorization` element into the root `web.config` file, all anonymous users are denied access to your web site:

```
<configuration>
    ...
    <system.web>
        ...
        <authorization>
            <deny users="?"/>
        </authorization>
    </system.web>
</configuration>
```

 Even if you deny access to all anonymous users, the login page is still accessible to anonymous users.

The `authorization` element can include multiple `deny` and `allow` elements. These elements are used to deny and grant access to resources, respectively. These are the attributes of the `deny` and `allow` elements:

➤ **users** — This attribute is used to identify one or more users. You can identify users by name or you can use the question mark (?) to represent all anonymous users and the asterisk (*) to represent all authenticated users.

➤ **roles** — This attribute is used to identify one or more roles.

➤ **verbs** — This attribute is used to identify the HTTP verb. The default is all.

The `deny` and `allow` elements must include at least one user or role attribute. The following example grants access to twright, rjoseph, and all members of the Admins role and denies access to jsmith and all anonymous users:

```
<authorization>
    <allow users="twright, rjoseph"/>
    <allow roles="Admins"/>
    <deny users="jsmith"/>
    <deny users="?"/>
</authorization>
```

If a user tries to access a page to which he does not have access and Forms authentication is enabled, he is redirected to the login page. By default all users are granted access to your web application. This is the default `authorization` element:

```
<authorization>
    <allow users="*"/>
</authorization>
```

If there is a folder for which you want to configure authorization, you can either place a `web.config` directly in the folder or you can use the `location` element to identify the folder from the root `web.config` file. For example, if you have a folder named SystemAdmin that you want only members of the Admin role to be able to access, you can place the following `web.config` file directly into the SystemAdmin folder:

```
<configuration>
   <system.web>
        <authorization>
            <allow roles="Admins"/>
            <deny users="*"/>
        </authorization>
    </system.web>
</configuration>
```

Or, you can add the following section to the root `web.config` file:

```
<configuration>
    ...
    <location path="SystemAdmin">
        <system.web>
            <authorization>
                <allow roles="Admins"/>
```

```
            <deny users="*"/>
        </authorization>
    </system.web>
</location>
</configuration>
```

> It is a better practice to configure all of the folders via the root web.config file because it consolidates all of the authorization information into one file. Maintenance is more complicated if you use multiple web.config files to authorize the users.

You can also use the location element to provide authorization settings for an individual file. The following example denies anonymous access to the Private.aspx page:

```
<configuration>
    ...
    <location path="Private.aspx">
        <system.web>
            <authorization>
                <deny users="?"/>
            </authorization>
        </system.web>
    </location>
</configuration>
```

The order in which you place the rules into the authorization element is very important. The ASP.NET framework uses a first-match algorithm to determine a user's rights. It starts at the top of the list and works its way down. The first rule that matches the current user is applied. Therefore, if the authorization element includes the following, all users will be denied access:

```
<deny users="*"/>
<allow roles="Admins"/>
```

Also, if the authorization element only contains the following, all users will be granted access:

```
<allow roles="Admins"/>
```

The reason for this is that by default, all users are granted access, so, if a user does not match any of the rules on the list, that user is granted access.

ASP.NET WEB SITE ADMINISTRATION TOOL

The ASP.NET Web Site Administration Tool (WSAT) demonstrated in both Lesson 5 and Lesson 26 can be used to configure authentication. To open the WSAT from within a Web Project, select ASP.NET Configuration from the Project menu. Figure 28A-1 shows the WSAT.

Figure 28A-2 shows the Security tab of the WSAT. As you can see, the Security tab allows you both to create and manage access rules.

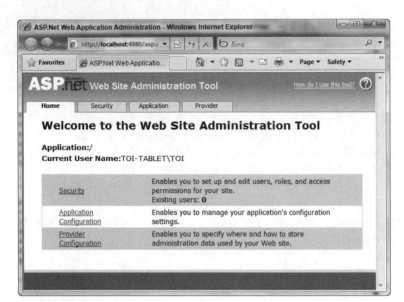

FIGURE 28A-1

FIGURE 28A-2

Figure 28A-3 shows the page used to add new access rules to your web application. In this case, the page is being used to deny access to all anonymous users.

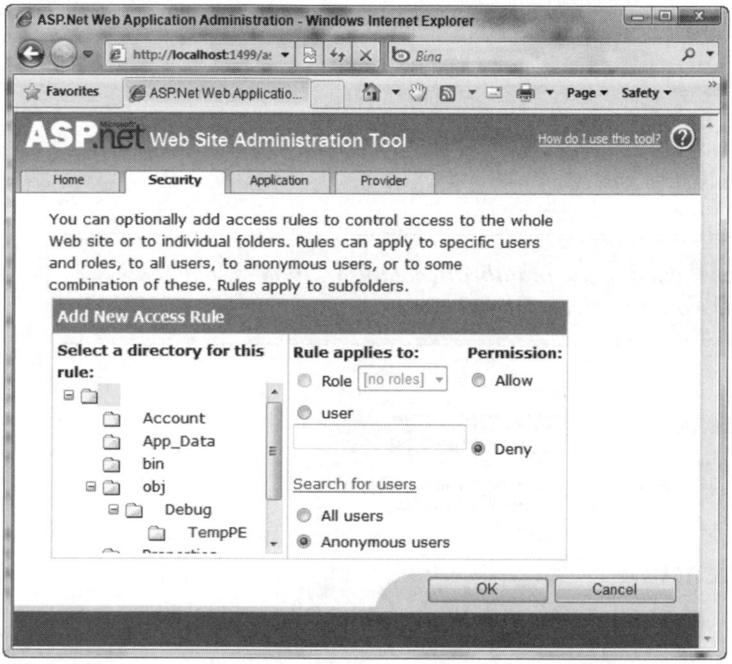

FIGURE 28A-3

TRY IT

In this lesson you deny access to your web application for all unauthenticated users.

Lesson Requirements

None.

Hints

➤ Use the ASP.NET Web Site Administration Tool (WSAT) to configure the `authorization` element of your `web.config` file.

Step-by-Step

1. Open Microsoft Visual Web Developer 2010 Express.

2. Select **New Project** from the File menu.

3. Select **Visual C#** on the left side of the dialog box.

4. Select the **ASP.NET Web Application** template.

5. Enter **Lesson28a** in the Name field and **c:\ASPNETTrainer** in the Location field. Click the OK button.

6. Open the `web.config` file and add the following element to the `system.web` element:

```
<authorization>
    <deny users="?" />
</authorization>
```

7. Press the F5 button, see Figure 28A-4.

> *Because access has been denied to all unauthenticated users, you will be redirected to the login page shown in Figure 28A-4.*

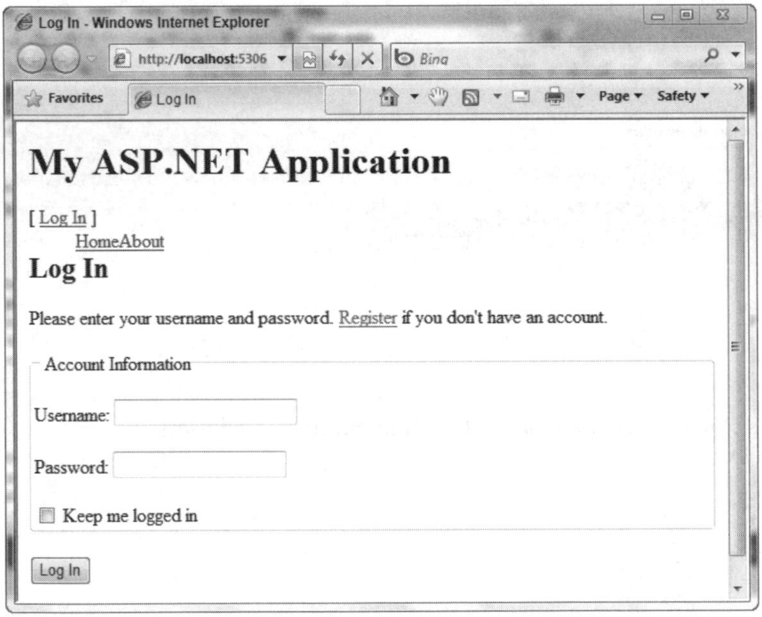

FIGURE 28A-4

8. Add the following to the bottom of the configuration element of the root `web.config` file:

```
<location path="Styles/Site.css">
    <system.web>
        <authorization>
            <allow users="*"/>
        </authorization>
    </system.web>
</location>
```

9. Click the F5 buttons (see Figure 28A-5).

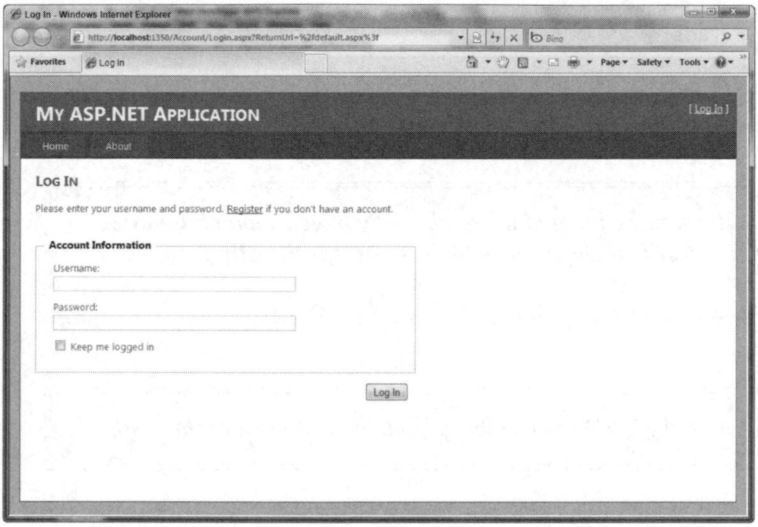

FIGURE 28A-5

10. Click the `Register` link to create a new account. Although access has been denied to all unauthenticated users, you are redirected to the Registration page shown in Figure 28A-6.

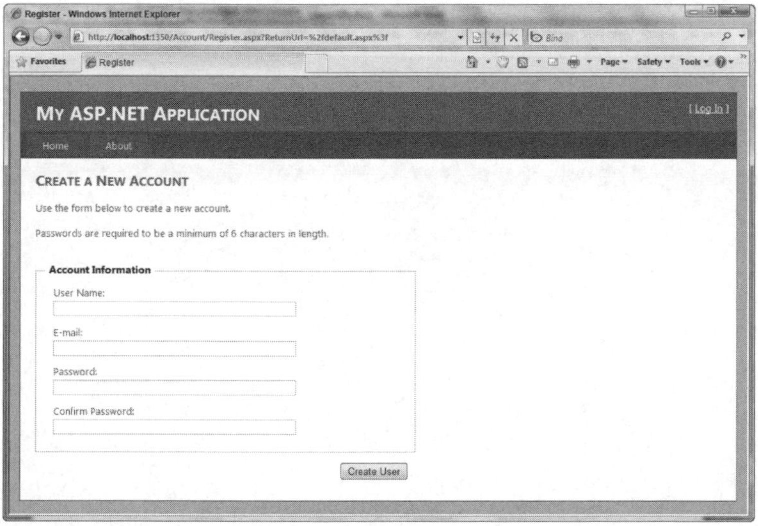

FIGURE 28A-6

11. Stop debugging by closing the browser.

12. Open the Account folder and double-click the `web.config` file to open it. The following rule is what allows everyone access to the `Register.aspx` page:

```
<location path="Register.aspx">
    <system.web>
```

```
<authorization>
    <allow users="*"/>
</authorization>
</system.web>
</location>
```

 If you deny access to all unauthenticated users, the only page to which unauthenticated users will have access is the login page unless you specifically grant them access to other pages.

 Please select Lesson 28A on the DVD to view the video that accompanies this lesson.

28B

Authorization in MVC

Authorization refers to the process of determining what a user is authorized to do in your web application. In Lessons 26 and 27 you learned how to use various types of authentication to determine who the user is. In this lesson you learn how to control to which pages users have access.

Authorization works the same way regardless of how the user is authenticated. Authorization is configured in the ASP.NET MVC framework by using the authorization action filter.

> *An action filter is an attribute that is used to decorate either an action method or a controller. For more information on action filters, see Lesson 14B.*

If you decorate an action method with the `Authorize` attribute without specifying any additional properties, all anonymous users are prevented from invoking the action. The following example denies access to the `About` action method for all users who have not been authenticated:

```
[Authorize]
public ActionResult About()
{
    return View();
}
```

If a user tries to invoke an action method to which he does not have access and Forms authentication is enabled, he is redirected to the login page. By default all users can invoke any action method.

The `Authorize` attribute takes three named properties:

➤ **Order** — This property indicates the order in which an action filter is executed in relation to the other action filters on the same action method.

➤ **Roles** — This property contains a comma-separated list of roles that are able to invoke the action method.

➤ **Users** — This property contains a comma-separated list of users who are able to invoke the action method.

The following example allows twright, rjoseph, and all of the members of the Admins role to invoke the About action method and denies all anonymous users the right to invoke the About action method:

```
[Authorize(Users="twright, rjoseph", Roles="Admins")]
public ActionResult About()
{
    return View();
}
```

> In Lesson 28A I showed you how to use the web configuration files to configure authorization for your web application. However, you should not use this method to configure authorization for an MVC application. The reason is that the authorization sections in a web.config file map to pages, whereas in an MVC application you need to protect controllers and actions. Therefore, authorization must be done at the controller and action level rather than the page level.

TRY IT

In this lesson you deny access to the web application for all unauthenticated users. Also, you see that you cannot use the authorize attribute of the web.config file to reliably deny access to users who have not been authenticated.

Lesson Requirements

None.

Hints

None.

Step-by-Step

1. Open Microsoft Visual Web Developer 2010 Express.

2. Select **New Project** from the File menu.

3. Select **Visual C#** on the left side of the dialog box.

4. Select the **ASP.NET MVC 2 Web Application** template.

5. Enter **Lesson28b** in the Name field and **c:\ASPNETTrainer** in the Location field. Click the OK button.

6. Open the Home subfolder that is located in the Views subfolder.

7. Right-click the Home folder and select New Item from the Add menu to open Add New Item dialog box. Select the **Web Configuration File** template and click the Add button (see Figure 28B-1).

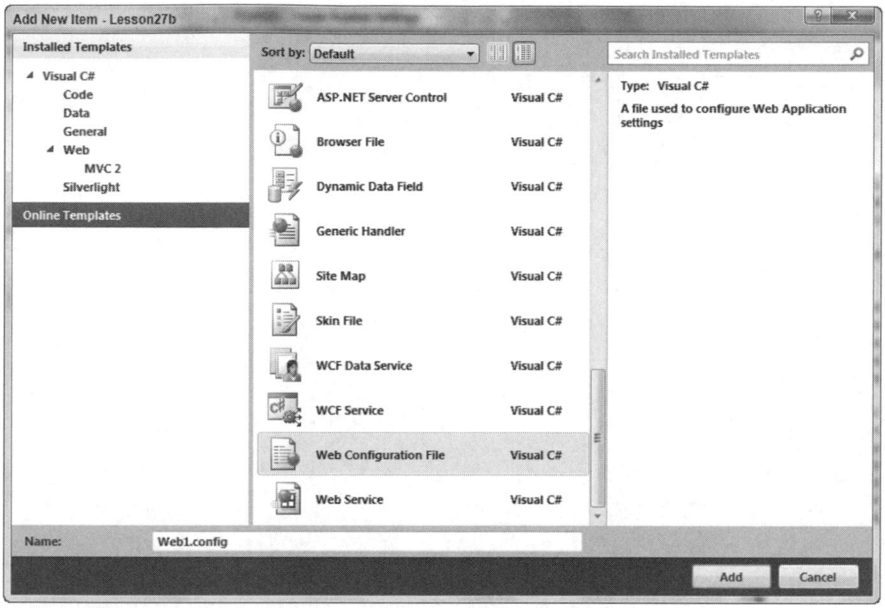

FIGURE 28B-1

8. Update the contents of the web.config to the following:

```
<?xml version="1.0"?>
<configuration>
    <system.web>
      <authorization>
        <deny users="?"/>
      </authorization>
    </system.web>
</configuration>
```

9. Click the F5 button.

10. Navigate to the About page. Because the Authorize attribute is restricting access to pages and not to action methods, you still have access to all of the pages in the Home folder.

11. Stop debugging by closing the browser.

12. Right-click the web.config file in the Home subfolder of the Views folder and select Delete from the menu. Click the OK button to confirm the deletion.

13. Open the HomeController.cs file and decorate the HomeController class with the following attribute:

```
[Authorize]
```

14. Click the F5 button. Access is now denied to all of the action methods in the HomeController.

Please select Lesson 28B on the DVD to view the video that accompanies this lesson.

A

Ajax Control Toolkit

The Ajax Control Toolkit is a free set of more than 40 Ajax-enabled controls that can be used with both the ASP.NET Web Forms framework and the ASP.NET MVC framework. The Ajax Control Toolkit is an open-source project that was originally developed by Microsoft employees, but is now part of the CodePlex Foundation (www.codeplex.org). It is part of the ASP.NET Ajax Library.

> The mission of the CodePlex Foundation is to enable the exchange of code and understanding among software companies and open source communities. It was founded by Microsoft in 2009.

Because the Ajax Control Toolkit is a separate download, it needs to be installed on your computer before you use it. You can download it from the following URL:

```
http://www.asp.net/ajaxlibrary/
```

There is an excellent Readme.doc file that is included as part of the download that will guide you through the installation process. Figure A-1 shows just some of the controls that are included as part of the Ajax Control Toolkit.

As you can see from Figure A-1, the Ajax Control Toolkit includes two types of controls: extenders and controls. Extenders add properties or methods to existing controls, whereas controls provide entirely new functionality. Most of the controls in the Ajax Control Toolkit are extenders. Although not a common practice, one control can have more than one extender applied to it.

CALENDAR EXTENDER

One of my favorite extenders is the Calendar extender. The Calendar extender displays a client-side date picker. Figure A-2 shows the calendar date picker that is rendered when the associated textbox is clicked.

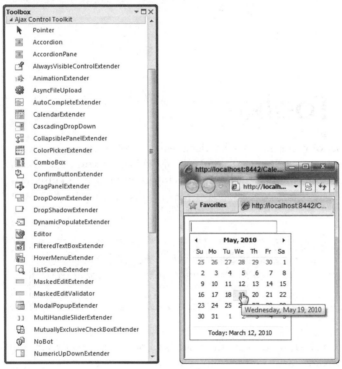

FIGURE A-1   **FIGURE A-2**

When the user clicks on a day, the textbox is set to the date that was clicked. The left and right arrows move the calendar forward or back a month. Clicking the title of the calendar changes the view from the days in the month to the months in the year. Another click switches the view to the years in the current decade.

ASP.NET Web Forms Framework

Once you have added the controls from the Ajax Control Toolkit to the Toolbox, it is easy to start using the controls in an ASP.NET Web Forms application. Like the other controls in the Toolbox, you can simply drag and drop them onto your form.

Before you can use any of the controls from the Ajax Control Toolkit you must add a `ToolkitScript Manager` to the page. The `ToolkitScriptManager` derives from the `ScriptManager` class and enables the automatic combining of script files in the web page. This is important because the controls in the

Ajax Control Toolkit use multiple JavaScript files. You can simply drag a `ToolkitScriptManager` from the Toolbox. This is a sample `ToolkitScriptManager`:

```
<asp:ToolkitScriptManager ID="ToolkitScriptManager1" runat="server">
</asp:ToolkitScriptManager>
```

This is the markup for a `TextBox` that has been extended using the `CalendarExtender`:

```
<asp:TextBox ID="TextBoxCalendar" runat="server"></asp:TextBox>
<asp:CalendarExtender ID="TextBoxCalendar_CalendarExtender" runat="server"
    Enabled="True" TargetControlID="TextBoxCalendar">
</asp:CalendarExtender>
```

You can also add an extender control by using the Add Extender option on the `TextBox` Tasks smart tag that is available in Design view (see Figure A-3) to open the Extender Wizard.

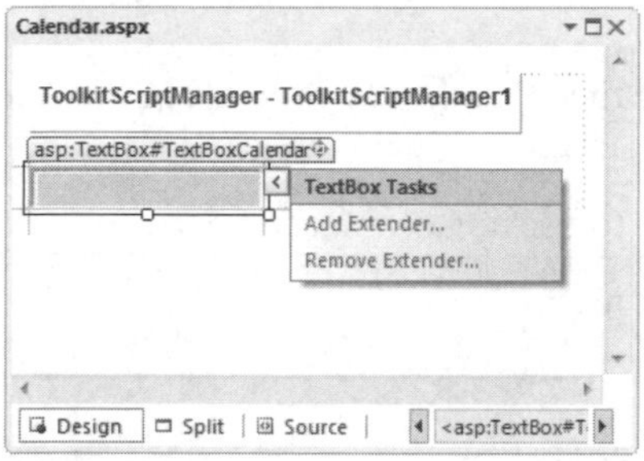

FIGURE A-3

Figure A-4 shows the Extender Wizard.

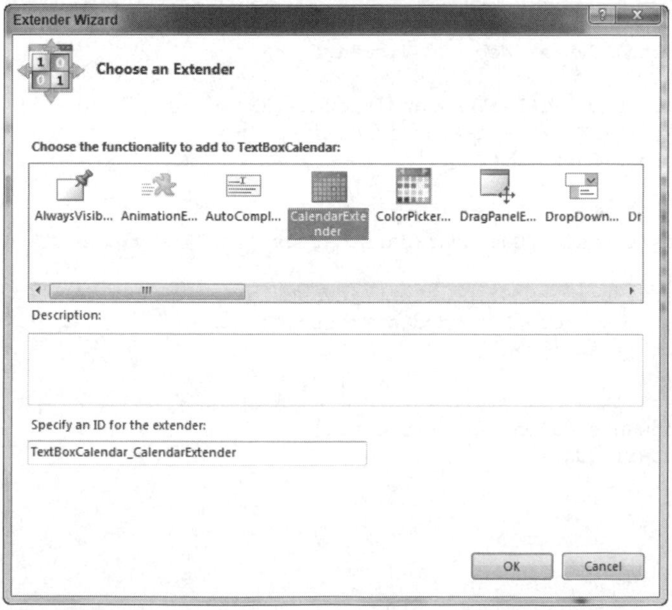

FIGURE A-4

To use the Extender Wizard all you need to do is select an extender and click the OK button.

> *The default calendar is rather plain; however, the calendar can be fully customized via its cascading style sheet to complement any design.*

ASP.NET MVC Framework

Most of the controls in the Ajax Control Toolkit can be used with the ASP.NET MVC framework. However, it is not possible to drag a control from the Toolbox. To use the ASP.NET MVC framework, you must copy the JavaScript files that are provided with the Ajax Control Toolkit into the Script folder of your application. In the case of the CalendarExtender you need the following files and folders:

➤ **Start.js** — This JavaScript file is required to use any of the extenders or controls in the Ajax Control Library.

➤ **ExtendedControls.js** — This JavaScript file is required to use any of the extenders.

➤ **Extended Folder** — This folder contains the following files:

 ➤ **arrow-left.gif** — This is the graphic for the left arrow.

 ➤ **arrow-right.gif** — This is the graphic for the right arrow.

 ➤ **Calendar.css** — This cascading style sheet contains the styles used by the calendar.

 ➤ **CalendarBehavior.js** — This file contains the JavaScript for the calendar.

This is a View that uses the CalendarExtender to render the same calendar shown in Figure A-4:

```
<%@ Page Language="C#" Inherits="System.Web.Mvc.ViewPage" %>

<!DOCTYPE html PUBLIC "-//W3C//DTD XHTML 1.0 Transitional//EN"
    "http://www.w3.org/TR/xhtml1/DTD/xhtml1-transitional.dtd">
<html xmlns="http://www.w3.org/1999/xhtml">
<head runat="server">
    <title>Calendar</title>
    <link href="../../Scripts/extended/Calendar/Calendar.css" rel="stylesheet"
        type="text/css" />
    <script src="../../Scripts/Start.js" type="text/javascript"></script>
    <script src="../../Scripts/Extended/ExtendedControls.js"
        type="text/javascript"></script>

    <script type="text/javascript">
        Sys.require(Sys.components.calendar, function () {
            Sys.create.calendar("#date");
        });
    </script>

</head>
<body>
```

```
    <div>
        <input type="text" id="date" />
    </div>
</body>
</html>
```

MORE EXTENDERS

The other extenders in the Ajax Control Toolkit work much like the `CalendarExtender`. They can be applied to extend either a server control or an HTML element. Some favorites are the extender that adds a watermark to a textbox and the extender that rounds the corners of a `Panel` server control or a `div` element.

TextBoxWatermark Extender

The `TextBoxWatermark` extender adds a watermark to a text-box. An empty watermarked textbox displays a message to the user, and after the user types text into the watermarked textbox the watermark disappears. Figure A-5 shows a watermarked textbox.

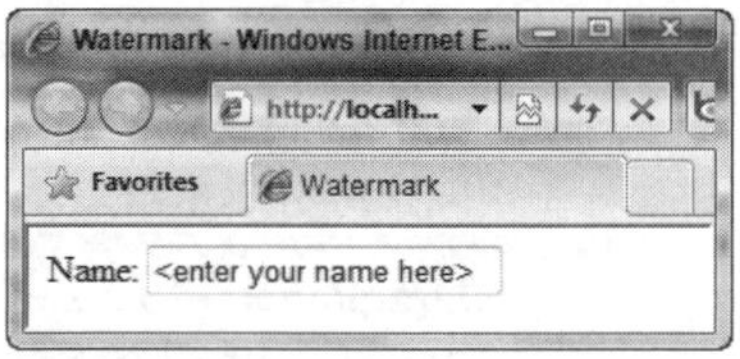

FIGURE A-5

This is the markup used by an ASP.NET Web Forms application to render the preceding watermarked textbox:

```
<asp:TextBox ID="TextBoxName" runat="server"></asp:TextBox>
<asp:TextBoxWatermarkExtender ID="TextBoxWatermarkExtender1" runat="server"
    TargetControlID="TextBoxName" WatermarkText="<enter your name here>">
</asp:TextBoxWatermarkExtender>
```

This is the View used by an ASP.NET MVC application to render the same watermarked textbox:

```
<%@ Page Language="C#" Inherits="System.Web.Mvc.ViewPage" %>

<!DOCTYPE html PUBLIC "-//W3C//DTD XHTML 1.0 Transitional//EN"
    "http://www.w3.org/TR/xhtml1/DTD/xhtml1-transitional.dtd">
<html xmlns="http://www.w3.org/1999/xhtml">
<head id="Head1" runat="server">
    <title>Watermark</title>
    <script src="http://ajax.microsoft.com/ajax/jquery/jquery-1.3.2.js"
        type="text/javascript"></script>
    <script src="../../Scripts/Start.debug.js" type="text/javascript"></script>
    <script src="../../Scripts/Extended/ExtendedControls.debug.js"
        type="text/javascript"></script>

    <script type="text/javascript">
        Sys.require(Sys.components.watermark, function () {
            $("#name").watermark("<enter your name here>", "wm");
        });
    </script>

</head>
```

```
<body>
    <div>
        <input type="text" id="name" />
    </div>
</body>
</html>
```

Other Extenders

This is a list of the some of the other extenders in the Ajax Control
Toolkit:

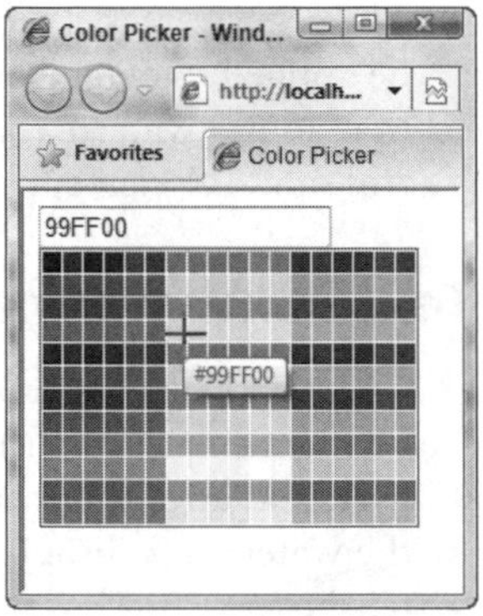

➤ **AlwaysVisibleControl** — This extender allows you to pin any
ASP.NET control or `div` element to a particular location on
the page.

➤ **Animation** — This extender enables you to add animation
effects to your web page.

➤ **ColorPicker** — This extender provides a client-side color picker
(see Figure A-6).

➤ **DragPanel** — This extender allows you to drag any ASP.NET
`Panel` control or `div` element.

➤ **DropShadow** — This extender allows you to add a fully customized drop shadow to an ASP.NET `Panel` control or `span` element (see Figure A-7).

➤ **DynamicPopulate** — This extender allows you to dynamically
replace the contents of another control.

➤ **FilteredTextBox** — This extender restricts the types of
characters that can be entered into a textbox.

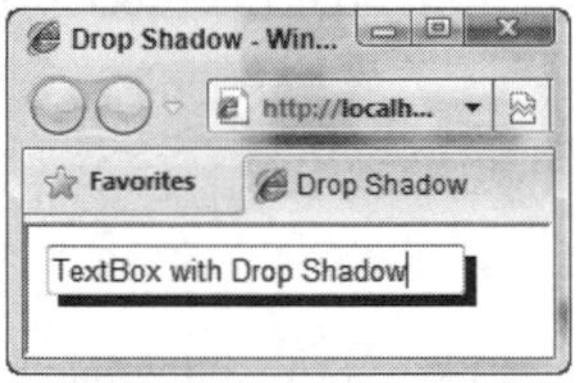

➤ **HoverMenu** — This extender associates a popup menu with any ASP.NET WebControl or
`div` element.

➤ **MaskedEdit** — This extender allows only certain types of text to be entered into a textbox.
The supported types are Number, Date, Time, and DateTime.

➤ **ModalPopup** — This extender creates a modal popup window.

➤ **MutuallyExclusiveCheckBox** — This extender allows you to
designate a group of checkboxes that can have only one item
checked.

➤ **NumericUpDown** — This extender adds up and down buttons
to a textbox to increment and decrement the value in the textbox
(see Figure A-8).

➤ **PagingBulletedList** — This extender adds client-side sorted paging
to a BulletedList control or `ul` element.

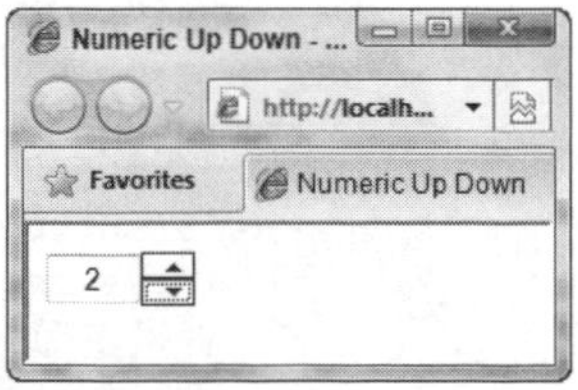

FIGURE A-6

FIGURE A-7

FIGURE A-8

> ➤ **PopupControl** — This extender adds a popup menu to any control.

> ➤ **ResizableControl** — This extender adds a handle to any element on a web page that the user can use to resize the control.

> ➤ **RoundedCorners** — This extender adds round corners to any element (see Figure A-9).

> ➤ **Slider** — This extender converts a textbox into a graphical slider.

> ➤ **SlideShow** — This extender is applied to image controls to configure a slideshow.

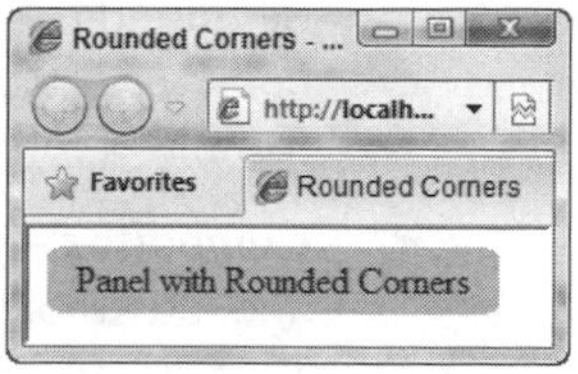

FIGURE A-9

> ➤ **ToggleButton** — This extender is used to replace the standard checkboxes associated with a `CheckBox` control or `checkbox` element with custom images.

CONTROLS

The Ajax Control Toolkit also contains a number of controls. The most impressive control that is provided is the HTML Editor, shown in Figure A-10.

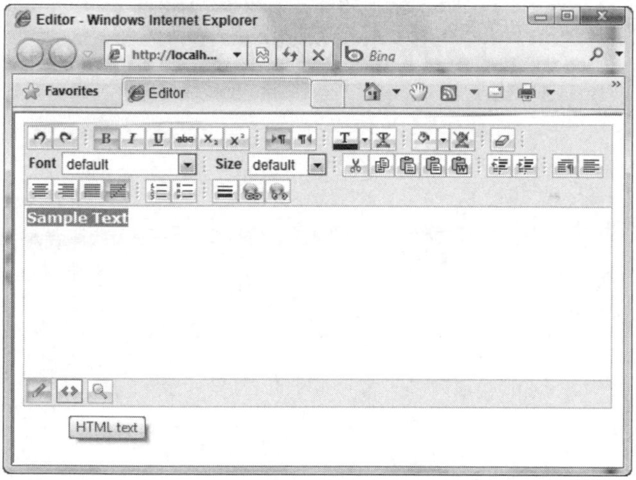

FIGURE A-10

The HTML Editor allows the user to edit text. Simply by dropping this control on a page, your user can select a font, change the background color, cut, copy, and paste text, add images, align text, and more. This is the markup for the control:

```
<cc1:Editor ID="Editor1" runat="server" />
```

> ⊗ *The HTML Editor cannot be used with the ASP.MVC framework. It can be used only on pages that use the ASP.NET Web Forms framework.*

This is a list of the some of the other controls in the Ajax Control Toolkit:

➤ **Accordion** — This control provides multiple collapsible panels.

➤ **AsyncFileUpload** — This control enables you to upload files asynchronously to the server. Because the `FileUpload` control that comes with ASP.NET does not work within an `UpdatePanel`, you must use this control if you want to perform file uploads without performing a full page postback.

➤ **ComboBox** — This control is a combination of a dropdown list and a textbox.

➤ **ReorderList** — This control provides a bulleted list with items that the user can drag from one position to another position in the list.

➤ **Seadragon** — This control enables the user to pan and zoom images.

➤ **TabContainer** — This control creates a set of tabs (see Figure A-11).

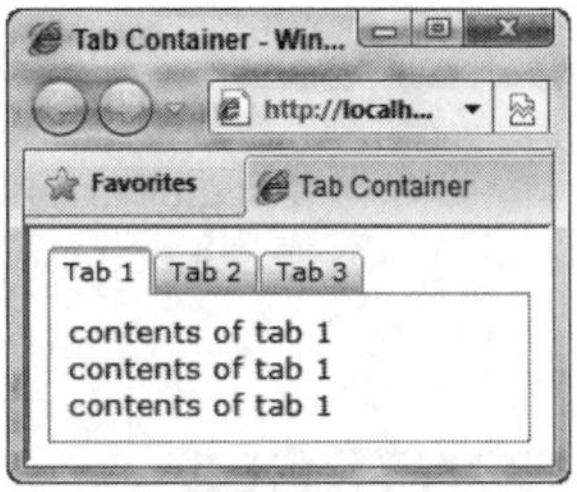

FIGURE A-11

> *The* `http://www.asp.net/ajax/AjaxControlToolkit/Samples/` *web site includes samples of all of the controls included in the Ajax Control Toolkit.*

B

What's on the DVD?

This appendix provides you with information on the contents of the DVD that accompanies this book. For the latest and greatest information, please refer to the ReadMe file located at the root of the DVD. Here is what you will find in this appendix:

➤ System Requirements

➤ Using the DVD

➤ What's on the DVD

➤ Troubleshooting

SYSTEM REQUIREMENTS

Make sure that your computer meets the minimum system requirements listed in this section. If your computer doesn't match up to most of these requirements, you may have a problem using the contents of the DVD.

➤ PC running Windows XP, Windows Vista, Windows 7, or later

➤ An Internet connection

➤ At least 512MB of RAM

➤ A DVD-ROM drive

USING THE DVD

To access the content from the DVD, follow these steps.

1. Insert the DVD into your computer's DVD-ROM drive. The license agreement appears.

2. Read through the license agreement, and then click the Accept button if you want to use the DVD.

   The DVD interface appears. Simply select the lesson number for the video you want to view.

> *The interface won't launch if you have autorun disabled. In that case, click Start ⇨ Run (For Windows Vista, Start ⇨ All Programs ⇨ Accessories ⇨ Run). In the dialog box that appears, type D:\Start.exe. (Replace D with the proper letter if your DVD drive uses a different letter. If you don't know the letter, see how your CD drive is listed under My Computer.) Click OK.*

WHAT'S ON THE DVD

This DVD is the most exciting part of this book. With this DVD, you can listen to me work through the lessons you've been reading throughout the book. Because I believe strongly in the value of video training, this DVD contains hours of instructional video. At the end of each lesson in the book, you will find a reference to an instructional video on the DVD that accompanies that lesson. In that video, I will walk you through the content and examples contained in that lesson. All you need to do is play the DVD and select the lesson you want to watch.

TROUBLESHOOTING

If you have difficulty installing or using any of the materials on the companion DVD, try the following solutions:

➤ **Reboot if necessary.** As with many troubleshooting situations, it may make sense to reboot your machine to reset any faults in your environment.

➤ **Turn off any anti-virus software that you may have running.** Installers sometimes mimic virus activity and can make your computer incorrectly believe that it is being infected by a virus. (Be sure to turn the anti-virus software back on later.)

➤ **Close all running programs.** The more programs you're running, the less memory is available to other programs. Installers also typically update files and programs; if you keep other programs running, installation may not work properly.

➤ **Refer to the ReadMe.** Please refer to the ReadMe file located at the root of the CD-ROM for the latest product information at the time of publication.

CUSTOMER CARE

If you have trouble with the CD-ROM, please call the Wiley Product Technical Support phone number at (800) 762-2974. Outside the United States, call (317) 572-3994. You can also contact Wiley Product Technical Support at `http://support.wiley.com`. John Wiley & Sons will provide technical support only for installation and other general quality control items. For technical support on the applications themselves, consult the program's vendor or author.

To place additional orders or to request information about other Wiley products, please call (877) 762-2974.

INDEX

G